INSTEAD OF HEADING NORTH THE TWO OR THREE MILES to Leann's parents' home, the Dakota turned south. The couple, Mick would tell police later, had decided to take advantage of Hannah's absence and race home for some time together. It is about 15 minutes from the Double Action in Sterling Heights to the house on Hazelwood Avenue. So that would have gotten them there about 12:30, 12:35.

Much of what happened next is disputed. Leann went to the bathroom, removed her blue shorts and underpants, washed her hands and returned to the small bedroom.

At some point very soon, the Smith & Wesson boomed out with a roar made deafening by the closeness of the wet-plaster walls.

At 12:48 P.M., Mick Fletcher called 911 at the Hazel Park police station. His wife, he said between gasps of hysterics and a high, keening whine, had shot herself . . . .

Titles by

TOM HENDERSON

Darker Than Night

Blood Justice

A Deadly Affair

Afraid of the Dark

Blood in the Snow

From the True Crime Library of St. Martin's Paperbacks

A DEADLY AFFAIR

TOM HENDERSON

St. Martin's Paperbacks

Permission to quote Brian Dickerson's newspaper columns granted by the author and the *Detroit Free Press*.

Permission to quote Laura Berman's newspaper columns granted by the author and the *Detroit News*.

A DEADLY AFFAIR

Copyright © 2001 by Tom Henderson.
Cover photograph of Leann Fletcher courtesy Jack Misener.
Cover photograph of Michael Fletcher courtesy AP/Wide World Photos.
Cover photograph of Susan Chrzanowski © Vaughn Gurganian/*Oakland Press*.

ISBN: 0-312-97764-6
EAN: 9780312-97764-1

Printed in the United States of America

St. Martin's Paperbacks edition / August 2001

20   19   18   17   16   15   14   13

ACKNOWLEDGMENTS

As Red Smith, the legendary *New York Times* sports writer, once said when someone suggested that writing must be a simple way to make a living: "It's easy to write. You just sit down at a typewriter and open a vein."

This book was particularly tough, especially the way it evolved. It was tough because of the circumstances—a beautiful young wife and her unborn child shot to death. It was tough, too, because what was needed to do the story justice was to get to know both families, whose lives were forever ruined in one loud, brief moment late in the summer of 1999. If you think it's an easy or fun job to come into a mother and father's home and talk to them about their dead daughter, or about a son accused of murder, give it a try.

And it was made all the tougher because at the end of the eight months that it had consumed of my life, to my great surprise and that of my editors, I was no longer sure I even had a villain to blame. Things were not as simple as they had seemed.

I will forever be grateful to Jack and Gloria Misener for not only inviting me into their home repeatedly, but for making me feel welcome. I will forever be grateful to Darla and John Fletcher, too, who against the advice of their attorneys finally gave in to my entreaties and believed me when I said I wanted to tell their son's side of the story. They also are wonderful people.

I want to thank Leann's sisters and friends for sharing their stories and tears, and Michael Fletcher's siblings and friends for doing the same.

I also want to thank Hazel Park Police Chief David Niedermeier for asking his troops to cooperate; Assistant Prosecutor Greg Townsend for being gracious and accommodating and down to earth from the moment I introduced myself during jury selection; Dr. Ljubisa Dragovic, the engaging, colorful shoot-from-the-hip medical examiner who was so generous with his time and spirit; Judge Jessica Cooper, who told me she had nothing to say and then charmingly proved otherwise; defense attorney Brian Legghio, who, against the advice of *his* co-counsel, took a chance that I would be fair and finally opened up his files and his feelings as the deadline loomed; and court reporter Karen Hollen, who provided encouraging words and court transcripts at way-below-market rates.

My apologies, too, to the Miseners and to Leann's sisters, who certainly envisioned this book would end up as something rather different than it did. They will likely feel some sense of betrayal by me, for which I am sorry. The book, as books tend to do, just became what it became, and it fooled me, too. I, like the prosecutors, had assumed going in this was an open-and-shut case.

That's what made this book so difficult. A beautiful, warm woman—beloved by most of those who knew her—is dead. Two families are shattered. And there is not even a clear "why."

All the characters who follow are real. Where possible, all quotes came from trial transcripts, police reports, court documents or the many interviews I conducted. In recounting some scenes, I have relied on people's memories of what was said, and, with only a rare exception, when it could be verified by others.

No quotes were made up. Nothing is fiction. Any deviation from reality is a mistake and my fault alone.

Hannah Fletcher, precocious, charming, witty, as pretty as her mother, is the biggest loser in this book of losses. One hopes at least a few readers will care enough about her loss to send a check to her trust fund, a registered non-profit and tax-deductible charity, at: The Hannah Fletcher Trust Fund, c/o First Federal of Michigan, 2225 Eighteen Mile Road, Sterling Heights, MI 48083.

Mick, if you did it, may Gloria's curse for you come true. If you didn't, you're the unluckiest guy on earth. What ultimately made this book so tough to live with is that, all these months and all these words later, those last two sentences can be written one after the other.

PROLOGUE

Mid-August of 1999 seemed the best of times in the tumultuous marriage of Michael and Leann Fletcher.

His fledgling legal career was finally taking off, with regular assignments to handle cases for the indigent who came before Judge Susan Chrzanowski of the bustling 37th District Court in Warren, Michigan, Detroit's largest suburb and the third-largest city in the state with a population of 144,864. The court was easily the busiest in Macomb County and a good place to be making the kinds of contacts Fletcher had made.

Their marriage, which had survived several separations in the last two years, was better than it had ever been since Mick—that's what everyone called him—moved back into their suburban Detroit house over Easter. Everyone had noticed how sweet he had been toward Leann the last few months, cooing in her ear at family functions, calling her "honey" and "sweetheart," and Leann told her friends and sisters she'd never been happier.

However, her parents, Jack and Gloria Misener, thought Mick was laying it on a little thick. "Every time he walks by her, he's got to bend his head and kiss her. It really looked stupid, when he started kissing her all over the place," Jack would say later. And Mick was doing stuff he'd never done before, like help load the car when they were leaving the Miseners' after family get-togethers.

On Thursday, August 12, Leann had given Mick the happy news that she was nearly a month pregnant with their second child.

Saturday, they double-dated with her oldest sister and best friend, Lindy, and her husband, Mark. The sisters squealed and hugged over the pregnancy. Sunday, the Fletchers took her parents, Gloria and Jack Misener, out to the nearby Outback Steakhouse, a place the Miseners had heard about for its monster steaks but had never been to. The dinner was two-fold—to celebrate the new baby and to thank the Miseners for loaning them money to pay various bills over the last few months as Mick waited for invoices to be paid by the court.

Monday morning, the good mood and good times continued. Mick stopped off at drugstore to buy a card for Leann, the kind of thoughtful, loving act he'd been doing with some regularity lately. He wrote a message inside expressing his love for her and his excitement over the baby. When he came back from the office, he handed her the card, which she read with joy, then tucked into her purse to show Lindy later.

They dropped Hannah off at her parents', chatted a few minutes, then left for the short ride to the range. Leann's good mood held until just inside the doors, where the joy quickly turned to discomfort bordering on chagrin upon arriving at the gun range at noon. Too loud, too scary. She hated the gun, she hated firing it, she asked if they could leave before their time was up.

Like many young parents who have some time away from a young child, they decided to take advantage of it. Though Leann had told her parents she'd be back in about an hour, they raced the ten miles or so in Mick's Dodge Dakota truck back to their house in the working-class suburb of Hazel Park for an early-afternoon quickie.

Within minutes, Leann was dead, shot behind the right ear with the Smith & Wesson and lying naked from the waist down in a swamp of her own blood on their bedroom floor. Mick's hysterical 911 call summoned police from the Hazel Park police station three blocks away. There'd been a horrible accident while he was in the bathroom, he told them. His wife had picked up the gun and somehow it had gone off.

Soon, two judges would be under a cloud of suspicion because of affairs with the young, extremely handsome attorney, and one of their careers would end up in tatters. Mick had gone with Leann to church on Sunday, and out with her and her parents to dinner Sunday. But after the steak and the beers, he hadn't gone back to his nearby office to wrap up some work, as he'd claimed. He'd gone to Judge Susan Chrzanowski's house, where, she told police, he'd had sex with her and told her he loved her. Mick hadn't told her Leann was pregnant; the police broke that news to her.

By Thursday Mick Fletcher would be in the Oakland County jail, accused of first-degree murder in the deaths of his beautiful young wife and his new baby. Prosecutors would allege that he was so cold-hearted and brutal that, moments after he'd had sex with his wife, while she was still kneeling on the floor near their bed with his freshly deposited semen in her vagina, he'd picked up the Smith & Wesson and shot her in the right ear.

All that week, and continuing on until after his trial in the summer of 2000, headline writers, talk radio and local TV news made the most of one of those stories too good to be true—the beautiful wife, the equally beautiful judge, the movie-star handsome attorney who had them both. And a big gun, a bloody corpse and sex in the afternoon.

It seemed so clear cut. At the least, Fletcher was a cold-blooded murderer motivated by his love for another woman. At the worst, as one local half-hour TV show would luridly and breathlessly claim following Fletcher's arraignment, the murder was the bloody, logical last act for a psychopath who had been a Satanist and devil worshipper in college, and who was fixated on ultraviolent computer games.

Or was it clear cut? Before the often-delayed trial was finally over, the defense would raise legitimate doubts about the forensic evidence; rookie investigators, it would be clear, had made more than their share of mistakes in what seemed to some a rush to judgment. How could a cotton shirt that prosecutors alleged was splattered with a fine mist of blood blown out of Leann's head—the linchpin of the case against Fletcher—flunk a test for a DNA match with her blood? Had a mother-in-law's anger and accusations sent cops on the wrong path?

An hour-long "20/20 Downtown" ABC news show after the trial would reveal a jury torn by doubt, disbelieving the prosecution evidence and bent on solving the case itself with its own theory of what happened and how—even going so far as to reconstruct the crime scene with masking tape and reenact a sequence of events different from that alleged by the prosecution, which the defense never had a chance to rebut.

Was Mick Fletcher an evil psychotic who had planned and carried out the most brutal and heinous of crimes? Absolutely, say prosecutors and state and local police. Or the unluckiest man on the face of the earth, a modern-day Job who lost his wife and child to a deadly accident only to be charged with the murder and stripped of his parental rights to his beloved daughter because of an unfortunate string of coincidences, police malfeasance and prosecutorial zeal? Firearms expert Frederick Wentling, a Pennsylvania state cop for 26 years, says Fletcher is an innocent man and that the case against him was a result of police and prosecutorial malfeasance so gross he describes it as "a railroad job."

Deranged murderer or hapless pawn? He was one or the other. There was no middle ground. Even after the verdict, for many the question would remain unanswered.

GOOD TIMES

It was Thursday, August 12, and Leann Fletcher wasn't sure if she should be happy or not. Her instinct was for joy. She had just administered a home pregnancy test and it came back positive, and there was nothing she loved more in life than parenthood and her only child, Hannah, who had turned three just weeks earlier. If there one thing in the world she was truly gifted at, it was motherhood.

But her marriage had been a struggle the last two years, and while she and Mick had never been happier—he'd been everything she wanted since his last return at Easter—it was still too soon. Better to wait a year or so and make sure she and her husband were going to make it, make sure the judge she suspected of being his lover was really out of the picture.

Maternal instincts gained sway over rational thought. She was pregnant, again! Yes! She couldn't wait to tell Mick when he got home from work.

Though Lindy was her oldest sister, fully ten years her senior, she was Leann's best friend. Facially, they were nearly identical. They looked nothing like their other sisters, Lori and Lisa. They talked on the phone every day and they and their husbands socialized, as well.

Tonight, Saturday, August 14, they were double-dating, going out to dinner, then catching a movie. But this was going to be a special night. She hadn't told Lindy about the baby, yet, and couldn't wait.

This Saturday night movie thing was going to be fun, too. The week before, she and Mick, Lindy and her husband, Mark Termarsch, and a close friend, Jeni Hughes, and her husband, Jeff, had gone out to the movies and promised each other they'd start doing this regularly. Jeni had never really been close to Mick but he was so much nicer now since moving back in April.

Leann called Jeni to ask her if they were coming. They couldn't. Jeff had to work.

"Come on, you can come without him," said Leann. "Please."

"Nah, I don't want to go without Jeff."

"Come on, please?"

"No, I really can't. I'm waiting for my sister, Wendy."

"Well, she can come."

"No, she's gonna be here later. I really can't."

They said their goodbyes. It was the last time Jeni would ever talk to Leann. She would tell a courtroom more than nine months later that she had never forgiven herself for saying no to Leann, for missing out on seeing her one last time.

Lindy and Leann talked on the phone and looked at the movie guides. *The Sixth Sense* was playing at the Oakland Mall, a few miles away. People'd been raving about that. There was a Red Robin, there, too, where they could eat. It was set.

Lindy and Mark, Mick, Leann and Hannah all met at the Red Robin. "Tell her, Hannah," said Leann after they'd been seated awhile. "Go on, Hannah, tell her."

Hannah, a round-faced cutie, sharp as a tack, with a big vocabulary and an endearing way of substituting her "R's" with "W's," had been coached ahead of time to break the news. "I'm going to have a baby bwothuh oh sistuh."

Lindy squealed. She and Leann stood up and hugged. Mark congratulated Mick.

She'd found out Thursday, she told them. It was early, just three or four weeks along, but there was no way she could hold the news and wait till the pregnancy was past its most dangerous stage.

"I just asked Mick if we could move from Hazel Park by the time the new baby comes," said Leann, referring to the need for a larger, more suburban house.

"I might have to get a second job," said Mick. It was no secret his law practice hadn't exactly taken off. He was doing okay, but that was about it. Still, he was making some contacts and applying for high-paid assistant prosecutor positions around the area.

After the meal, Mick and Leann took Hannah in his truck to the Miseners', just a couple of miles up the road, then returned for the movie, which they loved. The movies shocking trick ending surprised the heck out of all of them. It was a night for surprises, and Leann had one more in store.

Out in the parking lot, Leann asked Lindy and Mark to swing by the Miseners'. She couldn't wait to break the news to her parents. The Termarsches wanted to head home, instead.

"You don't need me."

"Ple-ease," said Leann, stretching the word out. Since the time she'd come home from the hospital, she'd had her siblings wrapped around whatever finger she chose. She gave Lindy that special, pleading, so-cute look that always worked. "Come on. Please."

"All right," said Lindy.

When they got there, it was Mick's turn to prod Hannah as they all sat around the family room in the back of the house. Jack was in his La-Z-Boy chair, as usual. The Miseners' only son, Chris, was there, too. "Come on, Princess, tell Grandma and Grandpa. Tell Grandma and Grandpa."

Hannah said her lines. Jack and Gloria were elated. There were hugs, handshakes, words of congratulations. Jack couldn't stop beaming. He'd traded in his beloved Taurus for a van just so he could haul his grandkids around, and now he was going to have another one. Leann said she had planned on waiting till Hannah was five, but she was really happy it happened, anyway.

"Leann was a great mother and it was nice to see she was going to have another one," Jack would say later. "That's all she wanted in life, to get married and stay home and have a family."

Before they left, the Fletchers made plans to stretch this happy day into two. How about if the Miseners and Fletchers went to church together in the morning—a rarity for the family—and then went out to dinner Sunday night? The Outback, our treat, said Mick. The Miseners hadn't been there, but had heard it was something special. That was the place with the line out the door, wasn't it? And that fancy thing they did with the onion and those big steaks? Yep, that was the place.

If Sunday dinner on Mick was a surprise, there was an even bigger one before they left. Leann had a habit of borrowing money from her parents in dribs and drabs to pay for bills. She was only working part-time at Incognito, a hair and nail salon, and Mick's invoices for his work at court could be really slow in getting processed. They had, in fact, built up a little more than $2,500 in debt to the Miseners in the last year or two, doled out in a series of small checks. It included $500 Jack had given Leann for her attorney when Mick had filed for divorce in January, but once she took Mick back, instead of figuring it was a gift, he added it to the debt. Jack had no real expectation of ever getting any of it back.

But—holy cow!—there on the kitchen table, Gloria found an envelope Leann had slyly set down when they arrived. When Gloria opened it, there was a check inside, paying them back for the entire amount. And a note, reading: "Dinner comes with this." Mick had sold his old clunker of a truck and Leann said it had been his idea. "Let's pay your parents off," he said.

Jack drove the five of them in his van to the Outback, near the huge Lakeside Mall, one of the nation's first monster malls, built in the middle of a cornfield twenty years ago and now surrounded by other malls, strip centers, restaurants and office buildings. They got there about 5 p.m., peak time. There was a line, as usual, and the place didn't take reservations, but Leann, ever outgoing, went in and was able to get them a table in the bar right off, no waiting. Jack ordered a beer, a Bud or Miller, something American. Mick ordered something Jack had never heard of; he didn't even know if it was a beer or not. A Foster's, he called it. It was a beer, a huge, blue-canned Australian beer.

They ate their steaks. Good as the reputation. Mick had another one of the giant beers.

They got back to the Miseners' about 7 p.m. Half an hour later, the Fletchers got ready to go. Hannah got in the back seat of the Dakota truck, Mick got behind the wheel, and Leann went back in the house with Gloria to get Hannah something to drink for the ride home. Jack stood at the passenger door, which was open.

Mick leaned over and said, "Are you going to be home tomorrow?"

"Yeah, I suppose we are."

"I'd like you to babysit for one hour while Lee and I go to the firing range. Just an hour."

Leann by now had returned to the truck and Jack turned to her and looked quizzically. She didn't like guns. It seemed odd she'd be going to the range to shoot one.

Leann looked at him, according to Jack's later testimony at Fletcher's arraignment, "just kind of meeky, like, 'cause I knew my daughter didn't like weapons."

Jack said sure, he'd babysit. Leann got in and the Dakota pulled out of the driveway and took off. Hmm, thought Jack, that was odd. Odd she'd go shooting. And odd Mick would ask. In six years, he had never asked the Miseners to babysit. It was always Leann who asked. They babysat every Wednesday and Friday regularly, and other days as the need arose, and never once had Mick done the asking.

Jack went back in, turned on the TV and sat back in his La-Z-Boy.

Twenty minutes later, the Fletchers pulled into their driveway on Hazelwood. The sun was still high in the sky—Michigan is at the far western edge of the Eastern time zone, really ought to be in the Central zone, and gets the latest light in the continental United States.

There was another surprise left in the weekend. Mick told Leann he had some work at the office that he really needed to wrap up. He had a hearing at the court in Warren first thing in the morning that required his attention. He wouldn't be long. Leann went inside with Hannah and Mick drove off. He didn't go to his office in Center Line, though—he went to Judge Chrzanowski's house in Warren, had sex with her and told her he loved her.

"HOW MUCH MY LIFE WAS ABOUT TO BE CHANGED"

Monday, August 16, dawned, already a scorcher. Newcomers to Michigan, especially those from the south, are shocked to find how hot and humid it can be that far north. The state is surrounded by the Great Lakes and is filled with thousands of lakes, creeks, rivers and streams. Close your eyes in the summer months and you might as well be in the Everglades, or the Mississippi Delta, the air's that heavy and wet. This day would be no exception.

The sun rises early here and sets late, and in between it bakes down on the morass of concrete highways and freeways that snake throughout southeastern Michigan and down, too, upon the acres of blacktop parking lots at the malls and shopping centers that replaced the wetlands and cornfields of a generation or two ago. The sun bakes from above and the cement and blacktop bake from below.

"Ozone action" days are declared, meaning no one is supposed to fill their gas tanks or cut their lawns between sunrise and sunset, though no one pays attention.

Cops on traffic patrol worry about road rage.

Mick Fletcher slipped out of bed, took a shower, put on one of his conservative dark business suits and headed out at 8:55 for his 9 a.m. pre-trial in Warren's 37th District Court. He left the court at 10 for his office in nearby Center Line, then stopped at the Rite Aid drug store across the street to pick up a can of Coke and a Hallmark greeting card for Leann. When she had told him she was pregnant, his first words were that he hoped it was a boy. She'd taken it the wrong way.

Leann was on the phone to Lindy when Mick pulled in the driveway about 10:30. Leann was feeling kind of punk, a little morning sickness she thought, and was lying on the couch. She and Lindy made plans to go for a walk, after the trip to the shooting range. Mick had to go back to the office later, and Leann had to pick up Hannah at her parents'. Lindy said she'd meet her there, and she and Lindy and Hannah—maybe Jack and Gloria, too—could go for a walk on the trails at a park near the Miseners'.

Leann heard Mick pull in, told Lindy she'd have to go. She hadn't realized the time; she'd planned to be dressed and up off the couch before he got back. She didn't want him thinking that's all she did all day, lie around and talk on the phone.

They hadn't broken off the call when Mick came in. He handed her the card. She was thrilled, bragged about it to her sister, then hung up so she could open it and read it, then she stuck it in her purse to read again later. To show Lindy and her mom. Whatever had caused it, he was a changed man since Easter, better than she'd ever hoped for.

The printing on the front of the card said:

My Love,
When I met you, I had no idea
how much my life
was about to be changed . . .
but then, how could I have known?
A love like ours happens
once in a lifetime.
You were a miracle to me,
the one who was everything
I had ever dreamed of,
the one I thought existed
only in my imagination.
And when you came into my life,
I realized that what I
had always thought
was happiness
couldn't compare to the joy
loving you brought me."

Inside, Mick had written:

Leann,

I might not always tell you, but you mean the world to me.

I love you so much, sweetheart; and girl or boy, so long as they are a part of you, our children will all be beautiful.

I love you!

The Fletchers drove separate cars to Leann's parents', so Mick could just drop her off there later. Leann stopped for gas along the way at a Citgo. When they got there, Jack and Gloria both walked outside to greet them as they pulled into the driveway, then all five of them walked back inside.

Leann and Mick were inside just a minute or two. They said they'd be gone for an hour. Mick would drop Leann off and go back to work. Leann said she'd made plans to go to the park with Lindy and Hannah. Jack and Gloria had just started exercising, and they asked if they could go, too. As they were leaving, Gloria pulled her daughter aside, just outside the house, and said, "How come you guys are going to the firing range?"

"Mick wants to teach me how to shoot, in case I ever need to use the gun. And he's been so good lately, I want to keep him happy."

Then, joking, Gloria said, "Mick didn't take out an extra insurance policy on you, did he?"

Leann rolled her eyes and said, "Oh, Mom, he's not going to shoot me."

Those were the last words Gloria would ever hear her daughter speak.

It was 11:50 a.m. when Mick and Leann got into the Dakota truck and left for the Double Action firing range a five-minute drive away.

The Double Action range is off Dequindre, the same main north–south road the Miseners live near. It looks like any of the myriad other low-slung, cookie-cutter buildings that line Dequindre—engineering firms, small manufacturing facilities making auto parts, medical offices.

Inside, the action was sparse, but still deafening. Most of the alleys were vacant. Paul Yaeck, the head of security at

St. John Hospital, was there with a couple of other men testing new firearms.

They noticed the young couple at the far end of the range. Yaeck knows his weapons, and knew that Leann was using a .45, a big, powerful gun for a fairly small woman. Heck, a big gun for anybody, for that matter. It has a terrific recoil, and it seemed clear to him that Leann was neither proficient, nor comfortable firing it.

About 12:15, maybe 12:20, the young couple stopped shooting. They were calling it quits a little early. An employee who just happened to be watching thought it was kind of cute, endearing even, that the woman bent over and picked up her spent cartridges. A rookie, obviously, who didn't know it was okay to leave your cartridges where they lay.

Instead of heading north the two or three miles to the Miseners', the Dakota turned south. The couple, Mick would tell police later, had decided to take advantage of Hannah's absence and race home for a quickie. It is about 15 minutes from the Double Action in Sterling Heights to the house on Hazelwood Avenue. So that would have gotten them there about 12:30, 12:35.

Much of what happened next is disputed. Leann went to the bathroom, removed her blue shorts and underpants, washed her hands and returned to the small bedroom.

At some point very soon, the Smith & Wesson boomed out with a roar made deafening by the closeness of the wet-plaster walls. Leann was shot in the right ear, her brain stem severed, death a certainty even before gravity could exert its tug. A mist of high-velocity blood, an aerosolized spray of red, shot out her right ear the instant the bullet went in. Blood poured out her nostrils. She fell to the carpet and soon a pool of thick red had formed around her.

At 12:48 p.m., Mick Fletcher called 911 at the Hazel Park police station. His wife, he said between gasps of hysterics and a high, keening whine, had shot herself. He'd gone to the bathroom. He was in there when the gun went off. He came out. His wife was shot. His honey was dead. The dispatcher told him to stay on the the line, not to touch anything. Mick called out to his his wife, got hysterical. The dispatcher tried to calm him down. He told him again not to touch anything. "I'm not, I can't even be in there," said Mick, who had

walked outside with the cell phone. He lit a cigarette and
stayed on the phone with the dispatcher.

Months later, in his only media interview, Fletcher, wearing the bright orange jumpsuit of an Oakland County prisoner, would tell ABC's "20/20 Downtown": "I thought I'd
see Leann standing there staring at a hole in the wall. When
I came out and saw that, it's almost like it didn't even register."

At 12:52, Hazel Park Police Officer Ronald Lehman pulled
up in front of the house. Fletcher was on the porch. The storm
door was still closing behind him. Lehman was the first of
many city and state police who would visit the Hazelwood
house that day.

"WOMAN SHOT"

John Heisler, a baby-faced nine-year veteran of the Hazel Park PD, was eating his lunch at the station when the call came in to 911. The jolting words, "woman shot," came over the station's PA system. Lunch would have to wait. Heisler is an evidence technician, so he grabbed his tools, including his camera, and raced to his car. Hazelwood is just four blocks from the station, and four minutes after Fletcher picked up the phone, Heisler was at the scene.

Lehman had got there seconds ahead of him and was approaching Fletcher, who was on the porch. "She's inside. She's inside," he said.

"What happened?" said Lehman.

"She shot herself. She's in the back bedroom."

Heisler noticed that Fletcher's belt buckle was undone. At that point, the officers didn't know who was in the house, if this had been a suicide or murder, if there was a shooter still alive in the house or if there were kids inside. As with all such calls—Hazel Park, a tiny city, didn't get many and in fact had no homicide detectives on its force, just an all-purpose detective bureau—this would be treated as a crime scene until proven otherwise.

Lehman entered the house. A third officer, William Hamel, just arriving at the scene, was told by Heisler to stay with Fletcher outside. Heisler followed Lehman inside and was hit with the acrid smell of gunpowder. Eerily, there was a large target splayed over the front room couch, a target with a crouching human figure aiming a gun at whoever would do the target shooting. There were five holes in the bullseye and it had been shot maybe 30 or 40 times. It was the same target the Fletchers had fired at minutes earlier.

The front room was to Heisler's right as he entered. To the left was the dining room and kitchen. An opened 30-pack of Busch Light was visible on the kitchen floor. The hallway went down the center of the house to two bedrooms and a bathroom.

They entered the southwest bedroom. Here, the smell of gunpowder was even stronger. Lehman bent down, checked for a pulse at Leann's wrist and neck, found none. She was sprawled out on the floor, a massive amount of blood soaking into the beige carpet in a huge stain billowing out from her head. She was naked from the waist down, wearing white cotton socks, a beige bra and a red cotton tank top. Her eyes were half open, staring out, so lifelike it seemed surreal. Thick streaks of blood ran across her face and under her chin. Her right foot was under the bed, as was the toe of her left foot. She was lying at a 45-degree angle to the bed. Her legs were thighs down, with her torso rotated so she was on her right shoulder blade and chest, her stomach aiming up. A black Smith & Wesson.45 gun was lying near her right arm, aiming at and almost touching her wrist. There was a magazine with several bullets in it near the gun, and a single bullet lying next to it. There was a swath of blood on her left thigh and blood on both her hands.

The tiny bedroom was crammed with a computer stand, a computer tower on the floor next to the stand, and a large chest. There was gun paraphernalia scattered about, much of which Lehman would begin collecting in plastic bags. There was a gun safe, a gun cleaning kit, a loaded clip, spare bullets and a shell casing standing, incongruously, on its end on the carpet.

The computer stand, near her right hand, was splattered with blood. There were several kids' CDs on the stand—a *Sesame Street Learning Series*, *Elmo's Preschool Deluxe* and a *Freddie Fish*.

The four emergency medical technicians had arrived and were in the hallway awaiting orders. Heisler told two of them to enter the room. He was worried that if too many of them went in, they might contaminate the scene, disturb evidence. They checked for signs, too. They checked the carotid artery. One put his ear to her chest. They hooked up three wires from the cardiac monitor. It showed pulseless electrical activity, which meant she'd been dead only a few minutes. They put a pen-light to her eyes; they were fixed and dilated. They hooked up two electrodes, one to each side of her chest, part of a telemetry system to beam her lack of vital signs to a nearby hospital, where a doctor made the official pronouncement of death.

The stain around her head continued to spread. The blood was mixed with a gelatin-like substance, brain fluid.

The paramedics left the room, gathered up their stuff and left the house. It was 1:20 p.m. The heat outside was oppressive, but it was a relief from the atmosphere inside, the smell of the blood mixing with the smell of the gunpowder, a smell that remains in the mind long after it's cleared the nostrils.

Heisler began snapping Polaroids of everything he could think of—the bullet casing, what appeared to be the entry wound in her right ear, the furniture, the blood stain on the bed, the godawful bloody carpet. He filled his evidence bags. He'd be busy for two hours.

While Heisler did his work, Lehman went back outside and talked to Fletcher, who had been taken to the yard next door to keep out of the way of the comings and goings.

Other cops began arriving.

Soon, a van from Classic Removal Service pulled up. The company has contracts with various funeral homes, as well as the Oakland County Medical Examiner's Office, for the removal of dead bodies. The driver went in, wrapped Leann in a sheet, then put her into a plastic body bag and zipped it shut. He wheeled her out of the house, down the steps and into the van, to take her to the ME for Tuesday morning's autopsy.

The driver didn't think anything of it, but when he wrapped her in the sheet, Leann's hands weren't bagged. One of the police officers at the scene should have put plastic bags over her hands to preserve such potential evidence as blood patterns and gunpowder. But, inexplicably, one of the ranking cops who had arrived in the meantime—later, no one seemed to remember who it was—ordered that her hands *not* be bagged.

The missing bags would play a bigger part in the months-away defense of Michael Fletcher than anyone could have imagined watching the Classic Removal Service van pull away. It was 2 p.m.

In the meantime, Hamel walked Fletcher to the yard next door, to keep out of the way. "Oh my God, this can't be happening!" said Fletcher, who was crying. Hamel asked him to sit down on the porch.

Hamel asked what had happened and Mick recounted the recent events. They'd gone to the gun range, then returned home "to play around," said Fletcher. He told Hamel he'd gone into the bathroom to take a pee before putting the gun away. While he was in there, he heard a gunshot, came out and found Leann on the floor. He wasn't sure, he might have moved his wife's arm. Fletcher kept interrupting his narrative with sobs and several times said: "Oh my God, what am I going to tell my daughter?" and, "This can't be happening!"

Hamel later wrote in his report that Fletcher appeared somewhat orderly. He was wearing a long-sleeve green dress shirt tucked into his pants, a multi-colored tie, dark dress pants, black socks and no shoes. He even noticed that Fletcher's top shirt button was undone and his tie loosened around the neck.

Sgt. Dennis Welch, known as Muggs, the first detective on the scene, arrived about 1:10. He'd been on the road on the way back from another crime scene, heard the call and raced over. Welch kept an eye on the scene for a couple of minutes, making sure nothing was disturbed, either by his own men or by the paramedics. Soon, Lt. Daniel Smick arrived. He headed up the detective bureau and relieved Welch.

Welch then asked if Fletcher would come with him back to the station to make a statement. "He gave the appearance of being very upset about the fact his wife was shot," Welch would say later. "Very upset. He was crying. Very, very upset. Nothing I would have thought unusual. I brought him to the station, calmed him down a bit and began the interview."

First, Welch retrieved a pair of Fletcher's shoes from the house. Fletcher cried the four blocks back to the station. "I can't believe this is happening," he said. "How can I tell my daughter? Everything was going so good, I can't believe this."

When they got out of the car, Welch had to physically

help him walk into the station and down the stairs to the interview room.

"Can I get you anything to make you more comfortable?" Welch asked.

"I'm fine," said Fletcher, who started to cry again and said: "I'm not fine."

Welch brought him a glass of water and some tissues, then asked him if he felt up to making a statement. In movies and TV, that's the point detectives turn on the tape recorder or the video camera. In real life, standard operating procedure is to do neither. Welch took brief notes in his own version of shorthand during the interview, the briefer the better so as to keep the flow going. Real-life detectives want to keep the subject talking. Later, they make a hand-written narrative report of their interpretation of what was said. Fletcher was not warned of his rights. Miranda wasn't mentioned. Though other cops had already decided he was a killer, he wasn't officially a suspect. Under recent Supreme Court rulings, Miranda rights need to be read only when there is a constraint on a subject's departure. Fletcher was free to terminate the interview at any time. Besides, he was a defense attorney. If he didn't know his rights, it wasn't Welch's obligation to make sure he did. The interview began at 1:30 p.m. and finished about 2:30.

"I'm a lawyer. I know you've got a job to do and I want to cooperate," said Fletcher. But he needed a cigarette first. Smoking in public buildings in Michigan is illegal, so Welch walked him back outside. Fletcher lit up and Welch went back in the building. When he came out a couple of minutes later, Fletcher was kneeling on the ground with his head down, crying. Welch knelt down next to him, helped him to his feet and they went back inside to the interview room.

In the office, Fletcher told them about the card he'd bought because he had felt bad for saying he really wanted a boy. He broke down again in tears, then resumed.

When they got back from the firing range, Leann carried in the gun case and he carried in the target and ammunition bag. Leann set the gun case down on the bed and went into the bathroom. He loaded the gun's clip with Federal ammunition, then picked up the second clip. He'd gotten an automatic loader for Christmas but never got it to work correctly, so he began loading the bullets into it by hand. He got two or three bullets into it before Leann came out of the bathroom. He handed the clip and ammunition to her and asked her to finish loading the clip.

(This would later be very important at trial. The prosecution would ask, and the jury would consider it damning, why Fletcher would hand a clip he was having trouble loading to his wife, an inexperienced shooter who didn't like guns. But according to Welch's written report, Fletcher never said he was having trouble loading the gun; he said he was loading it by hand because the automatic loader didn't work properly. Cleyman's written report, though, said Fletcher was having trouble with the second clip.)

Fletcher went into the bathroom, ran some water and splashed his face, undid his belt and heard a gunshot. He thought he'd see Leann standing there with a hole in the wall but instead she was lying on the floor.

Fletcher began sobbing, again. When he calmed down, he resumed.

He'd grabbed her right arm and rolled her over and could see she was bleeding from a wound on the right side of her head. At that point he freaked, grabbed the cell phone and called 911, then waited for police to arrive.

Welch asked him if he would give a written statement and he agreed. Then he asked him if there was anyone he wanted to call.

Fletcher told him he wanted to call Jack and Gloria Misener, Leann's parents, but didn't know what to say.

About the time Welch was finishing his first go-round with Fletcher, Lehman returned to the station and hand-printed a four-page report. It was sparse, to the point, understated the way Sgt. Friday might have done it. He said when he arrived at the scene, "Michael was shaking but was not crying." Lehman described his participation in the events in the bedroom, then told of his brief interview with Fletcher afterward.

"Officer asked Michael what happened and he stated he and Leann just got home from Double Action shooting range on Dequindre, where they were both shooting. Michael stated that the gun they both used at Double Action was the same gun that was next to her on the floor. Michael also stated this was the first time he had taken Leann shooting. Both subjects arrived at location in listed Dakota. (Officer found Leann's purse in the truck.) Michael then stated he and Leann were going to have sex in the southwest bedroom.

"Leann began taking off her clothes and Michael went into the bathroom and *closed the door*." For some reason, Lehman thought that particularly significant and underlined the words "closed the door." "Michael states he heard a loud bang and went back into the bedroom and saw Leann on the floor bleeding. Michael stated he moved her slightly but could not say what part of her body he touched, or if he moved her before or after he called 911. Officer observed a small amount of blood on each of Michael's hands.

"Neighbors near the location said they did not know Michael and Leann very well and never saw or heard about any problems."

Lehman's report—and testimony about it at subsequent court proceedings—would be used by prosecutors to imply that the Fletcher whom Lehman encountered was far calmer than the Fletcher heard over the 911 line, that his hysterics on the phone had been mere theatrics.

It would also be used by the defense. He noted blood on Fletcher's hands. The prosecution would later claim in court that Fletcher had washed blood off his hands, and Cleyman would testify that the lack of blood on Fletcher convinced him on first sight that he was a murderer. It was a theme that would run throughout the case—there was and would be two ways of looking at nearly everything.

And what Lehman described in his report on August 16 as "a small amount of blood" would be described in his testimony, at Fletcher's pre-trial hearing to decide if he should be bound over for trial, as "just small specks" of blood. The word "specks" was important. By then, the prosecution had claimed to have found tiny dots of high-velocity blood mist on the shirt Fletcher wore at the time of the shooting, blood that could only come from being at close range when Leann was shot. Specks of blood on Fletcher's hands would fit that scenario.

After finishing his report, Lehman returned to the Hazelwood house. He would stand guard outside till he was relieved at 9:30, making sure the house was secure.

*   *   *

At 3:30, Fletcher wrote his statement. In just less than one lined page, he wrote about his morning at court, stopping for a card, dropping off Hannah, going to the gun range, "then decided to go home together for 'personal time.' She carried gun case into house. I carried target and ammo bag. Laid target on couch, took ammo into room, sat on bed by gun case. She went into bathroom. I completed loading one clip, placed in gun and rounded chamber. Removed clip & replaced round in clip (uncertain). Placed 2 or 3 rounds in 2nd clip. She came into room (half-dressed), and I asked her to finish loading 2nd clip. (The 1st clip was put in gun.)

"I went into bathroom, undid pants & heard explosion. Ran back into room, saw her face down in front of computer. I held her right arm and rolled her back. Uncertain as to remainder."

If he had racked and chambered a bullet as he claimed, and left the safety off, it would have left the Smith & Wesson in single-action position. Cocked, it would be easier to fire than if it had been left uncocked, in double-action position, which required a certain pull on the trigger to cock it and a further pull to fire.

Detective Tom Cleyman had been on the Hazel Park police force since 1989, making him something of a veteran on the youthful force. Blond, ruddy faced, he looks a bit like a stouter, shorter version of Nick Nolte, and he would joke after the trial that he wanted Nolte to play him in the made-for-TV movie everyone seemed to think was inevitable. Hazel Park boasted many good athletes in its ranks, and in his 20s, Cleyman had been a fierce softball player. He was in the detective bureau when the 911 call came in. He had to go to the Michigan State Police crime lab in nearby Sterling Heights on unrelated business and returned to the station a little before 2. He and Sgt. Larry Dale Hendricks—L. D. to everybody, whose youthful, unlined face didn't seem to go with the chew of tobacco often wedged behind his lip, and whose dark hair was combed straight back from his forehead, tooth marks from his comb clearly defined—were about to head over to the scene. "We're small. We don't have a major crimes unit," Hendricks would say later. "When we get something like this, we basically drop everything. We do what we can and if we feel there's something we can't handle, we'll call an outside agency."

(The defense would later claim the inexperienced Hazel Park police were incapable of handling the scene from the start and should have called in county sheriffs, an allegation the Hazel Park police would angrily deny.)

A bit later, Welch walked Fletcher in from one of his smoking breaks and passed Cleyman. Cleyman eyed him suspiciously. He was too clean. No blood. This is a murderer, he told himself. He killed his wife. He would later testify in court that upon seeing Fletcher, he was "stone-cold certain" the lawyer was also a murderer. That quick assessment would be a key factor at the trial. Cleyman might not have made so much of Fletcher's blood-free appearance, but a couple of nights earlier, the detective had been watching the History Channel on cable, a show on the Kennedy assassination, and the image of Jackie all bloody in her pink outfit was fresh in his mind. How come Fletcher wasn't bloody Cleyman wondered. How come he hadn't cradled his spouse?

Many months later, after the trial, in an interview for this book, Cleyman would say: "When I saw him dressed like that, in a tie and suit and no blood, I said instantly that he was guilty."

As Cleyman and Hendricks pulled up to the curb, Leann's shrouded body was coming down the sidewalk on a gurney. It rolled past, then they entered the house.

"The crime scene bothered me right off the bat," Cleyman would say later.

"The scene seemed staged to us," said Hendricks. "No way would the gun have fallen to within a foot diameter of her right hand if she'd shot herself."

Hendricks made sure the scene was properly secured, gave Heisler some instructions and then he and Cleyman went back to the station, where they would be busy much of the afternoon conducting interviews.

After Heisler finished his work, police continued to secure the scene, awaiting a search warrant. It was issued at 4:17 p.m., and called for "evidence of a fatal shooting . . . weapons and ammunition, spent casings, blood and/or any objects which appear to have blood stains on them, including a computer."

They thought they had a routine murder. Not that murder was routine for Hazel Park, but a routine murder, nonetheless. What they'd find with the search warrant was about to turn it into a soap opera.

THE MISENERS WAIT

The Miseners expected Leann to be back about 1, maybe a little after. By 1:30 they were getting worried. She had a cell phone and was faithful about calling when she'd be late.

Two o'clock came and went. Then three. They were very nervous, now. No way would she just let them and Hannah sit there waiting without a call unless something bad had happened.

Jack was sitting in the front room, looking out the window when his heart sank. First one Troy police car pulled up in front of the house, then another.

"Oh my God, they're coming here," he said to Gloria, even before they'd got out of their cars.

They knocked on the door, identified themselves, came into the front room.

"I'm afraid there's been an accident with your daughter," one of them said.

Gloria and Jack both thought: car accident; she's at the hospital.

"What kind of accident?" said Gloria.

"There's been a shooting."

"Oh my God, Jack, he shot her," said Gloria, setting the tone for much of what would follow. Her absolute and instant certainty would strike all the police she would subsequently talk to as important and revealing.

(Many months later, she would say: "We knew from the minute the police came exactly what happened.")

"What happened? How bad is it?" asked Jack.

"We don't know. Here's the number to call," said the Troy policeman.

They were to ask for Dennis Welch. He's the one who

called the Troy police. A wiry, popular cop, he was normally quick with a joke and a laugh. This hit him hard from the start. Cops usually joke their way through tragedy and turmoil, a defense mechanism, but he'd do no joking this day. He felt guilty about turning a nasty job over to the Troy police but he didn't think it was right that the Miseners should get such bad news over the phone. When Jack called him, Welch said: "Can you come down here?"

"How bad is my daughter?"

"Would you please just come down, sir?"

"You can't tell me how my daughter is?"

"Would you please just come down?"

"All right."

Jack was on the verge of hysterics. Gloria, exhibiting the strength that she'd show her family and the outside world for the next year, was surprisingly calm. And very, very angry. She knew her daughter was dead. If she were injured, they'd have sent them to a hospital.

"Jack," she said, "he's smart. He's going to get away with it." She was sure Mick had murdered her daughter, but she figured he'd done it at the range, somehow, did it there to look like an accident.

Leann's car was behind theirs in the driveway. It had a child's car seat. So they loaded Hannah into the car and made the 15- to 20-minute drive to the Hazel Park police station. They knew the way well. It was the same way they'd take to Leann's house; instead of turning left on Hazelwood, they just kept going four more blocks and turned left into the parking lot.

The Miseners walked down the flight of stairs to the basement police station. They identified themselves to the officer at the desk behind the thick Plexiglas. He told Welch they were there and Welch came out to let them in.

One officer took Hannah into a room they kept for that purpose, filled with toys and stuffed animals.

Welch told them their daughter had been shot and killed.

"Oh my God," said Jack. He'd thought the worst, but hearing it was something else.

According to the report Welch filled out later, "Gloria also became upset but quickly became grim and looked this officer directly in the eye and stated: 'That son of a bitch killed her.' "

The words had a stunning effect. The defense would later claim Gloria's declaration was the rudder that steered everything that followed.

"Do you feel like making a statement?" Welch asked.

"Get the paper."

Jack was in shock. He couldn't talk. He couldn't begin to think about putting words to paper.

In a firm hand, writing quickly and without need for pause, she filled out one page of a standard statement form. It read:

Leann and Mick had a rocky relationship for the last 2 years. Mick has left 3 or 4 times, but always talked her into taking him back. She is a loving mother & wife. She suspected he was having an affair, but could never prove it. He turned from a loving husband after the first few years to a cold & distant person. He wanted to file for divorce (he did) & we loaned her the money for a lawyer. The day he was served, he started sending her flowers again & wanted her to take him back and he said he changed, so out of consideration for their daughter, Hannah, she gave him one more chance. He has went overboard on the loving husband routine & when he asked us to watch Hannah for 1 hour today while he showed her how to shoot a gun, I said to her before they left—Leann, has he taken out a new insurance policy on you? & she laughed & said mother he isn't going to shoot me. He was trained at a police academy & can handle guns. This was no accident.

It was signed: "Gloria Misener" and witnessed by Sgt. Hendricks.

He interviewed the Miseners for half an hour, forty minutes, and none of Mick's story rang true to Cleyman. He thought it ridiculously fishy the first time Mick asks Jack to babysit, the first time he takes his wife, who's scared of guns, to a firing range, that she ends up dead. He didn't like the absence of blood. He was pumped up. Something like this, it's what cops live for.

The Miseners left the station with Hannah. They had been kept apart from Mick and never saw him.

After the trial, in an interview for this book, Welch admitted that up till the Miseners arrived, he'd been sympathetic toward Fletcher, viewing him as a possible victim, too. But once Gloria arrived and stared him in the eyes and told him her son-in-law was a murderer, "To me, this is where everything fell into place. Because when I explained to them that their daughter was dead, and that she had been shot . . . the mom's reaction tightened it all up for me. I knew we were moving in the right direction because I can't picture anybody coming in—I know how mother-in-laws are and how in-laws can be—but that wouldn't be the first thing out of a person's mouth."

Gloria's cocksure attitude, her calm anger, her fortitude all energized the Hazel Park police. Her "That son of a bitch killed her" had been a jolt of adrenaline, not that the small force working a possible homicide needed any.

By law, the cops at the scene had a right to be in the bedroom and anything in plain view there could be used as evidence. It was clear, now, that a search warrant would be needed for the rest of the house. If this was a murder, it would have a motive, and a warrant might tell them what it was.

Welch went over his interview with Hendricks, who read Fletcher's written statement. It was time for round two. Time also to turn it up a notch. "We moved the interview into more of an investigation," said Welch.

"A lot of things didn't add up, so we went back in and turned the screws up a little bit on him," said Hendricks.

Hendricks took first crack. He didn't read him his rights. Though by now he, Welch and Cleyman were all convinced they had a murderer in the interview room, he was still free to leave of his own volition.

Midway through the interview, Roy Gruenburg showed up. A former district judge in Warren, he was now a defense attorney. His daughter, Dawnn, was a judge in Warren. She would soon be involved in the case, as well, to everybody's surprise—and titillation.

Gruenburg was a well-connected legal heavyweight and Mick's boss of sorts. He didn't actually employ him, but he provided Fletcher office space, threw overflow cases his way and even let him sleep on a bed at the office during his and Leann's separations. It was Gruenburg's office Fletcher had stopped off at on the way home that morning from court in Warren.

Fletcher hadn't made any phone calls and police were puzzled how Gruenburg knew to show up. They figured out later he had been called by reporters who had picked up the news on their police scanners.

Cleyman escorted him to the interview room and Gruenburg asked Hendricks if he could have five minutes alone with Fletcher. Cleyman and Hendricks left the room. Roy then came back out and asked if there was anything else they needed.

"We have some more questions for Michael," said Hendricks.

"I thought he already gave a statement."

"Are you representing Michael?"

"I am, but I might not remain the attorney of record."

"Well, we've got just a couple more questions."

Gruenburg, Cleyman and Hendricks went back into the room.

Hendricks knew he wouldn't have Fletcher long, not with Gruenburg there. He asked him about his loading the clip, then about Leann loading it. Why would Leann load the clip if she was afraid of guns? Fletcher said it didn't seem to bother her. Hendricks decided to make it clear where they were heading. As he would recount later: "We called him on why Leann would pick up the gun, if she was afraid of it. I said, 'You know, Michael, the only thing I can't understand is if she was deadly afraid of the gun—that she left the firing range because the gun scared her—why would she pick the gun up?'"

Gruenburg said quickly: "He's answered enough questions for today."

That was the last time police would talk to Fletcher. Before the week was out, Brian Legghio was his attorney, and he wasn't about to let Mick talk to anybody.

As Cleyman escorted Fletcher out of the station, he said to him: "You have a very beautiful daughter."

Fletcher replied: "Yes. She is my everything. She is my angel."

Cleyman took that as incriminating, too. Though Fletcher several times had broken down in front of Welch and while crying had told him how he and Leann had been getting along so well and how could this happen, now, Cleyman would later say about Fletcher's parting remark about Hannah: "That struck me funny. Supposedly your wife has just accidentally shot herself. Your daughter's important, but he never brought up his wife. He never said a word—nothing—about her."

Fletcher and Gruenburg went back to the office. Later, Hendricks and Weimer, on their way back from interviewing people at Double Action range, stopped by the law office. The first search warrant had been approved, and allowed them to take Fletcher's clothes. Fletcher took them off, the police put them in brown paper bags and left.

At some point early in the evening, Gruenburg drove Fletcher over to the Miseners' to see Hannah. Mick banged on the door but the Miseners, who saw them pull up, wouldn't answer. Mick, wearing borrowed clothes, gave up, turned around and walked back to Gruenburg's car. There was a very real chance he would never see his daughter again.

THE WORD GOES OUT

When Gloria and Jack Misener returned home from the Hazel Park police station, she got on the phone for the task of summoning the family, so she could tell them the tragic news in person.

Her second-youngest daughter, Lisa Felice, had just got home with her husband, Mike. They work together doing home remodeling and repairs and had just finished up a job in the Miseners' family room. So when Gloria called and asked, sternly, "Let me speak to Mike," Lisa thought she had called to complain about the job, to perhaps get them back to fix it right.

"We'll be right there," said Mike. He put the phone down and told Lisa that something had happened. Something bad, but Gloria wouldn't explain. She just said they had to come over right away—the Felices live in nearby Shelby Township, about eight or nine miles from the Miseners—and to call Lindy and pick her up if they could.

Lisa, panicked, knowing it had to be bad for her mother to act this way, ran out of the house, cell phone in hand. She called Lindy's home. No answer. Called her husband Mark's cell phone. No answer. Called Lindy's cell phone, and got her in the middle of a checkout lane at the grocery store.

"Where are you?" asked Lisa. Then, "Leave the cart, walk outside and we'll pick you up."

"What do you mean? My cart's full. I've got these perfect steaks. I just have to cash out. I've got like a month's worth of groceries."

"*No!* Leave your cart and come outside. Something's happened. We've got to go to Mom's."

Lindy flagged down a passing employee, said an emer-

gency had come up and she was sorry but she'd have to leave
her cart and the groceries, and she ran outside. While she
paced, waiting for her sister to pull up, she called Gloria.

"Mom, what's going on?"

"Just get over here."

"Is it Dad? Is it Dad?"

"It's not your father. Just get over here."

Lindy ended the call, thinking to herself, "I bet Leann lost
the baby. She's miscarried."

Lisa and Mike pulled up. They paged Mark, who was at
the gym working out, and headed to Troy.

They pulled up to the Miseners', got out and ran inside.
Lindy remembers seeing her dad standing there and thinking,
"That's a relief."

Gloria came up to them. "Mick's murdered Leann."

"What! What are you talking about?" said Lindy. "I'm
supposed to meet her. I was on the phone with her."

"Mick shot Leann. He murdered her."

Lisa and Lindy both fell to their knees, screaming. Hannah
was sleeping in a nearby room, and Jack and Gloria helped
their two daughters into the family room so as not to wake
the little girl.

"Take me to her! Take me to her!" screamed Lindy. "She
cannot be alone. She cannot be alone." Later, she'd explain:
"She was in the morgue and it was like, 'I don't care. You
take me there.' I couldn't stand that she was there, alone."

"I'll never forget walking into the house and hearing those
words," says Lisa. "I'll never forget that as long as I live.
And I'll never work on that day again, ever."

Two days before the shooting, Leann had called Lori Mayes
at her home in China Township, a community far enough
north of Detroit, running along the St. Clair River that divides
Michigan from Ontario, that it doesn't consider itself a suburb. Lori is a year older than Lisa, four years younger than
Lindy. She wasn't as close to Leann as Lindy was, but they
talked a couple of times a week, anyway.

Lori's phone had been acting up, so she told Leann she'd
call her back in the next day or two, after she got a new
phone. Leann told her the happy news, that she was pregnant,
Lori congratulated her and said call back ASAP.

The afternoon of the shooting, new phone in hand, Lori tried calling Leann, but the phone was static-y. She was in a rush, she'd try back later. The family was piling into the van for a ride north on I-94 to Port Huron. Michigan is hockey-mad, with recreation leagues for kids of all ages. The medi-ocre players compete in what are known as house leagues, with all or most of their games at one home arena. The better kids play on travel teams, with an expanded schedule and games throughout southeastern Michigan, and even into Can-ada.

This was a big day for the family. Jessie, 8, was good enough to be trying out for a travel team based out of Port Huron, and that's where they were headed, Lori and her hus-band, Gary, their four kids, one of her daughter's friends and three nieces and nephews.

They were heading north on I-94 when the phone rang. It was Gloria, who asked her what she was doing.

"You've got to turn around and come over here right away."

"What? What, Mom?"

"Just do it."

The directness of the request—and coming so decidedly just after telling her she was on her way to hockey tryouts with a van full of kids—well, Lori reacted immediately, cer-tain it was tragic news. "I knew somebody was dead. I told Gary, turn around, and then I started calling friends on the way back." She was looking for someone to take her kids for a while. Finally she reached a girlfriend who said it would be fine. "I didn't tell her I had eight," she is able to say with a laugh more than a year later.

She cried the whole way over. Lisa and Mike Felice are motorcycle enthusiasts and over the weekend they'd gone on a biker weekend up north. "I'm thinking Lisa and Mike are dead. I thought 'Oh my gosh, they got hit!' And I remember thinking, 'Lisa is never going to get to see Leann's baby.' "

Lori, too, felt like the ride over was in slow motion. Finally they get there. Gloria is standing outside, next to the garage that adjoins the house.

"It's Lisa and Mike," says Lori.

"No," says Gloria, "Mick murdered Leann."

Lori spins half around, falls back against the garage,

slumps to the ground. Gets up quickly, looks at her mom and says: "That motherfucker is dead."

They go in the garage. Lisa walks out of the kitchen. "Is she dead?" asks Lori.

When Lori and Gary had pulled up, Jack had started crying. As they walk into the kitchen he is standing there. "The normal reaction would be to run over and grab him and hug him," says Lori. "But I couldn't do anything. We just stared at each other."

Jeni Hughes, Leann's best friend, worked late that day. When she got home, there was a message from Gloria to call her when she got in.

"Is Jeff home with you?" Gloria asked.

"No, he's at work."

"Well, come on over."

"Why?"

"Just come over."

"Did something happen?"

"Yes. Just come over."

"Something really bad?"

"Yes, Jeni"—Gloria calm, as she will be throughout this day, but forceful, a power—"Just get in your car and come on over."

Jeni called her husband at work and recounted the conversation.

"What do you think it is?" he asked.

"Maybe they won the lottery or something and they want us to think it's something bad and we'll get over there and they'll tell us. She'll make it seem really bad and I'll get over there and then she'll say: 'Guess what? We won the lottery.' "

And all the way over, Jeni kept telling herself the same thing: Maybe it's kind of a joke. Maybe they won the lottery. Alternating that with, "If I get to the YIELD sign by their house and I see a lot of cars there, it's going to be really, really bad. Please don't let there be a lot of cars there."

She pulled off Dequindre onto the Miseners' street, drove up a block to the YIELD sign. Scared, afraid to look, lifted her eyes and saw . . . a lot of cars.

She pulled up, got out, walked up the driveway. Lindy and Gloria were walking toward her. It all seemed dreamlike. Jeni knew it was something horrible, but saw Leann's car in the driveway and without conscious thought was relieved it wasn't something horrible that had happened to Leann. Then, thinking it must be Mick. Something's happened to Mick.

Gloria took her hand. "Mick and Leann went to the gun range together and Mick shot Leann." Jeni had a scene in her mind. An accidental shooting at the range. Leann at the hospital. Everything going to be okay. "So, she's at the hospital?"

"No, Jeni, she's dead."

"What?" said Jeni. In a fog—"I felt like my whole head went blank"—she turned to Lindy. "Is your mom telling the truth? Is she lying?"

"No, she's telling the truth."

More than a year later, Jeni would say: "I felt like my eyes were going to roll into the back of my head, and I was going to pass out. I still feel that way today."

The Miseners say they had another visit from a family member later that night—Mick, along with Roy Gruenburg.

The Miseners said they saw it was Mick coming up to the door. Unwilling or unable to face him, they ignored his knocking, sitting there silently, looking at each other and hoping he'd go away.

He knocked, waited, knocked again. Gloria and Jack say they're sure he knew they were inside, and that finally Mick said loudly enough through the door for them to hear:

"I didn't do it. I didn't do it. I'm tired of this bullshit."

And then he and Gruenburg turned, walked back to their car and left.

THE FLETCHERS FIND OUT

August 16 was going to be a bad day for Mick's parents and their household in Marysville, even before Leann's shooting. Bad would, of course, get unspeakably horrible. Mick's mother, Darla had been out in San Diego, visiting her daughter Amy, while her son-in-law, Phil, attended a religious retreat for two weeks. Darla's prized 15-year-old shi-tzu, Gabby, had been ailing, and Mick's dad, John, thought it would be easier to have her put to sleep while Darla was out of town.

Darla, who had been told about Gabby while out in San Diego, was flying back on the 16th, arriving at Metropolitan Airport in the late evening. Originally, John had been scheduled to pull a night shift at Detroit Edison and Mick's younger brother, Ben, was going to pick her up. But John decided he didn't want her to spend her first night back in the Gabby-less house alone. So he changed his work schedule and told Ben he'd pick her up, instead.

Ben worked late on the day shift at his job at an auto-parts manufacturer in Marysville and got home to his apartment about 5:45 p.m. He had been a cook at Big Boy's and was the cook in the family now, and he set about getting everything ready for a spaghetti dinner.

The phone rang. He didn't recognize the voice, decided to let the machine get it, then saw on the caller ID that it was Mick's work number, at Roy Gruenburg's law firm. Ben picked up. It was the secretary. "Ben, there's been a horrible accident. Leann shot herself."

Knowing the recent ups and downs in their relationship, his immediate reaction was that she'd committed suicide.

Mick got on the phone. Ben says he'll never forget the

moment, made all the more shocking by his brother's tone, the brother who had always been the level-headed rock of stability. "Whenever you talked to him, he was just real clear and very thoughtful about what he was saying," he would recall after the trial. "When I heard him on the phone, he was in just so much desperation, and just so much pain."

Mick told him to come get him, tried to give him directions, couldn't. The secretary got on the line and told him how to get there.

The police had got a search warrant allowing them to confiscate the clothes Mick had been wearing and would soon be combing through the home on Hazelwood. They would gather evidence, then present their findings in the next day or so to the Oakland County Prosecutor's Office, which would have the say-so on whether or not to charge Fletcher with a crime and issue a warrant for his arrest. For now, he was a free man. Legally, he was free to fly to Zaire if he wanted.

Ben, his wife, Nicole, next to him, tore the speed limit apart the whole way down I-94, still thinking Leann had killed herself. When he walked into Gruenburg's office in suburban Center Line, he was greeted by the incongruous sight of Mick in a white jumpsuit, the first hint of legal trouble to come.

Ben went over to give him a hug, and Mick collapsed into his arms. "I felt all 220 pounds of his dead weight."

"They think I did it. They think I did it," said his brother. "They think I've killed my wife. They think I've killed my honey."

And then he got incoherent. "He was just spouting off everything that came into his head. Just thinking out of his mouth," recalled Ben. "I had never in my life seen my brother like that. Never."

Gruenburg was out, attending to something on Mick's behalf. They waited for him. Finally he called and told them to go on, to get Mick some clothes from his house, a few miles away.

They got there about 10 p.m. The heat of the day was still oppressive. Mick asked Ben if he could get his clothes for him, that he couldn't stand to go in. Four cops were still executing the search warrant. Mick stood on the front lawn smoking one of an endless chain of cigarettes. Ben stood on one side of him with his arm around him. Nicole had her arm around him from the other side.

Larry Hendricks walked out of the house, carrying a blood-soaked square of carpet that had been cut from the bedroom floor. Instead of taking it on a straight path to the police van, Ben said he made a loop past Mick, held up the carpet for him to see, then said: "You're free to go in, now."

"I thought it was probably one of the sickest things I've ever seen," recalled Ben many months later. "Just cold. I thought 'What kind of an asshole would do something like this?' I'm thinking, 'Here's a guy who just lost his wife, hasn't been able to see his daughter, and they're doing this?' It was clear. They thought from the get-go he did it. How are you going to do any kind of objective investigating? You're going to go around looking for things to incriminate someone instead of looking for the actual facts of the case."

Ben braced himself, walked up the steps and into the house, walked down the hall and into the bedroom. "I'll never get it out of my head. Not the sight of blood, but the smell of blood. It was overpowering. That amount of blood in that small a quarters. It just [emanated] throughout the entire house. As soon as you walked in, you smelled it. And then realizing it was someone you were close to. It's something I'll never be able to get out of my mind."

He grabbed some of Mick's clothes and they left. Ben drove Mick's Dakota back to Marysville. Nicole followed in their car. And then they began calling their parents, the seconds ticking by, Mick sobbing uncontrollably, as they waited for John and Darla to get back to what they thought was already a sad situation: a house without Gabby.

Mick's sister Amy dropped her mother off at the John Wayne airport in Orange County, then headed off to her job at the church preschool, where her husband is a pastor and musical director.

After school, she got in her car and got a block away when her cell phone rang. It was Phil. Leann had shot herself. He didn't have any details. Amy got hysterical. Sat there in the car crying, then managed to drive the block back to school. She went back in, still hysterical. "My sister-in-law shot herself. *I don't know where my brother is.* I don't know where my niece is."

She paged Ben. Ben picked up. He was crying. She could hear someone else crying in the background. It was Mick. Ben told her what he knew, which wasn't much. Leann had been killed and they thought Mick did it.

John and Darla got home at 11:25 p.m. Their house in Marysville isn't far from the St. Clair River, the deep, wide, blue expanse of water that separated Canada from Michigan. Its fast running water had just emptied out of Lake Huron a few miles to the north, a couple of days earlier, and had in turn emptied out of frigid Lake Superior. Lake Huron and the river are nature's air conditioning on hot, humid Michigan summer nights. The temperature felt 20 degrees cooler than it had at the airport.

Darla went to the answering machine. It was lit up, with about 20 messages. She listened to one. It was Ben. She could hear Mick's voice in the background saying, "They're not home." And then the line disconnected.

Just then the phone rang and John answered it. Darla, with a mother's instinct, could tell there was something wrong just from the stricken look on John's face. She picked up the other phone. "What's wrong? What's wrong?"

She could hear Ben on the other end saying, "She shot herself."

Darla: "Who? What?"

Ben: "She's dead."

Five minutes later, Ben, Nicole and Mick were at the door. Mick walked into the foyer and collapsed into his dad's arms. The two of them sank to their knees.

The rest of the night was a blur. Mick alternated between staring off into space and crying jags. Darla wanted to take him to the emergency ward, maybe get him some sedation. He wouldn't go. Somehow the night passed. No one slept. Mick would curl up into the fetal position crying.

"He'd cry a while, then go out and pace around the pool smoking," recalled John. "Then you'd hear him crying, again."

"He just kept saying, 'You don't know what it was like. You don't know what it was like. I tried to talk to her. I looked in her eyes. Her eyes open,' " said Darla many months later, the night still vivid in her memory.

It would be nearly a week before they remembered Gabby.

Amy called her dad late Monday night, early Tuesday morning. "I want to come home," she said.

The next night, she and Phil caught the red-eye back to Detroit, arriving at the airport early Wednesday morning. Ben picked them up. "I gotta warn you," he said. "It's not the Mick you know who's waiting for you."

They drove the hour and a half north to the Fletcher's Marysville home. When they walked in, Mick came over and collapsed into her arms, crying, dead weight. "I could hardly breathe," she recalled. "Mick said: 'They won't let me see my baby. They won't let me see Leann.' It was the most awful thing in the world. We all just cried together."

AUTOPSY

Dr. Ljubisa Dragovic was pumped up Monday morning as he made the long, 50-minute drive from his stately old home in old-monied Grosse Pointe to his office in the Oakland County government complex, rock and roll pumping out of the speakers as he battled rush hour.

He was the chief medical examiner, a colorful, high-profile character who was one of the best pathologists in the world. He was the boss, but he still liked cutting up bodies, too, looking for clues, helping put bad guys away. Today, this morning, there was something to look forward to as he drove in fits and starts through the clogged highways, the air already hot and steamy, the sun beating down. There was a big case starting, and the upcoming autopsy would be at the center of it, an autopsy he had decided to perform himself.

Oakland County has what he would argue is the best medical examiner's facility in the country, a state-of-the-art edifice that had opened the previous March. It was spacious, well lit, with all the modern, computerized amenities, unlike the cramped, dingy quarters he and his staff used to share.

He was alerted to the case the previous afternoon. His office is a moderate walk away from the Prosecutor's Office and the warrants people there had told him to be prepared. First word he'd had was that it appeared to be a suicide. A woman had shot herself. She and her husband were the only ones in the house and he'd been in the bathroom at the time of the shooting.

As always in such cases, Dragovic's inner alarms began clanging. "So many of these weird cases, it's either boyfriend and girlfriend drinking and suddenly girlfriend ends up shooting self using the boyfriend's gun," he would explain later in his thick accent—he is a native of Belgrade—dropping articles here and there. And, upon investigation, the reality is the girlfriend didn't shoot herself at all, the boyfriend did it. "Under those circumstances, you have to turn on all your antennae because after all, you are paid to be suspicious. The taxpayers of this county are paying me to be suspicious."

Dragovic had sent his own investigator to the house on Hazelwood as soon as he heard about the shooting, a retired Detroit cop named Bob Rossi, who would shoot some pictures, take some notes, size things up.

Rossi had called back. The body had been moved by the husband, turned over, at least. Did the husband have blood on him? Dragovic had asked. "Not really. He doesn't have any," said Rossi. "It was one of the coppers, and he told me he was real clean."

Rossi stayed in touch Monday night, too. The first word was wrong. Suicide was out and never alleged by the husband. He was saying accident, the cops thought otherwise.

Practically whistling, Dragovic got out of his Mercedes and went in to work. Hendricks was waiting for him. He'd stand outside the observation windows and watch the doctor work. Dragovic could talk into a microphone as he worked, with a speaker on the other side of the window letting Hendricks know what was going on.

Leann's body, purpled where gravity had pulled her remaining blood downward, was wheeled in and put on his cutting table. It was 8:30 a.m. He examined the body externally, then had an assistant take photos before any actual work began. At 9:10, he was ready to proceed with the noisy and messy tools of his trade. Unlike movie scenes, Dragovic wouldn't give a running account of the autopsy to be tape-recorded—you can't record much over the sound of a bone saw. He would make some notes as he went along and later fill out what was called an autopsy protocol, which would record some of the more mundane things he would get to later, the reductions of a human life to grams and centimeters and clinical analysis.

He would later remove her brain and measure it at 1,258 grams. Other reductions from flesh and blood, from a loved mother and daughter to statistics would include: liver, 1,168 grams; right lung, 399 grams; left lung, 255 grams; heart, 241 grams; left kidney, 142 grams; right kidney, 111 grams. He would find her stomach contained 1120 milliliters of partially digested food and her bladder 10 milliliters of urine.

She'd even gone from being a name to case number 99-2570, autopsy number 0638.

Dragovic would record that the woman on his table was 5-foot-3, 133 pounds, medium developed, medium nourished, with hair 10 inches in length, red-brown in color and saturated in blood. "The irises are blue, the corneae are clear and the sclereae and conjunctivae are unremarkable. The nostrils contain dry blood. The nasal skeleton is palpably intact. The lips are without evident injury. The oral cavity is without note. The neck and chest are unremarkable. There is a small scar in the upper right quadrant of the belly. The external genitalia show no evidence of trauma. The posterior torso and the anal orifice are without note. The length of arm from the top of the shoulder to the mid-knuckle is 23 inches."

All of that he would write later, after he'd finished with his hands-on work, which would take about an hour and 40 minutes.

Hendricks wouldn't need to wait for a written report. He wouldn't need to wait for the autopsy to be completed. He would be on his way in a few minutes.

Dragovic, as others would be in this case, was certain of what he was looking at right from the start, before he'd cleaned out the wound, before he'd figured out the angle of entry into the cleaned-out skull cavity, before he'd measured and weighed and recorded.

"The remains were brought in and right then and there it was clear," he would say later. There was a lot of caked blood, but no soot. A self-inflicted wound, one you'd expect to be caused at very close range, deposits soot and he saw none on her.

What he thought was clear got even clearer. He cleaned her up, shaved her hair away from her ear and was immediately able to see what is known as a stippling pattern, a kind of tattooing made by unburned gunpowder as it is exploded out of the front of the gun. The larger the pattern, the farther away the gun was when it discharged.

Tests at a firing range with Fletcher's Smith & Wesson would need to be conducted, but Dragovic was certain: The gun had been 12–18 inches from Leann's ear when it was fired, too far for her to have done it.

"This was not so much ingenuity, like in some other cases where you have to do a lot more to piece the puzzle together," he would say. "In this case, the pattern of injury was self-defining."

Dragovic told Hendricks to come into the room.

"She didn't shoot herself," said Dragovic.

"Well, Doc, what are you saying?"

"I'm saying, you've got a homicide," said Dragovic. Hendricks remembers the doctor getting excited then, his accent more pronounced.

"Okay," said Hendricks. He'd expected that, but still it was a jolt to hear it. A homicide!

Dragovic gave him some evidence to take with him—bullet fragments, clippings from her fingernails, a vaginal swab—and he hurried from the building. Dragovic says Hendricks was running. Hendricks says it wasn't running, but as close to it as he gets.

He got in the car and headed south. He called Cleyman, gave him the news. Cleyman told him they requested a second search warrant to go through the two computer systems and two laptops they'd seen in a brief search of the house the night before, items they hadn't included on the original warrant.

Hendricks stopped at the station, filled out the requisite paperwork for the morning's visit to the ME, then delivered the evidence to the state police crime lab.

Dragovic says he wasn't excited at the time of the autopsy, that his work requires a certain distancing and lack of emotion. The excitement came the next day, "when they told me they found the pinpoint droplets of blood on the cuff. *That* was exciting."

They told the press, too. The shirt was a giveaway, they said, its right sleeve covered with pinpoints of high-velocity bloodmist that would seal Fletcher's fate.

SEARCH WARRANT

The first warrant was issued at 4:17 p.m. Monday. About 9:30 p.m. a crew from the state police crime lab, headed up by Lt. David Woodford, a chemist, arrived at the scene to do some preliminary work. Most of the job, much of it tedious, involving the measurement of blood stains around the room to try to determine roughly where Leann was shot, would be done the next day. But it was important, in the meantime, to pull the drain trap in the bathroom sink. Blood is very water-soluble and any blood that might have been caught in the trap would need to be tested for as soon as possible. Tests for blood in the sink itself, and in the toilet, were negative.

The crew left at 11 P.M. after completing its quick plumbing jobs and taking 35-millimeter photos of the interior of the house. The gunk would be tested at the lab. At least one Hazel Park cop stood watch outside the house throughout the night. At one point, Fletcher, his brother, Ben, and his sister-in-law, stopped by to retrieve some clothes.

The next day, the search crew of Cleyman, Weimer and Welch arrived at the house about 8:45 a.m. They unplugged the PCs and removed them. A sheriff who was a computer specialist would later go through the files, as well as take the boxes apart, where he would find hidden several CDs which contained pornography Fletcher had downloaded from the Internet—garden-variety stuff, nothing involving kids or sadism and death.

The sheriff would find other stuff, too, which would make headlines for months.

At one point, Leann's sister, Lisa Felice, showed up to pick up the family pets. The cops gave her a cat, a rabbit and a tropical fish. Later, all three would be given to Leann's best friend, Jeni Hughes, who was as big an animal lover as Leann had been.

Cleyman went upstairs to the bedroom that served as Fletcher's home office. The entire house was a disaster area. By all accounts, Leann was a superb and loving mother, but she clearly didn't spend much time on housework. Clothes were scattered everywhere. The sink was filled with long-dirty dishes. There wasn't a step leading upstairs that wasn't covered with junk. Police officers get used to some pretty untidy homes, but this was near the far end of the bell curve. Mick's office was a mess, too. It was clear that its occupant liked Coke and Busch Light. Cans and bottles filled every level surface and were lying sideways across much of the carpet. It was hard imagining any work getting done here.

Over the back of a black desk chair, fitted over it like a seat cover, was a white T-shirt; printed on the back was: "BEST DAD IN THE WORLD, HANDS DOWN."

The bedroom filled half the upstairs. Doors led to storage areas under the sloping part of the roof. When Cleyman opened them, he saw junk of all sorts that had been tossed on top of the raw, pink insulation in the floor boards. The one room that didn't disgust him with its disheveledness was what was obviously a child's bedroom across the hall from where Leann was shot. Though a mess, it had been painted by Leann, with billowing white clouds and a brilliant big sun. It was filled with toys and stuffed animals and the presence of a mother who deeply loved her child. It filled Cleyman with sadness. So, too, did the pictures of Hannah in every room.

Later, he would say: "The only humanitarian thing to come out of this whole thing—if you want to call it that—was I'm glad he got her out of there. He knew what he was going to do and he got his daughter out. If he wanted to be totally evil, he could have done it while Hannah was taking a bath or something."

The state police, who would arrive soon, would look for forensic evidence. Cleyman and Welch, snapping photos as they searched, were looking for motive.

Cleyman didn't have to look hard. Almost immediately, in the desk, he found copies of divorce papers Fletcher had filed in St. Clair County. So, the marriage had been in deep trouble. He found a shipping bill from Gateway computers to the Hazelwood house, but it wasn't in Mick's name, it was in Sue Chrzanowski's. Cleyman knew her well from her days as a prosecutor in Oakland County when she'd worked the southern part of the county, where Hazel Park was. She was a judge in Warren. Fletcher was a lawyer there, and had been employed briefly by the Warren city attorney. Maybe the receipt was work-related.

In the closet, Cleyman found a brown, accordion-style folder, opened it up and hit the mother lode. Motive? A beaut. There were several Hallmark cards, love letters, poems, and three photos of a woman and one of a man. Cleyman recognized the woman in the photos right off. One of them was a picture she used when running for judge in 1996. It was Chrzanowski. The picture of Mick was taken at a lake; he was bare-chested. One of the poems was on court letterhead.

"I was stunned. Just stunned," Cleyman would say later. He liked Sue. He was disappointed in her. Worse than that, though, she was now, instantly, a suspect in a murder. She was apparently part of a love triangle, and one of its members had been shot to death less than 24 hours earlier.

The cards were love cards. And a poem.

Chrzanowski had written on State of Michigan, 37th District Court letterhead:

To: Mick
With all my love—
(Please forgive the massacre of this classic poem)
'TWAS THE NIGHT AFTER X-MAS

And then, on another sheet of paper, she wrote:

'Twas the night after Christmas and all through the home,
Not a creature was stirring, but my mind was a-roam.
Pretty garlands were hung by the chimney with care.
I admired the stereo wires my love put there."

[Note: When Chrzanowski was still married to Derek Zunker, before she and Fletcher had begun their affair, Fletcher had moonlighted on weekends at the Zunkers' new house, doing some wiring and networking their computers.]

I nestled myself all snug in my bed
While visions of him still danced in my head.
Till what did my wondering ears did hear
But the sound of my pager drawing me near.
With a little old message so lively & quick,
I knew in a minute it must be Sir Mick.
More rapid than eagles his pages they came,
He told me he loved me, and I felt the same.
His eyes how they twinkle, his voice makes me sigh,
His chest very sexy, his smile puts a sparkle into my eye
His droll little mouth—and his lips not to miss,
And the bump underneath them that I like to kiss.
No, he's not Santa—no reindeer in flight.
He is my Sir Michael, my own special knight.
He gave me a gift much better than a toy.
It is the lesson of faith—for true love and joy.
His pages are all I can have on this night.
I LOVE YOU, BABY!!

It didn't exactly scan but it was a blockbuster. Cleyman didn't have a murder case on his hands. He had a soap opera. One that would cause a frenzy in the local media, for Chrzanowski wasn't just a judge, she was a beauty. But more than that, she was from one of the most politically powerful families in southeastern Michigan. In the city of Warren or Macomb County, you could run for election with a first name of Butthead and win—so long as your last name was Chrzanowski.

The beautiful and powerful judge. The beautiful and powerless wife. The handsome husband who had them both. What else could you ask for? Court TV would be at the pre-trial hearing. ABC's "20/20" would cover the trial gavel-to-gavel. Book companies would scramble to find a writer on the scene. It was a career case for small-town cops. For big county prosecutors, too.

Chrzanowski, most agreed, had been destined for big things. She was connected, very bright, an able judge, extremely attractive, a hard worker who ran a tight courtroom, a rising political and judicial star with name recognition.

"I saw her with a very big future," said Margarete Sinclair, a former Warren city councilwoman and family friend. "I saw her in the Court of Appeals or the Supreme Court some day. Some people, you just know they are rising stars."

She was only 32 when the story broke, and had been on the bench since 1996, winning election to the 37th District Court for the first time after a losing effort two years earlier.

Her lawyer quickly walled her off from the media as the scandal unfolded, but friends, including many of the young attorneys who populated the bustling Warren court, said she was quick-witted, unpretentious, a good aunt to her young nieces and a lover of show tunes from big Broadway productions.

"A lot of people are going through the feeling of wanting to hug her and smack her at the same time and say, 'How could you? How could you have done something so dumb?'" Sinclair told the *Detroit Free Press*.

Her family would wonder the same thing. The Chrzanowskis, as a clan, had always been astute, politically and otherwise. Her father, Robert, had been chief judge of the circuit court that handled felony trials for Macomb County, where Warren was located; he'd also been Warren city attorney and was in private practice at the time of the shooting, preparing to run for county prosecutor in the fall of 2000. Her brother, Kenneth, was a county commissioner. Her sister, Janet, was an attorney. Her father's cousin, Mary Chrzanowski, was a Macomb County Circuit Judge.

(Mary, herself, has had her share of notoriety. In 1987, while in private practice, she was charged with drunk driving after hitting a parked car and then refusing a blood-alcohol test. Later that same year, she was fired from her new job as a member of the Macomb County Prosecutor's staff after getting into a loud altercation in a restaurant because the waitress gave free coffee to two cops but insisted she had to pay for hers. Then in January of 2001, while Susan was facing possible firing by the Michigan Judicial Tenure Commission, Mary was brought up before the same tribunal because, it was alleged, she had stormed into the office of newly elected Macomb County Sheriff Mark Hackel the month before and demanded he assign a certain deputy to her courtroom. She denied charges that she was drunk but accepted an offer by one of the other deputies to drive her home. She did admit,

"I became livid" because she couldn't get the deputy she wanted.)

Susan had been, it seemed, to the position bred. At Warren's Cousino High School, she had been class president three years running and delivered the commencement address. At the University of Michigan, she was an editor of the yearbook. At Wayne State law school in downtown Detroit, she graduated *magna cum laude*, then was hired as an assistant prosecutor in affluent Oakland County.

In 1994, just a year out of law school and riding the family name as fast and far as it would take her, she ran for judge in Warren and lost, then ran again two years later and won. Warren is a hotbed of family politics. Chrzanowski ran against Jennifer Faunce, the daughter of Sherman Faunce, the long-time Warren judge whose seat they were after. Faunce was considered the favorite. Because of her inexperience, the Macomb County Bar Association, normally a rubber stamp, gave Chrzanowski a rating of slightly below average, which is about equal to a D-minus. But despite that rating and the formidable name opposition, Chrzanowski pulled off victory.

She surprised everyone with her acumen on the bench. She started court on time, not always the case with her colleagues, and was a tough, conservative judge known for her compassion and probation policies for young offenders. Prosecutors and defense attorneys both liked her.

"She didn't have a good reputation, she had a sterling reputation," said Jun Munem, a political observer and consultant in Warren.

She was also known as a soft touch for local charities, someone who could be counted on to say yes to requests for time or money. She was on the board of the Warren YMCA, a member of Warren Goodfellows and a volunteer for several youth organizations.

"She is the first one to raise her hand to give time and energy to a worthy cause," said John Iras, the head of the Warren Coalition for a Healthy Community.

The only blot on the résumé, the only thing that said she, perhaps, wasn't a wonder woman after all, was her divorce from Zunker in September of 1998. By that time, it appears, Sir Michael had ridden to the damsel's aid.

PICKING UP STEAM

While Welch and Cleyman found more than they'd hoped for upstairs, forensic scientists Sheryl Tortigian and David Woodford of the Michigan State Police were doing their tedious, painstaking work in the downstairs bedroom. The scene was full of blood, and their job was to make it tell the story of how and where Leann died.

Blood is blood, except when it comes to a homicide, especially one involving a gunshot to the head. There are nearly as many types of blood drops and blood stains as there are Eskimo words for snow, and Woodford and Tortigian would be hunting for them, measuring them, applying fairly complex mathematics—dividing the width of a stain by the length, then taking the cosine of that to figure out the impact angle—to try to trace them back to a central focus, the space in three dimensions where the bullet entered Leann's right ear.

The first blood to exit a shooting victim is called blowback or high-velocity blood spatter. The bullet enters with such force that immediately it propels a cloud of microscopic blood drops—a sort of aerosolized mist—back toward the shooter. They would look for that at the scene and on the gun; about the same time they were looking for it in the house, Dragovic was looking for it on Leann's hands. The state police investigators would also look for it—and claim to find it—on the right sleeve of Fletcher's shirt, in tests conducted by Woodford back at the lab.

They'd be looking for other blood, too—blood that would have flown more slowly from the wound or that might have dripped from her nose. This blood would show a direction the body might have taken while falling. They'd be looking for contact stains, where a hand or foot of a possible killer might have come in contact with Leann's blood and left it on another surface.

They would hunt high and low for blood—and find it on the mirror, on a computer stand, on the carpet, on the bed, on the walls. Blood, like other liquids, forms drops that are perfectly spherical. The teardrop shapes we often imagine don't exist. Their shape after they hit a surface tells investigators from which direction they came—the drop hits and continues to spread in the direction of movement, leaving a tail.

So Woodford and Tortigian would look for drops with tails, measure the drops' width and length, measure angles of drops that had hit a surface while either rising or falling, would stretch string back from the various tails. Where the strings crossed, if they did their work correctly, would be where Leann was shot.

Their measurements painted an even more gruesome picture than the massive blood stain on the carpet. Leann Fletcher was shot, they would determine, while on her hands and knees, her head about 14 to 18 inches above the floor and about ten inches from the bed. Later, when Woodford's tests on the vaginal swabs taken by Dragovic from Leann came back positive for fresh sperm in her vagina, the picture was complete, at least to the prosecution—Fletcher had had sex with her from behind while she knelt on all fours, then seconds after ejaculating, had picked up his Smith & Wesson and blown her brains out.

Susan Chrzanowski was now a potential suspect in the murder of her lover's wife. She would need to be interviewed. More than that, she would need an alibi.

Hendricks and Weimer knocked on Chrzanowski's spacious Warren home about 5:30 p.m. Tuesday. Her sister, Janet, opened the door. The cops showed their badges, said why there were there.

"Just a minute," said Janet, closing the door on them.

She opened it a few seconds later. "Sue's not feeling well. Can she talk to you some other time?"

"No, I really need to talk to her today," said Hendricks.

"Hold on." She shut the door, harder this time.

A minute later, the door reopened. Sue was standing behind her sister. "Come on in," said the judge, and led them into the den.

"We already had the cards and love letters," Hendricks would say later. "We knew they had a serious relationship. We didn't know the dates, but we had a Christmas poem; we assumed that was from Christmas of '98. So now we were looking for motive, to see if it was an ongoing affair."

Chrzanowski lied to them, a lie that would eventually cause her to be removed from the bench. She admitted to an affair with Fletcher, but said it had been brief, in February and March of 1999, but that it was over.

Had she spoken to Fletcher recently? No.

She told them she'd met him at the Warren city attorney's office, had heard he was something of a handyman, a whiz with wiring and computers, and had hired him to do some work on her house. Her marriage had been struggling. She and Mick grew close during the time he worked for her, started having feelings for each other and eventually became lovers.

She said they dated only while he'd been separated, but that it was over and she hadn't dated him since he went back to his wife in the spring. She had heard at the office that Leann had committed suicide, which is why she was so distraught. What she didn't tell Hendricks is that after hearing the news, she'd left work early for the day, went looking for a church to pray in, and lit a candle in the chapel.

"I'm thinking, 'What you're telling me is not adding up,' " Hendricks would recount later, going over his thought processes at the time. " *'You dated this guy from February to March and now you're all busted up that his wife had committed suicide?' It just didn't add up."*

Not to mention the " 'Twas the Night Before Xmas" poem. Why write a Christmas poem in March?

Hendricks asked her if she'd talked to Fletcher since the shooting.

No. She'd been at the Cedar Point amusement park in Ohio on a family outing all day Monday and didn't get home until 1 a.m. Tuesday. He'd paged her at 7:30 p.m. and left a voice mail on her pager that something terrible had happened and she should call Roy Gruenburg.

"Did you call Mick back and talk to him?"

"No. I just got the voice mail. It was late. I was going to talk to Roy, but when I got to work I found out what happened."

That didn't make sense, either. The guy's getting grilled by police and is suspected of murdering his wife, so he's going to call a woman he hasn't seen in five months and ask her to call his lawyer? Two and two was still coming out three.

At that point, Chrzanowski's dad, Robert, showed up. Janet had called him and he'd driven over, pronto.

He didn't stop the interview, he stood outside the French doors to the den, listening quietly.

Hendricks began trying to pin her down on dates. Her dad stepped in and said, "Sue, I think you might need an attorney."

She looked at Hendricks. "Do you think I need an attorney?" she asked him.

"I don't know. Do you think you need an attorney?" said Hendricks. Later he would say, "Keep in mind, we're not dealing with Joe Blow off the street. The suspect is an attorney. The woman who has a relationship with him is a judge and an attorney, so they know their rights."

The judge looked at Hendricks, then over at her dad. "I think I'm going to get one. I might need to talk to one."

"Fine. Get yourself an attorney and have him call me and set up a time to talk."

At 6 p.m., Hendricks and Weimer left. Chrzanowski had lied to them—a judge lying to cops in the middle of a murder investigation—had gotten herself deeper in trouble, trouble she'd be fighting, trying to save her career, more than a year later. But one good thing had come out of it. She had an alibi, one they'd look into and would quickly check out. She was off the hook for murder, anyway.

As the police drove away, the judge began sobbing and apologized over and over again to her father for being an embarrassment to the family.

Hendricks, in the middle of his second straight 20-hour day, went back to the house on Hazelwood. They were still carting out stuff. They finished about 11 p.m. Fletcher was there, waiting for them to finish. They handed him the several-page tabulation of everything that had been confiscated, some 90 items.

At some point, Fletcher seemed to go "ooh" and slump a bit. Cleyman isn't sure, but he thinks it was when Fletcher saw they'd taken his computers and discs. There were e-mails in there, lovey-dovey stuff from the judge that would create headlines at trial, and titters around the Warren courtroom. And plenty of porno.

One thing the cops missed, somehow, was a role of exposed film sitting in a plastic canister on the bathroom sink. Fletcher's defense attorney, Brian Legghio, would find it later when he walked through the house and would have it developed. It was shots of Hannah's third birthday party at some indoor place with kids' rides, just 15 days earlier. One of the photos was of Fletcher, holding his daughter, both of them beaming at the camera.

While Hendricks and the state police finished executing the search warrant, another soap-opera development was taking place a few miles away, at the Miseners' house in Troy. Another judge was about to join the growing scandal.

The Miseners, Leann's siblings and close friends all gathered on short notice for a series of interviews. Police talked to everyone in turn. By then, they all were convinced of Fletcher's guilt, and for the most part the proceedings were foreordained. Each in turn told him their favorite anti-Mick anecdotes, much of it amounting to nothing useful except, perhaps, further convincing police the guy was a scumbag and murderer.

Interesting, though, was the statement given by Chris Misener, Jack and Gloria's eldest. As one officer later wrote in his report: "Chris did not think Michael was capable of hurting victim."

Jeni Hughes, Leann's confidante, told him something that made him sit up and take notice, though. Chrzanowski wasn't the first judge Mick had messed around with. He'd also had an affair with another, more senior judge named Dawnn Gruenburg, the daughter of the guy who'd driven Fletcher away from the Hazel Park jail the day before. Mick was her boy toy.

Gruenburg, said Hughes, had gotten mad when Fletcher started working at Chrzanowski's house and threatened to hurt his legal career if he kept seeing the younger judge. Mick had basically told her where to get off and the judge got so mad she sent one of her relatives—who was a customer of the hair salon where Leann worked—in to tell Leann that the judge wanted to meet with her and give her the lowdown on Mick.

Gruenburg, Jeni said, had always treated Leann meanly. Dawnn had been Mick's sponsor at the ceremony when Mick became a lawyer and Mick had thanked her, but hadn't mentioned his wife in his speech. Leann had been sure her husband was having an affair with Dawnn, and had driven by the judge's house hoping to catch Mick, but never had.

Leann hated the judge so much that she refused her request for a get-together.

Hmm, now that was some good stuff. Made the gathering worthwhile. Smick thanked everyone and left.

It had been a very interesting day for the Hazel Park PD. One to remember.

Wednesday was time for the overworked Hazel Park cops to take a bit of a breather. Hendricks filled out reports and waited for lab results and the inevitable arrest warrant.

Thursday morning, Chrzanowski and her attorney, Stephen Rabault, came in to the Hazel Park police station. It was time to set the record straight. Cleyman and Hendricks interviewed. She admitted that her affair with Fletcher was ongoing, that she had had sex with him the previous Sunday night, when he'd told her he'd been to church with Leann that morning and out to dinner with the Miseners before paging Chrzanowski. He hadn't, though, told her the reason for the dinner, that Leann was pregnant. The cops had broken that news to her.

She admitted talking to him after the murder. She had returned his page after she got back from Cedar Point, that he was extremely upset and told her to call Roy. She said she was in love with Fletcher, hoped something would come of it, had been assured by Mick that he wasn't having sex with his wife. When she pressed him about it, he'd said, "If you were a fly on the wall, you wouldn't need to ask me that."

"We got it all out," said Hendricks. "She was totally truthful, and from that point on she was totally cooperative."

Well, perhaps not totally truthful. Chrzanowski maintained then, and continued to maintain at subsequent hearings, that her affair with Fletcher began after her divorce in September of 1998. But in an e-mail sent to her months before her divorce, Fletcher wrote: "Knowing that you go home to someone who is not me is difficult. I know that he could not possibly look at you the way I do."

And another e-mail from Fletcher said: "I don't think I'll ever understand how your husband could stand being away from you so often as he is. Mind you, I'm not complaining."

Gruenburg came into the station on Friday with her attorney and was interviewed by Hendricks. She acknowledged an affair with Fletcher, saying it had been brief, from September to November of 1997 and inconsequential. It was for sex, not love. While it had been a sexual relationship it was, in the words of Hendricks' report, "not an intimate affair."

Gruenburg signed a consent form allowing police to search her office and computer. Since the computer was technically owned by the state of Michigan, state officials had to sign off, too, and did.

One of the things that would eventually enter the court file was a note sent to Gruenburg in December of 1997. She was clearly angry with Fletcher and he was trying to convince her of his friendship, even if their stint as lovers was finished. It read:

Dawnn,
I thought it might behoove me to write things I wanted to say, as opposed to trying to talk to you in person, given my addiction to breathing and all.
I did not want you to think that I was ungrateful for all the things you have done for me. . . . You have always acted in my best interests & for this I shall always be indebted to you.
I am concerned about your thinking that my friendship was limited only to that.
You have a heart of gold, Dawnn.

Referring to allegations Gruenburg had made to him about a possible affair with her rival judge, and subtly denying them, Fletcher went on.

If I am to suffer because of politicized gossip, so be it. To me, my freedom to associate with anyone I damn well please is far more important than any reward the legal profession can possibly bring.

And then he finished with a declaration of friendship.

If I were given the ultimatum of befriending Dawnn Gruenburg at the expense of my legal career, I would just as soon collect trash for a living. I would rather be known for being a good and true friend than the world's most successful attorney.
   I love you Dawnn. Your friend.

According to Hendricks' report, Gruenburg seemed hardly a friend. Not anymore. She ripped Fletcher up one side and down the other. He was a "user" of people and she had gotten tired of it. He was a "heavy drinker" who couldn't handle his alcohol and became "an embarrassing drunk."

He was a bad attorney, too. She'd referred her sister-in-law to Fletcher to handle a child-custody case, and both she and the sister-in-law were very unhappy with Mick's work.

And she confirmed that she had sent the same sister-in-law over to the Incognito salon to try to arrange a meeting between her and Leann, "because Leann did not need a husband like that."

Continuing, she said his affair with Chrzanowski was common knowledge among court employees and she described him as "sexually aggressive but not violent."

Hell hath less fury than a judge scorned.

SURVEILLANCE AND ARREST

Martin Barner was a late-comer to law enforcement. He was 38 when Leann was shot, and he'd been on the force just five and a half years. He was an entrepreneur before becoming a cop; he had a bachelor's degree in business administration and had owned his own direct-marketing company before deciding the headaches of owning his own business outweighed the positives.

He became a private investigator and then head of security at a huge flea market in the Detroit area, which gave him a taste for police work. He applied for a job as a real cop in Hazel Park and was hired. He got his calling late, but he got it big-time. He has a passion for the job.

At the time of the Fletcher case, he was part of a multijurisdictional force known as the Crime Suppression Unit, funded by a federal grant. Several local police agencies kick in one cop and one squad car to the unit, which worked out of an office in nearby Madison Heights. It was their job to take on some of the local crime that fell through the cracks.

Drug units and auto theft units are common. What the Crime Suppression Unit does is pool resources to take a more organized approach to crimes that might otherwise go relatively unnoticed by individual jurisdictions. If they got a tip, for example, that Joe Blow had been doing home invasions in the area, Barner could put a surveillance team in place, see what he was up to, follow him across city boundaries, where otherwise they would have been unable to go, wait for him to commit a crime, then arrest him on the spot.

With Fletcher as the obvious number-one suspect in Leann's death and an evolving situation with a number of unresolved questions—Did he have access to clients' money?

Did he have large funds of his own? Would he use his parents' home near the Canadian border as a springboard for flight abroad?—the CSU was asked to put him under 24-hour surveillance until, and if, a warrant for his arrest was issued.

Barner was point man for the unit. A big guy whose work attire is often a plaid flannel shirt, running shoes, baseball cap worn backwards and blue jeans, he looks more like the clean-up hitter on the neighborhood bar's softball team than he does an undercover cop. Which is the point.

Hazel Park is a small city but on the afternoon shift that he once worked as a patrolman, the action was non-stop. Routine, but busy. Pulling over speeders on I-75, the freeway that bisects the city, looking for drunks weaving away from bars at closing time, heading out on domestic violence calls in the working-class neighborhoods, busting kids with pot. Always enough doing to make the time fly by.

His first few months with the CSU, Barner was bored out of his mind. He hadn't yet learned how to handle the hard time of surveillance—the interminable waits while nothing is happening, sucking down coffee, fighting sleep, checking your watch yet again to see that time has stood still. "I was absolutely bored to tears," he admits.

But—and it's a big *but*—the adrenaline rush of catching a perp in action made up for all the slow time and drowsy hours. "When it happens, it's a major rush. It makes it all worthwhile. We sit there, watch someone rob a place, let 'em get back in their car and leave the scene, then, *Bam!*" Sirens wailing, lights flashing, guns drawn, you're-under-arrest-and-you-have-the-right, etc.

The day of the shooting, Barner was working a home-invasion target in Hazel Park. He was monitoring the frequency, heard the call to nearby Hazelwood Avenue and decided to drive over and help secure the scene pending the arrival of more police.

He ran into the house, saw Leann on the floor, hung around until the full contingent of crime-scene investigators was on hand, then left.

"I remember thinking at the time—and I told another crew member—'This guy killed his wife.' That was just my initial impression."

It was an impression he shared with other Hazel Park police. Smart, intuitive police work, or, as defense attorney Brian Legghio would contend, a rush to judgment by police altogether inexperienced in homicide scenes?

Two days later, and coming off a 12-hour day, Barner was back on the case. Lt. Smick called, said a warrant was being sought and they wanted Fletcher under surveillance, so they could prevent any flight, and so they could pull him in the minute word came down that a warrant had been issued.

The CSU unit knew his home address, of course, as well as the address for Judge Chrzanowski, his parents', and his office. They soon located his black 1999 Dodge Dakota pickup parked in the long curving driveway at his parents' home on 18th Street in Marysville.

A first glance was enough to send a jolt into Barner. There was a large fifth-wheel trailer attached to the vehicle, and there was a lot of activity. People were going back and forth between the house and the trailer. "It looked like maybe boxes of clothes and food. Our reaction was, 'Maybe this guy's getting ready to leave. Maybe he's packing up and getting out of here.' "

When the warrant would eventually come down, word would be leaked to the papers and show up high in the stories that Fletcher had been about to flee. Though eventually the trailer's license plate was traced to an out-of-town relative and the activity was found to be harmless and strictly coincidental to the arrival of surveillance units—and, in fact, the trailer was being unloaded, not loaded—it was impossible to know that in the dark. And the impression had been made, one that would be repeated on TV news shows and talk radio: The guy was about to make a run for it.

The corollary, of course, was that only a guilty person would be getting ready to flee before a warrant had even been issued.

Barner sat in his car throughout the night, in sight of the Fletchers' large corner house. Other surveillance units were parked nearby, one officer to a car. They had, in the vernacular, established "the eye." Whichever way Mick might head, Barner would put out the word, and someone would be ready to pull out in pursuit.

At one point in the long, boring shift, there was another jolt of activity for police. A car left the scene, with four occupants. It was followed to its destination. It turned out to be Mick's brother, Ben, his sister-in-law, and two of their friends.

Barner got his first clear sighting of Mick at 10:48 Thursday morning. There is a high wooden fence that runs along the back of the house, surrounding an in-ground swimming pool. Fletcher had come out the side door and was pacing a 10-foot swath, chain-smoking. Back and forth, one cigarette, two cigarettes, a third, in succession.

"He was like a caged animal," recounted Barner, freed by his chief, David Niedermeier, to speak after the trial, a year after events of the day. "He'd smoke three cigarettes in a row, then go back inside for a little while, then come back out and start all over again. Smoking like crazy."

At 1:30 p.m., Mick and his parents, John and Darla, got in John's black GMC Yukon, along with Amy and her husband, Phil. Brother Ben and his wife, Nicole, followed in their car. Surveillance units picked them up and followed them as they drove to I-94, a mile and a half away, then headed south, toward Detroit. They got off at the Mt. Clemens exit. Mt. Clemens had been a tourist destination known worldwide 100 years ago for the reputed powers of its numerous mineral baths.

Eventually the baths closed and prosperity went the way of the homing pigeons that used to fill the downtown squares. The town became, and remains, the county seat for sprawling Macomb County. Gentrification has begun, with abandoned blocks and buildings being saved from the wrecker's ball and remodeled back to their original high ceilings, wet plaster and wainscoting.

A new, expensive county courthouse serves as an anchor and much of the renovations have been financed by attorneys hoping to avoid the sterile look of suburban strip centers while at the same time being able to walk to work. Fletcher's defense attorney, Brian Legghio, is one of those in a renovated old brick building near the courthouse, and it was there the Fletchers were heading. It was their first meeting with Legghio and he wanted to meet the whole family. He told them that they were naive to think this would be dropped quickly. He told them to expect a full-court press by prosecutors and police. This was a high-profile case—"a made-for-

TV movie"—and the authorities were going to go all out with it.

"I know you don't want this to go to trial, but trust me, this *is* going to go to trial. They will not let up. They *will* be relentless. They are going to push this. I don't want you talking to anyone. I don't want you answering the phone."

But, he told them, he had just got off the phone with the prosecutor's office and he had a gentlemen's agreement that when and if a warrant was issued, he would be allowed to surrender his client. There would be no forceful arrest. At least there would be that.

Barner sat for 90 minutes while they huddled with Legghio, then followed them as they left downtown, drove back to I-94 and headed north toward Marysville.

Meanwhile, a Keystone Cops bit of business had continued. When Fletcher was put under surveillance, Barner had prudently notified the Border Patrol at the nearby Blue Water Bridge, one of the busiest entry points to Canada along the entire US–Canadian border, who Fletcher was, what vehicles he might be driving and their license plates. In the event of any apparent move by him toward the bridge, Barner promised to call and alert the Border Patrol.

That wasn't good enough for the federal officers on duty Thursday. "They were driving us nuts," recounted Barner. "They were calling us every 10 minutes. 'What's he doing? What's he doing? Is he coming? Is he coming?' They were driving me nuts. Finally, I had to tell them: 'I'm busy right now. If he comes your way, *trust me*, I'll call you. Believe me, I will.' "

At Hall Road, a couple of miles north of Mt. Clemens, word came over the radio that the arrest warrant had been issued. The normal procedure, according to Barner, when trying to arrest a potentially dangerous subject—and someone about to be charged with shooting his unarmed wife in the back of the head with a Smith & Wesson .45 certainly must be considered a danger—is to box the vehicle in front, back and side, then force it easy over. Given the circumstances—John Fletcher was at the wheel and he was a respectable member of the community, a supervisor with Detroit Edison—Barner decided such action was inappropriate.

Instead, he radioed the nearby state police outpost and asked for some marked units up ahead.

At 21 Mile Road—streets in southeastern Michigan from Detroit's northern border, which is Eight Mile Road, are named in one-mile increments—two marked state police cars put on their sirens and lights and effected a traffic stop along the shoulder of the freeway.

The Fletchers saw one state cop car up on the entrance ramp. When its lights came on, Mick sighed and said: "Here we go." He had prepared his parents that an arrest can be ugly and temporarily violent. The night before, he had his father leave the front door of the Marysville house, with the stained-glass window, open with just the screen door locked to minimize the damage if the police broke in to arrest him. And he had his mother take her porcelain figures off the front room tables. Given the tenor of the newspaper stories emanating from the prosecutor's office, Mick thought an arrest was imminent. And he didn't trust the agreement Legghio had made with prosecutors that if a warrant was issued, he would be allowed to walk his client in for arraignment.

Moreover they knew they were being tailed. "You'd have been pretty dumb not to know, with those unmarked cars," said Amy later. "We just didn't know we were being followed by so many cars. It looked like six or eight of them when we got out."

"We knew we were being surveilled," said John Fletcher. "In a small town like Marysville it'd be pretty hard not to notice."

Though police didn't really suspect trouble with his family in the car, this was, after all, an arrest on a homicide charge, so police carried out what Barner called a felony stop. He said the two state troopers approached the truck on foot with service revolvers drawn. The five unmarked surveillance units were also on the scene but Barner says those officers did not have their guns out.

Mick's sister, Amy, her husband Phil, a church pastor, and his parents, though, all swear the other cops had their shotguns out, too.

It has become part of Misener family lore that the Fletcher vehicle was quickly surrounded by a bunch of cops with drawn shotguns, with Mick quaking in fear. They love that part. Barner said it was less dramatic, though the Fletchers' version of events coincides with the Miseners'.

Mick put his hand on his sister's knee. "It's going to be all right." Then, "Mom, don't cry."

John Fletcher jumped out of the truck.

A voice on a bullhorn said: "Get back in your car, sir." Then, "Michael Fletcher, please step out."

Barner put the cuffs on Fletcher and put him in his unmarked car.

"I'll never forget Michael's mother: 'Remember what the lawyer told us. Don't say anything. Don't say anything,'" said Barner later. John Fletcher started to cry. No one protested the arrest or caused any trouble.

John asked if he could give his son a hug. Barner said: "No. You can talk to him through the glass." A Troy cop, though, said to go ahead, let him hug his son. The car window was rolled down and first the father, then the mother hugged Mick.

Amy was at the window, too, crying. "It's going to be all right," he told her.

Mick said two syllables on the 45-minute drive back to the Hazel Park police station.

"Are those cuffs too tight?" Barner asked.

"No."

"You need some air?"

"Yes."

Barner rolled down his window a bit and that was that.

As they approached the station, figuring the TV trucks and media would be out in force, Barner called a superior, Lt. Smick, to ask him how he should handle it—park by the front door, or do an end run and come in the back door?

Just come in the front, said Smick. Barner pulled into the parking lot, backed into a stall by the front door and brought Mick in. The TV crews were waiting.

"Any comment?" said one reporter.

"Did you do it?" hollered out another.

Fletcher was wearing a blue-gray suit. Thinking he was going to the funeral home later, he had worn Leann's favorite suit of his to Legghio's office.

The Fletchers continued on to Marysville to change and get ready for a visit to the funeral home, for the doubly dreadful duty of seeing Leann's body and facing the Miseners. Legghio called. "They're arraigning Mick. Get down here."

They piled back in the GMC and headed back down I-94 to the Hazel Park police station/courthouse. But the ubiquitous road construction that summer bogged them down in a hair-pulling delay. By the time they got there, the arraignment was over and Mick was on his way to the Oakland County jail, where he would spent the next nine months awaiting trial.

Legghio was still there. It was bad news. They had arraigned Mick on first-degree murder. And they were holding him without bail. The assistant prosecutor had labeled him a flight risk because of the incident with the fifth-wheel trailer, and the judge agreed.

"At least we got a laugh out of that," said Amy. The fifth-wheel, as it turned out, belonged to Mick's aunt and uncle, Ron and Jan Fletcher, who had driven in from Holland, on the far western edge of the state, to give some family support. "If Mick was going to flee, you'd think he'd take something that could go more than 50 miles an hour. This was a huge deluxe fifth-wheel. And it also had "The Fletchers" written in big letters on the back. That's not exactly a vehicle you'd flee in. You'd think he'd take one of my dad's Corvettes, instead."

Nine months after his arrest, on the eve of his trial, one of the reasons people had for assuming Fletcher's guilt was that, hey, the cops had caught him loading up a trailer and getting ready to run, right?

Meanwhile, Hendricks had called the Miseners at the funeral home to tell them Mick had been arrested and was in custody. The Miseners erupted in cheers. Lindy raced to the casket. "They got him! They got him!" she told Leann.

MISENERS: THE EARLY YEARS

Family and a sense of community had always been every-thing to the Miseners.

Jack and Gloria grew up five houses apart on Evelyn Street in Hazel Park. He'd moved there from Detroit with his par-ents when he was three, before Gloria was born. Later, Jack ran around with Gloria's brother, Richard, and she hung around with his sister, Joan.

But with five and a half years' difference between them, they didn't pay attention to each other much—until Jack re-turned home from what he still calls the Korean Campaign. Politicians then were careful not to call it a war, despite all the dying. It was either a "police action" or a "campaign," and war never was officially declared. Today, Gloria will tease him: "You can say 'war' now. They finally called it a war."

Jack never made it to Korea—he spent 18 months of his two-year Army tour of duty in Japan, making it to private first class—and first took serious notice of the fast-maturing Gloria at a party in the neighborhood soon after his return to civilian life.

"She was there and we just started dating," Jack recalls. She was 16, he was 21. The relationship never had any formal beginning. The young war vets and their friends did a lot of partying, and Jack and Gloria kept finding themselves at the same parties, hanging around. They hung around so much that by the time they actually got around to a real, formal date, it was no big deal. Today, they're not even sure what it was. "Probably a drive-in," says Gloria with a smile. "It must have been a drive-in. That's what we did all the time, then. That's what we did every weekend."

And if they weren't at the local drive-in, they were out square dancing. They loved that.

A year later, they were engaged. The circumstances weren't particularly dramatic or romantic in the storybook way, but more of an evolution in the relationship of two people who just seemed to fit, whose life seemed to be already heading along a predetermined path.

The fall of 1954 they were sitting there and Jack said: "Do you want a ring for Christmas?"

"I don't know," Gloria responded, "I'll have to think about it," which she did for a minute or two. And then said: "Sure, why not?"

Three years later, they were still engaged. "That was a long time to be engaged, then," she says. "I think we'd still be engaged if we weren't forced into getting married. It could have gone on forever. Engagement—that's the best time of your life. But my mother said, 'You ought to set a date. You've been engaged for three years.' So, she cashed in my insurance—it was like $500 back then—and that paid for the whole thing."

The neighborhood lovers were married on June 28, 1958, in a Lutheran church in Hazel Park, then had a reception for 200 guests at the nearby Knights of Columbus Hall. Her mother bought all the food and brought it to the hall, and friends and relatives cooked and served it. His aunt made the wedding cake.

They had grown up in Hazel Park, gone to school at Hazel Park High, gotten married in Hazel Park, and now they moved into their first house in Hazel Park, too, on Hazelwood Avenue, seven houses down from the home their youngest daughter, Leann, would buy when she was getting ready to be married herself.

Those were boom times in Detroit, the post-war 1950s. GI loans financed what had once been unattainable for young married couples—homes of their own. As the new thoroughfares called freeways were built leading out from the central cities, suburbs sprang up where cornfields used to wave in the wind. The corn gave way to FHA-financed housing and new streets that were soon filled with all the little kids who would one day be dubbed the Baby Boomers.

Hazel Park was an older suburb; no cornfields had made

way for the Miseners' home on Hazelwood. But I-75 went in just a few blocks away and in the not-so-distant future they would follow it north to the brand-new suburb of Troy, where cornfields did give way to new houses. The experts say the suburbs were invented when techniques of factory mass production built the from-scratch city of Levittown, but a better case could be made that they were invented in Detroit. The first mile of urban freeway in the country was poured in Detroit; city fathers thought high-speed, submerged highways would lead people into the city, take them downtown for shopping and culture, but it worked in reverse, giving them a fast way out. And the first suburban shopping center in the US Northland, opened in Southfield, just west of Hazel Park, in 1954. People would ride the buses way out there just to look at it, a cornfield turned cornucopia.

Detroit was the fifth-largest city in the US, then, with about 1.5 million people. The economy hummed. Anyone wanting a job got one. Unions made sure the jobs paid well and provided benefits and health care. The auto factories worked three shifts seven days a week. No one would hear of such words as "Honda" or "Toyota" or "Volkswagen" for years. (By the late 1960s, Detroit's downtown would be a ghost town, a third of its population would have fled to the suburbs, its factories would be turning out horrible cars no one wanted, unemployment lines went around the blocks and in winter those waiting in the lines would burn garbage in the trash cans to keep warm. Detroit became Murder City instead of Motor City). In the Fifties in southeastern Michigan, life seemed brimming with promise.

Jack's dad worked at the Young Spring and Wire Co. in Detroit and got Jack in there. He worked there before getting drafted, then went back to work there after his time in the Army. Then a better job opened up at John R Lumber, just a couple of miles away from their new house. He'd stay at the lumber company for 17 years and they'd stay in the Hazelwood house for seven years. In the meantime, they started a family.

Their boy, Chris, was born first, in 1959, a little more than a year after they were married. The next year Lindy was born. Lisa was born in 1964 and Lori in 1965. After they thought they were through adding to their brood, Gloria got pregnant again and Leann was born in 1970.

By the time Lori arrived, they had outgrown their Hazel Park home and, as thousands of other young married couples were doing, they moved up and out, following the freeway north into a larger lot, larger house and larger opportunities. The Miseners bought their first house for $10,500 and made a killing when they sold it seven years later for $15,500, which, after they paid off their mortgage, left them a sizable down payment for their new house in Troy, which seemed a steal at $16,000, and came with a six-percent GI loan.

Gloria came from an average-sized family—she has a brother, Richard, and a sister, Jean. (Her father, Richard Knisley, was a truck driver who died when she was three; he was just 32 and died of kidney failure caused by riding too many years on bad shock absorbers over bad roads; a sad parallel is that her granddaughter, Hannah, lost one of her parents when she was three, too.)

But Jack came from a large family, and having a large family of his own was always the plan. His youngest sister has ten kids and the other four siblings have twenty-five kids between them. At Christmas time, the Miseners and their in-laws rent a hall every year to handle the crowd of 80 or so. They chip in on the hall rent, everyone brings a dish and each year they take turns dressing as Santa Claus, showing up with gifts for the kids. In 1999, despite the tragedy of a few months earlier, Chris played Santa.

So when Gloria found out that she was pregnant, again, as Jack was nearing the age of 40, that was fine with him. The more the merrier. It'd make it a little more crowded when the family all piled into the car to go to the drive-in on those sweltering, humid Michigan summer nights, but, hey, so what?

(Drive-ins were hugely popular in southeastern Michigan in the 1950s and 1960s, and scattered throughout the area, fitting for the city that put the world on wheels. Lovers would come to the later shows, where some kinds of American Motor cars were banned because they had fully reclining seats and there was already enough trouble going on with bench seats, but families poured in early for the twilight shows. The kids would tear off for the playground, giving mom and dad a half hour or so of quiet while the on-screen cartoon characters, barely visible in twilight, counted down the minutes to the start of the feature, with Mr. Popcorn and Mr. Soda Pop dancing out enticements to visit the concession stand. Sometimes there'd be a fireworks show, too. Later, the Miseners would spread a blanket next to the car, turn up the little speaker that hung from the window up as high as it would go and sprawl out in the fresh air, or at least as fresh as it gets in July or August in Michigan when it's 90 degrees and 90 percent humidity. Today, one of the last drive-ins in America is still going strong in suburban Dearborn, with nine screens, all showing first-run movies to sold-out or nearly sold-out crowds.)

The four older Misener children were excited when they found out they'd have a new baby, the first to be born since they moved to Troy. With four kids already in the family, no one was about to get a nose out of joint or feel jealous over one more. While Gloria was in the hospital, they all made big signs on posterboards, and they were scattered all through the house, including one that greeted them as they came in the front door: "WELCOME HOME, LEANN."

"We had our dolls," says Lisa, "but she was a real baby for us to play with."

"She was the most spoiled of anybody, but she never took advantage of it," says Lori.

Lindy, the oldest sister at age 10, was particularly loving with the new baby. "She was my baby. I had her all the time. I'd take her shopping with me when I was older. Then, later, I'd go to her school functions as a chaperone. Later, we became best friends. We talked every day."

Shortly after Leann's birth, Jack had a career change. "The best move he ever made," says Gloria.

In 1971, older at age 39 than most people beginning their factory careers, Jack hired on at Ford Motor. Or, as he says it, "then I went to Ford's," with the possessive. It's a small thing, nuance, really, but today's workers call it Ford or Ford Motor. Older generations called it Ford's as in something owned by Henry. Long after it became a public company, the workers still called it Ford's, and somehow they seemed closer to the company, then, more invested in it psychologically, when they saw it as something owned and guided by a single man, or his family, than as a huge corporate entity.

Jack Misener's last day was Dec. 31, 1998, and he still speaks proudly of his time there, of how the company treated him and how he in turn treated the cars he made. Jack was not one of those auto workers of a succeeding generation who left loose bolts inside the frame on purpose, or who called in sick on Monday because he wanted to extend the weekend partying financed by Friday's paycheck, or who got drunk at lunch on Friday with all that money burning a hole in his pocket. (Smart buyers used to know that you never bought a car built on Friday or Monday, because the lines were short-staffed or manned by replacement workers, and demanded proof of the date of assembly from their dealers.)

No, Jack Misener was a Ford man. Still is.

Typical for a Misener, the career break was a result of family. One of his nephews came up to him one day and said, "Jack, I can get you in at Ford's."

"Great," Jack replied.

As he recalls today: "You had to have somebody get you in in those days. Later, I couldn't even get my son in. No one got in on their own. It was sons of union officials or sons of Ford management upstairs."

But his nephew had some clout and sent him to the Sterling Heights plant nearby. There weren't openings there, as it turned out, but the guy his nephew had sent him to had a buddy at the Utica trim plant who owed him a favor, so he wrote a note on a piece of paper, handed it to Jack and sent him on his way.

Jack drove over to Utica and was hired on the spot. Not one to burn any bridges, he took a week's vacation from John R Lumber to get the lay of the land at Ford, liked what he saw in his first week and told his old bosses he wasn't coming back. They understood. You couldn't beat the benefits and overtime of a factory job with the Big Three.

"I was lucky to get in and I was at a good plant," says Jack. "I think I was laid off once for two months in 27 years."

For many of those years, he worked six days a week, 12 hours a day, racking up the overtime. He did just about everything there was to do on the line over the years. He built door panels, head rests, arm rests, made bumpers, painted tail lamps, even acted as supervisor running the line for a good stretch.

Jack built parts for Tauruses and he bought them, too. Today, he leases a Ford van so he can haul the grandkids around, but, man, when they came out with that Taurus, it was the car for him. In 1997, when Leann decided to get a better car, she bought a Taurus, too. It was used, but it was low-mileage, looked new. She only had it a few months when she was killed. Jack cleaned it up, vacuumed it, sold it for what she owed on her note.

"It ran so beautiful," says Jack. "She got it because we love Tauruses."

Susick Elementary School was around the block from their home, with their back fence sharing the lot line. Gloria could watch her kids walk almost all the way to the school. Leann was the last to go there; when Hannah turned four, they enrolled her at preschool there, too. "Hannah will say, 'You can walk me to school, Grandpa, but you can't stay. But you don't have to walk me home 'cause I know the way,' " recounts Jack. "But it'll never happen." Grandpa waited faithfully at the door each day, waiting for her to come out for the short walk home.

The Miseners still live there, though the house is much larger, now, than when they bought it, and, in what has turned into an upscale community, they'd probably fetch upwards of $200,000 or more if they put it on the market. It's got five bedrooms, including the one in the basement where young Mick Fletcher spent the summer before he and Leann were married. Over the years, they had a dormer built upstairs, added on a garage, had a family room built out back. "We paid $1,000 cash for the family room," says Jack, the kind of man who's proud to let you know he had that kind of money on hand to pay for his expanding dreams.

It was a house that had grown as their family had grown, that was big enough now to hold all their grandkids at holidays. A perfect house to have grown a family in, a perfect house to enjoy a retirement, too, except that Jack didn't have long to enjoy his retirement.

Leann was shot eight months later and the next year and a half were pretty much filled with criminal proceedings against Mick and a bitter and protracted child-custody fight over Hannah.

"I can't wait to get all this behind us and get back to retirement. Do all the things we want to do," he said, a couple of months after the trial concluded. They made it to Branson, Missouri, once and can't wait to go back. Loved the shows.

Then Gloria's sister, Jean, and her husband live in Ocala, Florida. That's a nice place to visit. They'd like the Miseners to stay at their place, but Jack and Gloria like their time in the morning. Watch a little Weather Channel. Have some coffee. Look at the paper. So they prefer a motel. And there's one they like. It's nice, clean, quiet, and you can get a room cheap in the off-season. Last time they went, seven days for $117. Can't beat that with a stick.

Maybe Branson one year, Disneyworld the year after that. One site a year would be great.

EARLY FLETCHERS

The Fletchers and the Miseners were families in contrast from the start. While the Miseners epitomized the urban-becoming-suburban generation, born the in city, moving out to the brand-new suburbs as the jobs and the housing followed the freeways out of the central city, the Fletchers were small-town, farm-town born and raised.

John Fletcher was the youngest of four children, the kid of the family whose nearest sibling was a sister eight years older than him. His dad was a heating and cooling contractor, but most of their friends or neighbors were farmers in the small community of Peck, 600 or so in size, in the thumb of Michigan's mitten. The Thumb—that's what everyone in Michigan calls it—has a few scattered resort communities on Saginaw Bay or Lake Huron, but it was and still is farm country, flat and filled to the horizon with cornfields or soybean crops.

Darla Armstrong grew up in the nearby, larger (but still small) town of Brown City, the daughter of a postman who had had his dreams of playing pro baseball—he'd had several tryouts—cut short by World War II.

Though their moms worked together as nurses' aides at a nearby hospital, John and Darla didn't know each other. They met in the fall of 1964, when he was a junior at Peck High and she was a sophomore at Brown City. One week, Peck had a football game on Saturday afternoon. Brown City was playing Deckerville Friday night, and John went to that game with a friend to see a girl. Darla, sitting nearby, caught his eye and they talked.

"I didn't like him all that much, but he was cute," says

Darla. His cousin was dating her cousin and a double date was arranged. They've been together since.

By the next year they were going steady, and they got engaged just before she graduated in the spring of 1967. Her mom insisted she have something to fall back on, just in case, before she'd give her blessing to a marriage, so Darla got her cosmetician's license. "That was the quickest thing I could do," she says.

John went to Port Huron Junior College one year, dropped out, tried a couple of different jobs, didn't know what he wanted to do. It might not matter, anyway, he figured. Those were the days of the big drafts to feed the Vietnam War. Being married no longer was good for a deferment. Being in college full-time was, but when John dropped out, he lost his deferment. He thought he'd be sure to go to Vietnam, like all the buddies he'd had from high school who hadn't gone on to college.

John and Darla planned to get married when he got back from the war. In the meantime, he'd been hired for a training program at Detroit Edison. Detroit Edison's training school was in the poor downriver Detroit community of Delray; coincidentally, right across the street from the training center was the old and mammoth Fort Wayne, where all of Michigan's would-be draftees came for their physicals. Get a 1A, go to Vietnam was pretty much the program.

Soon, Fletcher's notice to take his physical came in the mail. He rode down on a bus from Peck, along with a bunch of the local kids and took it. One part included filling out the inevitable government forms. One asked him to check off if he'd ever had this or that ailment or trouble. He'd had a bleeding ulcer in college that had since healed, but he checked where it asked him to.

At the last station in the process—you went in long snaking lines past a series of stations, with one doctor looking in your eyes, another in your ears, another grabbing your testicles and asking you to turn your head to the side and cough, etc.—a doctor looked over his paperwork, saw the checkmark by "ulcers," asked him for the phone number of his family doctor, called to confirm the past history, came back and said those magic words: "Well, we're sorry. We won't be able to take you."

Like that, Fletcher was 4F. "I didn't know what to do," he recalls. "I didn't know whether to laugh or cry or what to do. I knew guys who'd already been killed over there. It kind of made me feel like a heel; it's always kind of bugged me because I didn't go. Guys I knew in high school got killed there. And four of the guys I rode down with on the bus to take my physical ended up dying."

Darla had no mixed feelings, whatsoever. They began making plans to get married as soon as they could arrange a proper ceremony and became Mr. and Mrs. the following year. (The ulcer wouldn't rear its ugly head for many years; he suffered a recurrence when he was 49.)

They began their life together, and he continued on his career path at Edison. In those days, getting in at a utility like Edison, which handled the power for all of southeastern Michigan, meant top wages, great benefits and job security. "Back then, people used to be loyal," says Fletcher. "When you hired into Detroit Edison, once you were in, you didn't leave. It was like family."

He remembers his hire-in date as well as he remembers his birthday—Nov. 13, 1967. In 25 of his first 33 years, he had perfect attendance (storing up personal time that would come in handy when he needed time off to attend Mick's murder trial). Edison trained him to be an engineer, and over the years he moved steadily up the ranks. At the time of his son's trial in June and July of 2000, he was the operations supervisor of the big Belle River power plant north of Detroit. Four supervisors reported to him and more than 20 employees. Two weeks in a row he worked three 12-hour shifts, then for two weeks he'd work four 12-hour shifts, alternating nights and days in the various weeks.

The shift changes never quite allow you to feel caught up on your sleep, but they always left him plenty of time for the family.

In the meantime, Darla became a stay-at-home mom. Her cosmetician's license was something she never needed to fall back on.

They were married in April of 1968 and lived in an apartment for two years. Mick was born in October of 1969 and the following March they bought their first house. Amy was born in January of 1972 and Ben in July of 1974. All three kids were well behaved, did well in school, stayed out of trouble. "Mick was a joy," says his dad.

In 1976, John built a house on five acres of wooded land outside Peck, land he bought from his parents. He would build a second house in 1983, and his current house—in Marysville south of Port Huron, an hour north of Detroit—in 1987. He hired some craftsmen to help with things like hanging drywall, but did much of the work on the homes himself, including laying in the field stones for the fireplace and doing all the detailed woodworking.

A self-described "gearhead," John also rebuilds and restores vintage Corvettes. One that he rebuilt was later sold to a man in San Diego who has won numerous awards and trophies at auto shows around the country. His pride and joy, a 1957 Corvette that he modified with a 1991 Corvette front suspension, power rack-and-pinion steering, a five-speed transmission with overdrive and a 450-horsepower engine, was sold to help finance his son's legal defense.

Life in the pastures and woodlands on the Fletchers' five acres, surrounded by the farmland, was idyllic, say Amy and Ben. The kids didn't have a lot of playmates, out several miles from town as they were, but they all got along and kept each other company. There wasn't much in the way of sibling rivalry. Both of them adored their older brother, and wanted to tag along with him wherever he went.

John and Darla were, and are, conservative, evangelical Christians, and the church was always an anchor. Both parents and the kids were at Croswell Wesleyan Church every Wednesday night, most Saturday afternoons for one function or another, and every Sunday. Years after they moved from Peck, all three Fletcher kids would get married in the beautiful old Croswell church.

Their own land and all the surrounding farmers' fields were a magic place for kids to grow up. John made trails through the woods with his tractor for them to go hiking on. He built them a fort, with entry by secret passwords or knocks. There were sand dunes on the property, and wetlands. In the winter, their dad would hook up big tires to the tractor and take them off sledding through the woods, or they'd toboggan down the dunes. In one house, John even built a roller rink in the basement for the kids.

Mick, say Ben and Amy, was the perfect big brother. A prankster with them—he loved to jump out from behind trees or from around corners of the house and scare Amy to death—he was protective, too. Nobody ever got away with picking on them.

"He was always non-violent," says Amy. "He wouldn't get in fights to defend us, but if he saw somebody was picking on us, he'd come over and sit down or stand there. Just let the person know our big brother was there."

Once, a high school girl was picking on Amy when she and Mick were in junior high, and she got so mad at Mick when he came over to break things up that she stuck a wad of gum in his hair that later had to be cut out, leaving a bald spot.

Before he could read, Mick memorized his books, and he'd sit there pretending to read, saying the words by rote as he turned the pages. Later, he'd add plot elements of his own. Mick became an inveterate reader, and he loved reading to Amy and Ben, or regaling them with tales he'd make up on the spot as they sat in the fort or played in the family play-room, waving his arms, taking them with his passion into his made-up world.

(Amy says the passion for storytelling is shared by her three-year-old daughter, Bailey, and by Hannah. "They both open their books and pretend to read. They'll wave their arms and make up stories about big scary monsters or whatever. They're just like Mick in that regard.")

At five, he was already a fan of Jacques Cousteau and announced one day to Darla: "Momma, I know what I want to be when I grow up. I want to be a marine biologist."

Despite their age difference, Ben and Mick were particularly close. Mick had started reading to Ben when he was still in his crib. He read him his shark books, he read him his dinosaur books. Mick later became a shark expert; Ben knew all there was to know about dinosaurs. "My brother was the kind of guy who knew it all, he could do everything," says Ben. "I was always wanting to be around him, even when we were older and he was with his friends. I wanted to hang out with him. I think I got to be a little bit of a nuisance."

When Ben was just three, Mick started teaching him to read. He'd sit with him and point out words, tell him about syllables, teach him about pronunciation. "He loved to share the information he'd compiled by reading," says Ben.

By the time Mick was in second grade, he was reading at the twelfth-grade level, and he'd be sent down to the kindergarten of the Peck school—it was so small, all grades were housed in one building, from kindergarten through high school—to read to them. At conferences, teachers would apologize to the Fletchers for not calling on Mick enough; he was always waving his hand in the air and always knew the answers, but they had to give other kids a chance.

Mick, Amy and Ben would head out into the woods to hunt for treasures. Growing up with them, on that land, she was into frogs and adventure; dolls weren't her thing. Ben didn't quite get what fossils were. From his books they looked like things he found quite readily in the woods. He'd come back, his corduroy pants with the elastic waistbands halfway down his butt they were so loaded down with what he called "bossils." He'd dump them out on the kitchen floor; they were ordinary rocks that seemed anything but.

Amy was in awe of Mick's ability to climb trees. One day, dressed in a hunter-orange jacket, he climbed what she describes as "a humungous pine tree in the back yard. Mom looked out the window and saw an orange dot at the top of the tree. She came out screaming, 'Michael John Fletcher, you get down from that tree!' "

Later, when Ben got old enough, they began another tradition—fierce games of catch with whatever was at hand, baseballs, softballs, Frisbees. Two Christmases before Leann's death, the Fletchers were at a Christmas gathering with Ben's wife's family, at a church near Flint. The church had a gymnasium and somebody had left a Nerf ball on the floor. Sure enough, soon Mick and Ben were hurling it back and forth, hard, harder, hardest. Pretty soon, the spectators had cleared out of the gym, to safer ground. Eventually, exhausted, they were done. Ben's new wife, Nicole, who had never seen the tradition enacted before, came over and said, jokingly, "Okay, you done trying to kill each other, now?"

"We could stand out there for hours, just throwing the ball

back and forth at each other," says Ben. "We'd start off throwing the ball back and forth for a little while and then the arms would loosen up and we'd throw a little harder. You start throwing harder, you start throwing *harder*, and pretty soon you're chucking the ball at each other as hard as you can. Just whipping the ball at each other. Like we'd be doing it to see who'd quit first. That's how we bonded," says Ben.

Mick wasn't the first Fletcher to make headlines. Back in the heyday of Christian cable TV in the early and mid-1980s— before Jimmy Swaggert and Jim Bakker brought shame and scandal—Amy Fletcher was one of its stars. A pretty little girl with a big, booming adult voice, she was a frequent guest on various shows on the Trinity Broadcasting Network, which later became the Christian Broadcast Network and then the Family Channel.

Amy's short-lived career as a concert soloist and recording star began when she was eight, at Christmastime of 1980. She had always sung in church, without much notoriety or attention. But that year, at their church's annual Christmas program, all of a sudden this big, powerful voice starting blasting forth.

Darla had been a frequent speaker at church functions and breakfasts. People started asking if she could bring Amy to sing at her talks. Soon it evolved to where they were asking Darla if she wanted to talk at Amy's concerts.

The next year, a family friend asked if he could send in a tape of Amy singing for a contest that was part of the National Quarter Convention in Nashville. The Fletchers reluctantly agreed. They soon got a letter back from organizers telling them that Amy had passed the tape audition and was welcome to come down and take part.

The family packed into their Pontiac compact, drove to Nashville and found a hotel with a pool for the boys. Amy sang and was named Child Vocalist of the Year.

That night, country star Larry Gatlin asked Amy up on stage in front of 20,000 at the Nashville Convention Center to give her her trophy. To her surprise, he handed her a mike and said: "You're going to sing a song, little girl."

She remembers looking down at her family in a row of folding chairs in front of the stage, then, without fear, belting out a version of "Just a Closer Walk With Thee" that brought the house down, and the crowd to its feet for a standing ovation. Mick and Ben stood up in the chairs and screamed and hopped up and down, and Ben's chair collapsed.

A star was born.

The family began appearing at churches in the Port Huron/ Thumb area. Mick had learned to play piano by ear—"He really had a gift," says Amy—and he'd accompany Darla. Little Ben would sing, too. Mom did the bookings, Dad shlepped the equipment around, drove the car and handled the sound equipment, and the family would get paid a modest share of the offertory.

When she was 10, the family put out her first album of contemporary Christian music, which sold well on the Midwest church circuit. She cut another album at age 11, which caught the ear of Nashville-based Love Song Records, which signed her to a contract and nationally distributed a third album, cut at age 12 and called *By Invitation Only*.

Amy would fly out to California with Darla once a month or so to tape TV shows in 1983–84, had her own special one year called "The Amy Fletcher Christmas Special," sang at Robert Schuler's Crystal Cathedral, and at the zenith of Jim and Tammy Faye Bakker's fame, was a frequent opening act at concerts at their Heritage USA Christian theme park in North Carolina, the fund-raising for which later landed Bakker in prison.

"I'd get driven around in a limo and put up in big hotel rooms, so that was all pretty cool to me," says Amy. Her limo driver later married Tammy Faye's daughter.

In 1985, trying to figure out how to market this young girl with the big voice, the record company wanted to put her on the cover of her fourth album in makeup and a strapless dress. John and Darla said, "Enough," and pulled the plug on her career.

It was time, they said, for her to go back to being a normal kid, and for them to start paying more attention to Mick and Ben.

"I was mad at the time. But looking back on it, it was the best thing they could have done," says Amy. She cut her last Christian record in 1997 with a small Midwest label, and was happy when her three-year contract for live appearances expired.

Today, she still sings at a few weddings and in church—her husband, Phil Count, is music director at their church near San Diego, El Cajon Wesleyan—but is happily focused on raising her two young daughters and her part-time job in the church's day-care center.

In 1983, John built a house in Marysville, near the beautifully blue St. Clair River that separates Michigan from Ontario, and the family left Peck. Marysville is a small city by most standards, a downright metropolis compared to Peck.

At Peck, everyone went to one school. In Marysville, there were several elementary schools, a junior high and a high school. The adjustment for the kids, by all accounts, was pretty easy.

They all made friends readily. Ben later became a basketball star—he was honorable mention All-State—and ran cross-country and played baseball. Mick played sports, too—in 10th grade he was a defensive end on a JV team for one of the most renowned football programs in the state. "He wasn't big, but he could explode off the ball," says Ben, who used to go to Mick's games.

But as all the Fletcher kids were required to do, Mick got a part-time job, and decided he liked money more than football. After his sophomore season he quit sports so he could work more hours at a variety of fast-food jobs. "He liked making money," says his father. At 16, Mick was the closer at the nearby Pizza Hut, a rare job for a kid his age, in charge of making sure things were ready to go for the day crew, the money was safely put away and the doors locked.

Even in high school, Mick was still playing the good big brother at an age when many kids want nothing to do with their siblings.

Amy remembers when she was a freshman in high school and Mick was a junior, a popular jock who was also in the 11th grade asked her to the prom. She wasn't allowed to date, yet, so her parents told her no when she pleaded with them to let her go. Mick interceded. He offered to let his sister and her date double-date with him and his girlfriend, a girl named Rachel they went to church with. That way he would keep an eye out for his sister. Their parents reluctantly agreed.

"My date had sort of a reputation for being fast, and Mick didn't trust him," Amy recalls. As soon as they all got in Mick's car, Mick made a point of adjusting the rearview mirror so it aimed into the back seat and not out the back window. "It was his way of saying, 'I want you to know I'm watching you.' And he kept coming over during the prom to make sure I was having fun and my date was treating me right."

Needless to say, the two couples did not go, in the vernacular of the time, "parking" that night.

The next year, Amy remembers having a boyfriend, and giving him a kiss in the school hall one day. Mick happened to be nearby and saw it. He came over. "Ahem," he said, fatherlike, disapproving.

After graduating from Marysville High in 1988, Mick attended St. Clair Community College for two years. Unlike many kids, he knew from the start what he wanted to major in, criminal justice, and what he wanted to be, a cop. And he made sure to take courses that would keep him on track to graduate in the shortest time possible.

"I told him, if he graduated in four years, I'd pay his tuition. If not, he'd have to pay me back," recalls John. Despite transferring to Michigan State in two years—its criminal justice program is considered one of the best in the country—Mick graduated right on schedule. "That's the way Mick is, once he makes up his mind."

While attending a Halloween party after transferring to Michigan State, he'd meet a beautiful woman dressed like the devil. Their lives—and their families'—would never be the same.

LEANN

Who was Leann Fletcher? Down-to-earth, unpretentious, pretty, gregarious, a bit spoiled as the youngest of five kids, she had been the center of the Misener family since she came home from the hospital 29 years before she died, passionate in her likes and dislikes, sexy and uninhibited—she would cause her sister-in-law to blush and her mother-in-law to cover her ears when regaling them with stories of her apparently rich sex life with Mick—and, above all, a great mother, according to everyone who knew her.

Her life centered around Hannah. When she made cookies, Hannah got to make them, too, hands-on, who-cares-about-a-mess, let's-have-fun Hannah. Leann came from a large, happy family and wanted a large family herself.

She was always a good kid, say her parents, never any real trouble, if you don't count her penchant for long-haired rock-and-roll musicians in high school. She was unassuming, happy when she was a phone solicitor, happier when she was a nail technician. She didn't aspire to be much of anything except the Leann her family and friends knew and loved.

She was artistic, a prolific writer of poems, a lover of ceramics and porcelain who sold her creations at craft fairs around metropolitan Detroit, a gourmet cook, a talent for stained glass.

Most of all, she had a talent for making friends.

At Mick's trial, her oldest sister, Lindy, would grow her hair out to look like Leann's. "I wanted that jury to know I'm her sister." When Leann was little, "she was my baby," says Lindy, and when she was grown, "she was my best friend."

Jeni Hughes, who considered Leann her best friend almost since the day they met at a job in 1992, describes her as "a happy person. She got excited about everything. The smallest thing that would happen, she'd get excited about it." A year before her death, Leann went bowling with Jeni. She'd never been bowling before, and had so much fun, next thing Jeni knew, Leann had them joining a league. "Every time she bowled a strike, she got so excited. It was refreshing to see, she got so into it." At the end of the fall league, Leann got a patch for most-improved bowler.

An irrepressible but harmless flirt, Leann flirted with husbands, fathers, brothers and friends' sons. No one took it wrong. Men and boys had crushes on her, her friends admit. At family gatherings, she'd be out there tossing horseshoes with the guys or playing air hockey. When the action got slow, she'd round everyone up into the Misener family living room and get them singing songs or playing games.

She was, everyone acknowledges, madly in love with Mick, through good times and bad, from the time they met at Halloween of 1990 through their several separations and right up until the minute she died. When Mick asked to come back the last time, in a letter professing his love and regrets at Easter of 1999, Leann wavered briefly.

"What do you think I should do?" she asked Lindy.

"What do you want, Leann?"

"I want Hannah to grow up the way I did, with both of her parents. And I still love him."

"Then I'm behind you. Give it a shot," said Lindy, who vividly remembers the first time she and others in the family met Mick, a week or two after that fateful party at Michigan State. "He was everything she wanted. Leann had dated some people we didn't care for, so when Mick walked in, we were like, 'Yeah!' He was clean-cut, short hair, successful. This soon-to-be-graduating guy from Michigan State."

"She loved him. Without a doubt," says Hughes. "I asked her once what the attraction was and she said, 'I don't know what it is, but I am *so* attracted to him.' It was just one of those things."

Jeni and Leann shared a love of animals. One night Leann called her, all excited. She'd found an injured bird and brought it into the house, fearful a cat would get it. She told Jeni to race over, help her figure out what to do. They ended up getting out the Yellow Pages and calling all over town before they found a vet who'd take the bird in for the night. It took them 40 minutes to drive there, each way.

"Leann said prayers over road kill," says Lindy.

"Three hundred people were at her funeral, and *every person there thought Leann was their best friend*," said Lindy. "Her clientele? They came in droves to tell you what an impact she had on their lives. Young girls. Old women. One woman came in a motorized wheelchair. We didn't know her. And she didn't know Leann. Leann did her daughter's nails and Leann had given her daughter some advice that turned her life around."

The woman would later come to trial nearly every day, a woman who had never met Leann but felt she had to be there to pay her back.

Leann's funeral was delayed because of the investigation and the need for an autopsy. The first day of viewing at the Price Funeral Home in Troy was scheduled for Thursday. Wednesday night, says Lindy, "I prayed to God that if—*if*—I walked in there and it didn't look like my sister, if it did not look like my sister, 'Please, God, give me the strength to make her look like her.' I knew she wouldn't let me lie there not looking good. 'Please, God, please, God, give me the strength.' "

Lindy got to the funeral home an hour before viewing was to begin. She walked in, took a look and freaked. It didn't look like Leann, the make-up was all wrong. The hair was wrong.

Lindy got her make-up and hair gear. The funeral director was adamant. No. Lindy was more adamant. *Yes*. "The funeral director was grabbing stuff out of my hand, saying 'What do you want us to do?' And I was, *'No! this is my sister and you will let me do this for her.'*"

Lindy re-did Leann's hair and make-up, ordering her hands to be calm, her heart to slow down. "She would have done it for me."

Kim McGowan, the co-owner of the Incognito salon where Leann worked, in the northern Detroit suburb of Sterling Heights, had to shut down for the day when Gloria Misener called to tell her what happened.

When she reopened the next day, she had a bucket on the

front counter, by the cash register, to collect money for Hannah, next to a framed poem titled "Remember Me" that one of Leann's clients brought in.

Later, they put a sunflower plaque out in front of the store in honor of Leann and her favorite flower. As a nail technician, Leann, who worked in the shop three days a week, did manicures, pedicures, paraffin dips for those with joint or arthritis trouble, and free-hand artwork on customers' nails. Doing nothing but holding a customer's hand or feet every time they come in requires someone comfortable with intimate contact, and able to put the client at ease.

"You have to have a certain persona, and Leann had it," said McGowan. "Leann possessed a deep passion for people. The people she did, she was very close with. You get closer than a psychiatrist. She had that rapport with people. They trusted her. They could tell her anything.

"She made everyone feel as if they were her best friends. She knew everybody. She had some kind of connection with people all over the place. When she smiled at you, you knew you were smiled at. Everyone just fell in love with her. I've met a lot of people, but I've never met anyone with quite that connection.

"People would meet her one time and be touched by her. After it happened, we'd have people come in off the street and we didn't know who the hell they were, and they'd come in and drop money in the bucket for Hannah. It was after she passed away that we found out how many people she had touched."

One old woman would come in, everybody thought she was a bitch, wouldn't want to work on her. Leann'd start her pedicure, they'd get to talking about the woman's dead husband, and pretty soon Leann and the woman would be crying away together, best friends.

"My boys were in love with her," said McGowan. "She was my oldest son's first love. Nicholas is 14 and he adored her. And she knew it, too. She'd flirt with him. He was just crushed."

Lisa Rodela met Leann at a dental supply company, where they handled phone orders. It was about the time she went up to MSU and met Mick. In 1994, Lisa's daughter, Elizabeth, then three, was diagnosed with leukemia. The daughter spent a month in the hospital during treatment, with Lisa at her side much of the time. Compounding the family's troubles was the fact they'd just moved into a new home and had only begun furnishing it when Elizabeth was diagnosed.

Leann got their boss to commit the company to match whatever funds Leann could raise. By the end of the month, the Rodelas had a new washer and drier and a month's payment on the mortgage. Moreover, Leann would come over after work and make dinner for Lisa's husband and son.

"She was our angel," said Rodela.

The day of the shooting, Leann called her at 10:20 a.m. to firm up plans for a get-together Thursday night. Lisa was at a sales meeting and could only talk a minute. "She said, 'I've some great news for you. Great news.'" But she wouldn't say what it was. Lisa had to get back to her meeting and hung up. "I always told her I loved her. 'I love you. I love you.' And I didn't tell her that day. I'll never forgive myself."

Lori Mayes, another of Leann's sisters, had a birthday party for two of her kids, Adam and Jessie, a couple of weeks before the shooting. Leann brought 200 water balloons, then sat there patiently filling them one by one. The kids at the party kept trying to grab them and Leann kept fighting them off until they were all filled. Then, it was a free-for-all grab-all. The kids bombarded her; the wetter she got, the harder she laughed. The harder they all laughed.

Later, the kids were starting to get on Lori's nerves, as a pile of kids aged five to eight will tend to do. "I was getting frustrated with all the games—the kids were like animals—I was getting ready to quit doing it and Leann took over. She said to them, 'This is what we're going to do.' She loved kids."

When Lori finally got around to taking the party photographs to be developed, then going back to get them, Leann was dead. She never saw the shots of herself, shirt soaking wet, hair bedraggled, huge smile across her face. Lori's oldest child, Jessie, 13 at the time, was so grief-stricken at Leann's death he later had to go into counseling.

Lori said that for months after the shooting, she'd be sitting there thinking, "Oh, I gotta call Leann.' Forgetting I couldn't.

I'd be getting the phone, getting ready to call her. I think I was in shock a long time. For months and months. I remember going through Christmas and I couldn't put up all the decorations. I put up some for the kids, but that was about it. I feel like I sat on my couch looking at her picture in a fog for like eight months."

More than a year after the shooting, Lori's daughter, Shannon, who had just turned 13, had to write an essay for school on one of her heroes. Her choice? Leann. Shannon turned six the day Leann was married. Leann called Shannon up to the front of the church, in front of everybody, and gave her a Cabbage Patch doll so she'd feel special, too.

The Miseners and their kids are big on cookouts and bonfires. Whenever they have a bonfire, now, they roast some octadogs in honor of Leann. Octadogs? It was something she learned in Girl Scouts. You take a hotdog and make two deep slits perpendicular to each other at each end, moving in toward the center of the hotdog. When the hotdog heats up over the fire, the four splits at each end curl up, forming an eight-ended treat. An octadog.

For one of their recent anniversaries, Leann wrote them a poem, then had it framed. The first stanza reads:

What can we say about our mom and dad?
How can we think of the phrase?
Simple words can't describe what we're feeling inside.
We love you in so many ways.

A second poem sits in another frame in their family room, part of a collage of photos.

I wish I could recapture all the memories we've had
And put them in a bottle for the times when I'm sad,
For all it takes is just one thought of my family
To quickly make me realize I'm as happy as can be.
I know I can be unmanageable, stubborn and selfish,
    too,
But my family will always come first in my life.
And don't ever forget, I love you.

DELAYED FUNERAL

As hundreds of mourners who had been touched by Leann Fletcher—from siblings and relatives who had known her her whole life to clients who had known her only for weeks or months, but felt they knew her intimately—made their plans to attend her funeral on Saturday, August 21, dramatic events were unfolding in two courts on Friday.

In the morning, an Oakland County Family Court referee awarded temporary custody of three-year-old Hannah to her maternal grandparents, Jack and Gloria Misener. "Hannah is suffering from a double whammy," said Referee Jean Dohanyos. "She has lost her mother. She has lost her father."

Fletcher appeared at the hearing in handcuffs and ankle chains. He gave brief answers to Dohanyos' questions and was accompanied by an attorney, Raymond Correll, but did not fight the custody ruling. "Frankly, we're in concurrence that the maternal grandparents' is an appropriate place for Hannah to be staying," he told reporters.

His request that Fletcher be allowed to speak to his daughter by phone was turned down by Dohanyos, who said it would be disruptive for the child in such traumatic circumstances. "I'm ruling that your contact, all contact, be suspended pending further court order," said the referee.

The Miseners then left for the Price Funeral Home in Troy to continue visitation. Early in the afternoon, though, they were told to hurry over to the Hazel Park courthouse nearby, that a motion had been filed by Brian Legghio asking that Saturday's scheduled funeral be postponed until an expert hired by the defense could examine Leann's body and come up with his own report.

The Miseners and their entourage, stunned, fled from the

funeral home en masse. They sat in court sobbing as assistant county prosecutor Gregory Townsend argued against a delay. "To me, this is the final insult to the family. This request is horrendous," he said, arguing that any available evidence from Leann's body had already been documented in reports and photographs.

Legghio countered: "The warrant for his arrest was obtained on the forensic evidence of the pathologist. To deny him the right to an independent examination is to deny him due process."

At 4:06 p.m. Judge Keith Hunt issued the order granting Legghio his request. He would have up to 48 hours to arrange for another examination of Leann's body, on site at the funeral home.

Hunt said the decision was "as difficult as any I have had to make as a judge. The community suffers with the family but I must insure the proper administration of justice. This case is heavily dependent, if not entirely dependent, on forensic evidence."

Townsend consoled the family that in the long run, the decision might be in their best interest. "I'm sure if the court had denied the request, it would have been brought up on appeal."

Over the weekend, one of the most prominent pathologists in the United States, Warner Spitz, conducted a post-mortem on Leann Fletcher's body at the funeral home. Ironically, Spitz had been Dragovic's boss at Wayne County before he took the Medical Examiner's position in Oakland County. Another headline-making name and element had been added to the case.

Spitz was the ME in neighboring Macomb County, now, and had a long and prominent history of taking part in famous murder mysteries and trials over the years. It was his testimony against O. J. Simpson that was crucial in the outcome of the civil trial against the former football star, with Spitz saying that injuries on the back of O. J.'s left hand weren't caused by broken glass, as claimed, but by acrylic fingernails. In 1969, he was hired by the family of Mary Joe Kopechne and affirmed she had died by drowning in the accident that forever ended Ted Kennedy's chances as a presidential contender. In 1963, he was part of a committee led by Nelson Rockefeller that concluded that only one gunman was involved in the assassination of John Kennedy. And he had written a guidebook on crime investigations that was in its fourth printing.

On Monday, August 26, after the longest week of the Miseners' lives, Leann was finally buried. More than 300 mourners filled the Price Funeral Home and shared stories of the young woman who had touched them all. TV and radio crews—prohibited all week from the lot of the funeral home itself—filled the parking lot of the 7-Eleven across the street, aiming their lenses and microphones at the mourners as they first arrived and then left in the funeral cortege.

Several days later, Legghio released Spitz's findings. His report, said Legghio, was that "it is inconclusive that Ms. Fletcher died as a result of homicide. She may have died by her own hand."

"Hazel Park Case Splits Medical Experts," read the headline in September 3's *Detroit Free Press*.

Many months later, courtroom observers were disappointed by the lack of a forensic showdown at trial between the two heavyweights, Dragovic and Spitz. Spitz, a colorful character with, like Dragovic, a thick accent—he was born in Germany and educated in Israel—who enjoyed talking with the media, had, jokingly or otherwise, responded to criticism that he was a gun-for-hire by saying he'd dance naked on top of a table for a thousand dollars. Townsend subsequently had used the quote to impugn Spitz in court. Legghio, not eager to have a jury hear such an utterance about one of his witnesses in a murder case, chose to seek expert opinions elsewhere.

In the meantime, though, the idea had been planted. Perhaps this wasn't a murder, after all. Maybe Leann had even committed suicide.

PRELIMINARY EXAM

Brian Dickerson, a columnist for the *Detroit Free Press*, had the best line to come out of Michael Fletcher's preliminary examination before Hazel Park District Court Judge Keith Hunt.

"Susan R. Chrzanowski entered the courtroom a little before 4 p.m. She wore a prim white blouse, a navy blue suit, and a look of absolute mortification," read the lead for his column of September 29, the day after the judge's appearance.

Mick's father, John, would gain some notoriety—as well as some enmity from the Miseners—when he would tell the press in later months that if this case had involved a pizza cook and a waitress, none of this would have happened. That overstated things, certainly—cooks and waitresses get tried for murder, too—but the media glare and public attention certainly grew out of the soap-operatic convergence of the handsome young attorney, his beautiful wife and the lovely judge he worked for and bedded.

Chrzanowski was the last witness in the two-day examination to see if there was enough evidence to bind Fletcher over for felony trial in Oakland County Circuit Court, but last certainly wasn't least. She was the star of this two-day show and the one everyone had been waiting for.

That Fletcher would be bound over was a foregone conclusion—it is very, very rare that a preliminary exam doesn't lead to an advancement of the proceedings into Circuit Court, where felonies are tried in Michigan. After all, police and prosecutors already had enough to convince the district judge at his arraignment in August that a crime had been committed and that there was reason to believe Fletcher did it; barring the dramatic, preliminary exams are a *pro forma* next step. The case is laid out in more detail but that's about it. In many cases, defense attorneys simply waive the right to a hearing and save a step in the process.

So, while everyone in court on September 27 and 28 knew the outcome, what they didn't know and hoped to find out were some of the juicy, salacious details the papers had only been able to hint at or allude to. They wouldn't be disappointed. They might have been surprised, though, at the gentle treatment Chrzanowski would get at the hands of assistant prosecutor Lisa Ortlieb.

What few knew watching the proceedings was that Chrzanowski and Ortlieb had once worked together in the Oakland County Prosecutor's Office, and in fact, Chrzanowski had succeeded Ortlieb in handling cases in the Clarkston District Court in the northern end of the county. There was no love lost between Ortlieb and Chrzanowski—Ortlieb didn't think very highly of Chrzanowski's skills as a prosecutor and, like many, if not most, on the staff, was resentful that she had so quickly traded on her father's name, even dropping her own married name of Zunker in her judicial compaign. (Soon after Chrzanowski's election in 1996, the Michigan State Legislature adopted new legislation unofficially dubbed "the Chrzanowski law" that required a minimum of five years of experience before one could run for judge.)

Still, there is a pecking order and Ortlieb respected it, as would her boss, Gregory Townsend, when the case finally would come to trial the following June. Ortlieb was an assistant prosecutor, Chrzanowski was a judge, and one was going to be deferential to the other.

"There was no hint of hostility in Chrzanowski's demeanor as she answered questions about her year-long affair with the defendant," wrote Dickerson. "But there was little doubt she would have been happy to forgo her appearance, given the option of boiling in oil."

The judge's stint on the stand was preceded by eight other witnesses including Leann's father and sister Lindy, and before the gathered media and assorted cameras could get to the judge, they would have to listen to Ortlieb lay out the state's case.

Jack Misener went first and recounted that Mick and Leann had told them Saturday night that she was pregnant, again, and that late Sunday afternoon they'd all gone out, Hannah included, in Jack's van for a steak dinner. After dinner, back at Jack's house, Mick had asked if he would babysit for Hannah for an hour during the day Monday so he could take Leann to the firing range.

Eye-witness testimony is the most trusted by juries, and the least reliable. The next witness, Paul Yaeck, showed why. A security guard at a hospital, he placed Mick and Leann at the Double Action gun range in Madison Heights on August 16. He was there testing some new semiautomatic pistols used by the hospital's security crew, and was emphatic in his observations.

Yaeck said his visual contact of Leann was limited to 30 seconds, but in that time, he deduced that she was firing a gun for the first time, that "she was startled by the weapon," that she "held the weapon in her hand is if it scared her," that after firing, she had "a surprised look on her face," and that at one point he and Leann had eye contact after she had fired the Smith & Wesson and she gave him an awkward smile like those "you see with folks who may not be that proficient with firearms."

He also said that the man helping her hold and aim the gun was "an older man with gray hair." Mick Fletcher was 29 at the time, with an unlined face and jet-black hair.

Yaeck was followed by Ron Lehman, a Hazel Park cop who testified that he was dispatched to the Hazelwood house in response to a 911 call and found Fletcher on the front lawn, smoking a cigarette and holding a cell phone. (A transcript of the 911 tape later introduced as evidence in the trial itself would show that Fletcher was, in fact, inside the house when police arrived. They are heard on the tape asking him to step out of the house.)

Lehman told of the strong smell of gunpowder inside the house, the description of the body ("she was lying on the bedroom floor, and she was bleeding from the head area, and she had on a red shirt and white socks; that's all") and a description of the bedroom (carpeted) and the presence of the gun on the floor, a magazine containing several rounds, a bullet near the gun, an open box of ammunition and a gun casing standing on its end on the carpet, about five feet from the body.

He checked for a pulse and found none. He saw a lot of blood on the floor and a "gelatin-like substance in the blood which looked like brain fluid" still oozing from the wound.

Four paramedics arrived, tried to revive her, were unsuccessful and left.

Dr. Ljubisa Dragovic, the county's colorful medical examiner, was next. He testified that he conducted the autopsy on Leann's body the next day, beginning at 9:10 a.m. In the passive tones of those who conduct autopsies and deal with death, Leann the warm, vibrant woman became "the body that was five-foot-three inches in length and 133 pounds, medium developed, medium nourished, white female." She also, in his opinion, was a homicide victim based on the pattern of gunpowder burns, called stippling, on her face. The tighter the pattern, the closer the shot. The pattern on her face led him to believe she had been shot from 12 to 18 inches away, making self-infliction impossible.

Dragovic also said he could find no traces of blood mist on her hands, a mist you'd expect to find on someone who has shot herself, and that he'd detected seminal fluid in her vagina.

And he described in clinical terms the catastrophic damage done to the Miseners' youngest daughter, as they sat in the courtroom, listening in shock. "The wound path went through the skin of the right ear and subcutaneous tissue. It fragmented the right temporal bone . . . a bone that is integral part"—Dragovic, in his thick Eastern European accent often drops articles like "the" and "an"—"of the human skull that's on the right side and includes the middle ear and a squamous part of the right side of the skull.

"This was perforated with a shattering of the petrous part of the skull, the hard, dense bone where the middle ear is placed. And it perforated the hard coverings of the brain that divides the front part of the skull from the back part bottom of the skull. It injured the right cerebellum, transected the upper part of the brain stem and tore the left side of the cerebellum."

The injury, he concluded "caused instantaneous damage to

the brain stem and would have rendered the person immediately unconscious, instantaneously unconscious, and within seconds there will be the cessation of all the vital functions in the rest of the body."

And so it went. David Woodford of the Michigan State Police crime lab testified that from examining various blood stains in the room he determined that Leann had been shot while on the floor, with her head nearly a foot from the bed and from 14–18 inches off the floor. He also said that the spermatozoa in her vagina was fresh. And that they found fresh blood in the trap of the bathroom sink.

A pattern was emerging: that of a woman kneeling on the floor, having just had sex, her head bowed, when she was shot to death. And of a shooter who had washed his hands in the bathroom sink.

Finally, Sgt. Tom Cleyman of the Hazel Park police testified that when the Miseners arrived at the police station, Gloria told him immediately that Mick had killed her daughter and was eager to fill out a report to that effect. He said Fletcher had told him he was having trouble loading a clip for the gun and asked Leann to do it, and that she must have tried to load the gun while he was in the bathroom. Cleyman provided details of the evidence that had been uncovered during the search of the Hazelwood Avenue house, evidence that pointed directly at Judge Chrzanowski and turned this into the headline-producing, soap-opera affair it had become.

The testimony seemed compelling evidence of Fletcher's guilt. But it was often tedious, mind-numbing in its detail, as it stretched into a second day. Judge Chrzanowski's appearance was compelling, too, and riveting. It lasted just 20 minutes but lived up to the anticipation, providing scintillating details of the love affair between the former Warren law clerk and the Warren judge who had been deemed to be a rising star in the judicial firmament.

Executing the search warrant, police had found photos of the lovers in a brown folder in Fletcher's home office. They had found cards and love letters. They had even found a sales slip for computer equipment that the judge had bought for her financially struggling paramour. Cleyman had provided the facts. Chrzanowski would breathe passion into them.

"For a riveting 20 minutes, Oakland County Assistant Prosecutor Lisa Ortlieb questioned Chrzanowski. It was a gentle interrogation, conducted in the deferential tone of voice favored by bereavement counselors," wrote Dickerson. "At times, the prosecutor's delicacy ('Did you have a relationship that grew with the defendant?') verged on the Victorian.

"But there was no lack of moral indignation in the gallery, where a mute Greek chorus composed of the late Leann Fletcher's friends and relatives looked on malevolently, their reproval more than compensated for Ortlieb's restraint."

Dickerson continued: "It was hard not to feel a twinge of sympathy for the pale, petite Chrzanowski. You date a married man, you have to factor in that you may one day find yourself confronting an angry wife. But the wife's parents, siblings, colleagues and bowling teammates? In a public courtroom? With television and still cameras recording the scene?"

What did the judge tell them?

That she'd met Fletcher while campaigning for office during the summer or fall of 1996, during a visit to the Warren City Hall, and that their relationship had blossomed after her divorce in August of 1998. (Later, evidence would emerge that seemed to show their affair started earlier than that, and the discrepancy in her testimony would later be one of the reasons the state's Judicial Tenure Commission would cite in trying to have her booted from the bench.)

The relationship "was romantic, it was on and off."

After he filed for divorce in January of 1999, did she think they had a future together? "I had certainly hoped that; but yes, he would say things about us in the future together."

The judge said she briefly stopped seeing Mick when he went back with his wife the last time, at Easter of 1999, but in June began again, with liaisons "approximately three times a week."

Had they seen each other on Sunday, August 15? "Yes."

Had it been planned? "It was spur of the moment."

How had it come about? "I was paged. It was later in the evening."

What had Fletcher said when she called him back on his cell phone? "That he had about an hour of free time and could we meet?"

Did they have sex? "Yes."

What did Fletcher say that night when they were together? "It was just, in a way, a very typical meeting that we had. He told me he loved me very much."

Did they make future plans? "I was going to have some time on Tuesday afternoon. I thought we would be able to see each other Tuesday afternoon."

Did she speak to Fletcher on Monday? "Yes. Technically it would have been after midnight. So, it would have been very early morning of Tuesday. I was in Cedar Point [the amusement park] and when I returned home, which was sometime after midnight, I had received a page. And he sounded very upset on the pager, very distraught. And he said to page him when I got home. And it was already, like I said, I think after midnight. So, this is really the morning of the 17th that I did page him."

Did he return the page? What did he say? "He said something very awful has happened and that he could not talk about it. And that I was to call Roy Gruenburg, his employer, in the morning and that he would explain, but that he couldn't talk. He couldn't say anything. And he sounded extremely upset and distraught."

Did they ever talk, again, after that night? "No."

At 4:28 p.m., Judge Hunt, as expected, found there was probable cause to bind Fletcher over for trial in Oakland County Circuit Court, and the defendant was led out in handcuffs.

THE DEVIL MICK

"If you're the Devil, take me to Hell."
  —Mick Fletcher to Leann Misener, dressed in a sexy
    red cape and horns the night they met at a
    Halloween party in 1990 at Michigan State
    University.

Leann Fletcher's murder created headlines and water-cooler gossip from the start. And Mick Fletcher was the too-good-looking, spit-curled smug-seeming lawyer people loved to hate. Something about even his head shots in the papers just made people want to smack him. He was the heavy, no doubt about it.

If there was a demonization process at work, it didn't seem like it. After all, you can't demonize the devil. He somehow, in pictures in the newspapers or the TV news, just looked evil. Handsome yet repulsive, but you couldn't put your finger on it. Of course, nobody who looked at him was ignorant of the fact that he'd been accused of shooting his wife in the head. And none of the newspaper readers or TV watchers would ever read or hear anything about his childhood or close family or any of the things that made him human, not in the months leading up to his trial, not through it, not in the months after it.

He'd been the heavy since his arrest on August 19, but the image was most clearly painted in a prominently played story in the joint edition of *The Detroit News* and *Detroit Free Press* on Sunday, September 25. Headlined "A Journey in Hell," it was written by Tamara Audi and included Mick's infamous come-on line to Leann.

The story would continue one of the dynamics that had

started the day of Leann's shooting—a lot of juicy quotes by her friends and innately media-savvy relatives, who took a large framed photo of Leann with them in the days after her death, much to the delight of all the photographers and TV crews following them around.

The article would also help create one of the many myths that would later be repeated as dogma. "Her savings bought their Hazel Park home in 1993," wrote Audi. It wasn't true—she didn't even have the $1,000 in earnest money to put a bid in on the house, and got the money from Darla Fletcher—but the Fletchers weren't talking, the Miseners were, and that's what they said.

Audi's story, and subsequent stories, didn't paint a pretty picture. It was one that seemed consistent with someone who could shoot his wife in the head.

The story accurately described the differences in the Misener and Fletcher families—the Miseners are gregarious, fun-loving types who show up places with their coolers of beer, many of them smoking cigarettes. The Fletchers are reserved, teetotalers, non-smokers who never felt at ease with their in-laws.

It detailed what seemed to be a growing rift between Leann, who'd never had an interest in college and was employed part-time as a nail technician, and her young attorney husband.

"It was like he had this attitude that she wasn't good enough for him, not good enough to be married to a lawyer," it quoted one of Leann's bowling buddies, Maddy Glefke, who had also been one of her customers.

Glefke told of Leann coming to her in puzzlement one day, saying she'd found a credit-card application Mick had filled out that listed his wife's occupation as "consultant."

"Why would he do that?" Leann had asked her.

"Because he's ashamed of what you do, honey," said Glefke.

This was played up big in the press. The point no one cared to make was that there might be a more innocent explanation than shame—don't people routinely inflate earnings or puff up job descriptions on credit-card applications? Nonetheless, it fixed in many people's minds the notion that Mick was now ashamed of his nail-tech wife.

He was, wrote Audi, a frequent attendee at social events put on by the Young Lawyer's Section of the Macomb County Bar Association, coming alone. "We never met his wife. I don't recall him wearing a wedding ring," Jacob Femminineo, Jr., chair-elect of the organization, was quoted.

"But he wasn't alone at the parties," wrote Audi. "Lawyers said he usually showed up with Chrzanowski, a Warren judge. Sometimes, they were seen holding hands or kissing at parties, other lawyers said."

That might have been what they were telling Audi after the fact, with Fletcher in jail and Chrzanowski in disgrace. But Kevin Schneider, an up-and-coming young criminal defense attorney who is frequently in the Warren district court, and also counts himself among the young Warren lawyers who routinely get together after work for a drink, tells a different story. He was in a good position to know—he was Fletcher's best friend in law school and a good friend of Chrzanowski's. He never saw them kissing or snuggling, never suspected they were having an affair until it came out after Leann's death.

And it seems unlikely the prominent judge would blatantly advertise her romantic relationship with an attorney she gave so much work to, not in front of other attorneys eager for that work themselves. Certainly she was aware of the conflict of interest, and while she allowed it to continue, she wouldn't have wanted it widely known.

"Generally, the prosecution is much more adept at using the press than the defense. And they use it. They use it," said defense attorney Legghio after Fletcher's trial.

If the prosecution took an advantage by getting its side out to the media, Legghio can share the blame. He kept a tight lid on, preferring to try the case in the court of law, not in the court of public opinion. But reporters had stories to write and space to fill.

The day after his arrest, the *Detroit Free Press* ran a story on Fletcher's arraignment in Hazel Park district court by Brian Murphy. Its lead paragraph was: "An apparently grieving Michael Fletcher told police he was in another room in their Hazel Park home, but authorities said Thursday the blood-spattered shirt he was wearing told them he is a killer."

Jennifer Stout, an assistant Oakland County prosecutor, said at the arraignment and in the article that the blood spatters on the right sleeve of Fletcher's shirt could only have come from his having fired a shot at close range—"this is a cold, calculated murder," she said.

Moreover, she asked that Fletcher be held without bond as a flight risk. Murphy wrote in paragraphs number four and five: "Fletcher was arrested Thursday afternoon at his parents' St. Clair County home. Hazel Park police had him under surveillance since Wednesday, and officers observed him packing a trailer, Stout said."

It was a strong image—the accused murderer packing his getaway vehicle while surveillance officers kept an eye on him. As a result the judge ordered him held without bail. In fact, Stout's allegations were without merit. Whether she didn't know the truth or chose to play fancy with it isn't clear. In interviews for this book, police say they never saw Fletcher load anything into the trailer. The trailer was a huge fifth-wheel owned by his uncle and trailered across the state from the Lake Michigan town of Holland. The trailer wasn't being loaded, it was being unloaded. (And, just for the record, Fletcher wasn't arrested at his parents' home, but on the freeway many miles away.)

Up until his trial more than eight months later, the image persisted in people's minds that Fletcher had been ready to skedaddle.

The image of the blood-spattered sleeve stayed in people's minds, too. And in the press. There was also another damaging image—that of Fletcher handing the gun to his wife, who was afraid of guns, and asking her to load it because he was having trouble. It sounded ridiculous, an obvious lie to cover up a murder. Another *Free Press* story by Murphy on August 19 was headlined: "He Asked His Wife to Load Handgun, Police Say." In fact, the handgun was already loaded. Fletcher said he gave her a second clip to load while he went to the bathroom. Police reports written the day of the murder even differ on whether Fletcher was having trouble loading that clip; one report said he was loading the clip by hand because an automatic loader he owned had never worked properly. In any event, it would be a red-herring throughout the trial and jury deliberations, as well. It sounded ominous but in fact had nothing to do with the shooting. The clip wasn't in the gun, and the bullet he handed Leann never was put in the clip, but the impression remained that his alibi was that he'd given her a balky gun, told her to finish loading it and that it had later discharged.

On September 3, 1999, Murphy wrote a follow-up story with Dr. Ljubisa Dragovic as the main source. "What's more," Murphy wrote, "blood spatters were found on the right sleeve of the shirt Michael Fletcher wore that day. None was found on Leann Fletcher's right arm that would be consistent with a self-inflicted shot, he said."

An article by Mark Truby in *The Detroit News* on September 27 repeated the refrain, under the sub-headline of "Story Falls Apart." Truby wrote: "His story fell apart, though, when forensic tests on his shirt cuff showed a distinctive blood spatter pattern that prosecutors say prove his right hand was inches away from her when the gun went off."

That same day, Fletcher was bound over for trial in Circuit Court in Oakland County. Audi wrote in the next day's *Free Press*: "Blood was found on Fletcher's shirt, but no blood was found on his wife's hands or arms."

In that article, assistant prosecutor Lisa Ortlieb laid out the prosecution's motive: "We know that four days before the killing, Leann told him she was pregnant, and that triggered something in Michael Fletcher."

Truby also covered the hearing and recounted the testimony of David Woodford, a forensic scientist with the state police, who said he found blood spray on Fletcher's shirt and, wrote Truby, "Woodford also said he found fresh blood in the Fletchers' bathroom sink."

The shirt would be crucial to the case, and in the trial the following June. But in ways no one could imagine. As for the blood in the sink, its presence would turn out to be less of a sure thing—but far more important—than anyone could imagine as the tests were being run.

Proving motive isn't an essential part of a prosecution—it's not a required element of the case under Michigan law—but prosecutors always feel better if they can come up with one. Juries don't like motiveless murder, especially when it's the husband being accused.

Prosecutors floated three different motives in the weeks after his arrest. First and most obvious—the only one that would still be floating come the trial—there was Fletcher's love for another woman, a love that could have been jeopardized if the judge found out his wife was pregnant. As Ortlieb said, something snapped.

Then, there was the porno angle. Police had found several discs containing pornography in his computer, and there was potential testimony that Leann had found a credit-card bill showing Fletcher had made charges on an Internet porn site. Judge Keith Hunt wouldn't let any of it into evidence, but the press and public had heard the arguments being made to allow it in, and so another stroke was added to the picture. Fletcher was a pornographer, too.

The motive? That maybe Fletcher killed Leann because he wanted custody of Hannah and was afraid Leann would use the pornography against him in court.

The third motive? As Audi wrote in the *Free Press* on September 28, "The Fletchers separated in January and he filed for divorce that month. Michael Fletcher stood to collect a large settlement from a malpractice suit, Termarsch testified, and her sister wanted that to be part of any divorce settlement."

Love, pornography and greed—three good reasons to pull the trigger.

Or so it seemed. But what no one in the media knew, or would find out, was that the fear of pornography affecting a potential child-custody divorce couldn't possibly have been a motive. Sure, police found porn, but some of it involved Mick and Leann together, and there were explicit sexual photos that had clearly been taken by Leann.

At trial, greed as motive was never even alluded to. While the Miseners continued to believe—and hope, for the sake of Hannah's trust fund—that there was a settlement in the millions coming Fletcher's way, investigators concluded that if Fletcher had, as the family claimed, talked about a huge settlement, it was just that: talk. His share of any windfall would be so small that, in the word of assistant prosecutor Greg Townsend after the trial, "We didn't think it was a motive."

But it was a motive in September, and it added yet another brushstroke to the image of the evil young attorney.

*   *   *

Mick Fletcher seemed an easy guy to dislike. Lord knows the Miseners hated him, with good reason. They were convinced, along with the general public, that he had brutally murdered the family's favorite member, their gregarious, cheerful daughter/youngest sister who seemed to have touched everyone she ever met.

They had liked him well enough in the early days. He was, they thought, the answer to their prayers when she brought him home, smitten and hopelessly in love, to meet her parents and siblings a week or two after meeting him at Michigan State. She'd been going out with a rock musician with a bad Rod Stewart haircut and they didn't like him at all.

Leann had gone up to MSU for a Halloween party, which she attended in a sexy red cape and horns. Mick had captured her fancy when he walked right up to her and said: "If you're the Devil, take me to hell."

Fletcher seemed perfect. "Oh, boy!" said Gloria Misener to herself when she met him. He was the answer to their prayers—clean-cut, good looking and a college boy.

"He seemed to be an awfully nice guy. And she was in love. They were inseparable," said Jack.

Soon, she was spending every weekend at his dorm at Michigan State. It was a fairytale romance. Both were good looking, both had good senses of humor and laughter came easy. And, the uninhibited Leann would tell her friends—and even Mick's shocked, conservative sister—the sex was great. Great!

Three years after meeting, on September 18, 1993, Leann and Mick were married at his family's old church in Croswell. They honeymooned in Jamaica—Leann came back with her hair in beads—and settled into the small, sturdy brick home they bought on Hazelwood Avenue, just down the block from the first home Leann's parents had owned.

Things were perfect, everyone agreed. Sure, they fought— even her family admits Leann was spoiled and liked to get her way, and she had a lively temper. She could blow up and cool off in a hurry and didn't think much of it. She liked a good fight and never took one too seriously.

Mick enrolled in law school full-time at the University of Detroit–Mercy and worked part-time at Radio Shack. It was, say the Miseners, the beginning of the end, now that they look back on it.

"When he became a lawyer, he changed. He wasn't the same guy," said Gloria. It is a Misener family mantra: Mick got too good for Leann when he got out of law school.

After graduation, there was a ceremony at the court in Warren where Fletcher was sworn in as a member of the State Bar. The other attorneys getting sworn in thanked their families and wives. Instead, say the Miseners, Mick thanked his sponsor, Warren Judge Dawnn Gruenburg, and never mentioned Leann. And Dawnn, they say, treated Leann rudely.

Soon, Leann, with one or another of her friends or family, would be cruising past Gruenburg's house, looking for Mick's truck. They never saw it, but they were sure something was up.

Lindy Termarsch, Leann's oldest sister, has some kind words for Fletcher—"There was nothing that would steer me to say, 'No, Leann, he's trouble. He's bad.' Even my husband, who's zoomed in on a lot of guys my friends date, said there was nothing, not a clue that he could do this."

But she recounts a litany of sins—Fletcher was always out with his lawyer friends, telling Leann no one ever brought their spouses. Lindy said that he was a bad father, never showing any warmth to Hannah. "If I was holding her or someone else was, he'd come up and coo, 'How's my princess?' She would literally look at him like he was nuts. She'd never reach out her arms to him. She didn't know him. She didn't see him much. He was just pretending to be this wonderful father. Just like he pretended for the judge."

Saturday was Fletcher's day to babysit for Hannah while Leann worked. According to Lindy, when Leann would get home, Mick'd be lying on the couch, the house would be a wreck, the dishes would be piled up and Hannah would often still be in pajamas.

The only reason Mick wanted to go back with Leann the last time, at Easter of 1999, was that she'd decided to move on with her life. She'd decided the marriage wasn't going to work and "she started remodeling the house. She dropped like 10 pounds. She was dressing up, feeling really good about herself. I remember babysitting for her when she was going out with the girls and she'd be so giddy. She'd borrow clothes and be trying things on in the mirror. She was much happier."

Whether Fletcher thought she was seeing other guys—she had dated a pizza delivery guy who worked in the same strip mall she did—or just felt lonely, "He came crawling back with this letter," said Lindy. " 'Oh my gosh, I've made the biggest mistake of my life. I'll do whatever it takes. I swear, please take me back. We'll be a family. I'll be the husband you always wanted. I'll be involved in everything. I'll make you involved in everything.' "

Soon after their reconciliation, though, Mick was up to his old tricks, staying out and blaming it on the young lawyers' club. "He was just the master of manipulation."

Lindy is a hairdresser. Once a month she cuts everyone's hair in the family, for free. When Mick sat in the chair and began talking, she said, "It was always Mick, Mick, Mick, Mick. He would never say, How are you, What are you doing? All I had to say was, 'What are you working on now?' and it was like, woooh, I'd get done with the haircut and say 'Next!' before he could even finish his story, which I wasn't even listening to."

Lindy and others in the Misener clan all had a favorite Fletcher-as-villain story—the time a bird flew in their chimney and instead of opening a window and trying to shoo it out, he picked up a broom and, as Leann begged for the bird's life and Hannah watched in horror, Fletcher beat the bird to death. "Leann was hysterical. Hannah was going, 'Don't cry, Mommy, don't cry.' Hannah still tells that story."

And the New Year's Eve party of 1998, when Leann was the prettiest woman in the place but Mick ignored her all night. He got a page at midnight, then moments later said he had a headache and wanted to go home. She was, he said, free to stay. Suspicious, she insisted on leaving with him. Within weeks, Mick had moved out once again.

By the time Mick's trial rolled around, Jeni Hughes had compiled, based on her own diaries, a two-page typewritten chronology of lowlights in the Fletchers' marriage, in case anyone was interested. The Michigan Judicial Tenure Commission was, and it used her timeline in helping to build its case for removing Chrzanowski from the bench. (The dates aren't entirely accurate but are close.)

It read:

1996—Mick is attending law school. Dawnn Gruenburg is his "sponsor." Leann suspects that Dawnn is after Mick.

Jan. 1997—Leann and Mick are having problems. Dawnn is a factor in their problems. Leann moves to her parents for a week.

May 1997—Leann throws a surprise party for Mick for finishing law school.

May or June 1997—Mick passes the bar exam. He attends a party [where] Dawnn gives a speech about him. Mick then says a few words and thanks only Dawnn. Leann is very upset that he never mentions or thanks his family, Leann and Hannah.

Dec. 1997—Mick and Leann sit with Sue Chrzanowski and her husband at a Christmas party. Leann tells me that she and Sue talk all night about Dawnn Gruenburg and it turns out Sue conveniently dislikes Dawnn as much as Leann. Leann is happy to have an ally. She thinks that Sue and her husband are very nice.

March 1998—Mick starts wiring Sue's house for phones and computers. He said it was a side job for extra money. However, there was never any "extra money" to be found.

April 1998—Leann is sick one evening and Mick is supposed to be taking care of Hannah. While Leann is in bed, Mick gets a phone call from Sue at the house. He tells Sue that he will be right over. He then tells Leann that he has to go to Sue's to fix her computer line. Leann is mad that he is leaving because she is so sick and she cannot take care of Hannah. She tells him that he can't go. Mick gets very angry and calls Sue in front of Leann and tells her that he can't come over because he is on babysitting duty.

May 1998—Mick starts making negative comments about Dawnn to Leann. He tells Leann that Dawnn is angry that he is talking to Sue and that Dawnn told him that it didn't look very good for Mick to be associating with Sue [another judge] when he was working for Dawnn. So

Mick supposedly told Dawnn, "Well, I guess I don't work for you, anymore." At first Leann is happy about this, but then she gradually begins to wonder now if something is going on between Mick and Sue.

June 1998—Mick moves out for a few weeks. Leann and I begin staking out Sue's house to see if Mick's truck is there. We also check his office. We could never catch him or find any proof.

July 1998—Mick moves back home.

Aug. 1998—Leann's sister has a cookout and Mick is drinking. Later that night, Mick and Leann get into an argument and I try to talk to Mick. He tells me that he thinks the only reason he is still married is because of Hannah.

Oct.–Nov. 1998—Mick moves out for a week, then moves home for a week, then moves out for a few more weeks. He is finally home before Christmas.

Dec. 1999—New Year's Eve. We are at a hall party and Mick receives a page at 12:00 midnight. Lindy notices and tells Mrs. Misener. She then follows him to the pay phone. The line, however, is too long and he returns to the table. Ten minutes later, he tells Leann that he has a headache and needs to go home. He tells her that she can stay if she would like to. Leann doesn't trust Mick, so she calls his bluff and leaves with him.

Jan. 1999—Mick moves out and files for divorce. He claims that he doesn't think he is capable of loving anyone.

April 1999—Mick begs Leann to take him back. He tells her that he will now be the husband that she deserves and he should have been all along.

All in all, it wasn't a pretty picture Leann's family and friends painted of Mick, a picture the media avidly bought and sold. Just when it seemed it couldn't get any worse, it did. In a half-hour news show on Detroit's local ABC affiliate, Fletcher was about to be "exposed" as a Devil worshipper.

A DEVIL IN DISGUISE

On November 3, the demonization of Mick Fletcher stopped being a metaphor. The local ABC affiliate in Detroit ran a half-hour special featuring the sensational news that he had been a devil worshipper, and that one of his favorite evening pastimes was playing a violent bloody video game with Leann. He sat at the computer terminal in his upstairs office and she sat at the computer in their downstairs basement; with all the lights out in the house, he would play the game with a frenzy, usually resulting in her bloody, simulated death by dismemberment.

The Fletcher murder case attracted national attention from the start. Court TV aired his arraignment in August and made plans to televise the trial live, plans it scuttled when it found out that "20/20" had lined up family members on both sides, some exclusively, for an hour-long program that would air after the trial.

"First Edition" ran a piece on the arraignment, too, and named both judges, Susan Chrzanowski and Dawnn Gruenburg. It showed a shot of Mick being escorted to jail in hand-cuffs and a shot of his by-now-famous spit curl dangling over his forehead as he sat in court. It showed Chrzanowski on the stand referring to her sexual encounter the night before the shooting: "He told me he loved me very much." And it showed Jack Misener in a bright blue suit as he expressed his feelings toward his son-in-law: "Hatred. Pure hatred. That's all I'll ever feel for him. He was a piece of ice sitting there. A piece of steel. He loves nobody."

Channel 7, the local ABC affiliate, got into the act belatedly, with its half hour on the Fletcher case broadcast on its weekly "Impact" news show on November 3. Its revelations by reporter Shelly Smith were sensational. It portrayed a sick and evil man whose life had long been unraveling, a twisted Satanist who fed on games of murder and mayhem.

The setup was classic TV—the earnest, heavily intoning reporter standing outside the murder scene on Hazelwood Avenue, walking slowly toward the camera and then on the sidewalk and up the stairs to the front door as the camera tracked along next to her and she said her lines:

"From the outside looking in, the young attractive couple had it all. So how did Leann Fletcher wind up on the floor with a bullet in her head, lying dead in a pool of blood on her bedroom floor?"

Smith said they'd contacted people who had gone to law school and college with Fletcher, tried to find someone who had been his friend, but no one would talk about him. Kevin Schneider, a criminal defense attorney who was Fletcher's best friend in law school, said, though, there was a good reason he refused to speak to her on the record. He said he had one informal conversation with her and soon after got a call from another former classmate whom Smith had called. "He said Smith had told him I'd said Mick talked about guns all the time. He said, 'Did you say all that stuff?' " Kevin responded that he didn't, and this led to others deciding not to cooperate with her.

The show had a brief history lesson—a yearbook shot of Mick in stage get-up at Marysville High School north of Detroit: he'd been an actor there, though one who was a loner, without friends; he'd majored in criminal justice at Michigan State, where he'd met Leann at a Halloween party where, Smith said ominously, Mick had gone up to her and said: "If you're the Devil, take me to Hell."

The devil line at Halloween was old news to those familiar with the case, having gotten plenty of play in the papers in the days after the murder, as reporters wrote their follow-up features.

But what came next was news. And it was shocking.

Lisa Rodela, one of Leann's friends, said on camera that Mick had said he'd practiced black magic in college and was into Satanism. As for Leann: "She was totally shocked," said Rodela. "He said he had a relationship with Lucifer."

There was more, said Rodela. Leann had told her that Mick

would wake her up in the middle of the night, talking in his sleep—talking in different languages. Mick would be calling her name in his voice, then would be Lucifer in another voice, recounted Rodela. As Mick, he'd say: "Leave my angel alone. Don't touch her." Then, as Lucifer: "What about the girl?" Mick: "Don't touch our angel." Leann would wake him up, petrified.

Then came a video clip the producers had gotten from the Miseners, a tape of Mick moments after inhaling helium at a New Year's Eve party, in the first few minutes of January 1, 1996. The foreshadowing was so eerie, it made the hair stand up on your neck as Mick, in his helium-induced falsetto, said, looking into the camera: "I would not, could not possibly have committed these crimes."

Smith then segued into Mick the Lothario, recounting his affair with Dawnn Gruenburg, saying the senior 37th District Judge first sponsored him when he passed the bar but then later threatened his livelihood when she found out "he was in the arms of another judge in the 37th District Court."

It was time for a break. The show cut from Smith to studio host Guy Gordon, who told viewers, "He is teetering on the edge," as they broke for commercial.

Back from commercial, Smith continued the theme they broke on: "Mick was unraveling."

The show then recounted Chrzanowski's rise to the bench, how Mick started wiring her house and they fell in love, her divorce, her summoning him to her house to supposedly work on a computer even as Leann was sick in bed and Mick was supposed to babysit, how Mick hung out with other young lawyers in Warren bars.

All signs of a busy social life and a philandering husband but none of it evidence of "unraveling" or "teetering on the edge."

But then the payoff. Suddenly on screen came violent scenes from the video game "Quake," whose robot monsters do the worst kinds of bloody violence. Leann would join him in the game he loved, said Smith, the house lights all turned off, Mick upstairs, Leann downstairs as he did his best to kill her. The game would always end in Leann's bloody death.

Rodela was back on screen, saying she used to ask Leann about the game: "What fun is that?" To which Leann would respond, said Rodela: " 'Well, he just really likes it.' She always said he took it too seriously."

The show ended with a recounting of the final months together, when Mick seemed so much in love. "The former teen-age actor was putting on the performance of his life," said Shelly Smith.

Soon, Leann was dead on the bedroom floor, and Mick was charged with murder and awaiting trial.

It was amazing stuff. It certainly broke ground, the devil worship, the bloody video games in the darkened house each night, that other news organizations—print and electronic—hadn't stumbled upon. And much of it was exaggerated. It was TV news at its most sensational, stretching bits of truth into something else and weaving the sheerest of suggestions into a cloak of terror, witchcraft and the macabre. It was fun TV, but hardly probing investigative journalism.

Leann's best friend, Jeni Hughes, who ate dinner at the Fletchers' many nights and who routinely watched TV sitcoms with Leann while Mick was upstairs at the computer, said she never heard about "Quake" and never knew Leann to play it. Leann's sister, Lindy, with whom she talked every day, said her sister never mentioned "Quake," either. Neither they nor anyone else in Leann's family ever heard her say anything about Satanism or Mick worshipping the devil.

After the show aired, Lindy called Lisa and tried to pin her down as to what Leann had said about Mick and what he had said about the devil. The revelations had come as a shock, and Lindy, as mad as she was at Mick over the shooting, didn't believe them.

"I said, 'Did she actually that? Say *Satan*?' " recalled Lindy. "And she'd say, 'Well, ah, no. Ah, I don't know.' And I'd say, 'What do you mean? Did she say that?' 'I don't know.' *'Did she say that?'* "

The more Lindy tried to pin her down, the more elusive Lisa was. She wouldn't say what had or hadn't been said.

"I was just so mad at her," said Lindy, who discounted nearly all that had been said on the show. She said she was equally mad at Shelly Smith, assuming she'd goaded Lisa on. She, and others of the Misener family, figured it was more a case of Lisa enjoying her 15 minutes of fame than it was about Leann and Mick.

One other thing, said Lindy: "Leann was never scared of Mick, never. She trusted him completely."

As for the voices in his sleep, Lindy said: "My husband talks in his sleep, too."

In her first interview for this book, Rodela never mentioned either "Quake" or Mick's alleged Satanism. In a subsequent interview, to ask her about the charges on *Impact*, the entire Satan tale seemed to fall apart in under 10 minutes of polite but firm questioning.

Rodela said Leann had told her about the devil stuff "near the end of their relationship." But Rodela said she couldn't even remember if Leann actually used the word "devil" or "Satan," but said she might have used those words or maybe the word "Lucifer."

But she didn't remember? No. By devil worship, had she meant Mick lit candles and drew pentangles on the floor? Definitely not, said Lisa. Had he actually prayed to Satan? She didn't know. What were Leann's words? She couldn't remember. In fact, said Rodela, her own feeling was: "I don't think he was a devil worshipper." A far cry from what she had said on camera.

What, then, had she been alluding to? Well, she hemmed and hawed, she was sure that Mick had said something to Leann about having always communicated with a certain spirit. That he'd talked about this spirit "in the third person."

Since Mick was the son of evangelical Christians, talking about being in communication with a spirit is hardly proof of devil worship. It's the rare evangelical who doesn't talk about being moved by, or in communication with, the spirit. (During the college days he was supposedly worshipping the devil, his sister, Amy, remembers him coming home from college one weekend and rummaging in the basement for his old, childhood Bible. He'd read it front to back three times and had underlined numerous passages in yellow marker. Its spine was held together with brown tape. He told her that Leann hadn't had much of a church background and he wanted to take his Bible back to school to point some things out to her.)

Rodela even denied that Mick scared Leann, either through video games or talking in his sleep. Rodela maintained that Mick *did* talk in voices in his sleep, but "Leann wasn't fearful of it. She had a strong faith that allowed her not to be scared of it."

And she did say that once Leann expressed some concern about Mick's so-called spirit because maybe it explained why he was so smart. Said Rodela: "She said, 'Lisa, what if he does have some kind of connection? He's so smart. He knows everything about every subject. How can somebody know everything about everything?' "

Mick hadn't even been an aspiring actor. He'd had two bit parts in high school plays, never anything approaching a lead—at Marysville, as with many schools, so few kids tried out for plays that just about everyone who did got a part— and he never took any theater classes in high school or college.

Rodela's claims about the devil and "Quake" were the juiciest, most memorable parts of the "Impact" show. They were also allegations easily challenged, refuted even by those who hated Mick, thought him guilty of the most heinous crime imaginable and couldn't wait to see him held accountable at trial.

But the show had left an indelible image in the minds of those who saw it. Presumption of innocence be damned: this was an evil man, a devil worshipper gone mad who'd practiced on home video games what he would later do in real life. He was a cold-blooded killer of his wife and baby.

THE ANGEL MICK

Mick Fletcher, the strange loner who didn't even have a friend at his wedding. Who was a loner in college and law school. Who beat birds to death. A lazy lawyer who preferred pornography to practicing law, who was happy to let his wife put him through law school and buy the house and roof over his head. A user and abuser who, said Channel 7, worshipped Satan and insisted on playing cruel and bloody video games with his wife, trying to murder her electronic image on the computer screen as they sat in their separate darkened rooms in the ill-fated house on Hazelwood Avenue.

Those images formed in the public consciousness during the months between arrest and trial. The Fletcher family refused interview requests on Legghio's orders. But the Miseners had plenty to say about Fletcher, and so did the prosecutors—and the media had air time or column inches to fill.

These things became accepted fact:

- Leann saved up her money and bought the house on Hazelwood that he moved into after their marriage.
- Leann put him through law school with her earnings as a phone solicitor or nail technician.
- Mick was a loner who'd had no friends. No one, even, to come to his wedding.
- He had to have the best. His Dakota truck, for example, had to have the special bed liner, had to have the fancy gizmo to get rid of the smoke from his cigarettes, had to have the nice sound system. Nothing was too good for him, even if it meant building up a large debt to his in-laws.

- Mick spent no time with his daughter unless he wanted to put on a show for Leann's family.
- He was lazy. First, he was content to let Leann work while he went to school. Then, he was an underachieving attorney who'd rather sit in his room watching pornography on the computer than trying to make a living.

Perception isn't always reality. There was far more to Fletcher, as it turned out, than the images presented on TV or in the local papers. Perceptions are sometimes myths, too. For example:

- Leann didn't buy the house on Hazelwood. The purchase agreement was signed with Re/Max realty on March 2, 1993, with the house selling for $50,465.46, including county and city taxes. Leann's name was the only one appearing because Fletcher had to finance his way through law school with student loans, and he was afraid that if the loan for the house was in his name, too, it might damage his ability to get enough student loans.

    First American Mortgage Services financed a loan of $48,850. The $1,000 in earnest money to hold the house pending loan approval was paid by Darla Fletcher, in a check dated March 23 on an account at Citizens Federal Savings Bank in Port Huron. If Leann's savings paid for anything, it was the balance due on the settlement statement of $615.46.

- Fletcher had always worked, from the time he got his first job when he was at Marysville High. The summer before they got married, Fletcher worked full-time at a machine shop in Lexington, north of Port Huron, and spent his paychecks buying furniture and appliances for the house.

    During law school, he worked at a Radio Shack and then as a clerk in the Warren City Attorney's Office. His earnings paid the bills, too. And his law school bills were paid by his loans, not Leann.

- He did have friends at his wedding. His brother, Ben, was best man. Phil Count, his brother-in-law, who was such a family friend that he and Ben had Tigers season tickets together, also stood up at the wedding. None of his other friends stood up with him, says his sister, because Leann wanted the spouses and boyfriends of her sisters to be in the wedding party. Mick had other friends in attendance, and would have had more, said Amy, except the Miseners insisted the Fletchers trim their initial wedding-invitation list down to 75.

- Sure, his truck was his pride and joy. He'd bought it several months before the shooting, but it was the first new vehicle he'd ever owned. Until then, he'd had a series of clunkers, first a Chevette, then an old Chevy S10 truck with a blown engine he'd bought for $1,000 (John put another engine in it and Mick was able to get another 80,000 miles on it), then another S10 held together with duct tape. When he had clients to meet or on hot summer days when he had a couple of courts to get to and didn't want to wrinkle his suits too badly— he didn't have air conditioning—his mother would drive down to Hazel Park and switch her car for his rattletrap truck.

  Leann always had the better vehicles, a Ford Probe, then a Villager, then a Taurus. Mick couldn't trade vehicles with her when he needed something nicer to drive because his truck was a manual shift and she never learned how to drive one.

- Fletcher seemed to his friends and family, at least, to be anything but an inattentive dad. He built a computer file for Hannah called "The Pontificating Two-Year-Old," and filled it with Veggie Tales and Barney videos. During his separations from Leann, Mick took Hannah every Saturday. According to Amy, who was visiting her parents where Mick, recently separated, was staying at the time, Leann called during a rainstorm to say she was having trouble closing a window. Mick, she says, got in his truck and drove an hour to Hazel Park to lower the window, then drove back to his parents'.

  "Hannah has the vocabulary of a third-grader because Mick was the one sitting there playing computer-education games with her," said Amy after the trial. "She'd come up and say, 'Are you impwessed with me?'—she couldn't say her 'R's'—and it was like, 'Yes, I am impressed with you, because you're a three-year-old saying 'impressed.' He was the one who was always reading to her."

- His law career was anything but foundering. Most criminal defense attorneys scuffle to pay the bills the first few years out of law school, and he was no exception. But a key to success is forming productive alliances with local judges, who pass out assignments for the indigent, and with powerful attorneys.

     If anything, Fletcher was too successful in this regard. His alliance with Chrzanowski was both lucrative and sexual. And Roy Gruenburg, one of the most powerful attorneys in Warren and a former district judge, had taken Fletcher under his wing. He provided him office space—even a place to sleep during Mick and Leann's separations—and threw work his way. And Mick had an affair with Roy's daughter, Dawnn Gruenburg, another Warren judge.

     Fletcher's connections, in fact, were things to envy in the eyes of the other young struggling attorneys working their way up the ladder in the busy Warren courtroom.

Mick the loner? Perception, yes, even during his trial. Legghio played things close to the vest, as defense attorneys do. Family members who could—and wanted desperately—to speak up for him weren't allowed to.

Fed information by the prosecutors, and with ready access to the Miseners, those on deadline cranked out their stories or filmed their pieces.

But Mick had never been a loner. He was, others say, affable, gregarious, well-liked, with a quick laugh and a sharp sense of humor. The stoic face presented before and during trial was not the only one he had for the world. And he had friends who were willing and able to speak up for him, for those who took the time to find them—friends who say they loved and love him and will never believe the Mick Fletcher they knew had any resemblance to the guy they kept reading and hearing about—the guy accused of murdering his wife while she knelt on the bedroom floor.

Rachael Schmidt knew Mick most of her life, through the Croswell Wesleyan Church. "He and Amy and I were inseparable. We were bosom buddies," she said after the trial. "Everything we did was with Mick. He made everything more fun. He had a great sense of humor."

At some point the friendship blossomed into romance. She was one year behind Fletcher in school and went out with him her freshman and sophomore years. She and Mick and Amy and her boyfriend double-dated to Mick's junior prom at Marysville High. Rachael went to school at Croswell–Lexington and she said that geography more than anything broke them up. "But even after we stopped dating, we remained great friends. There was never a fight that broke us up. There was never any bad feelings. He was always super, super nice. Whenever we went anywhere, it was always more fun with Mick. He was just a great guy all round."

Schmidt, a German linguist, said that other than his sense of humor, she best remembers Fletcher for his intelligence. "His brain works so uniquely. He's just got an amazing brain. When synthesizers first came out, he got one and taught himself music theory and he was great on it."

Though they lost contact after high school, Schmidt said she never doubted his innocence. "It's absurd. He's way too smart. If he wanted to kill somebody he'd come up with a better plan than that, something that made sense. It's impossible. Never once for a second did I think he did it. There's just no way. It had to be an accident."

He had friends in high school. And he had friends in law school.

Kevin Schneider, now a defense attorney in Warren who considers both Judge Chrzanowski and Fletcher close friends, said they became friends because they had a common habit. Smoking inside buildings at the University of Detroit–Mercy law school was prohibited. "We pretty much smoked all day long together, for three years," said Schneider in an interview after the trial. "Mick's a gentleman. He's a very civil man and you could tell that the first time you met him."

He said Fletcher was affable but "not a giant socialite." Unlike a lot of the other students, who, says Schneider, "got schnockered up every Thursday night and most Fridays and Saturdays, too," Mick would grab a beer here and there but usually went straight home at the end of the school day.

He and Schneider talked politics—Mick was big on Second Amendment issues and was one of the more conservative classmates. Later, their career paths took them both to Warren, where young attorneys ran from court to court at the busiest, most bustling court in suburban Detroit. Mick fit right in, hanging out in the halls with the other attorneys while they waited for judges to take the bench or for cases to be called.

"You can't say he was a social animal, but for people to say that he was a loner, that he had no friends—that's completely absurd," says Schneider. "He knew all of us. He was a regular guy. There was nothing loner or reclusive about him."

When word came out that Fletcher had been having an affair with the judge, "I was very impressed. When I heard that he was sleeping with Susan, I was like, 'You know, Mick, I didn't know you had it in you.' I was surprised. I mean, he's a good looking guy, but . . ."

Schneider considered himself in the know in the Warren court and Chrzanowski was a good friend—"she's a fine judge and one of the first judges to help me out when I first started practicing law, very nice, very knowledgeable"—but other than a secretary or two and one or two of Chrzanowski's confidants, he and most other courthouse hangers-on hadn't an inkling of the affair. They'd been discreet, even at many of the social functions where the lawyers and judges would find themselves.

When he heard of the charges against Fletcher, Schneider said, "I was floored. It just didn't make sense. It never made sense to me." He practices in Hazel Park, too, and even being privy to the cops' point of view—"almost immediately you heard from the cops that they had blood-soaked shirts, they'd found blood in the drain trap, they got him, they have him, but even based on that amount of evidence I didn't believe it. I still don't believe it. Pulling the trigger on the gun? He would not have proceeded in that manner. He's a pretty smart guy—he's not a brain surgeon but he's not that dumb."

"I've known Mickie my entire life," said Danielle Blais, a telecommunications specialist for Ameritech. Her parents go to church with the Fletchers and the siblings of both families grew up together. Amy Count, Mick's sister, is her best friend. She and Amy would drive up to spend weekends with Fletcher at Michigan State, and saw his relationship with

Leann evolve from its beginnings. She remained friends with
Leann until her death, and saw her for the last time at church
the week before the shooting. She congratulated Danielle on
her new baby and they talked briefly about maybe Leann and
Mick having another one in the not-too-distant future. Five
days later, Leann found out she was pregnant.

"Mickie is a great guy. He really is," she said. "Very car-
ing. Loving. It's hard for me to even think somebody would
think he'd do that. I've never known him to have a mean
bone in his body. Never a bad word for anyone. He was an
easy guy to love. Obviously he was very good looking, and
he had a heart of gold. He'd do anything for anybody. He'd
always, always do things for Amy and me. If we called him
and said we were broke down on the road, he'd be the first
one there to help you out. Any time of day or night, if you
needed him, he was there."

"People say, 'Oh, people snap.' Not this guy. Not this guy.
I cried when I saw him on TV in his orange [jail] jumpsuit."

She remembers him growing up—he is four years older
than she is—as a big brother, smart, joking, fun to be with.
Her brother, Buck, was Mick's best friend. "We couldn't believe it when they'd say he had no friends. My friends and I
said, 'They never asked us.' He always had friends. Absolutely.

"He would always console people who were in love trouble. He'd say, 'Don't you worry about it. You're a beautiful
person. You'll be fine.' "

Her words were hauntingly similar to words of his in one
of the e-mails to Judge Chrzanowski that would make headlines at his trial. They would be seen by some, then, as part
of a con job by a wheeler and dealer trying to keep the judge
on the line. As always with Fletcher, and with this case, there
were two ways of looking at things.

"And as far as being a father, he was amazing with that
baby. He adored her. And he loved Leann. He absolutely
loved her. Everybody makes mistakes and he made his, but
he loved her," said Blais. "You know, I loved Leann, but she
didn't make things easy. She could be hard to live with. I
remember when they were separated the last time and Amy
and I were talking to him. He said he was going to go back
and we said, 'Are you sure you want to do this?' And he

said, 'Yes, I do. I really love her.' And we told him we'd support him 100 percent whatever he did."

Blais said the day she heard Fletcher had been arrested, "I cried. I could not believe it. They had the wrong person. There's never been any doubt in my mind. I've never, ever had a second guess, or a doubt about that. Never. And I never will. Of all the people this could have happened to, it happened to him, the most undeserving of all. That's the hard part. I feel so much pain for him and his family.

"My heart goes out to the Miseners because they lost a beautiful daughter. But Mick did not do it," she said, finishing the interview by saying: "Thank you so much for the opportunity to tell you what a wonderful person Mick is."

Jennifer Davis, a funeral director in the small town of Flushing, west of Flint, has known Amy Count for 15 years, since meeting her at a church summer camp. They later went to college together and she has known Mick well for much of that time.

"Mick—actually, we all call him Mickie—is easy going, friendly, thoughtful. I've never seen him in a bad mood. I've never known him to be nasty to anybody. He'd hold doors open for people. He always thought about other people before himself," she said several months after the trial. "He's very humorous, a great sense of humor. I can't think of anything negative about him. He reminds me a lot of my brother."

Like Blais, she was friends with Leann, as well, and was at the hospital the day Leann gave birth, and she recalls happy times baking cookies with Leann and Amy at John and Darla's house in Marysville.

Her reaction to hearing that Fletcher had been arrested for Leann's death? "It was a sickening feeling. I couldn't believe they thought he did it."

Could he have? "No way. Nope."

Was he a loner? "He was the farthest thing from a loner you could imagine. He could be anybody's friend. The Miseners say he looked down on people. He never looked down on anybody."

As for Fletcher the dad, she says: "He was always carrying Hannah around. Whenever I'd see them, he'd always be the one holding her. I mean, my dad loves me, but there's no way my dad ever held me or treated me the way Mick did Hannah. He was an exceptional dad."

Marshall Hook, whose parents had worshipped with the Fletchers in the Croswell Wesleyan Church where Leann and Mick were married, was 19 when Mick went on trial. His memories of Mick were formed during a week-long fishing trip to a small lake in Chapleau, Ontario, about 120 miles north of the Canadian Sault.

Marshall says Mick took him under his wing, recounting one long hike around the lake, through deep woods and nearly impenetrable marsh and thickets. "Mick led the way. I was grumbling most of the way. He was trying to keep my spirits up. 'We can make it. We can do it. It's only a little bit more.' " Later, around the campfire, Mick helped Marshall whittle a walking stick and carve a face into the handle; for years, the stick was a proudly displayed souvenir in Marshall's bedroom at home.

Amy Count has always been close to her brother. They had the kind of relationship where, even after she moved out to San Diego, they'd call each other and spend small fortunes in long conversations, real conversations, about life and what they were up to.

She says her husband was, in fact, envious of how close she and Mick were, that he and his siblings kept in touch but it seemed far more perfunctory.

She and other Fletchers were baffled that the Miseners so quickly and readily believed the worst, that Mick could have shot Leann, and not only shot her, but in such a lurid, evil manner as the prosecutors allege.

And she is baffled, too, at the picture the Miseners and Leann's friends now paint of a cold, aloof, non-caring husband and father who had changed so much after getting out of law school. "I mean, if he was such a bad guy and had been for so long, why were the Miseners out celebrating with Mick and Leann the night before? Why would you be happy that your daughter was going to have another baby with such a guy?

"And even that morning of the shooting, they were fine with Mick. They were willing to babysit so he could take

Leann shooting. If you thought for one instant he was capable of doing that to your daughter, why would you be babysitting? If my parents thought my husband was capable of shooting me, they'd never let me anywhere near him. They'd have me so far from him. But they were out celebrating with him the night before."

John and Darla sent "20/20" video tapes of the Miseners and Mick at family parties. One showed Gloria dancing and laughing with Mick; another had Gloria jokingly warning Lindy's second husband to give his new wife everything she wanted because they had a lawyer in the family.

Her brother, she says, was the kind of guy who'd call home if he heard a report about tornado watches to remind his mother and sister which corner of the basement to go to. If he was going to be late, he'd call so no one would worry. When Amy visited him one time in jail, it was getting late when she was leaving. "This was the way Mick always was: He was, 'Do you have Mom's car phone? If something happens, make sure you pull over in a well-lit area.' He was always like that."

Buck Martin is a building contractor in Port Huron who has known Fletcher as long as he can remember. They went to church together, played on the church-league softball team when they were 14 and 15 and went to community college together. Like most kids their age in the Port Huron and Marysville area, when they turned 19, they'd head across the Blue Water Bridge with four or five other guys to Sarnia in Canada to drink beer legally—they were still underage in Michigan—and try to pick up girls. "Canada was a happening place. That's where all the girls were," said Martin.

After Fletcher transferred to Michigan State and met Leann, Buck and his future wife, Melissa, frequently double-dated with Leann and Mick. Later, Leann would come to Melissa's wedding shower and Melissa would go to Leann's baby shower for Hannah.

"I was shocked. I'm still shocked," said Martin of his reaction to Fletcher's arrest. "It hurts my heart to even think about it."

He was the kind of guy, said Martin, who, when he got a new sound system for his car, would take the old one out and install it in your car, free of charge, which he did with Martin's hot-rod Camaro.

As for Fletcher's reputation as a loner, Martin said, "He got along with everybody. He was a great guy. I could name ten guys right now that he hung with. He never had any problem making friends. What a crock! I tell you, it was hard for me to listen to Drew and Mike rip him apart. That wasn't the guy I knew. I don't know where they got that stuff."

(Martin was referring to a popular drive-time radio show on WRIF-FM. For some reason, the Fletcher case became something of a cottage industry for the two co-hosts: Drew and Mike. For months, up and through the trial, they savaged Fletcher and interviewed a series of Miseners and friends of Leann.)

Martin said he is convinced of Fletcher's innocence. "Let's put it this way. If something happened and he got out of jail and needed a place to stay, I've got a bedroom here and he's welcome to stay here any time. And if he ever needed a job, he could slip a tool belt on and go to work with me."

A TIE AT JURY SELECTION

After months of delays and rescheduling, things were finally underway in the case of the *People of the State of Michigan* vs. *Michael Fletcher*. It was 8:30 a.m. Tuesday, June 6, 2000. The long-awaited DNA tests on what the prosecution said would be a crucial, damning piece of evidence—presumed blood-mist stains on Fletcher's green cotton Oxford shirt, which would prove that he was near Leann when she was shot and not, as he claimed, in the bathroom—had finally come back months late from the overworked Michigan State Police crime lab.

And now, the last bit of routine work—jury selection— was about to commence. Several days of the dull and mundane—the analyzing of jury surveys by both prosecution and defense and the actual picking of a jury—and then, finally, things could get underway in what promised to be one of the highest-profile, most dramatic murder trials in recent memory in Michigan.

Judge Jessica Cooper's courtroom on the third floor of the Oakland County Courthouse was nearly empty. Six members of the Misener family, including Jack and Gloria, sat in the front row. The attorneys—lead defender Brian Legghio; his assistant, Marla McCowan, who had been a classmate of Fletcher's at the University of Detroit–Mercy Law School; Gregory Townsend, who would head up the prosecution; and his assistant, Lisa Ortlieb—would spend all day today going over the surveys potential jurors had filled out, looking for reasons for rejection or approval and to prepare themselves for the jury interviews later in the week.

On a hanger near the defense table was a very dark, near-black suit and starched white shirt encased in clear plastic. It awaited Fletcher. When he faced his prospective jurors for the first time on Thursday, he'd be able to look more like an attorney, which he was, than like a prisoner, which he also was, in a bright orange jumpsuit which he'd been wearing for 10 months.

Lisa Ortlieb got up and came over to the Miseners. She leaned down in front of them and said quietly but excitedly: "We got the shirt in," she said. One of her duties during the trial would be family liaison, explaining decisions, calming them down during low spots when Legghio's case would be going well, letting them know what was coming up. The Oakland County Prosecutor's Office took very seriously its secondary role as victim's advocate, and so did Ortlieb.

The attorneys had been busy the day before with Cooper, laying the ground work for the trial, discussing procedures and deciding on potential motions regarding evidence. Legghio had said many months earlier that he would fight the admission of the shirt as evidence, as it had been improperly seized the day of the shooting, but he told Cooper he was dropping his objections.

The family was all smiles, yesses and greats at the news.

They wouldn't have been so happy if they knew why Legghio was suddenly so agreeable. The DNA report had come back, but with hardly the result Townsend had expected. The test showed no positive match between what had been described to the press as the forensics equivalent of a smoking gun—blood mist that could only have come from shooting Leann at close range—and Leann's actual DNA.

Ortlieb would let that bad news wait a bit. The prosecution would later claim victory over the test, anyway—while there had been no DNA match because the sample was too small, it had tested as human blood—but clearly the prosecution had overstated the volume on the shirt and its ramifications on the case. It would, in fact, turn out to be nearly irrelevant to the proceedings.

Friday, June 9, 8:20 a.m. All day yesterday, dozens of prospective jurors had been questioned closely. Some had been dismissed upon agreement of both attorneys—those who said they couldn't give fair judgment to an admitted adulterer, for example, or those who admitted a bias against police—and others under the preemptory challenges allowed each side, where jurors could be eliminated without explanation in the combination of science, art and wishful thinking that is jury selection.

Today the process will be completed and on Monday the trial will begin.

Fletcher is brought into the courtroom, dressed in the near-black suit and white shirt, open at the collar. His hair is slicked back, a bit too much hair gel evident as it formed a small duck's tail in the back, a spit curl dangling over his forehead, teeth marks from the comb visible from 15 feet away.

Five of the Miseners sit across the right half of the front row. Also in the row, to the far left, are Mick's parents, John and Darla. Five or six feet of hard wood separate the two intertwined families.

Judge Cooper enters at 8:26. All rise.

At 8:27, Marla McCowan walks in with a pre-knotted tie and hands it to her client. The jurors who have thus far passed muster, and the dozens of others who are ready to be grilled, have yet to be brought in. Other than the families, just one reporter is on hand.

The tie is bluish-purple and clearly something about it displeases Fletcher. He nods his head "no." Marla says something, nods her head in a "yes," and tries to reassure him. He seems put out, puts the tie up against his shoulder. The color, apparently, displeases him. He lays the tie down on the table in front of him. Legghio has noticed the exchange. He comes over, says something to his client, picks the tie up, puts it up against Fletcher's suit and nods encouragement.

"Sure, it matches," he seems to be saying.

Finally, Fletcher grabs the tie, still clearly unhappy, buttons his top shirt button, puts the loose tie on over his head and knots it in place.

The whole exchange has taken just a minute or so and has gone unnoticed by most. But not by Ortlieb. She sees it, too, and thinks: "What ego! The guy's life is basically on the line and he's worried about whether his tie matches?"

Later, during the trial, she makes a mental note whenever she sees Fletcher borrow Marla McCowan's mirror so he can see how he looks.

*   *   *

The jurors and prospective jurors, each wearing a large number affixed to the chest, are brought in. As the day begins, 13 jurors have tentatively been selected and are seated in the jury box. Fourteen are needed. After the trial itself and before deliberations, two of them will be dismissed randomly and the other 12 will decide guilt or innocence.

A middle-aged woman who works as an operations manager for a trucking concern is called up to the witness stand. Legghio asks her if it would bother her if the people at the heart of this case had been involved in extramarital affairs. "I don't think so. My father did it. My husband did it. Everyone does it."

She is then shown graphic photos of the crime scene and Leann's lifeless body, pieces of evidence she will have to ponder at trial. She says she can handle such graphic displays and do her job as a juror. She is told to join the others.

Legghio then uses one of his challenges and tells one of those in the box to step down.

A young kid is called up and Townsend eventually asks him to be removed for cause, and Cooper agrees. One prospective juror turns out to be an attorney who knows Judge Chrzanowski and has represented police before. He is excused.

Another man is seated, bringing the total to 14. Legghio uses another challenge and dismisses a juror.

The owner of a dog bakery in nearby affluent Birmingham—part of a small franchise operation called the Three Dog Bakery founded in New Orleans' French Quarter—is seated. (She will later be one of the strongest proponents on the jury for conviction on the charge of first-degree murder.)

Townsend uses one of his challenges. Back to 13.

A kid who says he can't stand cops is dismissed. A man who hates philanderers because his ex-wife was a two-timer is excused.

Finally, at 10:11 both Legghio and Townsend say they are satisfied with the 14 in the jury box. They are all white, 10 of them are men, three of the men are engineers.

At 10:13 Judge Cooper gives them their instructions. They will be allowed to go home at night. They cannot discuss the case, amongst themselves or with loved ones. They cannot eat in the court cafeteria. They can eat in the jury room or leave the building for lunch. The trial will be on Monday, Tuesday, Thursday and Friday. Wednesday will be a day off for them, since that is the judge's day to hear motions in other cases and attend to other duties. The case may last for three or four weeks, and if any of them have any trouble from their employers, let her know and she will handle it forthwith. Fletcher may or may not testify and they may not draw any conclusions about his innocence or guilt if he chooses not to.

At 10:30, court is adjourned for the day, and the weekend. It will resume at 8:30 a.m. on Monday. Legghio comes over to Darla Fletcher and has some advice for her. He has seen her slumped, looking depressed, as any mother might who is watching a jury being picked that's going to be voting soon on whether or not her son shot his wife in the back of the head with a Smith & Wesson.

Sit up straighter, he says. He offers the advice gently but firmly. You have to look more alert, focused even when you're not, or when you're bored. Don't let the jury see you bored or disinterested.

Legghio then greets a reporter and says: "This is really going to be a fun trial to watch. I don't say that because I am part of it. It's just that there's such good issues at stake. It's going to be very interesting for people who like these things."

On the way out, Legghio introduces the reporter to Townsend and the three of them share an elevator down. Townsend is on his way out to smoke his pipe. It is a sunny, warm day, and while he has his smoke, he and Legghio have some odds and ends of procedural business to discuss.

The elevator stops at the second floor and on walks a court employee who knows Townsend and Legghio. "I wanted to come in and get a look at your guy, see if he's as good looking as they say," she says to Legghio.

"He's a good looking kid," says Legghio. "I wish I looked like that."

"Yeah," says Townsend. "Then you could have had a couple of judges."

The three erupt in laughter. The elevator door opens and out they go.

THE ATTORNEYS

Greg Townsend is an unlikely legal star. He isn't particularly glib. He's not a fancy dresser like others at the top of his profession. He's plain to look at, maybe even a touch homely. He drives a Ford 150 truck. On his off days, in black shirt and cowboy hat, he looks more like a guy on the line—or a line dancer on one of the cable shows on the Nashville Network—than the Oakland County Prosecutor's expert in criminal forensics.

His delivery in court is workmanlike, straightforward, lacking in histrionics or dramatics. Despite that, or maybe in part because of it, juries love the guy. They trust him and they believe him.

Townsend is a native Detroiter and grew up in Dearborn Heights, once the locus of Henry Ford's factory workers and now the center of the largest Arab population anywhere in the world outside of the Middle East. For generations of immigrants, Dearborn has been at the center of the prototypical American dream. People worked hard and made better lives for their kids.

Townsend went to school briefly at Detroit's Wayne State, an urban campus without much pretension, either. He dropped out, joined the Navy, did a tour in Korea, then returned home to get serious about his education.

He completed his undergraduate degree at the University of Michigan campus in Dearborn, then graduated with honors from the Detroit College of Law in 1983. He was 46 when the Fletcher trial began, and he had never worked anywhere else as a lawyer except the Oakland County Prosecutor's Office.

He was, and is, a lifer, a term he uses with pride. The way

to make real money in lawyering is to pay your dues on the prosecutorial side of things, then switch sides and go into criminal defense. That was Brian Legghio's route. But Townsend realized early on he liked putting bad guys away, and he was good at it.

At the time of the trial, he was the resident expert in forensics and the senior prosecutor on a staff of more than 100. His official title was assistant to Prosecutor David Gorcyca, an elected official whom the electorate put in office in 1996 when they got tired of former Prosecutor Richard Thompson's series of losing trials in assisted-suicide/murder cases involving the notorious Doctor Death, Jack Kevorkian, whose flamboyant attorney, Geoffrey Fieger, became a national celebrity more for his court-steps outbursts than for his string of victories.

Townsend had prosecuted upwards of 90 murder cases when he was assigned the Fletcher case. He had seen way more than his share of ugly, headline cases—the firebomber who killed three kids and their father; the punk who'd sodomized a woman, then kept her in the trunk of her car while he drove her around town for a week (she got so thirsty she drank the antifreeze in the trunk and died); a kid who liked to beat older gays to death; a psychopath who shot a high school football star to death because he'd dared brush shoulders with him in a McDonald's in 1992.

Townsend has a small, relatively unadorned office on the third floor of the building that houses the prosecutor's staff, across a driveway from the Oakland County Courthouse. There are several photos of Alcatraz on his walls, and several small monuments to evil people put in jail. If he put Fletcher away, he'd make room for one to him, too, on the small table that already bore the framed picture of Dr. Death, the one with a caption reading: "Do I look like a criminal?"

The football player who'd been shot to death at the McDonald's? After his killer was put away for life, the family put a framed plaque together thanking Townsend. It included a small football helmet and a jersey bearing the number 72. It hangs on the wall and is one of the first things a visitor sees.

*   *   *

Lisa Ortlieb preceded Mick Fletcher as a criminal justice major at Michigan State, class of 1989. Like him, she went to law school in Detroit, graduating from the Detroit College of Law in 1993. Like him, she applied for a prosecutor's position at Oakland County. There, their paths diverted. She got hired. Mick didn't, and began relying more and more on Susan Chrzanowski.

Ortlieb also shared a career path with Chrzanowski. She preceded the soon-to-be judge in handling cases in the Clarkston District Court in northern Oakland County.

Where Townsend is plain, Ortlieb is striking—tall, model-thin, pretty and something of a head-turner in Oakland County courts. She would help Townsend with tactical planning before the trial and in end-of-the-day strategy sessions during it. The arguments in court would be left to him.

Her main task, at least insofar as the Miseners saw it, was hand-holding and liaison. She would keep them informed of what was coming every step of the way. If she and Townsend hit some bumps in the trial road, she explained them and helped paint them as smaller rather than larger.

During breaks she'd come over to chat. She'd explain procedures or rulings during recesses. She'd huddle with them in the hall before sessions began.

It was a role that came naturally to her, having been the section leader of the Domestic Violence Section for half of her seven years with the Prosecutor's Office.

(During the trial, the Miseners would have made a bunch of sterling silver medallions with an angel on the front and the words "I Watch Over You" on the back, in honor of their fallen angel. Months after the trial, Ortlieb would still have one on her person.)

"My aspiration is to follow in Greg Townsend's footsteps," she laughs, then gets serious. "I'm a lifer. Just like Greg. We get paid in other ways besides big paychecks. Our rewards come in different ways. Prosecuting rapists. Fighting for the victims. Helping people. Making a difference in their lives. Having a family crying and hugging you and saying you made a difference, that justice was served."

Already grown close to the Miseners—she had been involved in the case since Fletcher's arraignment in August of 1999—she said: "I love the Miseners. They are a remarkable family and I wish I never would have met them. They are unlike any victims I have ever met. They're great people, and the fact that the apple of their eye was taken from them by their son-in-law and they were able to maintain their spirit and composure is amazing."

Brian Legghio was one of the Detroit area's best criminal defense attorneys, but compared to Fieger, relatively unknown in the local media until he got the Fletcher case. Where Fieger would have had an ear-splitting field day with it, playing to the press more vigorously than he'd play to the jury, Legghio would keep a very low profile. It would be, he decided early on, a case that would be settled by forensics; he thought the prosecution's case was far less substantial than the local media had been led to believe, and in turn had led its viewers, listeners or readers to believe.

A native of the working-class Detroit suburb of Roseville, his dad, Adam, was a construction worker and ditch digger. Legghio did his undergraduate work at the University of Michigan, then got his law degree from Franklin Pierce Law School in New Hampshire in 1978. He worked as an attorney with the US Secret Service in Washington until 1982, then until 1988 served as an assistant prosecutor for the US Attorney's Office in Detroit. He took a job at a Detroit firm for the next three years, then put out his own shingle in 1991.

Gentlemanly and polite for the most part, he can be sharp-tongued, sarcastic and downright nasty when needed, and the Fletcher trial would eventually need all three.

His highest-profile case to date had been something that seemed more suited to a Carl Hiaasen or Donald Westlake comedy/mystery than real life—the infamous Chicken Condom Case in Manhattan in 1992. His client, Timothy Mucciante, like him a resident of the posh Grosse Pointe suburb and a lawyer, to boot, had been charged in federal court with operating a bogus $3.3 million investment scheme that involved . . . No, this was better than Hiaasen or Westlake, way too funny for fiction.

Mucciante specialized in international law, namely, the arranging the adoption of Romanian orphans. In 1988 he hooked up with Dr. Stuart Berger, a 400-pound doctor, an image in itself too good for fiction. *The Wall Street Journal* described Berger as looking like what you might get if you inflated Billy Joel.

Berger and Mucciante distributed diet products in a licensing deal that allowed them to use comedian Dick Gregory's name. Mucciante and Berger grew close; soon the attorney was wheeling around Manhattan in Berger's Silver Shadow Rolls Royce and trying to entice Berger's friends, including the congresswoman Bella Abzug, into investing in a deal to license Peter Max art works in Russia.

Mucciante had another good deal going, a pipeline down under, where he was able, or so he claimed, to get good deals on Australian bonds. Eventually he sold Berger $2.5 million of them. Berger never noticed such minor details as typographical errors and a lack of engraving, perhaps because he'd been blinded by the pre-payment of $143,000 in interest, delivered in cash to his office in a suitcase.

It gets better. Soon Berger and his Manhattan buddies were in on the ground floor of another deal, this, they were told, to take advantage of a seller's market for good condoms in Russia. Berger and pals had the money, Mucciante the contacts.

Mucciante could get top quality condoms and latex gloves in London—two million of each, in fact. They'd be swapped for frozen chickens in Russia. The chickens in themselves weren't of any value to the diet doctor, but they were worth plenty in Saudi Arabia, where it is well known that there are very few chickens. Mucciante collected $74,500 to get the project rolling; the business plan called for a profit of $3 million.

Months passed. The profits failed to materialize. Berger asked what was up. There was, Mucciante told him, a delay. The chickens were in quarantine.

Some more time passed when the light bulb starting going on over the investors' heads. As one of them told the *Journal*: "I began to get suspicious. If they were frozen, why were they in quarantine?"

Exactly. Mucciante hired Legghio to explain to them and to the feds. He did the best he could. Legghio used all his considerable oratorical skills, and nearly pulled it off. Mucciante was acquitted on 15 counts but found guilty by a jury of masterminding the scheme.

"That case was a blast. A blast," said Legghio.

Criminal defense attorneys are known for their egos, and the better ones for their stagecraft, as well. Legghio's strength, as it is in all good actors, is you don't notice him acting. He underplays the role to perfection.

"You're always conscious you're on stage," says Legghio. "I'll wear a suit that may look a little older or ruffled. I'll wear shoes that won't be as highly polished. You don't want the jury seeing the Palm Pilot." Or the Rolex.

"It's not about you. It's about the jury and their perceptions."

Legghio would impress in the Fletcher case, too, drawing the highest in post-mortem praise from one of the chief witnesses lined against him. Dr. Ljubisa Dragovic, the Oakland medical examiner. "A master," he would describe him. "A master. I didn't know him before the trial. I turned into his fan. He's a great defense attorney."

Marla McCowan, a slight, baby-faced woman who became pregnant shortly before the trial, had gone to law school with Fletcher at the University of Detroit–Mercy. She had him in several classes but didn't know him. She, like others, remained more or less aloof from most other students in the cutthroat environment of law school.

Their one encounter was hardly pleasant. Fletcher was one of those students who would gather outside before, during and after classes to smoke. McCowan briefly sat next to him in a criminal justice class. She is severely allergic, and he always smelled so strongly of cigarette smoke that she asked the professor to let her switch seats halfway though the semester.

McCowan read about the shooting on August 20, her birthday. "I saw his picture in the paper [and] when I was reading some snippet about the affair, I almost instinctively saw an injustice in the making." At the time she was working part-time for the State Appellate Defender's Office, the state-funding agency that would, if Fletcher were convicted, handle an appeal. If Ortlieb is a true believer and on a mission to put the bad guys away, McCowan is a true believer, too—in trying to keep good guys from being convicted as bad guys.

She cold-called Legghio, to offer her services. He met her

twice and finally accepted. "Quite frankly, I just bugged Brian until he let me in." She was bright, she had a good background in appellate law, which might be needed down the road, and she filled Legghio's need to have a woman on the team. Her presence might prove crucial, especially to female jurors.

When she showed up at jail the first time to meet with Fletcher, he didn't even recognize her from law school. By the time the trial would end McCowan would consider him a friend. "We have since become close, as a matter of circumstance," she would say after the trial, "but my guess is he became a totally different person after August 16, 1999, and that is the only person I know."

Another of her duties was to keep Fletcher socialized, to try to keep him from getting too demoralized or stir-crazy while sitting in solitary confinement. Every Monday for eight months McCowan visited him, partly to keep him abreast of developments, mostly to keep his spirits up, to keep him used to talking and interacting with people from the outside. "Part of my job was to keep Mick human," is how she put it. "I have seen guys who have spent a few months in solitary confinement come out drooling. This isn't by accident, it's by design. The Oakland County jail is run by a politician, not a warden. He doesn't understand rehabilitation, much less any aspect of the Eighth Amendment. He only knows he gets more votes if he says he is tough on criminals. So, without any real objectives, he just keeps everyone locked up and doesn't care how or when they come out."

Each trip she'd bring little but important things like cookies from his mother, vitamins, lip balm, Cokes and toothpaste.

"If I leaned over during trial and picked up a pen from him or said something in his ear, or whatever, I didn't want it to be just for show. I wanted it to come from a natural closeness that we had established from working together for a long time," she said.

After the trial, Dragovic also praised her highly. Not a great respecter of attorneys, dishing out accolades to both of Fletcher's attorneys was unusual. Generally he thinks of defense attorneys as lazy, shoot-from-the-hip types who come in unprepared. "She was astute," he'd say. "And worked very hard. She spent many hours with me in preparation . . . far more than the prosecution did."

OPENING ARGUMENTS

The long-awaited, often-postponed murder trial of the *State of Michigan* vs. *Michael Fletcher* finally began on Monday, June 12, 2000. Originally scheduled for January, it was pushed back to February, then April and finally June as both sides awaited the crucial DNA tests.

At 8:15 a.m. the courtroom of Judge Jessica Cooper, one of the most highly regarded judges in the state and, by luck of the draw, judge of seemingly every high-profile case in affluent Oakland County the last few years—including several trials of Dr. Jack Kevorkian—is packed to overflowing.

Fletcher's parents, Darla and John, his sister Amy, and a family friend sit at the very left of the front row. About 45 of Leann Fletcher's extended family—who had been hugging each other out in the hallway earlier, take up most of the rest of the seats, with reporters from local TV and radio stations and the area's numerous weekly and daily newspapers getting seats if they arrive half an hour early, getting sent down the hall to a media-overflow room to watch TV feeds if they don't. Two newspaper photographers and a free-lance camera crew working for ABC's "20/20" show position themselves in the back right-hand corner of the courtroom. A TV technician is duct-taping wires and checking microphones.

Leann's three sisters sit in the front pew. They and others of the Misener family have a certain look about them, almost a Sixties look of teased hair dyed blond and hairsprayed. The look may be passé elsewhere, but it speaks here, in Oakland County, to their working-class roots; it also visually represents their "family-ness." They are together in this spiritually and emotionally and their similarity of appearance announces their unity to anyone in the court who cares to look, Mick's parents included. Mrs. Misener shares the same look, though for now, she must remain out in the hall, until her testimony is concluded.

At 8:25, Mick Fletcher is led into the court, sheriff deputies in front and behind. His hands are cuffed in front of him. His face is fuller than at his arraignment last summer, his skin sallow from months of jail time. His black hair is slicked back into a bit of a duck's tail, teeth marks from his comb clearly visible, a small spit curl dangling over his forehead. He's wearing a black suit, white shirt open at the collar. Marla McCowan hands him a tie and he quickly puts it on. Today, there is no argument over whether or not it matches.

(Each time he leaves the court, for a recess or for lunch, he must remove the tie, presumably so he won't use it as a weapon or commit suicide. Each time he comes back, he has to retie it. It's another way the system reminds him of his status, suit or no suit.)

At 8:30, Judge Cooper enters, the courtroom stands, then sits. The jury is brought in, and Greg Townsend stands to deliver his opening statement.

"Ladies and gentlemen of the jury, a beautiful 29-year-old young woman named Leann Fletcher had a dream—of having a large family like the family she grew up in," he begins. Townsend is the antithesis of slick. An expert on forensic evidence, and presenting it to a jury, he depends on organization and fact, not showmanship or charisma. His suit looks off-the-rack. He has kind of a plain, everyman look that sits well with juries.

He recounts for the panel the events leading up to Leann's death—the dinner with the Miseners on August 15 and the Fletchers' seeming happiness over the news of Leann's pregnancy. He tells them, too, that after the dinner was over, Mick had claimed a need to go to the office, but instead had driven over to Judge Susan Chrzanowski's for sex, where he professed his love for her and his hope they would have a life together.

The next day, "On August 16, Leann's dreams of a large family disappeared. Leann Fletcher was dead. She died when a .45-caliber bullet went in her head right here," says Townsend, pointing behind his right ear, a moment of rare theatricality for him. "It went through her brain and killed her instantly. If this case wasn't so sad, it could almost be a made-for-TV movie. But in a movie the actress gets up and walks away."

Why had Fletcher pulled the trigger? What was his motive? "Susan Chrzanowski had demanded he not have sex with his wife. And he had promised her he wasn't. But this lie would soon be exposed, because he had found out his wife was expecting."

Townsend lays out a timeline. In November of 1998, Mick had bought the Smith & Wesson .45. But it wasn't till August 16 that he had ever taken her to the gun range; it wasn't till then that she had ever so much as picked it up. The day ended in her death but began so much sweeter, with Fletcher giving her a card, in which he had written, recounts Townsend to the jury, "I love you so much, sweetheart. Whether our child is a boy or a girl, I'll love it because it's part of you."

He'd bought the card in the morning, after a stint at the office and before the trip to the gun range.

Townsend then tells the jury about the evidence it will hear—that a state police scientist will testify that he found blood in the trap of the bathroom sink, the first time he had ever found blood in a trap in 19 years; that it usually washes away, so this is proof of fresh blood and lots of it. They will hear about something called stippling, a tattooing of Leann's skin caused by gunpowder residue, and that the pattern of the stippling will prove that the shot was fired too far from her head to be self-inflicted.

He tells them there was no gunpowder residue on Leann's hand, that she must have washed her hands after getting home from the gun range. Had she pulled the trigger, there should have been some there. He tells them there were blood droplets on the right cuff of Fletcher's shirt, droplets that were part of a mist of blood blown out of Leann's head.

And he paints a chilling scene for the jury members, one they will remember long after the trial—he tells them that fresh semen, Mick Fletcher's semen, was found in Leann's vaginal cavity, that she had been found naked from the waist down and that she had been shot with her head nine to fourteen inches from the bedroom floor. The implication is clear: Mick Fletcher is such a cold-blooded murderer that he has sex with his wife while she kneels on their bedroom carpet-

ing, and while his sperm is fresh in her vagina, he picks up
his Smith & Wesson and shoots her behind the right ear.

The opening statement is powerful. And it is brief, just 25
minutes of quickly moving narrative.

At 9:35, Brian Legghio stands up and takes his turn before
the jury. He paints a picture of a different Mick Fletcher, a
picture of an All-American kid who grew up in the small
town of Marysville on the St. Clair River an hour northeast
of Detroit.

He has a brother and a sister and loving parents. He meets
Leann at a Halloween party while a student at Michigan State
and falls in love. They buy a 900-square-foot bungalow in
the working-class suburb of Hazel Park. Mick works at Radio
Shack and Leann styles nails at a beauty shop, a typical struggling young couple. He goes to law school at night. He had
wanted to be a cop but Leann wants something better for him,
for them, and so she urges him to become a lawyer.

Their daughter, Hannah, is born in 1996. And, yes, there
are marital troubles. From June of 1998 to April of 1999,
Mick moves in and out of the family home. But through the
various separations, there is never, not once, any assaultive
behavior.

In 1997, Mick begins working in the Warren city attorney's office, and it is there that he meets a young judge, Susan
Chrzanowski.

"He found some solace, or what he thought to be solace,
in another human being," says Legghio. "We can talk about
sex and have a good giggle, but that's not what this was
about. This was about two human beings finding something
in another human being they wanted—social, intellectual and
emotional."

In January of 1999, Fletcher moves out and files for divorce. In March or April, he decides to move back with Leann
and Hannah, telling the judge he has to go back and give it
a try.

On August 12 Leann finds out she's pregnant. On Saturday, August 14, the Fletchers go out to dinner with Leann's
sister, Lindy, and break the happy news to her. On Sunday,
they take her parents out to dinner, Mick says he wants a boy,
which upsets Leann. On Monday, Mick buys a card of apol-

ogy and writes a note to Leann telling her he will love the child with all his heart, boy or girl. "He's telling her, 'Leann, I might not always tell you, but you mean the world to me.' "

Mick drives a pick-up truck, Legghio tells the jury. They live in a small house. He's not overly motivated or hard driven in his job. He often works in the morning, then takes a long lunch or the afternoon off. And that's what they decide to do Monday. He'll work in the morning, they'll drop Hannah off at her parents' house and go to the gun range over lunch.

They take two cars to the Miseners' house in the nearby city of Troy. That way, he can drop her off and go straight back to work, and she can go to the park with her sister and parents for an afternoon stroll.

But, as young couples will, especially young couples in the midst of a reconciliation and happy with the news of a new baby, the Fletchers decide to prolong their time together—they decide to go back to their bungalow and have sex first, before going back to the Miseners'.

But something tragic happens, a horrible accident. Mick is loading the gun, has to go to the bathroom and asks Leann to put the last bullet in the clip. While in the bathroom, he hears a loud roar, finds his wife on the floor in a pool of blood and calls 911. The 911 operator asks him to feel for a pulse. He can't find one and is told to leave the room.

The police arrive and from the start don't believe him. One Hazel Park investigator—Legghio tells the jury with disdain dripping from his voice—even rushes to judgment because of a TV show a few days earlier on the History Channel. The show was on the Kennedy murder and showed Jackie in her pink dress, covered with blood from holding Jack as he died. And since Fletcher wasn't drenched in blood, he must not have been holding Leann, and if he wasn't holding her, he must not have loved her, and if he didn't love her, he must have killed her.

And then there's the cop who figures Fletcher must be guilty because he hasn't been able to get his wife to the shooting range in 13 years on the force, and if his wife didn't want to go to the range, why would Fletcher's?

"That's the Hazel Park Police Department," sneers Legghio.

Legghio then tells the jury that his experts will corroborate Fletcher's innocence. He says the prosecution will tell them about a dime-sized spot of blood found on Mick's shirt and supposed blood mist, but that the state police's own crime lab could not get a positive DNA match, "and you can get sufficient DNA from a single cell."

The DNA tests confirm the defense's own expert on blood evidence that the spots on Fletcher's shirt were not from blood-mist blown out from Leann's head.

"It's not our job to tell you how Leann was shot. I don't know how she was shot. I don't think there will be any clear answer. But that's not our burden. I urge you to listen to the forensic evidence, for as the prosecutor says, that's where the case lies. Without any DNA, we suggest to you there just is no compelling forensic evidence."

Legghio's opening has lasted for 50 minutes. At 10:25 a.m. on the first day of two weeks of testimony, the court takes its first recess.

DR. DRAGOVIC TESTIFIES

At 10:40 a.m., the state's star witness, Dr. Ljubisa Jovan Dragovic, is called to the stand. Today, Monday, June 12, 2000, is his 50th birthday. The Oakland County medical examiner, he is straight from central casting. Hair cut so short it's nearly shaved bald, thick Eastern European accent that drops the occasional article from the associated noun—as in "victim was brought to office"—loud, even booming voice, walrus mustache, large, natty bowtie, he appears larger than life in a courtroom. He can fill it with his presence.

With a reputation for not suffering fools well, or at all, he can be intimidating for a cross-examiner. He chews up and spits out bad or weak interrogators. He's even tough on good ones. He became the chief antagonist for Dr. Death, Jack Kevorkian, and his high-profile lawyer, Geoffrey Fieger, testifying in several trials that the cause of death in Kevorkian cases was murder and not suicide.

Fieger kept getting Kevorkian off. He lambasted Dragovic as "Dr. Dracula," though in fact Dragovic was one of the few who ever gave as good as he got when it came time for trading quips, or verbal blasts, with Fieger. (The insistence of Oakland County's former prosecutor, Dick Thompson, to keep indicting Kevorkian led to his ouster from office by a young unknown, Dave Gorcyca, whose office brought charges against Fletcher. When Kevorkian was finally convicted, a case based on his infamous "60 Minutes" appearance on CBS where he was shown fiddling with the dials of his killing machinery, Fieger no longer represented him.)

Although Dragovic appears fresh, he feels anything but. He has just spent nine days touring Europe with his wife and another couple. Yesterday, they had suffered through a five-hour delay at the airport before finally taking off and getting in late. He is badly jet-lagged.

The beginning of Dragovic's testimony is *pro forma*—he is asked to state his name and spell it for the record. Where is he employed? What are the duties of a medical examiner? Then, to establish his credibility as an expert witness, he is asked about his professional background (10 years in Oakland County; three and a half years with the Wayne County Medical Examiner, when Detroit was the murder capital of the US and there was no better place to work for a fast-track forensic pathologist; the Chief Medical Examiner for the state of Maryland) and his educational background (medical school, University of Belgrade, Yugoslavia; rotating internship and military medical service in Yugoslavia; 10 months general practice; Department of Pathology at Queens University in Kingston, Ontario; board certification by the American Board of Pathology; senior fellowship in Toronto specializing in neuropathology, which involves injuries and diseases of the brain and spinal cord, and related nerves and muscles; Fisher Fellowship for advanced neuropathology and forensic training in Baltimore with that city's Chief Medical Examiner; certification by the American Board of Pathology in the specialty of neuropathology).

And he is asked how many autopsies he has conducted or supervised in his career. "Well, last time it was about two weeks ago in one of the Circuit Courts. Sometimes it happens a couple times a day, sometimes it's once a week—hundreds of times, if not thousands of times."

Townsend moves to have him qualified as an expert witness and Legghio has no objections.

Townsend hands Dragovic People's Exhibit 1, a photo of Leann Fletcher, and asks him if he can identify the picture and if he conducted the autopsy on her body on August 17, 1999.

"Well, I examined the body as it came to our facility, documented any pertinent departures from normal on the body as I saw it on the outside of the body, and then I proceeded to examine the inside of the body and documented the findings within the body cavities, the cranial cavity, the head and chest and belly. In the meantime, photographs were taken as needed."

A diagram made by Dragovic is entered as People's Exhibit 2, and he is asked to explain it. It is part of an autopsy protocol, his written report and related materials explaining his autopsy findings. Dragovic takes the diagram and, leaning toward the jury so they can follow along as he points with his finger, he says it is a not-to-scale representation of both the left and right sides of Leann's head with numbers to pinpoint the location of her injury. There is, says Dragovic, still pointing, "a wound that is present in the upper part of the right ear and it is four and three-quarters of an inch below the top of the head, five and a half inches to the right of the front midline—that's the measuring line that goes through the front—and this is three-eighths of an inch in diameter, the actual defect. It has concentric marginal scraping."

The large, extended Misener family stares at him impassively, not reacting as he pinpoints her injury and describes the hole caused by the bullet that killed her as a defect.

"What do you mean by that?" asks Townsend.

"This is a particular finding, a physical feature of every gunshot entrance where the projectile, the bullet, coming through the skin punches out a hole and at the same time rubs the sides, the margins of the skin, with its sides and causes the scraping we refer to as marginal abrasion. So I indicated there that there was concentric marginal abrasion and I indicated no soot and underlined that."

"Why did you find that significant, that there was no soot?"

"Soot is gunpowder residue . . . a very fine carbon dust that is only found in contact and near-contact gunshot wounds. The farther the muzzle of the firearm from the target, that is, the surface of the skin, the less likely there will be any evidence of soot. Soot can only travel so far, maybe a couple of inches at the most, and it is important to see in any assessment of any gunshot wound if there is soot present or there isn't, and also if soot is present within the margins of the wound or around the margins of the wound."

"What does that indicate, if you found nothing within or around it?"

"That indicates that the muzzle of the firearm when discharged, when this person sustained this gunshot wound, was farther away than being within a couple of inches or so."

Townsend is laying a foundation that Leann did not shoot

herself. The farther the gun is away from the head when it fires, the less chance there is that the firing was self-inflicted. That segues into the next line of questioning, about something called gunpowder stippling. When a gun discharges, not all the powder is burned. Some is discharged from the barrel of the gun as tiny projectiles. They form multiple dots on the skin of a victim, a sort of deadly tattoo, and how far the stippling pattern has spread on the skin indicates how far away the gun was when it was fired.

A very tight stippling pattern means the gun was near the skin. A wider pattern means it was farther back. A wide enough pattern is proof a victim couldn't have shot herself. Contact or near-contact range means from two inches in, close range is out to two feet and distant is beyond two feet.

"There were multiple dots in the upper part of the head on the right side, above the right ear, and it extended all the way up about two and a half inches," says Dragovic.

Townsend then enters a photo into evidence. Dragovic had shaved part of her hair away to show the stippling, and the photo is of her face, with a ruler in place to show the width of the tattooing. He leaves the witness chair to show the jury the photo and to point out the stippling on Leann's face.

Townsend, saying he will return to the stippling later, then asks Dragovic about the course the bullet took through Leann's head. There was no exit wound, says Dragovic. "I examined the cranial cavity, that is the head, and removed the brain and established that the bullet went through and across the base of the skull and through the brain and struck the opposite side of the base of the skull, and I recovered the fragmented bullet in the cerebellum, in the lower part of the brain."

Leann's sisters and father listen to his clinical testimony impassively. Later, they will hear worse, that "there was blood in both ears, as a matter of fact. The blood present in the left ear is the result of the blast of the bullet causing transverse fracture, a hinge-type fracture, at the base of the skull and tearing the tympanic membrane of the left middle ear and allowing the blood to gush out from the left ear canal." Her mother, who will testify later in the day, is outside in the hallway. Until she testifies, she must remain there, so as not to be influenced by other testimony.

Townsend then asks if Dragovic looked for anything on Leann's hands or arms, and the reason for doing so.

"The information that I received at the time was that there was suggestion of a self-inflicted gunshot wound and I looked for some evidence of fine mist that would be the pinpoint blood dots on the hand if the person had shot self. Every time there is an impact of a projectile onto the surface of the skin, there is a blowback type of mist [which] consists of aerosolized blood because of the high speed and kinetic energy that the bullet delivers to the surface of the skin. There will be a blowback of fine mist just like if you spray for a fraction of a second a can of aerosol, and that will travel for some distance. How far? It's quite variable, but for the most part, this will land on the objects that are in front of the target and a gun may be the object that they land on and the hands of the person that is discharging the firearm.

"There was a lot of smudged blood, there was a lot of coarse blood spatter, like droplets of blood of a rather large size. What I was looking for is fine needlepoint dots on the surface of the skin that would reflect this type of phenomenon of mist being generated as a blowback from the wound."

"Did you find any?"

"No, sir."

And then Townsend returns to the stippling. "With regard to the stippling pattern, can that be used at times to make a determination of the distance between the muzzle of a gun and the point of entry?"

"You can only give a projection, of how far would the gun of that category likely be away from the head. I'm talking about the muzzle of the gun, not the gun itself. . . . I believe, based on what I found on this particular gunpowder stippling pattern, that the gun was discharged with the muzzle being approximately 12 to 18 inches away from the head."

Townsend then shows him People's Exhibits 75 through 80, which were test firings from the gun that killed Leann. The tests were conducted weeks after the shooting by Michigan State Police, who fired the gun into a cloth target from a variety of distances to show various stippling patterns. Fletcher's Smith & Wesson was shot at contact range with the target, at six inches away, and at further six-inch increments out to 30 inches.

Exhibit 75 was firing done at contact range. Exhibit 76 was at six inches; the gun produced stippling, but it also left soot.

"Was there any soot at all found on Leann Fletcher?" asks Townsend.

"No, sir."

"Seventy-seven?"

"Exhibit 77 reflects the findings where this gun was discharged at 12 inches away from the target and it shows the gunpowder stippling, the dots. It does not show evidence of soot."

"And then People's 78?"

"At the distance of 18 inches, this gun shows sparse gunpowder stippling pattern."

"People's 79?"

"The test firing of the gun at 24 inches' distance, that is two feet, muzzle to the target, created some very sparse minimal gunpowder stippling pattern, just a few dots there."

Based on the stippling pattern of the test firings, what were his conclusions?

"That it would be from 12 to 18 inches when the gun was fired."

"Do you believe it to be closer to 12 or closer to 18?"

"Possibly more toward the 18-inch pattern, but I cannot tell with certainty."

Then followed testimony by Dragovic of Leann's body dimensions—again the family sat impassively as their loved one was reduced to "29 years of age, five-foot-three inches in height and 133 pounds; she was medium developed, medium nourished white female"—as Townsend tried to show that a woman of her size couldn't pull the trigger of a gun that far from the entry wound.

"Did you take additional measurements?"

"There were additional things that I did after finding the gunpowder stippling pattern, because you have to establish some physical parameters to ascertain if it was actually feasible for someone to self-inflict. As I was informed prior to the autopsy, the notion was there was self-infliction by the decedent."

"And what was the measurement?"

"The length from top of the shoulder to the mid-knuckle was 23 inches."

"Okay. And did you find that significant?"

"I found it significant because that offers some physical limitations. In order for someone to hold a gun in a fashion that could result in self-infliction, one had to have far longer an arm than this. That's as simple as it is."

Anticlimactically, Dragovic goes on to testify that Leann was in the very early stages of pregnancy, that oral, anal and vaginal swabs were taken, and as part of his autopsy he had to make one of five possible determinations regarding manner of death—natural, homicide, suicide, accidental or undetermined.

"Do you have an expert opinion, Doctor, with regard to the manner of death of Leann Fletcher?"

"Yes, sir."

"Can you tell the jury what your opinion is?"

"In my opinion, this decedent, Leann Dawn Fletcher, died as a result of homicide. The manner of death was homicide."

At 11:50, Dragovic steps down from the witness stand and the court breaks early for lunch. Legghio will have the luxury of an hour and a half to prepare his cross-examination.

DRAGOVIC PROFILE

Jump forward to September 6. The Fletcher trial has been over for two months and a verdict rendered. A reporter looking for background has called Dragovic's office, expecting a secretary to take a message. Instead, the doctor had answered himself, looked at his appointment book and told the reporter to come out for a two-hour block of time, with a caveat: things get hectic here, said the doctor, so be prepared to put up with some distractions.

Sure enough, at the appointed time, something has come up that requires a staff meeting. Dragovic ushers the visitor into his office, first taking him by a small kitchen to let the reporter grab a newspaper, bagel, cream cheese and coffee and leaves him. A glance around the new, spacious office of Dr. Ljubisa J. Dragovic is revealing.

Consider: On one wall is a framed saying, "Blessed are they who can laugh at themselves, for they shall inherit the earth"; a framed, 18-by-12-inch diagram of all the parts of a Smith & Wesson revolver, the same gun, coincidentally, that shot Leann Fletcher; a staff photo from 1991, early on in his stint as ME of Oakland County, with all but one of the 16 staff members wearing Groucho Marx mustaches in imitation of him; and a variety of framed posters and maps of Europe— Saint Tropez, French Wine Country, Musée Picasso Antibes, Galeries des Papes, Monaco Yacht Show.

It has been a busy few weeks since his appearance at the Mick Fletcher trial. He testified in another hugely controversial high-profile local case immediately afterward, this time on behalf of the defense, saying that a black security guard at a suburban shopping mall did not cause the death of a black shoplifter in a scuffle, testimony that led to the judge setting him free despite protests and picket lines outside the court. A glowing profile in the fine city magazine, *Hour Detroit*, has just come out and is hitting the coffee tables of the affluent throughout the region. Jack Klugman's been calling, needing some information on a case he wants to use for an upcoming made-for-TV *Quincy, M.E.* movie. And a TV crew from Ivanhoe Productions, which films and distributes segments of medical-related news to some 300 TV stations around the country, is setting up for an interview later this morning on the Matt Smith case, which is a primer in how Dragovic approaches his job.

In March of 2000, Matt Smith was a healthy-seeming 14-year-old who was skateboarding in his aunt's basement when he collapsed and died. No one could figure out why. The fall hadn't killed him, certainly, as there were no broken bones and he hadn't hit his head.

And so in came Dragovic to solve the mystery, to pull a big answer out of tiny clues. Or as Jack Lessenberry, *Hour* magazine's fine contributing editor, put it in his profile of the good doctor:

> He's smelled things we don't even want to imagine, seen things we'd give years of our lives not to see. He's looked into tens of thousands of eyes that can't look back, and stood in the hot Wyoming sun to exhume the mummified remains of a man who just might have been the Oakland County child killer.
>
> Sometimes, finding out why they died isn't very hard; large bullet holes are dead giveaways. So is the bitter almond smell of cyanide, or lungs filled with water. Matthew's case had no such easy answers. Nor is it ever easy for him to take lightly the death of a child, even when you see more bodies in the course of a year than most people see invoices. Especially not when you have seven children of your own.

Quickly, Dragovic determined the young boy had died of a heart attack. But why? That was the rub, and the reason Klugman and Ivanhoe Productions would come calling. Dragovic found perplexing changes in the blood vessels leading to Smith's heart, the kind of microscopic changes you associate with years of cocaine or amphetamine use. Or, in this case, he would rule, the controversial drug Ritalin, a stimulant that acts the opposite in hyperactive children.

Smith was hyperactive, and he'd been taking Ritalin for years.

Dragovic ruled that the Ritalin had caused the boy's death. It was controversial, especially within a medical community that dispenses prescriptions for Ritalin the way it used to tell folks to take an aspirin and call back in the morning. Pediatricians went nuts, writing to local papers or calling in to talk radio. To Dragovic, it was simply doing what one of his literary heroes—Sherlock Holmes—does best: eliminating the impossible until there's just one thing left, no matter how controversial.

Dragovic likes to paraphrase Arthur Conan Doyle. "The number 1 rule for everybody is one spelled out by Sir Arthur Conan Doyle through the mouth of Sherlock Holmes," he tells a visitor here to inquire about the Fletcher case. " 'You cannot advance theories before knowing facts.' If you create a theory, you fall in the trap of trying to fit the facts to your theory." (Dragovic and Legghio's star witness, Dr. Herbert McDonell, had disagreed in court on a variety of forensics; later, with the trial over, Dragovic will criticize McDonell's theory of how Leann could have been shot as fitting fact to theory: "This was a means that was at fault for the same reason Arthur Conan Doyle explained originally," he'll say.)

He likes to quote proverbs, too, first in their original Latin, then in his heavily accented English. "The worst truth is better than the sweetest lie," he'll say, which is a central professional philosophy.

There's a co-equal central thought to his work. "Minutiae are not trivial," he says, repeating it in caps: "MINUTIAE ARE NOT TRIVIAL. You cannot say, 'Okay, just because they are little things, they do not mean truth.' Actually, it is the little things that give you the critical sentinel positions of the jigsaw puzzle you want to piece together."

They were little things—microscopic changes to blood vessels—that led to a big thing: a nationally renowned forensic pathologist ruling that Ritalin kills kids. The ensuing multi-million-dollar lawsuit against the drug's makers and dispensers has enormous ramifications for the drug and medical communities.

"The use of Ritalin is well known to be extremely safe. We use this so widely . . . it doesn't seem very likely or plausible," Dr. James Shaya, a pediatrician in upscale Clarkston, north of Detroit, told a reporter for the Oakland Press. Shaya is the co-author of a book: *What You Need to Know About Ritalin*.

Dragovic is willing to go against the grain if that's where his view of truth takes him; he is one of those rare folks who have acquired reputations as expert witnesses who testify equally for defense and prosecution; and he's not afraid, even though he's often part of the prosecution team in Oakland County, to testify against prosecutors and police in very high profile cases in nearby counties.

He became Geoffrey Fieger's chief foil in several high-profile cases against Dr. Death, Jack Kevorkian, insisting that Kevorkian's so-called patients had died as a result of homicide, not suicide. Juries kept disagreeing. He was one of the few who held their own verbally against the peripatetic Fieger. Unable to get him to take the verbal bait in their encounters in court, out of court, Fieger played to the press by calling him "Dracula" and "the Transylvanian vampire." (Dragovic's staff and friends call him "Dr. D.")

Typically, Dragovic got the best of the name-calling, too. "I may be a Montenegrin vampire," Dragovic told the delighted press in response. "But I regretfully must correct 'Doctor' Fieger on his geography, as I occasionally must on medicine." He would also say: "I think 'Doctor' Fieger needs humility. If he had humility, he could have been among the very best of the finest people. But there's always hope for everyone."

Also, typically, Dragovic attended a Halloween party afterwards dressed as—what else?—Dracula. And, now, there sits atop the front corner of his desk, nearest to where visitors sit, a 15-inch-high plastic Dracula with a Don King hairdo, clutching a coffin to his chest as he stands amidst the skeleton and skulls of past victims.

On the other side of things, he testified in opposition to the Wayne County Medical Examiner several years ago in the trials of two Detroit cops accused and eventually convicted of killing a small-time black street character named Malice Green. The Wayne County ME ruled that Green died as a result of a beating by the cops; Dragovic said the death was a direct result of Green's cocaine abuse, which drew the enmity of black activists. The two cops were convicted, won retrials on appeal and were convicted again. (Coincidentally, one of the co-counsels in one of those cases was Marla McCowan, who would later be on the opposing side in the Fletcher trial.)

Though he testified for the prosecution in the Fletcher trial, he makes it clear that even then he didn't see himself as part of the prosecution team. "I don't hide behind the prosecutor's office. A lot of medical examiners do," he says. When Marla McCowan wanted to interview him about the Fletcher case in preparation for the trial, he opened up his office and his files. He saw it just as much a part of his duties to prepare her and Legghio as it was to prepare Townsend, and in fact he spent far more time with McCowan pre-trial than with Townsend.

One of Dragovic's favorite autopsy stories goes back to his days in Detroit, where bodies came in by the truckload, and no one was encouraged to look too hard or too long for explanations. One apparently routine suicide came in, a young woman who had been drinking with her boyfriend, grabbed his gun and shot herself in the mouth. It was being treated as routine, too, though Dragovic says that such cases should always provoke extreme skepticism. The same skepticism with which he entered the examination room on August 17 to do the autopsy on a young woman named Leann Fletcher, who was killed with her husband's gun.

The examiner in the Detroit case gave the body just a superficial, external going over, pronounced it a suicide and moved on to the next job. "People did not generally maintain a desirable index of suspicion. And I was unhappy about that," says Dragovic. He said to himself, "This is a fishy story."

Dragovic asked his boss if he could do a full-fledged autopsy. "He started calling me paranoid. I wasn't very popular back in that environment. They said I was a paranoid type seeing murders where no one else could see them."

He grabbed the body, anyway, went downstairs and did a

full autopsy. He discovered the muzzle had been pushed quite forcefully into the tongue before the trigger was pulled. "Which would require quite a bit of pain. No one that's shooting self will do that. I mean, unnecessary additional infliction of discomfort in your last moment of life, just before the lights went out?"

Dragovic ruled it a homicide, forcing the police to investigate further. "A funny story. I come back and say it's a homicide and they're all upset. The police go back to talk to the boyfriend and they say, 'We know you shot her.' He says 'How do you know?' They say, 'The doctor told us. The doctor who did the autopsy.' 'What autopsy?' he says. 'I called the Coroner's Office a couple of weeks ago and they told me they never did autopsies on suicides."

His statement is proof of premeditation and he is convicted of first-degree murder.

Dragovic, quite frankly, is far more colorful than Jack Klugman ever dreamed of being. If you put him at the heart of a TV show purporting to be about forensic pathology and the workings of an ME's office, the part would seem too broad, overwritten.

Dragovic speaks passionately and dramatically in a heavy Serbian accent, punctuating his statements with loud laughter and a waving of his hands. He works in Oakland County, an affluent area pockmarked with numerous small lakes and multi-million-dollar homes. New money lives there. A generation ago, it was semi-rural; today, the farms and woods have been replaced by golf courses and huge, gated communities. The county population is 1.2 million and climbing. He, however, lives on the far east side of town, in the old-money capital of Grosse Pointe Farms, whose older mansions and stately homes lie along Lake St. Clair, just north and east of Detroit.

Dragovic isn't old money, though between what he makes and the income of his wife, Jadranka, a doctor herself and director of the cancer-care center at St. Joseph's Mercy Hospital, they can live anywhere they choose. Grosse Pointe Farms, while more blue-blooded, is in some ways less pretentious than Oakland County, with much smaller, easier-to-tend properties and, with a few exceptions, more tasteful houses.

The Dragovics live in an Italianate mansion that has seen better days. It was built for the scion of the Crowley department-store family in the 1920s; in the 1940s, famed World War II pilot Eddie Rickenbacker lived there.

As his walls indicate, Dragovic is something of a man of the world. He has, and hasn't, made his escape from the Balkans. A martial arts student, while in medical school, he brags that "Everyone went in for martial arts. We [from the Balkans] were fierce people, always ready and willing to fight."

Too fierce, as the world keeps learning.

In World War II, Tito's pro-Communist partisans in Yugoslavia were in civil war against royalists like Dragovic's grandfather. They threw him into a mountain crevice. His father, Jovan, fought against the occupying Nazis and later won a medal for bravery. As a boy, Dragovic knew he wanted to be a doctor—he comes from a family of doctors; though his father went to law school, his aunts, uncles and a sister, now in Australia, are doctors—and he knew he wanted out of Yugoslavia.

When he was 22, he accepted an internship in San Francisco that gave him some coveted time away from his studies at the University of Belgrade. When the internship was over, on the plane home, he heard a young woman saying she was going to the University of Belgrade to become a doctor, and he turned around. If there isn't love at first sight, then this was the nearest thing. They saw each other a few times on campus, turned up at the same dinner party and were soon married. He was 24, she was 20.

Instead of pouring money into landscaping their large house, or on refurbishing it with the latest marbles, Pewabic Pottery or whatever happens to be hot in the tony Grosse Pointe community, where lawn perfection and remodeling are practically required pastimes, the Dragovics spend it on taking all or some of their seven kids (two are in law school) to Washington, or to Italy, or wherever the mood leads.

After medical school and a stint in the Yugoslav military, Dragovic and his growing family headed first to Ontario, Canada, and then into the US on a string of residencies. Eventually he ended up in Detroit as assistant ME to a politically connected boss named Bader Cassin. Dragovic, who refuses to suffer fools and others, privately and not-so-privately referred to his boss as "Master Bader."

"I was a sore thumb there, and constantly criticizing," he admits.

Though he has been working for Oakland County for more than a decade, his kids liked the east side, and he and his wife liked their Italianate mansion. So rather than move, Dragovic decided to commute. At rush hour, it frequently takes an hour or more to drive across town to the Oakland County government complex in Pontiac, a trip he makes in his white C280 Mercedes, old rock and roll cranking out of the speakers.

When he gets there, he oversees a staff of 35. Five of them conduct autopsies, about 1,200 a year—all the suspicious deaths, sudden, unexplained deaths, murders, suicides and traffic fatalities that might later result in criminal charges. Though he's the head, he still takes a regular turn at cutting and sawing, himself, depending on staff workload, holidays, vacations and whatnot. On a recent busy Sunday, he performed three routine autopsies. Cutting the body open, measuring organs, weighing the brain and the like take 30–35 minutes, with the more detailed work that might be required, depending on the circumstances, taking another hour.

A month after his autopsy findings in the Fletcher case, Dragovic even got to do some Holmesian sleuthing in a Wyoming cemetery. In the 1970s, four Oakland County children were abducted and killed in a 14-month period; all the evidence points to a single killer. As quickly as the serial murders started, they stopped. A pubic hair on one of the victims was one of the few clues. One of the chief suspects in the case moved to Wyoming after questioning and died in a car crash in 1981.

Advances in DNA research led Dragovic and a team of gravediggers to exhume the body. Alas, after a year, tests came back from the FBI's overworked crime lab that the pubic hair found on the dead child was not a match for the long-dead suspect.

One year, in 1988, when Detroit was rightly called the Murder Capital and he worked downtown, Dragovic did

1,200 autopsies, himself. "I think that was probably the world record."

Dragovic is witty, urbane, dapper—and extremely cocky, feisty and self-assured. There's nothing like a tough cross-examination to bring out that cockiness and feistiness. Little did he suspect, though, when he was about to go up against Brian Legghio in that first day of the trial, how poorly his testimony—or, more accurately, the attitude that went with it—would play for the jury. They—as they later told Townsend in the post-mortem examination of the trial that accompanies such cases—had a visceral dislike for him.

DRAGOVIC CROSS-EXAM

The jury returns at 1:38 p.m. Legghio's questions are pointed, brief, calmly put but clearly adversarial. Dragovic admits that when filling out his autopsy protocol, he didn't know the make of the murder weapon, the length of its barrel or its caliber.

"What types of gunpowder are there?"

"All kinds of gunpowder. I am not a particular specialist in various types and combinations of gunpowder."

"I didn't ask you if you were a specialist, Doctor. I asked you to the extent that you provide a professional opinion on stippling."

"Yes."

"And stippling is caused by gunpowder, right?"

"That's correct."

"And you're aware that there are different types of gunpowder, correct?"

"As far as physical appearances?"

"Are you aware that there are different types of gunpowder?"

"Yes. I told you that."

"And so can you tell the members of the jury what different types of gunpowder there are that you're aware of?"

He does so—powder comes in different shapes with different firing characteristics, such as cylinders, disks and balls, and it can come in different combinations of each.

"Now, are you aware of different types of powder that are called flake gunpowder?"

"Flakes, yes. Flakes are disks or variations of disks."

"Are you aware of gunpowder that is sometimes referred to as a flattened ball?"

"Flattened ball, sure."

"And those different types of gunpowders, they can result—or they have a significant impact, do they not, in the distance in which they would travel?"

"Sure, there is a variation based on the size of the actual gunpowder particle. There will be more capability to travel because of the actual size of the mass of the particle and they would have different kinetic energy in and of themselves."

"They travel differently, different speed, different velocities, correct?"

"That's correct."

"Because of that, they would have an impact on how they would stipple an individual's skin, correct?"

"Yes."

"Your determination that Leann Fletcher's death was homicide rested in some measure based upon the stippling of the skin that you just pointed out to the jurors?"

"The spread and the density, yes."

"Now, can you tell us, Doctor, what type of gunpowder was used in this gun when Mrs. Fletcher was shot?"

"No, sir."

"Why not?"

"Because I don't know."

"Was it listed anywhere in your report?"

"No, sir. If it was, I would have known."

"And, so, let me see—you then did not only not know the type, make, model of firearm, you didn't even know what type of gunpowder was used?"

"Precisely."

Legghio goes to a white board and begins making grease-pencil diagrams. He writes the date "AUG. 17," the day of the autopsy. He also writes "AUG. 25," the day of the gun-firing tests by the state police. He also writes a curious misspelling for a defense attorney: "HOMOCIDE."

"As I understand you correctly," he says to Dragovic, "you made your determination of homicide on the 17th, is that correct?"

"It's hom-EE-cide," says Dragovic giving an EE sound to the "i," stressing it to point out the lack of an "o."

Legghio looks at the board. "I misspelled it. Where am I wrong here?"

" 'I' instead of 'O.' "

"Thank you for your spelling correction," he says, erasing the grease "O" and replacing it. "So you made your determination of hom-I-cide on the 17th?"

"Yes, sir."

"But those test firings did not even occur until the 25th?"

"Correct."

"You did not use those test-firing patterns at all in determining homicide?"

"That's correct, sir."

Legghio elicits that Dragovic had no knowledge of whether Leann was right- or left-handed.

"This is a young woman who suffered a wound entry to her right ear. Did it not at all seem mildly important to you or significant to note whether she was right-hand or left-hand dominant?"

"There was no way to determine that from the autopsy."

Legghio attempts to link the ignorance of whether she was right- or left-handed with Dragovic's lack of knowledge regarding the type of weapon and gunpowder. Dragovic interrupts him, eliciting snickers from the crowd.

"We're mixing mangos and papayas with figs and melons, here."

"Sir," Legghio counters, "how about if we just stay with rifles and handguns?

"And so," Legghio continues, "at the point in time in which you rendered your decision, you really had no knowledge at all about either test-firing of this gun or the type of gun that was used?"

"I was informed by the people who went out to the scene who established the preliminary report that there was a semiautomatic gun, so that much I knew."

"Is that where your investigator indicated that it was a Smith & Wesson .9 millimeter?"

"I would think so, yes."

"But it was not a Smith & Wesson .9 millimeter, was it?"

"I don't know."

Later they get into the crucial issue of whether or not Leann's hands were bagged, that is, covered with loose plastic and tied off at the wrists to preserve evidence and keep blood from being wiped off or coming in contact with other items.

Legghio asks if any of the autopsy photos show her hands in bags. They do not. Dragovic says he is sure someone must have bagged them at the scene and that one of his staff people must have removed the bags prior to the autopsy.

Did his office keep custody of the bags? No. Why not? They may have been returned to investigators, the doctor replies. Is he aware that one of the police, for some reason, asked that her hands not be bagged at the scene? He didn't know that.

Legghio elicits that swabs were taken of her hands at the murder scene by Hamtramck police, to be tested later for gunpowder residue, that these are made with cotton swabs that have been moistened with a solution and that of the 28 color photos taken of her at the autopsy, none shows her right hand.

Why not?

"Had there been a particular finding of importance, evidentiary finding, that would have been included. Since there was no evidentiary finding of importance for me performing the autopsy, I did not insist on any particular region being photographed other than the areas of injury. The right hand had smudged a large amount of blood on it, on the back, and that's all that there was."

"It is true, is it not, that you said that one of the factors that led you to believe on August 17 that this was a homicide was the fact that there was a lack of mist?"

"That's correct."

"Did you not think, then, that if there was a lack of mist, it is as significant as mist being present and therefore a photograph would be in order?"

"If something is not there, I do not insist on photographs being taken," said Dragovic, a little more forcefully, perturbation entering his voice.

"So, then, why take a picture of the left hand?"

"I didn't insist in particular on taking a picture of the left hand. As a matter of fact, I was surprised afterwards not finding pictures of other areas of the body, because they try to cover the whole body as much as they can."

"So, we have this one picture of her left hand, none of the right, and yet in your determination of August 17th of whether or not this was homicide, accident, suicide, natural or unknown, no pictures whatsoever of her right hand were taken, correct?"

"We generally do not take negative pictures." Spoken with a little more emphasis.

Legghio then introduces Defendant's Exhibit B, a crime-scene photo of Leann's left hand, covered in blood.

"Can you tell the members of the jury what differences to note in terms of the amount of blood which are on her hands at the scene as distinguished from the amount of blood that is on her hands while at your office on August 17?"

"There is certainly less smeared blood on the left hand on the photograph taken during the autopsy than on the photograph that was taken at the scene."

"Well, Doctor, in part your determination that this situation was homicide—spelled correctly or incorrectly—was the lack of mist on the hands, correct?"

"Well, that's part of it, yes."

"Now, can you tell members of this jury how or why there was a difference in the amount of blood on Mrs. Fletcher's hands at the scene than when she shows up at your Medical Examiner's Office the next morning on the 17th?"

"It appears that some of the blood that was smeared on the outer aspect of the left hand was removed by some sort of procedure, might have been something that [was] done at the scene."

"Now, let me ask you this, Doctor: Did you know that the Hazel Park Police Department had come to your Medical Examiner Office on the evening of August 16 and swabbed or, you say, maybe took samples of her hands?"

"Now that you're mentioning it, I might have been aware of that at the time but not at the top of my head."

"Did you in your autopsy protocol indicate, 'that I as Medical Examiner am looking and notice that there is no fine mist on her hands. I'm aware that her hands have been swabbed for gunshot residue, but it doesn't affect my judgment or affects it to such-and-such degree.' Did you note that at all in your protocol?"

"I noted what I noted, sir." More of the famous Dragovic feistiness coming forth. "I said there was no evidence of mist."

"Did you at all indicate when you arrived at your conclusion that it was homicide and you arrived in part because there was lack of mist on the hands, did you at least mention or note that you were cognizant that a Hazel Park police officer had swabbed her hands the night before?"

"No, because that's not relevant."

Having drawn blood, so to speak, Legghio stays on the attack, going back to the issue of soot and whether Leann's thick hair could have absorbed soot in the shooting.

"That is correct."

"Now, you took samples of her hair, did you not?"

"That is correct, sir."

"You gave them to the state police?"

"Yes."

"And did they ever do an analysis for you to determine whether or not there was soot?"

"I did not receive any report from them. I didn't specifically request them to do the analysis for soot because I was not interested in that."

"But it is true that soot can be trapped in the hair, isn't it?"

"Yes, it is."

"And that soot may not readily be detectable to the naked eye, correct, because it is spent gunpowder particles?"

"Oh, sure, yes."

"And particularly if the hair is matted with blood?"

"True."

Another point made.

Legghio goes back to the white board and picks up a grease pencil and starts writing down some highlights of the autopsy reports. As he writes "AUTOPSY," he says to Dragovic, "Let's see if I can spell that."

He then writes the word "STIPPLING." And says to Dragovic: "*So* one of the findings is stippling, right?"

"One 'P,' " says Dragovic. It is his turn for misspelling and he says again: "One 'P.' "

"You know what?" responds Legghio. "I'm giving up on spelling today."

He then writes "RANGE," and "LACK OF MIST," then asks Dragovic what other factors he should write down.

"Well, length of the arm is a minor factor, but it is there."

"It is true, is it not, that with the length of arm, Mrs. Fletcher could have shot herself, correct?"

"Theoretically, yes."

"What do you mean by 'theoretically'?"

"By theoretically, yes, it is possible that the decedent could have self-inflicted the wound, but practically, it's just not— it doesn't make sense. It doesn't fit the physical relationships."

"But when you say 'theoretically,' it is as theoretically possible to shoot oneself as it is theoretically possible to be shot by someone else, is that correct? They're both theories, are they not?"

"Maybe in your concept, but . . ."

"No, I'm asking you, Doctor. To the extent that Mrs. Fletcher could have physically grabbed the gun and shot herself, either by accident, correct, or someone else could have shot her, they're both theories, are they not?"

"Sir, let me explain. The accident that you're bringing into the picture is out of the picture completely."

"It is, out of the picture completely?"

"Yes."

"Why is it out of the picture?"

"Homicide constitutes a category where there is purposeful action that results in injury and this injury leads to death. There are so many purposeful actions built in. Number one, loading a firearm is a purposeful action. It doesn't happen by a higher force, by nature, by lightning, by thunderstorm. Someone puts the load in the gun. A purposeful action is pointing to your own self or to someone else's head. That's purposeful act. There is nothing accidental about it. That's why, sir."

"Doctor, were you in the room when the gun went off?"

"No, sir."

"So, if the gun is loaded and we don't have to worry about thunderstorms or accident loading the gun, it is physically possible for Mrs. Fletcher to have picked up the weapon and either intentionally or unintentionally discharged the weapon into herself, isn't that correct?"

"Intentionally, yeah. That's a possibility, yes."

"And unintentionally, perhaps. Correct?"

At that point, Legghio asks his co-counsel, Marla Mc-

Cowan, to stand. McCowan's arms, as measured by Dragovic, are 24 inches long, an inch longer than Leann's. The actual murder weapon, having been checked and found unloaded by one of the Hazel Park police in the court at the direction of Judge Cooper, is given to McCowan. "Now, Ms. McCowan—hold it like this—could Ms. McCowan hold a weapon like this and inflict a wound?" She has the gun out about a foot and a half from her head and is clearly capable of holding it there and squeezing off a shot.

"That would be self-inflicted injury. Nothing accidental about that, sir."

"But you're not in the room at the time the firearm is discharged."

"Doesn't matter whether I'm in the room or you're in the room or whoever is in the room, I'm telling you this is common sense at work."

"I understand, Doctor."

"Not theories."

"I understand common sense. We're talking about medically. Ms. McCowan could physically—what's the range here, Doctor?"

Dragovic leaves the witness stand, goes over to a kneeling Marla McCowan, takes out a tape measure and measures 18 inches.

"And you said 12 inches, even."

"Twelve inches."

"Twelve inches. Thank you, Ms. McCowan." She rises and goes back to her seat. "So it is physically possible for Mrs. Fletcher to have discharged the weapon, whether intentionally or unintentionally, physically? Not theoretically, physically?"

"Physically it's possible. I told you that earlier."

"Did you at all, Doctor, in your report, address the potential aspect of maybe the weapon being dropped?"

"That's nonsense."

"Okay."

"That's a joke." Dragovic is angry, now. Voice louder than it has been. Each syllable forceful.

"I understand that."

"I mean . . ."

Legghio cuts him off. "Did you address it in your report?"

"No, *I do not address nonsense in my report, sir.*"

The sharp response draws snickers from the crowd.

Legghio finishes by getting an acknowledgment that the issue of distance becomes moot if the decedent had for some reason been holding the gun with her thumb on the trigger instead of her finger. In another Michigan case, the *People* vs. *Cynthia Lee McDonald*, Dragovic testified for the defense that a wound in the back of the head was self-inflicted by her husband and not a case of murder, with the trigger having been pulled by the thumb.

"This was a police officer inflicted by cancer, yes," says Dragovic.

"Thank you, I have no further questions."

Upon redirect, Dragovic testifies that while the thumb is often used to pull the trigger in suicides, nearly all suicides involve contact or near-contact wounds, and Leann's is neither. Townsend also has him expand on his claim that the theory of an accidental shooting was nonsense.

"That's nonsense, number one, because you would have to have a malfunctioning firearm in the first place. That malfunctioning weapon can discharge upon contact, upon being dropped on the floor or something like that, but then how can you drop a handgun on the floor and lean and align your head to the dropping of the trajectory?"

Since Townsend opted to redirect Dragovic, Legghio gets to recross. He hammers on two points, the missing blood on the left hand and the lack of an autopsy photo of the right hand of a woman shot in the right side of her head.

"Would you not agree with me that her hands [in photos at the crime scene] are pretty much covered with blood? And you can't indicate to the jury why Mrs. Fletcher's hands [in the autopsy photo] appear nearly clean?"

Dragovic has no explanation and says it is irrelevant to his findings. He is excused. It is 3:10 p.m. The court is recessed for 20 minutes.

During recess and after the trial is adjourned for the day, reporters and family, alike, are convinced Dragovic has been a highly effective, impressive witness who has gotten the best of Legghio. Townsend, Ortlieb and police congratulate him on his testimony, both the content and the form. He is all smiles, jokes and self-satisfaction as he rides the elevator out of the courtroom and returns to the Medical Examiner's Office across the way.

The family is still talking about his performance the next morning. "Great" is the most frequently used adjective. They think he has handled Legghio quite well.

What they don't know is that the jury's reaction is quite different. They don't like Dragovic at all. They regard him as arrogant. Worse, they don't see him as dispassionate. He's far too adversarial for their tastes. He comes across as a member of the prosecution team. Which of course he is, despite any pretense to objectivity. The fact is, the prosecution is based on his findings, so of course he has a vested interest.

Days later, when he takes the stand to rebut a defense witness, he will only reinforce the jury's first impression of him, which is not good at all.

Says jury foreman Rob Jensen: "He came off as an arrogant ass."

Legghio's most important point is duly noted: If Leann's hands have been wiped nearly clean of what had appeared hours earlier to be copious amounts of blood, how in the world can Dragovic say that a lack of blood mist helps prove this is a homicide? If gobs of blood have been wiped clean, obviously any fine mist would have, too.

As to the lack of a photo of the right hand, and blood being washed from her other hand, Jensen would later say that when jury deliberations would begin two weeks later and jurors could finally discuss the case amongst themselves, the word "conspiracy" was bandied about. "He gets on the stand and says, 'Why would we take a picture of something that's not there?' Is he that fricking stupid?"

It is not nearly so fine a day for the prosecution as Townsend and Ortlieb think when they go back to their offices at the end of the day to plot strategy for tomorrow.

A MOTHER TESTIFIES

"**C**an you state your full name and spell your last name for the record?"

"Gloria Anne Misener. M-I-S-E-N-E-R."

It is 3:50 p.m. After a half-hour recess following Dr. Dragovic's cross-examination—some members of the jury will need extra time to get out of the courthouse for a cigarette—Leann's mother takes the stand.

From the beginning of this tragedy—from the time Troy police knocked on her door to tell her she needed to go to the Hazel Park police station—she has been a bedrock of strength, an indomitable will holding her family together. She is at the center of the family both physically—when it gathers at court and when it leaves for lunch or recess, its members seem to surround and follow her—and emotionally.

From the beginning, she has been sure Mick intentionally murdered her daughter. Her hatred for him is palpable as she testifies, but it is a hatred all the more fierce for the way it comes through a more or less placid exterior. She has a job to do today, an important job, and she is ready for it.

Briefly, she tells the court and the jury some of the details that made up her daughter's life—married six years, a house on Hazelwood Avenue in Hazel Park, one brother, three sisters. "She was a nice person, very outgoing. She loved life."

As for Mick, he and Leann got along fine in the early days, she says. But a party Leann threw for him upon his graduation from the University of Detroit–Mercy Law School seemed to end that happy chapter of their marriage.

"When he graduated from law school, he changed from a nice, loving guy to a cold-hearted person," she says.

What about their marriage troubles? asks Townsend.

"She didn't tell us much about it. She said he'd moved out, that they were having troubles. That he'd changed when he got out of law school."

What about any possibility that Leann could have shot herself?

"That thought wouldn't have even entered her head. She loved life. She loved Hannah. She was pleased every day to do things with Hannah."

And then she described what she knew of Leann's last day. Mick and Leann would go to the gun range for an hour, then Leann would join her parents, along with Hannah and sister Lindy for a walk on the trails in a nearby park.

"I asked her, 'Why are you going to a gun range?' And she said, 'To keep Mick happy.' "

Was she depressed that day or the days before? "No. She was very happy."

Did she like guns? "No, she was very afraid of them. She didn't want to touch guns."

What had happened the night before the death? Leann and her parents had gone out to dinner, after which Mick did something that took both Gloria and Jack Misener by surprise. "He had never asked us to babysit before. Leann always asked, but she said she'd asked us to babysit so much, she wasn't going to ask anymore." And so Mick had asked Jack.

The next day, Mick and Leann came over in two cars, dropped Leann's car and Hannah off and headed to the shooting range in Mick's truck, just a mile and a half or so down the nearest main highway, Dequindre.

"They should have come back at one. Two came. Three came. We thought something must have happened, a traffic accident or something. Then the police came and said there had been an accident. We thought it had been a car accident, and they asked us to call the Hazel Park police. I said, 'Was it a car accident?' He said, 'No, a shooting accident.' And I said, 'Oh my God, he shot her!' "

Fletcher, as he will remain throughout the trial, is completely impassive, his expression unchanged. He seems to be staring off, not at Gloria but past her.

"Why did you say that?" asks Townsend.

"Because I knew it. She wouldn't have put a gun anywhere near her head."

"No further questions."

Gloria Misener has been on the stand for just ten minutes. The judge announces that since there is so much road construction on Telegraph Avenue, the main thoroughfare that leads to the court complex, she wants to get the jury out before rush hour, if possible, and so she calling it a day. The announcement jolts Legghio, since the week before, she had told both sides that the court day would run till 5 p.m., and Legghio is stunned to hear that he won't be able to cross-examine Mrs. Misener until the next morning.

The jury will spend the night with her declaration ringing in their heads: "Oh my God, he shot her!"

And it is that line that replaces the image of Dr. Dragovic holding the Smith & Wesson in the minds of the local TV people planning their evening news shows. Beginning at five and re-run periodically till 7 p.m. and then again at 11, viewers throughout southeastern Michigan will watch her say it again and again.

Out in the hallway the family clusters around her. Some of them are crying. They head down the hall and board an elevator, en masse.

Tuesday, June 13, 8:40 a.m. Before the jury is brought in, Legghio has a motion for the judge to consider. He asks Cooper to instruct Townsend not to ask prosecution witnesses questions intended to elicit testimony that Leann would not have committed suicide.

Since the defense will not be alleging suicide as an explanation, says Legghio, court rules prohibit the prosecution from pursuing that line. Townsend can only ask questions proving the elements of the charge of murder on direct examination.

"Mr. Townsend?" the judge asks. He stands at his table, near the jury box. "This is analogous to an arson case," he says. "You must exclude all possibilities of accidental ignition, and if you do, you are left with an intentional fire. If we rule out accident and suicide, we're left with murder."

The judge agrees. He will be allowed to ask the question of other witnesses, too.

At 9 a.m. the jury is brought in and Mrs. Misener is put back on the stand and reminded she is still under oath.

Legghio has her recount more details of the Fletchers' marriage. At the end, they had broken up and separated "so many times I couldn't keep it straight. It was three or four times. One time he left for five days, came back for five days and left again."

Leann worked part-time. And Mick, did he work full-time? "He left every day," she answers neatly, the implication being that while he might have been gone every day, he wasn't working full-time.

"You don't know if he was working?"

"No."

"Did the Hazel Park police tell you it was a suspicious shooting?"

"No, I told them. They wouldn't even tell me where she was shot."

What happened at the station? "They took us back into a room and sat us down and I told them, 'He shot her.' "

"Did you know your daughter was dead?"

"I knew she was dead as soon as they told us, because instead of sending us to the hospital, they sent us to the police station."

Mrs. Misener told how just before Easter of 1999, during one of their separations, Mick had sent a basket of flowers to the beauty shop where Leann worked, "begging her to take him back."

And from then on, Mrs. Misener told the court, "he'd gone overboard with love."

What did she mean by that? "He did things he never did before. Kissing her in public. He was filled with affection. He was helping her carry the baby things, which he'd never done before." She described how Mick and Leann came over to the Miseners' on Easter Sunday—Jack and Gloria always went overboard at all the holidays, decorating the house and yard, and Easter was one of their favorites; their kids and grandkids always spent the day there with egg hunts and dinner—and Mick later did something for the first time ever when the day was over: "He helped Leann carry their stuff out of the house. Before, she always did that. And he took the garbage out. He was putting on a big show."

He asked her about what happened the day after the shooting, when Hazel Park police came over to the Miseners' and took turns interviewing Jack and Gloria, their children and the kids' spouses, one by one in the back yard. At that session, Mrs. Misener gave them the letter Mick had sent to the beauty shop with the flowers, when he'd asked for the reconciliation.

Mrs. Misener, it was clear, thought the letter suspicious.

"He started to act too nice?" asked Legghio. "Too loving?"

"Yes. I think it was part of the plan."

"To kill your daughter?"

"Yes."

Legghio has brought her to this point brilliantly. He wants the jury to see that this is, and has been, an angry mother-in-law. Look, this is a woman who got mad when Mick took out the garbage for her, who thought being nice after a separation was just a big show. What do you expect her to say after her daughter is shot?

"You told police you asked your daughter when she told you about the gun range. 'Did he take out an insurance policy on you?' "

"It was a joke. She said, 'Mother, he's not going to shoot me.' But he did. I know he did it. I'd stake my life on it."

"You hate my client, don't you?"

"Yes."

"You want him convicted."

"Yes."

"There's something else at stake here, isn't there? Isn't there another court hearing going on?"

"Yes, there is."

"There's a probate hearing before Judge Sosnick and you and your husband are seeking custody of Hannah so your daughter can adopt her, correct?"

"Yes."

"And if my client is convicted of murder, you're going to keep custody of her, won't you?"

"I suppose so."

"You've told people you want your daughter to adopt her, haven't you?"

"Have I? I guess I have."

"No further questions."

*　　*　　*

Townsend asks several questions on redirect, including:

"You said something changed when Mick became a lawyer. What did you mean by that?"

"It went to his head when he became a lawyer. He was trying to sleep his way to the top of the legal system. He was mean to her and did cruel things."

Mrs. Misener steps off the stand. Her stint as witness over, she will be able to sit in the courtroom, now. She sits there, at the center of her family, nearly as impassive as Mick for the next two weeks.

A PRELUDE TO JUDGE SUE

With Mrs. Misener out of the way, interest begins building. The moment the media has been waiting for for months has arrived. Today, Judge Susan Chrzanowski, *the* star witness in these proceedings, will have the most unpleasant task of testifying about her role in the long, tragic series of events, in front of a packed court, a jury, hordes of media—including still and TV cameras, the reporters who will be here throughout the trial and the columnists who will be here for this day only—and the family of the woman whose husband she had sex with a few hours before Leann was shot.

Will Susan get on before lunch or after? Will those with early deadlines run into trouble? How soon can the TV stations break into regular programming with shots of the "other woman" answering questions about her now–high-profile affair? First, though, there is other business to attend to. The star will have to wait, while the excitement builds.

Lindy Termarsch, Leann's oldest sister, is up next. Townsend questions her for ten minutes. She describes Leann— "incredibly wonderful, very giving, very loving"—and their plans for that last day of her life: "I was supposed to meet her that day; she had a couple of pounds she was trying to lose, so we were going to walk in the park, on the trails; she was going to go grocery shopping after shooting, then call me on my cell phone."

Had she been unhappy? "No, she was happy."

Did Fletcher change after law school? "Definitely. He was very arrogant."

And their marriage? "He wasn't home a lot. When he was home, he was upstairs a lot on the computer. It wasn't what she hoped it would be. She was lonely."

What about Leann's future plans? "She wanted me to get pregnant with her. So our kids would be the same age."

Hannah? "Hannah was her life. She was her greatest accomplishment. She wanted a family like the family she had. A large family, with a mother and father who stayed together. A father who came home after work every day and had dinner at home."

About her fear of guns: "Mick wanted to go to the police academy, but she was opposed to him becoming a cop because she was afraid he'd get shot."

Legghio's turn. "Leann hated guns?"

"Yes."

"She was the kind of mom who'd go on a Million Moms March?"

"Yes."

"Did you know that Leann had bought accessories for the gun for Mick for Christmas?"

"No."

Legghio then shows her pictures of Mick, Leann and Hannah in the kind of old-fashioned period photos that some studios specialize in. The entire family is dressed in costume. Leann is holding a gun. So is Hannah.

"Do you hope to adopt Hannah?"

"Yes."

"If my client is convicted in this case, does it substantially increase your chances of adopting Hannah?"

"Yes."

Next comes Jennifer Hughes, Leann's best friend. She reiterates that the Fletchers had marriage troubles and that Mick seemed to change after law school. And she told of her last conversation with Leann, on Saturday, August 14.

"She was in a great mood. They were planning to go to the movies. My husband had to work at the last minute, so I wasn't going to go. She really wanted me to go, she wanted to come pick me up. But my sister was coming over and I had to wait for her. She said to call her on the cell phone when my sister came. But I ended up not calling because my sister came over too late, and I never talked to her again."

Townsend buttresses his arguments against suicide by having Hughes recount plans she and Leann had made—a trip they were to make to Cedar Point Amusement Park in

Ohio in September, flying to New York for a weekend in December for last-minute Christmas shopping, and beyond. "We were going to open an animal shelter together. Animals were a big part of our lives and we wanted to open a shelter for stray animals."

It is 10 a.m. Cooper recesses the court. It is called back into session at 10:30. Judge Susan Chrzanowski is announced.

JUDGE SUSAN

Judge Chrzanowski has more legal troubles on her mind than testifying in the murder trial of Mick Fletcher. Under her authority as a district judge in Warren, she had funneled many cases for the indigent his way. That was fine—until it came out in the days after Leann was shot that Chrzanowski was sleeping—or not, depending on their mood—with Fletcher.

Before, during and after the Fletcher trial, Chrzanowski and her attorney would wage a fierce legal battle with the Michigan Judicial Tenure Commission, an arm of the state Supreme Court, which wanted her fired from her job. In the meantime, she would temporarily be allowed to work, and collect her $118,285-a-year salary.

Five days before Fletcher's trial began, and a week before her crucial and riveting testimony Chrzanowski was busy at work, on the job, dispensing her brand of gentle, preachy justice.

District Court in Michigan is where the wheels of justice are lubed, greased and paid for. This is where felons are arraigned and bound over for trial in the larger Circuit Courts, but most of the people walking through the doors are here for minor driving infractions like speeding and running stop signs, for housing code violations like letting their grass grow too high, or for misdemeanor charges such as petty shoplifting, destruction of property and being minors in possession of alcohol. Judges here also hear civil suits involving sums of less than $10,000.

Most cities have their own district courts, but some share judges with larger, neighboring cities. Such is the case with Center Line, a tiny blue-collar community just one and a half miles square that shares a border with the city of Detroit. Many of its residents still make a living from the auto industry, either working at the sprawling GM, Ford or Daimler-Chrysler plants nearby, or at the hundreds of small job shops along the surrounding thoroughfares that make parts for the Big Three or their suppliers.

Center Line's tiny courthouse is staffed by judges from nearby Warren, which is the third-largest city in Michigan—2000 census figures are expected to put the city over 150,000—and Detroit's largest suburb. They spend most of their time on their home turf, visiting Center Line once a week to dish out justice the way many of those coming before them build cars—relentlessly, keep-the-line-moving, next case, *People* vs. *So and So*, one after another.

Judge Susan Chrzanowski—small, blondish, cute in a bookwormish way with her hair worn up when she's on the bench, far more striking when it's down and she's out of her robes—knows how to keep the line moving. Some judges at the district level are notorious for starting late and leaving early—one called "Half-a-Day" made a career out of four-hour days in a busy Detroit court, sandwiched between rounds of golf. His docket grew enormous.

But by 9:12 today, Chrzanowski enters the courtroom to her bailiff's cry of "All rise," and without ado she tells everyone to sit and calls her first case, herself, in a strong, clear voice: "*People* versus *Shannon Williams!*"

At 8:30 a.m., a seemingly chaotic line of people had snaked through the lobby, waiting to alert the clerk they were here. Late-comers cruised the parking lot in vain looking for places to park. Police with clipboards hollered out names, then went to huddle with those who had been called as they waited in line. The prosecutor met with others. By the time the judge had taken her seat, things were ready to roll. Deals had been offered and accepted.

Center Line's 37th District Court is no impressive hall of justice. There aren't the typical wooden rows found in most courts, just cheap aluminum-framed, padded chairs, and all 42 of them are filled. The state seal affixed to the wall behind the judge is so small it looks like a plastic plate. By 10:50, everyone here will have had their day in court. Nearly all of them will leave less solvent but somewhat mollified. Unless they screw up and ask for a trial, invariably they walk out guilty of something less onerous than what they had been facing when they arrived. They will have stood before the judge, pleaded guilty or asked for a break because of extenuating circumstances, gotten their lecture, gotten a reduced sentence, paid their fine and left.

Metropolitan Detroit is the most racially segregated area in the United States. The city is 80 percent black. The suburbs that surround it are, with rare exceptions, lily-white. The highway that divides Detroit from its suburbs, and Wayne County from Oakland and Macomb counties—Eight Mile Road—is as stark a demarcation line as any you'd find separating warring ethnic factions in Eastern Europe or the Middle East, but you'd never know that sitting in the courtroom on any given day in any suburban district court.

Blacks come to the suburbs for the service jobs whites no longer want in the full-employment economy of the late 20th and early 21st centuries. As they have for decades, they fill the auto assembly lines. And they come to shop at the modern, sprawling suburban shopping malls. On their way out of and into Detroit, they are arrested and ticketed by suburban police. Blacks call it "racial profiling." Cops and their supporters say that the poor, the uneducated and the underclass commit more crimes and offenses and are more likely to get arrested or ticketed, and that the poor, uneducated underclass of southeastern Michigan just happen to be black.

The cops in the suburb of Livonia used to alert each other on their car radios to the unofficial crime of NIL—nigger in Livonia. The cops and their chiefs say those days are long past; many of those sitting on plastic and aluminum chairs in Center Line might beg to differ.

Shannon Williams, like many of those here today, in this predominantly white suburb, is black. He was originally charged with driving without a valid license, which can mean jail time and points on his driving record. He has been offered a chance to plead guilty to not having his license on him.

"Do you wish an attorney?" Judge Chrzanowski asks for the record. If he does, the deal is off.

She fines him $309 and gives him 30 days to pay.

Next comes an old guy, what little hair he has left completely gray, who has just finished an alcohol-treatment pro-

"If you're the Devil, take me to Hell." Leann and Mick Fletcher at a Halloween party. She is wearing the same costume that she wore the night they met. *Jack Misener.*

The proud parents: Mick and Leann with their newborn daughter, Hannah. *John Fletcher.*

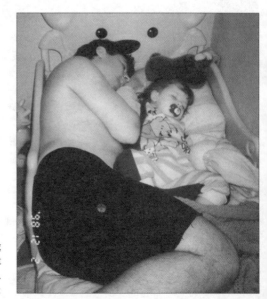

Mick sleeping in the bassinet with Hannah. *John Fletcher.*

The quiet suburban house where Leann Fletcher died from a gunshot wound to the head on August 17, 1999. *Tom Henderson.*

A sign outside the Double Action gun range, where the Fletchers went target shooting just before Leann's death. *Tom Henderson.*

OUR BELOVED ANGEL
LEANN DAWN FLETCHER
May 12, 1970 - August 17, 1999

If tears could build a stairway,
And memories a lane;
We'd climb right up to Heaven
And bring you back again.

Until we meet again we will forever love and miss you.

Love, Dad, Mom, Hannah, Chris, Lindy & Marc, Lisa & Mike,
Lori, Gary, Jamie, Shannon, Jessie, Adam,
Jenny & Jeff

Courtesy Jack Misener.

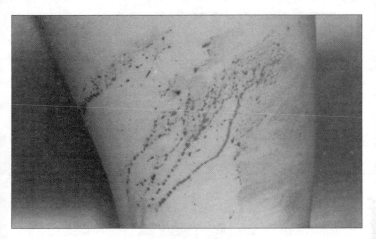

Critical evidence at the trial: State Police blood expert David Woodford did not answer how, if Leann was shot on her hands and knees, these rivulets of blood could end up on her left thigh.
Taken by the Oakland County Medical Examiner's Office.

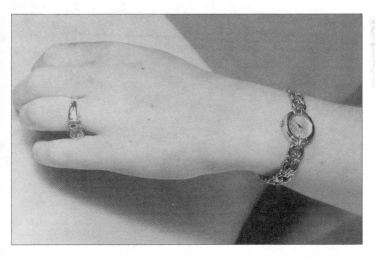

Leann's left hand was covered with blood at the scene, but nearly devoid of blood at the autopsy. Police should have ordered her hands covered in plastic bags, but they neglected to do so. Gunpowder and blood evidence was tainted. *Taken by the Oakland County Medical Examiner's Office.*

Authorities determined that Mick Fletcher was a flight risk after this trailer was parked in front of his parents' residence on August 19, 1999. They arrested him and held him without bail. The vehicle belonged to Mick's uncle, and the family name was painted on the spare tire. *John Fletcher.*

Leann at the wheel of John Fletcher's show-quality Corvette. The Fletchers argued that, had Mick been planning an escape, the fast Corvette would have served him better than the slow trailer. John Fletcher eventually sold the car to finance his son's defense. *John Fletcher.*

Michael Fletcher's attorney, Brian Legghio. *Vaughn Gurganian.*

Gloria Misener holds a portrait of her daughter, Leann, outside a preliminary hearing for her former son-in-law, Mick Fletcher. *David H. Schreiber.*

After the trial, the Miseners threw a party that many of the police and prosecutors involved in the case attended. *Left to right:* Prosecutor Greg Townsend, Gloria Misener, Leann's brother Chris, Jack Misener, and assistant prosecutor Lisa Ortlieb. *Jack Misener.*

The Miseners' monument to their daughter, Leann. *Tom Henderson.*

gram and is hoping to get a drunk-driving charge dismissed. He'd been here a year before and as part of his plea-bargain then, all charges would be dismissed in a year if he sought treatment, passed urinalysis tests and went to AA. He has complied on all counts.

"I hope I never see you again, though I don't mean that in a bad way," he tells her.

"I don't take it in a bad way," she says, dismissing the charge from his record. "You obviously can't touch alcohol. It's poison to you. Good luck."

A lawyer steps forward. His client hasn't shown; bond is revoked, an arrest warrant issued.

A defendant steps up, says his attorney was here 15 minutes ago, but went out to his car on the pretense of fetching something and instead drove off. He is here to have assessed his compliance with a set of her orders at a previous hearing.

"Have you attended the first-offenders' program, sir?"

"No."

"Why not? It's been a year."

"No money."

"Have you done your community service?"

"No."

"You haven't paid your fines and costs?"

"No."

And so it goes. He gets 30 days in county lockup and is ordered to pay more fines and costs. If he doesn't pay them in 90 days, it'll be more jail time and more fines and costs he won't pay, either.

A man driving on a suspended license pleads to no operator's license on his person; fine and costs of $359, two weeks to pay. A drunk driver who caused an accident, now in AA, gets 9 days in jail to be served on weekends and community service; fine of $909 with 90 days to pay. Drunk driving pleaded down to careless driving. Defective brake light fixed on the spot by a new fuse when the cop pulled him over dismissed; court costs of $10. Failure to dim lights, guilty, $85. Driving around a railroad gate, guilty, will come off the driver's record if no further tickets in six months, $95. Speeding for a teen-age girl reduced from fifteen over to five over with a lecture: "I want to warn you, don't drive through yellow lights, don't roll through stop signs—the Secretary of State loves to take away people's driver's licenses."

Up they march, face the judge for their minute or two, then are directed to the clerk's office down the hall to write a check. One after another, people versus, people versus, people versus.

In theory you can have a trial here. In practice, you'd be a fool to insist on it. It's a peculiar form of justice, but even critics admit it works remarkably well. The cities share in the court revenue. Paying for a modern police force, for high-paid judges and for city services means making arrests and writing tickets, lots of them. Claiming innocence, even if you are, is foolhardy. It's the cop's word against yours, and the cop always wins. Because trials here are for misdemeanors and are heard by the judge, only a preponderance of evidence need point to guilt, not the harsher standard in felony trials: evidence beyond a reasonable doubt. "Preponderance" means 51 percent, and a cop's word is always worth at least that to a judge who has to work with him or her year round.

Admit guilt, even if you aren't, claim extenuating circumstances, and almost always the charge is reduced or even dismissed. Even when the charge is dismissed, court costs are often assessed and the wheels turn.

Part of the greasing of the wheels involves the system supporting young attorneys in the process of building up a client roster—kids just out of law school who weren't good enough to land high-paying, long-hours jobs with the major law firms around town. Criminal law for young defense attorneys can be little more than a subsistence living, without alliances formed with sitting judges.

Many of the felons, who are required to enter the legal system in Michigan at the District Court level, where they are apprised of the charges against them and the judge determines whether there is enough evidence to bind them over to Circuit Court, are indigent. When they are, attorneys are appointed to their cases and paid for by the court. Judges are free to appoint cases to lawyers of their choosing, and frequently in many cities a handful of attorneys get almost all the cases.

They quickly learn once they start getting cases that if they want to keep getting them—and often the only work involved is to meet the client for the first time minutes before the case is called, then go through the expected steps of the dance when it is called—they better not slow things up with motions, arguments, protests and appeals to the letter of the law.

Judge Susan Chrzanowski, it had recently come to light, had her favorites—or favorite—when it came to assigning cases, too, and his name was Mick Fletcher. Today, though, nobody has needed her help in finding attorneys. There were no felony arraignments or pre-trials. No one asks for a trial on misdemeanor charges. The line has sped along.

Chrzanowski is a budding Judge Judy. She likes to lecture and admonish, especially youthful offenders. Near the end of her day's work here in Center Line, a thin, small 17-year-old black boy steps before her. Five months earlier he had been arrested for shoplifting. A search of his car had revealed some beer, and he subsequently blew .04 on a Breathalyzer test. While not legally drunk, he is in violation of Michigan's zero-tolerance laws for teens and alcohol.

As arranged beforehand between the prosecutor and his attorney—only four of the 42 in court today have attorneys—the teen will be allowed to plead no contest to a lesser charge of retail fraud if he also pleads guilty to consumption of alcohol by a minor. The boy has dropped out of high school, but works as a landscaper for his uncle, and his father, a factory foreman, is in court to tell the judge that he will be hiring him for the shop when he turns 18. A no-contest plea has the same legal repercussions as a guilty plea.

The judge is told by the defense attorney that an agreement has been reached. Playing her role in this organized charade, the judge tells the teen that he has a right to a trial and if he goes to trial he'll have certain rights he will be able to enforce. The reality is, if he pleads no contest or even guilty, his sentence will be far lighter than if he demands a trial and is found guilty.

Rights come with costs.

Before sentencing, Chrzanowski lectures: "It's time to start making some responsible decisions here. You seem pretty nonchalant here. Sometimes I have the impression the best thing I can do for young people is to send them to jail for a weekend or two. Let them see what it's like.

"You work landscaping with your uncle, and while I've known many good landscapers, it bothers me when family members bail out their relatives," she continued. "You have to think about the choices you make. Sooner or later you have to pay for your mistakes. We all do."

To the casual observer, it's a standard lecture line that precedes the sentence: House arrest on an electronic tether for six consecutive weekends and a stiff fine. To those few in the court in the know—a journalist with a book contract, her court reporter, the bailiff and the prosecutor, her words are beyond ironic.

A JUDGE TESTIFIES

Judge Chrzanowski used to work with Greg Townsend. She was a young kid out of law school whose first big break was getting hired in May of 1993 by the Oakland County prosecutor. In a quirk of fate, she replaced Lisa Ortlieb at the Clarkston District Court in the northern end of the county, and now it was Ortlieb who was helping Townsend try to put Fletcher in jail for the rest of his life.

Young judge or not, male or female, it's an old-boys' world. And the boys will take care of each other today. Chrzanowski has not had to sit out in the hall with the other witnesses. She hasn't had to worry about reporters asking for quotes, or passers-by snickering or pointing or asking, "Is that her?"

Chrzanowski and her parents—her father is running for prosecutor in Macomb County—come in through the doorway to the judge's office, jury room and court-officials' lounge.

At 10:29, Cooper tells the clerk to summon Chrzanowski. The two pool photographers in the court standup, their cameras trained on the door. The film crew for "20/20" is standing and aiming, too. This is one of *the* moments of this trial, second only, perhaps, to a verdict, or third to a verdict and the sentence.

The door swings open, the cameras begin click-click-clicking and . . . Lisa Ortlieb walks in. The crowd breaks out in laughter, a rare moment of levity in the course of what will be three weeks of testimony and jury deliberations.

Here comes the judge, too small it seems to be such a focus, too young, dressed in a pink suit. She is sworn in, spells her name for the record, gets just halfway through her last name, pauses nervously, says "excuse me" and spells it again. Her hair is down. She is wearing little or no makeup, but is pretty, feminine despite a lack of adornment. Mrs. Misener, her husband, her daughters, all of the extended family that makes up most of the overflow crowd, are staring at her with palpable anger, with pure intensity.

The court seems to freeze, and then Townsend asks her to describe her relationship with Mick. For the next two hours, as the cameras click roll after roll, the room will be riveted, straining to hear her so-soft replies, embarrassed at her tears but unable to look away.

Throughout the two hours, Townsend will treat her with kid gloves. There are many tough questions, but they will not be asked this day. He will ask her nothing directly about their last night together, the circumstances, where it was, how long they were together. He will mention nothing about the many cases she threw Fletcher's way in her role of judge. His deferential treatment of her is the one thing the Misener family will fault him on when things are over. And they will remain angry at a system that insisted on treating Chrzanowski as something special that day.

(Townsend will, in September, be a key witness in a Judicial Tenure Commission trial against her, testifying on her behalf, claiming that despite early falsehoods to Hazel Park police, she'd been forthright and honest with prosecutors.

Chrzanowski testifies that she met Fletcher briefly in 1996 when she stopped by the Warren city offices one day while campaigning for 37th District Court. "He was a law clerk, which was what I did there before I began working for you," she tells Townsend.

She took the bench in January of 1997. The following November, the affair began to take root. The judge and her husband were in a new home and needed someone to install computer wiring. Someone around the courthouse had heard that Mick was good at that sort of thing and picked up money moonlighting when he could.

"I asked him at a party the city employees threw for him for his passing the bar, and he said he'd be interested," she said.

Mick began the wiring on the Sunday after Thanksgiving. He would finish it after New Year's. The judge and her husband—she took the name Chrzanowski back when she decided to run for judge, Chrzanowskis being eminently electable in Macomb County—weren't living in the house, yet, but she'd stop by from time to time with coffee or food, and the two would talk. In fact, at a Christmas party that year, the Fletchers shared a table with Chrzanowski and her husband, and Leann and the judge spent a lot of the time talking about their mutual dislike for Gruenberg; Leann would later tell her friends how much she liked Susan.

"The first time we talked about lots of things—life, music, literature. I was having trouble in my marriage and at some point I expressed my troubles on a small level. He said his marriage was not good, either. That they were not very close and had not been close for a long time."

The judge loses her composure, again. Voice cracks. A tear. Takes a deep breath.

"He relayed to me his marriage was going to come to an end at some point. It was inevitable. That's not his word. It's my word. We'd mainly talked about happiness, what makes someone happy in life.

"He seemed like a nicer guy than he seemed in court. He told me I seemed a lot different off the bench, too. I can be very straightlaced and conservative on the bench. A lot of people tell me I'm nicer off."

Mick was paid for the job, but a new one cropped up. At the end of January, Chrzanowski bought her new computer and asked the young attorney with an aptitude for things electrical if he'd help her put it together and get it running.

It was then, she said, that she felt emotional stirrings for Mick and thought he did for her, too. "It was a gradual thing. In the months of February, March, April, as things deteriorated in my marriage—" she stops, begins crying softly, regains her composure again. "As I said, that was a difficult time for me. He was a very good friend. He gave me encouraging words, words of understanding, of faith. I began to have feelings for him and he began having feelings for me, as well."

The heartless killer portrayed by the prosecution has taken on a human face, at least in this telling. But in court, Mick Fletcher remains so impassive he could pass for a corpse with open eyes. He rarely shifts, never changes his facial expression, doesn't seem pleased to hear words of praise from his former lover, a woman he also betrayed but who seems still to love him.

The Miseners continue to stare daggers. She isn't melting any of their hearts.

Mick and Susan talked by phone and by e-mail. "He would tell me I was a wonderful person, that I should have happiness in my life. Some of them [e-mails] expressed his love for me, too." (As the prosecution well knew, all of his and her e-mails had been retrieved off hard drives and printed out by a computer technician for the Oakland County Sheriff's Department.)

"Mick had a wonderful way of saying things. I knew him to be poetic. I shared with him feelings of the heart because he seemed very wise in the ways of the heart. He'd say, 'Your happiness is important, too.' He'd try to point out to me that maybe I was being treated unfairly. Or I should listen to my heart. He could say it many ways."

And when, asked Townsend, did it get to the next level?

"Feelings were getting stronger, always. But the major change came when he separated from his wife in mid- to late June of 1998. I knew he was married and didn't feel like getting involved on that level. But when he moved out, it said to me his intentions were to divorce her, as well. He said our relationship was the kind of love that married people should have. Mick said he and Leann fought a lot, had always fought. He'd say, 'We argue all the time. She doesn't seem to care about my feelings.' People throughout the courtroom said she was bossy, that she kept a thumb on him. He'd say, 'She wants things her way and that's why we fight.' . . . The emotional relationship grew much faster than the physical relationship."

Sometime in June, Mick had moved back home with his parents. As for him and the judge, there was "kissing, hugging, things like that. I felt it was developing with a possible future. It was not so much what he said but how we were with each other. We talked. 'Would I like to have children?' Or, 'Would you go to Lamaze classes?' "

They would meet maybe twice a week, for day outings at parks on days she got out of court early, or they'd catch a bite to eat. By then, she was separated, too, so it was easier to work things out.

"It was a loving relationship. It was a relationship I hoped and believed would work, progress. He was separated from his wife, and I thought he'd file for divorce, as well. We didn't talk about marriage so much. We talked about what it would be like to have a life together. I took it to mean marriage. Those were the kinds of feelings I had toward him."

Over Legghio's objections to allowing copies of e-mails to be entered into evidence—"They're all lacking the originating and intended addresses, they have an inherent lack of credibility and trustworthiness and are harmful to my client"—Susan, in a moment of high drama, begins reading one of Mick's messages.

With the jury present, Chrzanowski starts to read, her voice cracks, she stops, she dabs at her right eye with a tissue, she sniffles, she wipes her nose. Jurors follow along on an overhead projector as she continues.

"You mean more to me than I could ever articulate," Mick says in the e-mail. It had been sent to her offices in the 37th District Court. "A fleeting glance from you can move my soul . . . you are my pretty lady for many reasons. Remember, I am here for your many reasons."

She reads another: "I am here for you, Susan, and everything you are. I miss you already. I am so anxious for the day when I never have to say that again. That's my hope for the future, anyway."

And: "I don't need to remind you how much you are loved by me . . . keep that lovely little chin up, pretty lady. I miss you. I can't wait for the day when I never have to say that, again."

She is, he says, "a creature of true beauty, gifted with the sweetest spirit."

But despite his glib ways, and her feeling he would get a divorce and her admission that "I thought we had a future," things were as rocky for Mick and Susan as they were for him and Leann. It seemed the grass was always greener. He was continually breaking things off with the judge to move back with his wife, then leaving his wife to rekindle things with the judge.

One thing should have told her all she needed to know.

After a profusion of love letters, cards and e-mails, Chrza-nowski's divorce became final in August of 1998. She was surer than ever that she and Mick had a life ahead of them. The day ended in tears and emotional bleakness when Mick chose that special day to tell her he was moving back in with Leann. "I was crying. It hurt. But I was supportive. I know how tough divorces can be . . . Divorce was a very hard decision for him. Hannah was the most important thing in the world to him. He didn't want it to be bitter. He wanted to make sure he was doing the right thing."

But by October, Mick and Leann were separated and he and the judge were an item, again. In November, Mick moved back in with Leann. In January, he filed for divorce and moved back out. In March, back he moved, home to Leann and Hannah, "and he never left her, again." This time, Chrza-nowski took the stuff he left at her house—some clothes, his toothbrush, his shaver and the like—and gave it to him in a garbage bag.

Somehow, each time he left her for his wife, even on the *day* her divorce became final, Chrzanowski forgave him. In June, they resumed their sexual relationship and would continue to meet three times a week for the rest of Leann's life.

Chrzanowski was willing to forgive him everything and anything. Except . . . except that the last time Mick moved back with his wife, and the judge, after a brief stint of restraint, decided to resume their sexual relationship, she made him promise he was no longer having sex with Leann. She could tolerate anything but that. And so Mick had promised, and promised, and promised. Whenever it came up, in those post-coital moments or otherwise, Mick would continue to deny it. "He said, 'If you were a fly on the wall, you would know there is nothing between us.' "

I'll stop seeing you if I find out, she told him again and again. That's my bottom line. Do what you have to for Hannah, but I cannot and will not stand for you having sex with both of us.

"If you had known Leann was pregnant, would you have stayed in the relationship?" asked Townsend.

"No. I didn't think anything was occurring. Yes, he might have slept in the same bed with her. But I didn't think there were any relations."

The last night Mick and the judge had sex, the night before Leann was killed—"We had relations and he told me he loved me"—Mick told Chrzanowski he'd been out with Leann and her parents. He didn't tell her they'd been celebrating her pregnancy.

After an hour and a half under direct examination, Chrzanowski is questioned for half an hour by Legghio. He finishes the portrait begun by Townsend of an altogether more human Mick Fletcher than the headlines have let on. Weak? Sure. Torn between two woman? Certainly. A womanizer? Plenty of evidence there. But all in all a pretty charming guy to be accused of shooting his wife behind the ear after he has sex with her, and while she is pregnant.

The afternoon session is anticlimactic. Chrzanowski says she even now doesn't regard Mick as manipulative. He hadn't talked her into her divorce—"I got divorced because my marriage was bad and I needed a divorce"; he had genuine love for his daughter—"he was a very adoring father, he babysat for her every Saturday when they were separated, he always talked about how he'd played with her and helped her read"; and he had concern for his wife—"he always moved back for the holidays and said he didn't want to hurt Leann"; and, while Mick continued to have sex with Susan after he went back to Leann at Easter of 1999, he never sent the judge another card, letter or e-mail after his last attempt at reconciliation.

Mick even admitted to her in March, just before the last time he'd move home, that he loved Leann and needed to give his marriage one last chance.

Their last bout of intimacy, which began in June, was initiated by the judge. She had begun dating someone else, it had gone badly, and, desperate, she had turned to Mick for advice. She got that, and more.

At 2:20 p.m., Chrzanowski is excused. The next day, she will be back in court—her own.

During recess, one of the friends of the Misener clan asks a reporter: "What did Fletcher ever see in her? Leann was ten times prettier than her. I thought she was supposed to be beautiful? She ain't so hot. Leann? She was enchanting. Sexy? Whoa! I hope there's a bunch of black guys in prison who think he's a pretty white boy."

REACTION TO THE JUDGE

Chrzanowski's testimony led the evening news, was the lead every eight or ten minutes on the talk/news radio stations and drew derisive headlines in most of the next day's dailies.

The media ate up the "pretty lady" quote. It got laughs the next day at the Warren courthouse. Judge Chrzanowski might have taken the appellation as personal, that it was his own little nickname for her. The media certainly took it that way.

Many of the women who worked at the court knew differently. "Pretty lady," as it turned out, was Fletcher's standard greeting for just about any female under the age of 40, from judges to clerks to secretaries to janitors.

He was a flirt, one of the few men who could routinely, in this day and age, get away with greeting women he only knew casually as "pretty lady."

The *Detroit Free Press* put readers to sleep with its headline, below the fold on its Local News section—"Judge Gives Testimony in Fletcher Murder Trial" while the *News* was far juicier: " 'Pretty Lady' Judge Tells of Affair, Lies" along with a photo of her on the stand and a liftout quote: "I loved him. I felt we would have a real future together."

Brian Dickerson, the *Free Press'* gifted columnist, who had nailed the situation so brilliantly in a column at Fletcher's arraignment 10 months earlier, was on his game, though.

"Hope is the thing with feathers," he began, quoting Emily Dickinson.

And even when it seemed Michael Fletcher had plucked that sucker clean, Susan Chrzanowski went on believing. As late as Tuesday, when prosecutors called her to testify at Fletcher's first-degree murder trial, the young Warren

District Court judge seemed not quite ready to let the affair go.

Speaking tearfully at times, but never bitterly, she described a 17-month liaison marked by frequent reversals, but sustained again and again by Chrzanowski's hope that her lover would leave his wife and make a life with her.

Prosecutors have painted Fletcher as an equal-opportunity liar who regularly deceived both the women in his life. But in Chrzanowski's retelling, the slaying suspect seemed less a master manipulator than a garden-variety scaredy-cat who benefited from his lover's almost breath-taking capacity for self-deception. . . .

" 'We talked about what makes people happy,' " Dickerson wrote, quoting the judge's testimony.

"We talked about what it would be like to have a life together." But that August—the same day her divorce became final—Fletcher told Chrzanowski he was going back to his wife. Another woman might have taken that as a clue Fletcher was not the long-term investment opportunity she had imagined. . . .

The night before his wife's death, Chrzanowski said, Fletcher paged her to a late-evening tryst. He told her he'd been to church that day and that he'd gone out with his wife and parents. He didn't mention that they'd been celebrating Leann Fletcher's pregnancy. She only learned about the baby her lover and wife were expecting, Chrzanowski said, when Hazel Park police investigators sought her out the day after Leann's death. . . .

In the least convincing part of her testimony, Chrzanowski insisted she would have left her lover for good if she'd known he was still sleeping with his wife. But if that was what Fletcher feared most, he needn't have worried. If Chrzanowski's testimony established anything, it's that she wouldn't have stayed away long.

Dickerson's opposite at the *News*, Laura Berman, didn't write about Chrzanowski's testimony. She'd been at court the day before and had asked an old friend, who had once co-written a lengthy magazine cover story with her back when she worked at the rival *Free Press*, if he had any good angles to suggest.

The reporter told her that everyone would be covering Chrzanowski in Cooper's court. What she ought to do, if she was interested in irony and writing about it, was go sit in on the Warren or Center Line court and catch Chrzanowski on the bench. She's a preacher, the reporter had told her. She loves to admonish people on their sins. Trust me, it will be worth your morning. It will be a hoot. Berman took him up on his advice.

More than two weeks later, on June 29, while the jury was still out on its extremely lengthy deliberations on a verdict, the *News'* Metro section ran a withering column by Berman, headlined: "Shame Takes Back Seat in the Halls of Justice for Illicit Lovers."

"Shame isn't what it used to be," Berman began.

> *Every weekday, Warren Judge Susan Chrzanowski dons the black robes of her office. She administers justice in Center Line and Warren. It is her role to be a moral and legal authority, an example to the man who fell asleep in his car and left a crack pipe on the seat, to the student who sped through a stop sign, to the guy with stringy hair who says he had a shot of Jack Daniel's and "a couple of beers." And then drove home.*
>
> *This is her job. To exemplify a high standard. To occupy a place of honor and authority. But how is a judge who has been publicly assigned a scarlet letter supposed to do this? Before the shooting death of Leann Fletcher, Macomb County prosecutors were happy to draw Chrzanowski on cases: She was fair and tough. Now, how tough can she be? How sternly can she lecture from the bench?*
>
> *How much credibility can the star witness in her lover's murder case muster before the assorted scofflaws, screwups and speedsters who troop before her? "Good luck with your driving," she said cheerily Wednesday, to a speeder. "You need to slow down, ma'am," she said to another, in one of her harsher moments. . . .*
>
> *The problem with Judge Chrzanowski isn't her passion for the wrong man, or her lapses in personal judgment that have been so publicly exposed. The problem is with a*

system that keeps giving her breaks, while the poor schmo who took a day off work to fight a 10 m.p.h.-over speeding ticket because he can't afford to pay the fine doesn't get a break.

Lying to police? Giving taxpayer-supported jobs to your lover? On Wednesday, I sat in her Center Line courtroom and watched her, a pleasant, pretty, 33-year-old woman who was kind, efficient, and friendly to everyone who came before her. Any woman might feel sympathetic toward another who happened to fall in love with the wrong man.

But she's a presiding judge. She might as well be wearing a big letter H for the hypocrisy of the justice system that lets her stay.

THE PROSECUTION
CONTINUES

Talk radio began running updates of Chrzanowski's testimony as soon as it began. TV would have to wait a bit. The newspaper columns would have to wait a day. When the star witness walked out Tuesday, so did half the media. The rest of Tuesday, at least, would be anticlimactic.

After a half-hour recess, passed by tittering in the hallways about the judge's testimony—"he went back to his wife the day her divorce was final?"—Ronald Lehman took the stand. He was now a cop in Shelby Township in neighboring Macomb County, but on August 16, he was the first Hazel Park cop to arrive at 23757 Hazelwood Avenue.

Fletcher was standing on the front lawn, he said, smoking a cigarette, shaking, trembling but not crying. Not too frantic. Fletcher told him where he'd find his wife and Lehman went in and checked for a pulse. A sketch he made of the scene was shown on an overhead projector; the screen was just a few feet from Fletcher, who stared past it.

Lehman said Fletcher told him that he and his wife had just gotten back from the Double Action shooting range and were going to have sex. His wife began taking off her clothes, he went in the bathroom, heard a loud bang and came rushing back out.

At that first interview, had Fletcher mentioned loading the gun? "No." Had he mentioned loading a second clip? "No." Had he said anything about asking Leann to help load a clip? "No."

Lehman said in cross-examination that he saw blood on Fletcher's hands but didn't remember where it was on his hands or how much there had been, and he acknowledged that no one ever took a photo of Fletcher, or his hands, at the scene.

He stepped down at 3:42 p.m. and dramatic day two was over.

Wednesday was a day of adjournment so Judge Cooper could attend to routine business in other upcoming cases. Thursday, the third day of the trial, the newspaper columnists were gone, as were most of the TV and radio folks. Judge Chrzanowski was done, and so were they, for now. They'd be back for closing arguments and the verdict, but now it was time for more mundane stuff.

"Mundane" is open to interpretation. It may have seemed like a day to stay home for the media heavyweights, and the testimony in day three looked as if it would be cut and dried—emergency technicians and police describing the scene and their duties the day Leann died—but there would still be plenty of drama and tragedy. The extended Misener family would hear more than they cared to about Leann's body, her blood, the blood-soaked carpet, pulseless electrical impulses and the rest of the details of a crime-scene investigation into everyone's favorite family member.

Richard Storey took the stand first. A firefighter and paramedic in Hazel Park, he told of arriving at the scene, checking for vital signs and finding none. Only two of the four paramedics went into the bedroom and the police stayed out while they conducted their business so as to not get in the way and possibly contaminate the scene in the small bedroom.

Storey's partner, Jeffrey Schmuezer, told of finding the pulseless electrical activity in her heart that indicated she'd died within minutes, but said there was so much that had bled out on the body and carpet, roughly two liters, that there was nothing left for the body to pump. He also said they'd visually inspected Leann's hands for gunpowder residue and didn't see any. They were in the bedroom for four or five minutes, out with the cops in the hall another couple of minutes, packed up their equipment and left at 1:20 p.m.

Under cross-examination, Legghio had Schmuezer look at a photo of Leann's left hand, taken at the scene.

"Does it appear her hand is covered in blood?" asked Legghio.

"There's some smearing of blood. Not a lot of blood, but a moderate amount of blood," said Schmuezer.

"I'm not asking you if it looks like she dipped her hand in a bucket of blood, but does it appear as if nearly every square inch of her hand has blood on it?"

"Yes."

"Is the right hand covered or tainted in blood?"

"All the way down to the elbow."

"Are you saying to the jury you examined her hand for gunpowder residue?"

"Yes."

The brief line of questioning was crucial for two reasons. Legghio was making an inference he would return to later: how could you see gunpowder when any powder that had been put there would soon be covered with blood?

More important, he had established that both her hands were covered in blood. Photos taken at the autopsy the next day would show her left hand was nearly devoid of blood. What had happened to it? Legghio would later argue very effectively that it was clear the blood had been wiped off somehow; if the blood could disappear, so too could blood mist and gunpowder residue. You couldn't remove one without removing the others.

Hazel Park policeman John Heisler took the stand and recounted his role as the evidence technician at the scene. He took photos, of the body before it was removed, and of the scene after the body was gone. He collected such obvious evidence as the gun cleaning kit, rags, the gun itself, the clip near the body with three rounds in it, a bullet next to the clip and the spent shell casing, and, after being at the scene for about an hour and a half, returned to the station.

Legghio got another crucial admission.

He got Heisler to detail how Leann's body had been put in a plastic body bag and zipped up, then wheeled outside to be taken to the Medical Examiner's Office.

"Did you see anybody bag her hands?"

"No."

"They didn't do it in this instance, did they?"

"No."

Then came Scott Breedlove of Classic Removal Service, which has contracts with funeral homes and the Medical Examiner's Office to remove bodies. He said he wrapped Leann in a white sheet, then put her in a body bag. And that he was careful to touch just the clothes, not the body, as per standard protocol.

On cross-exam, Legghio asked him if the removal service had any procedural manual from Dragovic's office regarding how they were to handle bodies.

"Yes. One piece of paper."

And what did it say?

"That we should use a clean, white sheet and it had a dress code. No sandals, no shorts, mostly stuff like that."

Did he bag her hands? "No. We don't do that. The police officers do that. I don't recall if her hands were bagged."

They broke for recess at 10:20 a.m. (During recess, a sheriff's deputy in the basement who was manning the metal detector by the door joked with an attorney as he entered the building: "Have you been having sex with Judge Chrzanowski?" They both laughed. There were lots of Judge Chrzanowski jokes in the upcoming days and weeks.)

Sgt. Thomas Cleyman took the stand after recess. He recounted for Townsend his career in Hazel Park, that he was a sergeant in the Detective Bureau the day the call came, that he had gone to the crime scene about 2 p.m., had returned to the station about 3, where he took a statement from the Miseners, then interviewed Fletcher.

He said Fletcher had told him about the visit to the gun range, a visit cut short because Leann wasn't enjoying it, they'd gone home to have a quickie, and that he'd been sitting on the bed loading the gun when Leann walked out of the bathroom, naked from the waist down.

She sat down at the head of the bed by the pillow. By then, Mick, said Cleyman, was loading the second clip, was having trouble, needed to go to the bathroom and handed it to Leann as he got up.

He then went into the bathroom, heard a shot, came out and saw his wife on the floor. Cleyman asked why his wife would lean over and pick up the gun if she was so afraid of guns and said Mick replied that he didn't know.

(Cleyman returned to the crime scene the next day, where he found the infamous brown folder that held the pictures of

Mick and Susan that would propel this case to the front pages for the next year.)

Legghio's cross-examination of Cleyman was one of the critical points in the trial. Jurors would later say Cleyman's admissions to Legghio tainted, in their minds, everything he had to say. It convinced them that he, at least, and perhaps other police, had not been dispassionate observers and seemed far too eager from the start to pin the murder on Fletcher.

When Cleyman was done with the Miseners, Fletcher was outside having a smoke. Cleyman's first sight of Mick was as he came back down the stairs to the basement offices of the police station.

"When you first saw my client come down the stairs, were you sure he had committed murder?"

"I had a suspicion, yes, sir."

"It was more than a suspicion, wasn't it?"

"For me, yes."

"In fact, you said you were stone-cold certain he'd killed her when you saw him come down the steps to the Detective Bureau."

"I won't say stone-cold, but I was pretty sure."

"You testified at the preliminary hearing that you were stone-cold certain, didn't you?"

"Yes."

"At the preliminary hearing, you were asked what factors led you to believe he'd shot his wife, you said, 'A defense attorney and he takes his wife to a shooting range? I've been married thirteen years and I've never taken my wife to a shooting range. Those are two things.' "

"Not because he was a defense attorney, but because he was knowledgeable about what police would look for. I'd have been suspicious of a police officer who'd taken his wife to a firing range, too."

Legghio asked him about a cable TV show on the Kennedy death. Cleyman said he'd watched a History Channel show the Thursday before the shooting "and I observed Jackie Kennedy in her pink business suit and she was red head-to-toe trying to save her husband. . . . [Mick] had no blood on him. I thought that was very suspicious."

"That was the first time you'd met my client and you were already stone-cold sure he'd committed murder?"

"Yes."

(Rob Jensen, the jury foreman, would later say after the trial: "To us on the jury, it scared the hell out of us. Here's a guy who hasn't even seen the crime scene, and bases this on nothing more but the fact that the mother said he did it and the fact that he'd watched a John F. Kennedy assassination show on TV. And that the guy's a lawyer. Great! You're a cop, you're supposed to be suspicious. But there's a difference between being suspicious and getting in front of a jury and saying, 'I'm stone-cold certain.' ")

Cleyman testified that he and officers Welch and Hendricks had interrogated Fletcher from about 4–5 p.m. (He had not yet been read his rights and was free to leave the station, or to terminate the interview at any time.) Cleyman said no one took notes and the interview was not tape-recorded or videotaped. Cleyman later wrote up his official report based on memory.

He also admitted that he hadn't read the statement Fletcher had finished about 10 minutes before their interrogation.

On redirect, Cleyman told Townsend that he'd be suspicious of an attorney or cop who'd taken a wife to a gun range who was later shot "because anyone familiar with police procedures would know we'd be looking for gunpowder residue on her hands."

Legghio scored on recross when he asked: "If you were so worried about gunpowder residue, did anyone test him for gunpowder in his three hours at the police station?"

"No."

Sgt. Larry Hendricks took the stand. His dark hair was swept back from his face, comb-teeth-marks running through it. He had ten years on the Hazel Park force and was 32 when he was assigned to head up the case, but he had a baby face and could pass for younger. As officer in charge, he would be in court each day helping the prosecution with a wide array of odd jobs—going over testimony with witnesses, planning strategy, setting up exhibits and the like.

He told of arriving at the scene after the body had been taken away, then taking as evidence Fletcher's tie, white T-shirt, green Oxford dress shirt, boxer shorts and black dress shoes, which he delivered later that day to the state police crime lab in Sterling Heights.

He testified that he conducted test fires with Fletcher's Smith & Wesson at the crime lab about two weeks after the shooting to see how it deposited gunpowder. He said he had a white shirt on that was flecked with black up the arm after shooting, and that Det. Sgt. Bruce Arthur of the Hazel Park police swabbed Hendricks' hands with an atomic-absorption kit, to see how much gunpowder was deposited, and that the kit was later sent to the Institute of Forensic Science in Dallas for analysis.

Then it was Arthur's turn. He confirmed that gunpowder was visible on Hendricks' shirt and hands after the test firing. He also said he'd conducted the atomic-absorption test swabs on Leann's hands at the Medical Examiner's Office at about 10 p.m. the night of the shooting. He had to unzip the bag to take her hands out, and neither hand was bagged.

Legghio got right to a common theme of his cross-examinations: These were relatively inexperienced police officers on a small force that handled few murder investigations.

Before he conducted the atomic absorption tests on Leann, how many had he conducted in his career? None.

Had he ever taken classes or seminars in the procedure? No.

And then right to another theme: What had happened to the blood on Leann's hands, so visible at the crime scene and pretty much gone by the time of the autopsy the next day?

Some blood could have been moved in swabbing for gunpowder? "Correct."

Had he been at the shooting scene?

"Yes."

Why hadn't the hands been bagged? He recalled that one of the officers at the scene said he didn't want the hands bagged. He said it casually, as if it were no big deal. And then he was excused. Standard operating police procedure everywhere in the Western world had been violated. Why? By whom? Legghio seemed to let it slide. It was an illusion. He would return to it later to great effect.

At 4 p.m., day three ended.

PROSECUTION DAY 4

The prosecution's fourth day began quietly enough. Sgt. Steven Nowicki of the Michigan State Police Crime Lab began things at 8:42. He was part of a four-person state police team that arrived at the Hazelwood house to gather and examine fingerprint and bloodspatter evidence. It was the first time he'd been involved with crime-scene bloodspatter.

He described how he looked for and identified fingerprints, which was done back at the lab. He had ink impressions of the fingerprints of both Leann and Mick so he could compare their prints with the prints he found—the protocol calls for eight matching points on a known and unknown print before they can be declared a match. Then, using a process involving Super Glue fumes to harden the prints so they can't be erased, and two different powders—a talcum called volcano white and a red fluorescent called redwop (*powder* spelled backwards) that is zapped with a laser to excite it—he searched for prints on the gun, on the magazine and on four bullets. He found no prints on the weapon and just a match for Mick's left thumb on a bullet.

He also found no match on the spent cartridge.

Under cross-exam by Marla McCowan, Nowicki said it was usual not to find prints, and that what comes out through the fingertips is 99 percent water and evaporates. It is the remaining one percent oil the experts have to work with.

Lt. Michael Thomas, a supervising firearms examiner, told the jury that bullets range from 29 grains in weight to 250, and that the Federal Hydroshock .45s in Fletcher's gun were at the far end of the scale, at 230 grains. He said he ran one test firing that showed that the fragments of the bullet that killed Leann came from Fletcher's Smith & Wesson, and that he also conducted a series of test fires to determine the gunpowder patterns exhibited by the gun.

He shot the gun at cloth targets from six inches, twelve inches, eighteen inches and so forth, until he could no longer detect residue, at thirty-six inches.

On cross-examination, Legghio asked him if he had measured the pull required to fire the gun. The Smith & Wesson fires either with double action or single action. With double action, pulling the trigger first cocks the hammer, then continuing to pull it releases the hammer, which strikes the cartridge and the gun goes off. In single action, if a bullet has been previously racked into the chamber, the gun fires with a single pull.

Thomas told him that he measured the force needed to fire it in double-action mode and found that it was just over twelve and a half pounds. He didn't test it for single action.

"Wouldn't you have thought it important to test this gun for single-action pull? Had you been informed that this firearm may have been placed in single-action status, wouldn't you have conducted a single-pull test?" asked Legghio.

"I likely would have."

(It was the defense claim that while Fletcher had been reloading the gun, he racked a bullet into the chamber, putting it into single-action mode, which presumably would have required less pull to fire it and made an accidental shooting more of a possibility.)

Legghio also asked if any tests had been done involving dropping the weapon to see if it could discharge accidentally. Thomas said he'd never heard of such tests and didn't conduct them.

He also asked Thomas if the kind of shoulder-length hair Leann had could act as "an effective intermediary" and block gunpowder from getting through to the skin and thus interfere with the stippling pattern.

Thomas acknowledged that it could.

And had any of Leann's hair been tested for gunpowder? It hadn't.

Following the morning recess, Sheryl Tortigian, a state police crime-scene investigator and member of the bloodspatter team that analyzed the bedroom, said that they didn't do much

Monday night, just pulled the drain trap from the bathroom sink, then came back on Tuesday to interpret the blood evidence.

There were, she told the jury, several types of blood patterns, and she showed them with drawings on white boards she'd made earlier, using real blood and a pair of scissors for demonstration purposes.

When she dipped the scissors in blood and then, holding on to one end, whipped them in front of a board, the pattern of drops that flew off and landed was called a *cast-off pattern*.

If the scissors with blood on them touched a surface, they left a *transfer* or *contact stain*.

If blood dripped from them under force of gravity and landed on a board, that created a *passive drop*.

If blood fell and then was walked on or wiped in some way, it left a *wipe pattern*.

Other forms of blood patterns, she said, included *projected blood*, where an artery was cut and blood spurted out onto a surface; a *void pattern*, where blood had been sprayed around an object that was later moved, revealing a pattern; *low-velocity blood spatter*, caused when someone stepped on a pool of blood, forcing some droplets to scatter; *medium-velocity spatter*, which might be caused by a hammer or weapon hitting a blood stain while being swung; and *high-velocity bloodspatter*, the kind of aerosolized mist of blood sent out into the air from the impact of a bullet.

Finally, she showed the jurors how a drop of blood forms different shapes when it hits surfaces at different angles, one shape for 10 degrees, another for 20 and so on through a 90-degree, vertical fall.

At the scene, she saw a large contact blood stain on the bed cover, high-velocity blood mist on the wall mirror, and lots of blood on the computer stand. They looked for blood drops consistent with projected blood. The object was to find various drops around the room that had been flung out from the body, which left a tail when they hit and splattered. Taking strings and running them back from the various tails, investigators could determine where the shot entered the head. That would be where the strings crossed.

The stage was being set, though no one yet knew it, for one of Legghio's critical arguments, and one of the critical elements of Fletcher's defense. The state police, testimony was about to show, had run those strings and the place they crossed was in the middle of the room, nine inches above the carpet. Leann, it would seem, had been shot while kneeling on the floor, her head bowed.

Legghio, and his witnesses, would argue that the police were clearly wrong when they did their string work, that such a theory actually violated the law of physics. The jury would agree with Legghio—but that's getting ahead of the story.

After lunch, Vickie Hall, a trace-evidence analyst for the Institute of Forensic Science in Dallas—a for-fee private lab that conducts forensic tests for police agencies and defense attorneys around the country—took the stand.

She described atomic absorption tests, used to find evidence that someone has fired a weapon. She said the tests show traces of antimony, lead and barium, three components of the primer mixture in the cartridge. The firing pin ignites the primer, which sets the gunpowder on fire, which launches the bullet.

She received two test kits from Oakland to analyze, the one used to test Leann's hands at the autopsy, and the one used on Hendricks' hands at the subsequent test firing. The kit from Leann's hands tested negative; the kit from Hendricks showed elevated levels of all three elements, meaning more than one part per million of lead, .5 part per million of barium and .05 part per million of antimony.

In the test firing, the levels came back at 4.95 for lead, 13.68 for barium and 2.226 for antimony. "That's an extremely high level of antimony," she said. "This particular weapon is a very good depositor of gunpowder residue on the shooter's hands."

On cross-exam, Legghio asked her if it was possible to shoot a weapon and not have the test show positive.

Yes, she said, "it may give negative results when a person actually fires a weapon. In the thousands of cases I've seen, I've seen numerous cases."

Then she put a smile on Legghio's face when she acknowledged that fully 50 percent of the known suicide cases in her lab come back with negative results. Hardly a precise science.

Legghio asked her if a scanning electronic microscope

could have been used instead of a spectrograph to do the analysis. "Yes." Was it? "No." Is it more expensive? "Yes."

And then he asked her if someone didn't have the gun in a traditional position, but was holding it with the thumb on the trigger when it went off, could that affect the results.

"Yes."

Townsend repaired some of the damage on redirect. Hall clarified that guns that are bad depositors of gunpowder residue cause most of the false negatives, and that Fletcher's was a good depositor of residue. And that she'd expect some residue even if it were fired with the thumb.

Up next was a prosecution witness Townsend thought would be key in piecing the forensic bits that were emerging into a clear picture of Mick Fletcher pulling the trigger and murdering Leann. The result was anything but what he anticipated, and would have a shocking effect on the jury.

Lt. David Woodford had nearly two decades of experience at the state police crime lab and was supervisor of the microchemistry unit, with expertise in trace fibers and body-fluid analysis. He was dressed in a dark suit, and was blond and bland looking, with a bit of a baby face. He had, he said, analyzed blood on clothing in thousands of cases and had worked on dozens of homicide scenes. He had testified more than 500 times in federal, state and local trials on forensic serology and was an expert in bloodstain-pattern analysis.

Legghio then *voir dire*'d, which meant he wanted to explore the witness's supposed expertise.

Of his more than 500 appearances as an expert witness, just one—in 1995 or 1996, he didn't remember which—was on bloodstain patterns.

Legghio objected to his being qualified as an expert in bloodstain patterns and was overruled by Judge Cooper. Woodford proceeded as Townsend continued with his direct examination.

He said that he ran the analysis on the gunk removed from the drain trap in the bathroom and that it had tested positive for the presence of blood.

Had he ever found blood in a sink trap before? "No."

But he did this time?

"Yes. Whoever used that sink last had blood on their

hands. To me it had to be a fair amount of blood on their hands for any blood to be in the debris. There had to be a significant amount of blood flowing through, especially since it was flowing through with water. And the next person to turn on that faucet would wash that blood away."

Woodford said he ran the test on Leann's vaginal swabs and on a microscope slide found an intact sperm, one he could tell from the shape was fresh. "The tail was intact with the head, and the head was perfectly round and not out of shape in any way."

He also conducted an acid phosphotase test on the boxer shorts confiscated from Fletcher and they tested positive for semen.

And he said he found blood, including high-velocity blood mist, on the gun and on both clips, but found no blood on Fletcher's socks, shoes or pants.

Next came a gripping power-point presentation—a computer controlled slide presentation—of the crime scene.

First, the living room—piano, TV set, red leather chair. The dining room, the small kitchen, with dishes stacked in the sink. The basement stairs off the kitchen. Another of the living room, with a black leather couch and a black-and-white painting hanging over it.

All the mundane ordinariness of mismatched furniture, clutter, dirty dishes, tacky paintings turned into high drama by the knowledge of what lay down the hall. The bedroom photos showed the blinds closed at the foot of the bed, a bed and headboard, a chest next to the bed, a sport coat on a dresser, a mirror, a plant, a five-drawer tall chest, a computer stand and computer, and now, finally, as the Miseners stare transfixed at the big screen, a full-color shot of the massive blood stain that seemed to fill the room, spreading out across much of the carpet, a deep, too deep, red. Red becoming black as the eye moved from the edge of the stain to the middle.

Woodford broke the tension by going over, again, the various kinds of blood droppings and their corresponding sizes—low-velocity, six millimeters in width; medium-velocity, three to six millimeters; high-velocity, three millimeters and smaller, down to one-tenth of a millimeter, so small the human eye could barely see it.

At one point Legghio objected to a piece of narrative involving blood and how close a gun must be to get it inside the barrel. Where does that information come from? he asked. From this book, said Woodford, pulling a book out of his briefcase and holding it up. "It's a book on bloodspatter by Professor MacDonell."

"Professor Herbert MacDonell?" Legghio asked incredulously.

"Yes."

"I withdraw my objection," said Legghio, barely able to contain himself.

Herbert MacDonell would be Legghio's star witness the next week. Woodford had just acknowledged that his guide book—the one he keeps in his briefcase so he can refer to it—was written by the very person who would shred Woodford's testimony in the next week. Legghio couldn't have scripted a better moment, the key forensic witness for the prosecution proclaiming the surpassing expertise of the defense's star—and certainly key—witness.

(Someone later crudely but colorfully asked Legghio if he "creamed his pants" when Woodford held up MacDonell's book. "Yes," he said, breaking into a big smile.)

The best was yet to come. Woodford was only just beginning to help the defense. It was 4 p.m. and his testimony was adjourned until Monday. The jurors were sent home for the weekend. The defense and prosecution went right to work on strategy for week two.

Woodford's return to the stand would be one of the keys in the trial, with one moment of cross-examination that was nothing short of pivotal. It would be a moment that would help galvanize the jury, help it become more of a single-minded entity with a common perception of the events and not merely a collection of individuals and individual thought processes. And the direction this single-mindedness would take was not what Townsend was hoping for when Woodford had taken his oath.

PROSECUTION DAY 5

Day 5 began with an inadvertent shock. There was a problem getting the power-point equipment to work, and Legghio and Hendricks began to fiddle with it for a while. Suddenly, without warning, there on the screen larger than life was a picture—it had accidentally slid in front of the projector and when it came on there it was in full view—of Leann, naked from the waist down.

She was wearing a red tank top. Her left arm was splayed. Her belly, drained of blood, was an unreal white.

Loud gasps.

"Hey!" someone screamed.

"Jesus!"

"Turn that off."

Those who had been chatting quietly turned their heads to see what was causing the ruckus. Legghio turned the machine off.

Five minutes later, at 9:16 a.m., the jury was brought in and Townsend's direct examination of Woodford continued.

Woodford said that blood mist is usually found within three or four feet of the impact site. Could someone get blood mist on their shirt if they were in another room? "Impossible."

Townsend had Woodford show the jury Fletcher's green Oxford shirt. Woodford told them he had placed straight pins at the various spots he detected blood mist. The right sleeve seemed filled with straight pins sticking out. He said the shirt tested positive for blood, that he had given it a visual examination first, then looked at it under a stereo microscope.

"I started noticing fine, almost microscopic particles that appeared to be blood," he said.

He then showed on the power-point several shots of the

shirt under high degrees of magnification. The first showed cotton fibers, but no blood was discernible. The second shot showed barely visible bits of red. The third showed clear red dots. Woodford said they were about 1/10th of a millimeter in size and were in a one-eighth-inch–square section of the right cuff.

Woodford said that the dots had penetrated the fibers and "that, to me, is a high-velocity bloodspatter. The blood on that cuff had to come from it being very close to Leann Fletcher when she was shot."

His power-point demonstration ended at 9:28. He then told the jury that there was other blood on the shirt, a big contact stain under the button, and that he had submitted the shirt for DNA analysis, along with various other pieces of evidence, including blood samples from both Leann and Mick, blood from Fletcher's tie and blood from the gun.

The testimony appeared quite powerful. Legghio would soon prove that under the glare of a powerful cross-examination, appearances aren't always what they seem.

Legghio began his grilling of Woodford at 9:35. He asked him how many courses he'd had in bloodstain analysis. Two, one in the late 1980s, one in 1994.

None since? "No."

He got Woodford to acknowledge that he had cut a blood-stain off a book and preserved it when he was first at the scene, thinking it was cast-off blood of some significance. But that two weeks before trial he had determined that the drop in question was actually a "gravity drop," and that it wouldn't help indicate where Leann had been shot.

Legghio read from a report Woodford had filed saying he'd gotten Fletcher's clothes at 2:15 p.m. on August 16, but pointed out that that date had to be an impossibility, because the initial state police involvement didn't occur until 7:30 p.m. the night of the shooting.

He also got Woodford to confirm that in one report he had written, there was blood mist on the mirror in the bedroom, that there appeared to be a contact stain on the bed, which was about four to five inches above Leann's head and about 10 inches to the left from where Woodford determined she'd been shot.

Woodford acknowledged he'd never mentioned that contact stain in any of his reports but said it was his conclusion that her head had gone up and over upon being shot. (This was a crucial conclusion and one the jury would determine was wrong; it would help them decide she had, in fact, not been shot on the floor as the prosecution insisted.)

"Didn't you think it was worth putting in a report?" Legghio asked, rhetorically, about the blood stain on the floral comforter on the bed.

Legghio then said there were 14 drops of blood near the comforter and asked if he put in his report any theory of how they got there.

"No."

"How did those gravity drops get there?"

"I don't know. You can't know how every drop gets there."

They recessed at 10:35. When they came back into session at 11:04, things would get even rougher for Townsend's forensic expert. Legghio referred to a report Woodford wrote on November 29, 1999, which included a detailed diagram of the Smith & Wesson, complete with sketches of various blood stains.

"You drew pictures of the bloodspatter on the gun but you didn't take a photo of it?"

"Correct."

"Even though you took photos through a microscope of other blood stains?"

"Yes."

"You said the gun had high-velocity blowback bloodspatter on it. Did you take any photos of it?"

"No. I don't take photographs of every single piece of evidence that comes into the lab," said Woodford. He was getting red of face and angry. He was a violin that Legghio was about to play in earnest.

The defense attorney made a segue to the vaginal swabs and Woodford's contention that the sperm was fresh, which fit with the prosecution's theory that Leann was shot just after finishing the act of sex.

"What does 'fresh' mean?"

It meant, said Woodford, that it had been deposited within 72 hours.

"Can you give a guess how old the sperm was you saw?"
"No."

And then a segue back to the blood on the shirt. With each tack, Woodford got more flustered.

Legghio asked about a report Woodford had written on September 15 about lab work done on Fletcher's shirt on September 4. It mentioned two small high-velocity blood stains on the right cuff, which he saw after looking through a stereoscope, and a contact stain about the size of a dime, also on the cuff.

But, Woodford acknowledged, that report didn't mention any of the numerous stains he now claimed to have seen and had marked with straight pins.

With that thought hanging, it was lunch time.

The jury came back in at 2:20 p.m.

The Misener family and friends were warned there would be some graphic photos shown on the projector and were told they could go down the hall to the media room and listen to a feed of the proceedings without having to sit through shots of Leann.

No one made a move. Townsend came over to and knelt by Jack and Gloria Misener and whispered something. They got up and left the room. Two of Leann's sisters followed. Two men got up and followed them out.

The "20/20" cameraman screwed his lens toward the projector screen. The press photographers took aim.

Judge Cooper warned the jury to brace themselves.

Legghio asked Woodford if he had found blood on the underside of one of Leann's white cotton socks. He had. How could he account for that if, according to his theory, she was shot while on her hands and knees? He couldn't.

Then Leann Fletcher's body came into view. It was a close-up of her from the waist down, taken at autopsy. Briefly her pubic triangle was visible but Legghio quickly covered that part of the photo with a yellow Post-it. There were two types of blood smears on her upper left leg, a lighter smear, and darker drips that seemed to have been running down her thigh. Woodford said the lighter blood appeared to be a swipe pattern, where blood had been wiped by another surface.

"How would you describe that blood?" asked Legghio, referring to what appeared to be darker drips. These drips, if that's what they were, were crucial to the defense. If Leann had been on her hands and knees when shot, how could so much blood have dripped onto the front of her thigh?

"I wouldn't even try to attempt to make a judgment off of a photograph," said Woodford.

"This blood here—would you agree it appears to be going down her leg?"

"Again, I wouldn't even try to hedge a comment on that."

"Well, let's take a look at this one. Does that not look as though it may have been some sort of a river type of action, generating or gravitating downward?"

"Again, you're getting into an area that I would feel totally uncomfortable testifying to."

"You've been qualified as a forensic bloodstain-evidence expert. Can you provide the jury any assistance on what that blood stain on her leg either looks like, how it might have been generated, which way the blood may have flowed—can you give us any assistance at all?"

"Unless I was actually at the autopsy of Leann Fletcher, unless I saw her whole body in totality where I could get a good look at different types of patterns and the way the body was and everything else, I cannot in good faith testify off a photograph."

"Ever?" said Legghio, drawing the word out, dripping disdain. "Are you saying that you can never look at bloodstain-pattern evidence and in good faith provide an opinion?"

"I don't feel comfortable doing it, so I will not," said Woodford. He was getting angry, his face flushed.

"My question is, are you saying never, you will not ever look at bloodstain evidence in a photographic reproduction and provide an opinion?" Legghio appeared genuinely surprised at the witness's truculence.

"I don't feel comfortable testifying off a photograph and I will not do that." Woodford was fully red-faced now, flustered, even angry.

"Ever?"

"In this case I will not do that."

"So you're basically unwilling to provide any information on this blood stain, whether the blood flowed down the leg, whether the blood flowed up the leg, where it generated, any information whatsoever?"

Legghio put another picture up, of the crime scene. Leann's leg was aimed toward the bed, with half her right foot disappearing beneath it. Blood was visible on her leg. Legghio asked if it appeared to be bloodspatter.

"Honestly, I cannot tell."

"You're not willing to render an opinion whether or not that appears to be bloodspatter?" asked Legghio, sure now what the answer would be, but feigning incredulity.

"Again, I wasn't there when Leann was present, so I cannot render an opinion if that's even what that is."

Townsend tried to mend the damage on redirect. He asked about the semen in Leann's vagina. Woodford characterized it as "extremely fresh." And could the stain in Fletcher's pants have been deposited there just before the shooting? "That would be consistent with my findings."

Ironically—the jury would note the irony and comment on it later—Townsend asked Woodford about the very photo he had refused further comment on moments earlier. He asked about the stain that had been characterized as a swipe and asked how it could occur. This time, Woodford had a clear, firm opinion. "A swipe occurs when you have blood on an object and you touch an unstained portion of that object. It's a transfer or contact stain."

"Or something or somebody had blood on it and then touched that leg?" asked Townsend. The implication was: If Fletcher had blood on him and touched her leg, could that stain result?

"Yes."

"Do you know how much would have been on that individual?"

"There had to have been enough to leave that big of a stain."

Woodford then asked him to comment on three other autopsy photos that showed blood stains on Leann's arms. "Again, I don't feel comfortable testifying off a photograph, but it appears to be some sort of a contact stain."

And what was his opinion about where Leann was shot? "I believe Leann Fletcher was shot while she was facing the computer stand while she was on her hands and knees."

Legghio resumed his cross.

Was Woodford aware that the medical examiner had found no abrasions on Leann's hands or knees? "I was not aware of that."

Was he aware her brain stem had been severed? Yes. And that in the event of a severed brain stem, the victim loses all muscle control? Yes.

He gave Wooodford two photos.

"If it is your theory that Leann Fletcher was on her hands and her knees, why doesn't she drop down here? Why is she way over here, probably perhaps as much as three feet away from that bed?"

"She was moved."

"Now, when the bullet hits the head, though, isn't there immediately an eruption of blood? Wouldn't there be a trail of blood that drips from where she was moved?"

"I don't know."

"How did her foot get under the bed?"

"I don't know. Again, I am contending that she was on her hands and her feet in front of the computer stand when she was shot. She was shot in the right ear. The left ear hit the comforter, she fell over."

"Is it your testimony that the bullet moved her entire body, while on her hands and knees, more than nine and a half inches, throwing her onto the bed, the force of a single bullet?"

"Yes, from a .45."

"Have you done any experiments with the force of a single bullet into a human body?"

"No."

"Have you ever shot a deer?"

"No."

"Have you ever been hunting with someone who shot a deer?"

"No."

"Have you ever been present when a bullet has gone into a live body, whether it's a deer, an elk, a moose, a human?"

"No."

"It's safe to say you don't have any expert forensic experience at all about what kind of energy it takes to move a body by virtue of one bullet?" asked Legghio dismissively.

It would prove to be an important line of questioning. Doctor Dragovic would describe Legghio as a master after the trial, and this was one of the heights of his mastery. Woodford, with no forensic experience involving the force a bullet exerts, had articulated what was at the center of the prosecution theory of events—Leann was on the floor, on her hands and knees. It fit Woodford's theory of the blood evidence, and it fit Townsend's theory of Fletcher as sexual sadist/murderer. Legghio's own witnesses would be able to prove conclusively, to the jury's satisfaction, at least, that Woodford's theory was an impossibility.

Legghio went back to the photo they'd gone round and round on earlier, the one Townsend was able to elicit comment about.

"Isn't it possible, Mr. Woodford, that if Mrs. Fletcher is up here where your head is, and she received a shot, that the blood might drip down onto her leg? Is that possible?"

"I don't think so."

"Based upon your forensic expert opinion, what would have contact with her to cause that kind of stain?"

"Again, I am not going to testify off a photograph."

He was done. It was 3:25. Townsend would say after the trial that he thought Woodford had been a good witness. The jury disagreed. In fact, it is hard to overstate the antipathy he created.

"Here was a guy who was actually getting upset on the stand," said jury foreman Rob Jensen after the trial. "You're a prosecution witness and you're getting upset? You're supposed to get on the stand and say what you think. He was refusing to testify off photographs for the defense but he'd testify off photos for the prosecution? There were people on the jury who literally were very aggressively hating this guy. They didn't like this guy at all.

"It seemed to me the witnesses were tailoring their testimony to meet whatever went against their case. I mean, I could have looked at the damn photo and said there was a drop of blood there. When he acted like that, it made it look as if he had something to hide. It created a lot of animosity with the jury. People got angry. It annoyed people."

"Animosity," "angry," "annoyed," "tailoring testimony"— hardly ideas and phrases your star forensic witness is supposed to leave in the minds of the jury. What began with Cleyman's assertion of "stone-cold certain" had continued through Woodford's anger and intransigence—the common mind that the jury was evolving would very much distrust and discredit the prosecution witnesses, right on through jury deliberations.

Their credibility was pretty much destroyed in the jury's mind, and Legghio had yet to put on a defense. "It was an example of how an artful defense attorney can corner a witness," Dr. Dragovic would say later, having successfully escaped being cornered by the best of them.

In the strong words of Jensen: "The prosecution witnesses were so obviously biased, you couldn't believe a word they said."

Lynne Helton, a supervisor and biologist with the state police crime lab in Northville was the last witness of the day. She told Townsend she'd been with the police 15 years, had a master's degree in chemistry from the University of Pittsburgh, oversaw a staff of four and had testified in court more than 100 times.

In *voir dire*, she acknowledged to Legghio that she had no academic training in DNA analysis, and had never done any research or published any papers or books on DNA.

Her lab identified Fletcher as the donor of the semen in Leann's vagina and found a mixture of Fletcher's and Leann's DNA on his tie. As for the green Oxford shirt he'd been wearing—the one the media had trumpeted many months earlier as being, metaphorically, the smoking gun because of what police and prosecutors said was the telltale blood mist on the sleeve—she cut pieces from the cuff and tested them. The test showed positive for human DNA, but didn't match Leann's or Mick's profile.

Why? "I don't know why that would be the case. It was insufficient DNA to get a type, or perhaps the DNA was degraded."

She tried two other samples but they were extremely small and there wasn't enough blood there to generate a profile.

It was 4 p.m. Time to adjourn.

PROSECUTION FINISHES

At 9:07 on Tuesday, June 20, the jury took its seats for day six. When the prosecution would rest its case later in the day, Legghio would move to have all charges dismissed, but first he had one last cross-examination to perform.

Lynne Helton took the stand, again.

After a few technical questions about how she conducts tests, Legghio asked: "The amount of DNA needed to get a profile is very, very tiny?"

"Correct."

And she went on to explain just how tiny "very, very tiny" is. One gram, about one twenty-eighth of an ounce, is 1,000 milligrams, she said. One milligram is 1,000 micrograms. One microgram is 1,000 nanograms. And just 1.25 nanograms of DNA is enough to get a matching profile.

In other words, just over one-billionth of a gram of Leann Fletcher's DNA was needed to confirm that it was, indeed, hers.

She confirmed for Legghio that Leann's DNA was found on the gun and the magazine, and that both her DNA and Fletcher's showed up on his tie. She said that while tests show a match for DNA, they can't tell you whether it is from skin cells, blood or other fluids.

She said they were able to extract enough DNA from the Oxford shirt to normally get a profile, yet "I did not detect any genetic information in this sample."

Why not?

"Occasionally it happens. There are no guarantees we will be able to get a DNA profile from the evidence we are given."

Could it have been somebody else's DNA on the shirt?

"Correct. There was no way for me to tell anything about the source of the DNA on that shirt."

She then combined the blood from three separate stains of what were thought to be high-velocity blood mist, and ran another test. She still could not get a match?

"Correct. I didn't detect any quantifiable stain."

"You weren't able to find any quantifiable DNA?"

"That is correct."

On redirect, Helton told Townsend that she was able to determine that there was, indeed, blood on the shirt, having conducted a test for heme, a molecule that is part of hemoglobin and helps carry oxygen.

"In your opinion, was that human blood?"

"Yes."

Legghio then asked her when she conducted the DNA testing.

"May 30." That was just a week before the trial began.

"Did you know the trial began on June 5?"

"Yes, I did."

"When did you get the samples?"

"We received them at the lab on April 30."

And then she told Legghio that, as per national testing standards, she had kept enough of the cut-out portions of the Oxford shirt to conduct a second test, but there hadn't been enough time to do so before trial.

She was excused.

At 9:57 a.m., Townsend said: "At this time, the people would rest."

More damage had been done in the jury's mind. The Oxford shirt was central to the case. The prosecution had proclaimed nine months earlier to the press that the blood mist on the sleeve would prove Fletcher to be a cold-blooded murderer. Yet, it didn't get to the police lab until more than eight months after the shooting? And when the first tests for DNA came back as a bust for the prosecution, there wasn't enough time to do a second test? The impression was building in the jury's mind that this was a bungled investigation.

And they wondered, they would later admit, how Woodford could see so much blood and put in so many straight pins on a shirt that could fail the DNA tests so convincingly.

*   *   *

As with many of the goings-on at a trial, there was much more involved with the shirt than met the eye. Townsend assumed all along that the shirt would be the smoking gun—or, more accurately, the direct result of the smoking gun. The press had been told, and had trumpeted the news way back in August, that blood mist on the shirt proved Fletcher a killer.

But just a week before the trial, they had to swallow the news that there was so little blood on the shirt—contrary to Woodford's assertions with all his pins—that they couldn't even get a DNA match.

The testing and the timing tell an interesting tale. Soon after Fletcher's clothes had been confiscated, the defense had filed a motion to quash the search warrant, saying it was defective, and to give back the clothes. Ultimately the motion was denied and the warrant deemed proper by a judge.

That was the first stage of a long process of wrangling over the shirt. Legghio didn't want it tested—he fully expected Leann's blood to be there, he just thought it wouldn't be high-velocity mist and that he'd be able to argue against its culpability—but the letters D, N and A resonate powerfully in a jury's mind. They hear "DNA match" and they start thinking "guilty."

So Legghio told Townsend he would agree to a stipulation that the blood on the shirt was Leann's. But he never got around to signing it. He was stonewalling, a delaying tactic that he figured couldn't hurt. Townsend would ask about the stipulation, he'd give the right answer, then never get around to doing anything about it.

Trial was approaching. Finally—to Legghio's surprise, he says—Fletcher himself ordered the shirt tested.

"Are you sure?" said Legghio.

"I want it tested."

Legghio would later say that Fletcher's demand "was much to our shock. I said, 'Are you sure you want this DNA flag going around the court that you've got her DNA on your shirt?' But he said, 'I want it tested. I'm instructing you to have it tested.'"

It was Townsend's turn to be shocked, when in late April Legghio called him and told him he'd be signing no stipulations. Go ahead and test it for DNA.

The shirt got to the lab on April 30. The week before trial, Townsend got the stunning news. Like so much else at this trial, things were not what they seemed. The gun wasn't smoking. It wasn't a gun, at all. For trial purposes the shirt was once again just that, a shirt.

The court came back from recess at 10:40 and Legghio promptly made motions, based on what he said was a lack of evidence, to dismiss charges against Fletcher in the death of the unborn fetus, and for Judge Cooper to order a directed verdict of not guilty on the first-degree murder charge.

The charges regarding the fetus were dismissed, as everyone knew they would be all along. Some critics of Cooper thought she should never have let the jury hear them in the first place, so preordained was their eventual dismissal. Moreover, they might constitute grounds for an appeal if Fletcher were found guilty of the murder charge. (In fact, one juror would later say he wanted a conviction for first-degree murder because the unborn baby had died, too, so he wanted Fletcher to go to jail for life.)

The Michigan law Fletcher was charged with involves an assault on a woman that subsequently results in stillbirth or miscarriage. But the prosecution's own witness, Dr. Dragovic, had testified that in this case, neither event happened. According to Michigan criminal law statute miscarriage is when a fetus is born alive, then dies. Stillbirth is when a dead fetus is expelled from the womb. Neither event had happened with Leann's fetus. Legislators would later rewrite the law to include the death of fetuses not stillborn or miscarried, but Fletcher was off the hook.

"I can't send it to a jury," Cooper said. "That's not my philosophy. That's the statute."

As for counts three and four—first-degree murder and using a firearm in the commission of a felony—Cooper was succinct. "There is sufficient evidence to go to the jury to make these deliberations. Therefore, the motion is denied."

Legghio then moved for the judge to declare a mistrial. He said the DNA evidence came back too late, just a week before trial, for him to properly respond, that the prosecution had the shirt all that time and delayed getting its work done. It wasn't fair. It wasn't right. A mistrial was in order.

It would have been a master stroke had it worked, but it didn't. After all, by his own admission months later, his own game of cat-and-mouse with Townsend had resulted in the test being done so late.

The judge would have none of it. The motion was denied. After recess, Legghio would begin his case. The Miseners thought Townsend had done well. The jury, though, went out thinking, as Rob Jensen would later say: "That's it? That's all they have?" The prosecution had been battered. Townsend's best evidence now seemed irrelevant, his witnesses largely discredited. And Legghio had yet to put a single witness on the stand.

A JAILHOUSE LAWYER

One of Brian Legghio's theorems of life in criminal court is that the prosecution is always more adept at using the media. He considered a story that broke in the combined Sunday edition of *The Detroit News* and *Free Press* on Sunday, August 20, a classic example.

With the trial four days old, *Detroit News* reporter Joel Kurth wrote that Fletcher was establishing quite a reputation as a jailhouse lawyer, a story that provided comic relief for observers during recesses when the trial resumed the next day.

The story ran on the front page of the Metro section under the headline: "Jailed lawyer busy with beefs."

"A novice attorney, Michael Fletcher's legal career never quite took off, but he's using his stay in Oakland County Jail to hone his skills," read Kurth's lead paragraph.

He was honing his skills and adding significantly to the enmity in which jail officials held him. In his months behind bars, Fletcher, given inmate number 267103 and assigned to cell D-2-10, had become the most litigious inmate in memory, filing complaints over the reading material he was allowed to bring to court, over not being allowed to hang his laundry in his cell on a clothesline fashioned from a sheet, and over what he said was a lack of exercise time.

Fletcher even filed grievances over not being given more than one grievance form at a time, over being asked what a grievance was about—he said, "the right to silence is absolute"—and over what he termed were one deputy's "two-toned grunt" and "simian gestures" when Fletcher asked him about how to prevent "mold, mildew and various forms of bacteria" in his cell. Fletcher alleged, among other things, that jail officials had violated his Fifth and First Amendment rights.

On May 19, 2000, in fact, Fletcher took the grievance process one step further, filing a federal lawsuit in the Eastern District of Michigan over the exercise issue.

The court file held copies of Fletcher's various typewritten complaints over the preceding months, as well as responses by jail officials. Excerpts are noteworthy for their insights into his thought processes, and for the haughtiness (spiced with convoluted syntax and occasionally poor punctuation) with which he addressed jail officials, even using the royal "we" in writing to them.

Dec. 15, 1999—A grievance by Fletcher reads, in part:

Please be advised that this grievance is being filed for purposes of notice and maintaining a record within this facility. The nature of this grievance is one of generality. That is, it seeks to address the problems at an administrative level as opposed to any individual agent or policy. I have requested the opportunity to review the policies/rules/regulations by which the inmates of this facility are required to adhere. My verbal requests were summarily denied, and a written request responded in like.

These "policies" (whether or not such exist), are cited generally as the authority for such actions by agents of this facility (examples): Destruction/confiscation of personal property, definition/restriction of religion and/or "religious materials," physical appearances for court proceedings.

Given the fact that policies are unavailable for review, it is impossible to determine which agents are acting in accordance and under what circumstances. The application of authority is terribly inconsistent from one officer to the next, or from one inmate to another. There is unfettered discretion of the personnel enforcing these policies, as inmates are forced to accept the word of such agents as to whether the particular policy actually exists, and/or whether such policy applies in a given circumstance, and/or whether such is being applied correctly . . . these practices are subject to civil liabilities, and given the number of possible claimants, such liabilities may be tried through class action status suits.

Please acknowledge the receipt of this grievance by sig-
nature, and maintain the yellow copy with my inmate file.
If there is a problem with this request, please advise.
Thank you.

Deputy James Smith filed a memorandum the next day.

I interviewed Mr. Fletcher at approximately 1400 hours
today with Deputy R. Garcia present. The interview lasted
approximately five minutes. I asked Mr. Fletcher if he had
received our inmate guide book when he was booked into
our facility, and he acknowledged that he had indeed received this item. I then informed him that just as I had
told him when he initially asked for the grievance forms
that I would be the officer investigating any allegations
contained in the grievance in an attempt to ascertain their
legitimacy. I asked what specific instances of "unreasonable behavior" by any of the Sheriff Dept. "agents" he was
referring to in his grievance form.
    He refused to tell me of any single instance. I was in-
formed that he was not an employee of the Sheriff's Dept.
and thus he was under no requirement to tell me anything.
He said the matter was strictly for the administration and
that they should know how to handle it or else they weren't
very good at their jobs. I informed him that I was acting
on behalf of the administration in an attempt to rectify any
problems he might be having and to ensure that he would
be treated professionally at all times while incarcerated
here.
    He would simply not list a single event that I could
then look into for any validity. When I asked him how he
expected me to answer these allegations of misconduct or
mismanagement he merely stated that was my problem and
he was under no obligation to aid me in the endeavor. At
this point I ended the interview as it was proving fruitless
and had Deputy Garcia place Mr. Fletcher back into cell
D-2-10.

Dec. 29, 1999—Mick writes on an inmate communication
form to jail officials:

Please be advised that on 12-15-99 a complaint (grievance) form was submitted [with] a request for a photocopy of the grievance and a signed acknowledgment . . . I have received no written response or photocopies. I am reiterating the request of 12–15. If said request is denied for any reason, please indicate such on this, returning the white copy to me (as indicated on form). Thank you for your attention in this regard.

Dec. 30, 1999—Fletcher writes on another inmate communication form:

Please be advised that on 12-14-99 I was informed by Sup. Smith that it was against regulation to allow me to possess any books that were not considered "religious material" while being held in the court lockup area. The book which I had in my possession at the time was confiscated, and returned to me when I was brought back. I am requesting the opportunity to review the regulation to which Sup. Smith refers, as well as the operable definition of the term "religious materials," insofar as such is defined for purposes of the aforementioned regulation. I further would request to review the policy which authorizes personnel of this facility to make determinations concerning "religious materials."

If this request is deemed unreasonable or is denied for any reason, please indicate below, and respond accordingly. Thank you for your attention in this regard.

Lt. Charles Swaney responded on the bottom of the form and returned it:

Mr. Fletcher,

It is sufficient for a supervisor to tell you what the rules are. I am not going to have a search done for a policy that was written several years ago when it became apparent the security for persons waiting to attend court proceedings needed measures established to prevent contraband being taken to court. Officer safety is the obvious reason for such a measure. I am not going to debate what is defined as

"religious material" with you, but for the purpose of the
rule, a bible or Holy Quran would be acceptable.

Jan. 9, 2000—Fletcher files another reply to Lt. Snarey
over the memo of Dec. 30.

Your response indicates that a misunderstanding exists.
Your apprehension, with regard to entering into debate
with me, is flattering, but altogether unnecessary. What I
requested was a definition of the term "religious materials," as applied. In the alternative, we would be satisfied
with an explanation as to why the book I was in possession
of on 12-14-99 did not fit said definition. One will, for
reasons apparent, obviate the other.
    I am appreciative of your offering of a rationale for this
particular policy. While the notion that "religious materials" offer a measure of safety to officers that other forms
of literature do not is not logically apparent to myself, we
would be interested as to why such is "obvious" to you.
At this time however, the purpose for such policies is not
urgent. If and when such becomes necessary, we will be
conducting exhaustive research in this regard.
    Furthermore, your use of the term "a bible" [sic] ob-
viates the need for any "religious" content whatsoever.
Ergo, I shall consider this an error as well.

Jan. 26—Fletcher files a grievance, saying:

On 1/22/00 Dep. D. Nash ordered myself to remove one
clothesline from my cell, said clothesline was full of wet
laundry at the time. Nash advised it was a violation to have
a clothesline in my cell. In over five months of residence,
this was the first time I had ever heard of this "rule."
    I inquired of Nash as to how we were to effectively dry
our clothing after washing it. His response was little more
than a two-tone grunt, accompanied by shrugged shoulders. To me, this simian gesture was indicative of two
things in his regard; the most relevant of which being his
inability to answer the question.
    This facility provides inmates with laundry soap. I as-
sumed that such provision is made in order to promote

proper hygiene, such as is conducive to a clean and healthy (in relative terms, of course) environment . . . Without the ability to dry clothes by more conventional means, it is necessary to suspend them evenly to dry in order to avoid undesirable (indeed, unhealthy) results. Without the ability to "hang one's laundry out to dry," the act of washing one's clothing becomes an exercise in the cultivation of mold, mildew and various forms of bacteria.

Given that this facility is responsible for the health and well-being of its' [sic] residents, I should think that this matter be addressed in timely fashion. Under the present circumstances, it appears as though cleanliness has itself become a proscribed condition.

Lt. Susan Steinhelper responds.

Your cell provides hooks for your clothing. The torn sheet that you were previously using as a clothes line is contraband as the sheet was being used for a purpose other than what a sheet is used for. Deputy Nash could have requested that you be issued a ticket for possession of contraband and/or destruction of jail property. In lieu of tickets, Deputy Nash chose to remove the torn sheet from your possession.

One solution to your personal dilemma would be not to wash all your clothes at one time. The second solution would be to dry flat. Your grievance is not a grievable issue; denied.

Feb. 10—Fletcher files another grievance.

Please be advised that on 2/5/00, an incident occurred which I believed necessary to document as a matter of record, and notify the department and facility of said occurrence. I requested of Dep. B. Mansell three (3) grievance forms. He stated that he would do so. Later, Mansell returned and handed one (1) form to me. He then began to interrogate me as to the nature of the grievance(s) I wished to file. I advised him that I wished to file two (2) separate grievances, one of which would require two (2) forms to complete. I further advised Mansell that I wished to file written grievances so that the record of such would be clear, and that I had a right not to be interrogated regarding the matter.

Mansell then advised me that Sup. Delagarza refused to provide me with the forms without my submission to his ordered interrogation . . . To my knowledge, this is the only established method of drawing the Dept.'s attention to grievous matters, allowing same to be addressed prior to entering into costly litigation, for which the insurance carrier(s) of the Dept. and Facility will be ultimately responsible for.

Copies of this grievance were also mailed to Oakland County Sheriff Michael Bouchard, who directed Snarey to review the grievance and to respond both to him and to Snarey's superior, Captain Wallace.

Snarey wrote:

I would be more than happy to give unlimited grievances to inmates like this, but if I don't require the Officers to communicate with the inmates, how are the Officers going to learn what they are supposed to be accused of doing? Mr. Fletcher has written several grievances and has had them answered, however, if he took the time to talk to the Officers, most of his perceived problems could have been taken care of before it came to the stage of filing a written grievance.

I don't believe the inmate's rights were infringed upon. The Officer simply wanted to know if he could do anything to head off a formal grievance being written, however, Mr. Fletcher was unreasonable thinking he didn't have to converse with the Officer at all.

Snarey then wrote Fletcher:

You are correct that you should have received blank grievance forms when you requested them, however, you are wrong to assume the Deputy shall not ask questions as to the nature of the grievance. How are the Deputies to correct perceived grievable issues if they are not aware of them. [sic] You will agree, in all grievance procedures, the first order is to settle grievances at the first step with a verbal communication. Even you, Mr. Fletcher, will be expected to verbally communicate your perceived grievance before you are given a blank form. Further, you will submit grievances on the forms provided. Any future grievances typed in free format will be returned to you in their entirety.

March 15—Uncharacteristically, Fletcher takes three weeks to respond to Snarey's orders, but does so with a flourish and this time sends a copy to Bill Martin, the state director of the Department of Corrections, in the state capital in Lansing.

The above named "response" that has been issued is in fact non-response with regard to the grievance it purports to address. It presumes that I will forgo and waive my absolute rights as a result of your coercive applications of policy. Further, it bespeaks expectations and/or duties which do not exist, and which you are without lawful authority to enforce.

The right to remain silent is absolute. I, along with every other resident of this facility, may exercise this right or not at our discretion. Even you, Mr. Snarey, are bound by restrictions placed upon the agents of government by state and federal constitutions. By subjecting myself and others to grievous acts and/or conditions, you are in effect, forcing inmates to waive constitutional rights in order to avail themselves of your policies, and any remedies which might be available. Your behavior in this regard is not only grievous in and of itself, it is illegal.

I will not agree that verbal communication is the first course of conduct a prisoner awaiting trial should engage in. Your use of the word "perceived" is most appropriate to support my premise. Assuming that the staff possesses some minimus of literacy, deputies should be able to read and respond . . . I disregard whatever expectations you may have as to what manner of correspondence I should utilize. I will correspond by whatever means best serves and/or satisfies any legal requirements or notice, for our purposes.

May 19—A class-action federal civil-rights lawsuit is filed by Fletcher and assigned to Judge Paul Borman of the U.S. District Court's Eastern District of Michigan. Named as defendants are Oakland County Sheriff Michael Bouchard and Lt. Charles Snarey.

Fletcher files suit over what he claims is a lack of outdoor exercise time.

> I have been awaiting trial in this facility since 8/19/99. During that time, I have only been allowed outside for fresh air and sunshine for one hour. My requests to be allowed outside have been repeatedly denied. They have advised me that one hour, per week in the gymnasium is adequate. The gymnasium has no windows, nor ventilation for fresh air. It is my understanding that this policy applies to all prisoners of this facility.

Fletcher asked that the court issue an order

> directing the Oakland County Sheriff's Department/Oakland County Jail, to allow all inmates the opportunity to have one hour, per day, five days per week out of doors, for fresh air and sunlight.

The Sheriff's Department filed a memorandum on May 22.

> According to the Recreation Log Book, Inmate Michael Fletcher #267103 has been offered recreation a minimum of 16 times since his incarceration. The recreation has been offered in the gym due to the winter season and bad weather. Inmate Fletcher has told our deputies repeatedly that he will only go to recreation when it is outside and has refused to attend recreation when it is in the gym. . . . Deputy Bailey advised me that Inmate Fletcher refused recreation this morning, 05-22-00, because it was in the gym and not outside.

MR. BLOOD SPATTER

On 11:22 a.m. on Tuesday, June 20, having lost his motions to either have the case dismissed or for a mistrial to be declared, Brian Legghio began his defense of Michael Fletcher. He had a star witness of his own to lead things off, Professor Herbert MacDonell, who wrote the book, literally, on blood-spatter evidence.

MacDonell made a marvelous first impression. Tall and thin with a neat gray beard, he came across as a combination of favorite uncle and the best, most memorable college professor you ever had. He had a folksy charm, with just the right amount of self-deprecation—here was a witness who obviously took himself seriously but at the same time didn't have that inflated air you usually get from professional witnesses with extensive *curricula vitae*.

Where Dr. Dragovic had come across as combative and insufferable and had irritated the jury no end, MacDonell won them over from the start, transfixing them with his combination of folksiness and scientific acumen expressed in the kind of everyday language even the non-engineers on the jury could understand.

By the time the direct examination was over and the court recessed before cross-examination, the Miseners would be disconsolate. Legghio would lead MacDonell through an alternate theory of events that would seem to shred Townsend's case, and when the Miseners walked, they had the look of deer staring at headlights.

Confident of a looming guilty verdict when Townsend rested his case and Legghio began his, they soon would fear the worst.

MacDonell told the court he came from upstate New York

and then he recited his lengthy and extensive background—director of the Laboratory of Forensic Science, which he founded in 1977; Master of Science degree in analytical chemistry from the University of Rhode Island; former head of the chemistry department at Milton College in Wisconsin; professor of criminalistics at Corning Community College in New York for 32 years; professor of criminalistics at Elmyra College for 12 years; a research chemist at DuPont in Philadelphia and Corning Glass in New York; attended numerous seminars and courses in crime-scene investigation, including those at MIT in infrared spectroscopy; forensic scientist at the Rhode Island State Crime Lab for two years.

It went on—he had more than 100 published articles, books or chapters of books in the field of forensics to his credit over a 40-year period; had provided forensic consultation in 18 foreign countries; had membership in numerous professional societies and associations, including being a fellow of the American Academy of Forensic Science since 1964 and a Distinguished Member of the same group, and membership in both the British and Canadian Forensic Science societies; and founded the International Association of Bloodstain Pattern Analysts in 1983, which had grown to more than 650 members worldwide.

On and on the recitation went. Oh, wait, an aw-shucks correction to make sure he hadn't overstated anything. "I should reflect back. I think I said I was a Distinguished Member of the Academy. I'm a Distinguished Member of the International Association for Identification. As yet, I'm not a Distinguished Member of the Academy."

And then came the eye-popper, or, more accurately, the ear-popper that caught everyone's attention.

Legghio asked MacDonell if he had authored any books, as opposed to articles, on the subject of bloodstain pattern and pattern interpretation.

Oh, yeah, it just so happened there was this 77-page book. The US Department of Justice asked him to submit a grant proposal in 1969 and the result was two years of research and a book for the FBI titled, *Flight Characteristics and Stain Patterns of Human Blood, the* text on blood stains and one which has undergone several revisions and has been retitled *Bloodstain Patterns.* It has been translated into Spanish and

German and at the time of the trial was being translated into Dutch.

This was the book that Townsend's bloodstain expert, David Woodford of the Michigan State Police Crime Lab, had pulled out of his briefcase and referred to during his testimony just days before.

Since the book was published in 1973, MacDonell testified, he had conducted 54 seminars based on its findings for more than 1,300 police professionals, including those of the FBI and Scotland Yard, and lectured on the topic throughout Europe, Iceland, New Zealand, Australia, the Bahamas and elsewhere. Typical of the tenor of his responses, MacDonell interjected a bit of folksy charm during his recitation of countries and lectures. "In Europe, I would say France, Germany, Spain, Switzerland, Hungary, and of course England and Scotland, which I like to keep separate, being Scottish."

Finally, MacDonell said he'd been qualified as an expert witness in bloodstain patterns in more than 200 trials in 28 states, including Michigan, and in more than 100 other trials as an expert in fingerprint identification and firearms. And he'd testified throughout Canada, in Europe, Bermuda, Grand Cayman and Australia.

Legghio then offered MacDonell as an expert witness. Townsend had no objections and Judge Cooper approved. And things went downhill fast for the Miseners.

(It wasn't brought up, but MacDonell had been involved in several famous cases over the years. His interpretation of the murder scene led to the indictment and criminal trial in 1969 of the Chicago police who murdered Black Panther Fred Hampton in his sleep and then claimed self-defense; that story was recently produced as an A&E special. His testimony in an appeal won the recent acquittal of a Canadian named Clayton Johnson, wrongfully accused of murdering his wife and subject of an NBC "Dateline" show in January of 2001. And MacDonell was responsible for the acquittal of Susie Mowbray in a 1998 retrial of her murder conviction in the death of her husband in 1988; MacDonell had written a report for the prosecution before the first trial saying Mowbray couldn't have shot her husband, but the prosecutor wrongfully suppressed the report, and he testified at the retrial.)

*   *   *

MacDonell had never met Fletcher. He was contacted about becoming a member of the defense team by co-counsel Marla McCowan—"the young lady over there with the strawberry-blond hair," MacDonell interjected—by phone on September 16, 1999.

The next month, MacDonell received some documents and photographs and began his own investigation, which would culminate in visits to the crime scene on Hazelwood and a drastically different interpretation of events—and the forensic evidence—than that arrived at by Woodford and others on the prosecution team.

Legghio asked MacDonell for his operating definition of bloodstain pattern.

"They are patterns made with blood and we're dealing now specifically with geometry, the geometric shape of a red stain or, later on, darker maroon and possibly even black. I realize that you have seen diagrams and sketches showing angles of impact. . . . I'm not sure they would have been done accurately because of the testimony, which was inaccurate in that regard."

MacDonell then asked to give a short dissertation on how and why the liquid known as blood behaves as it does. He got up from the witness stand, got a clean sheet of paper and began diagramming for the jury.

"The first thing I want to correct is what has been published in some fairly decent books but is totally wrong," he told the jury, while beginning to sketch, further reinforcing his image as the ultimate authority. "This is a medicine dropper, a pipette, a burette, your finger, your nose. Blood is flowing either out of it, or around it. The blood starts forming like this, and as it starts forming it gets bigger. Now, I'm not going to talk about the inverse square laws and things in Newtonian physics. You all know that when an apple grows big enough, at some point it's heavier than the support of its weight and it falls. Newton did that back in the 1600s. You also know that if your faucet is dripping, it starts dripping and dripping and the reason it drips is because the weight of the water exceeds what we call surface tension.

"So, to understand surface tension, you have to know the physics of it. This is now the beaker. You can tell it's a beaker and not a glass because it's got a lip. It's full of water, let's say up to this level," continued MacDonell at his folksy, professorial best. "We all know Archimedes' principle of flotation. Whether you know it technically or not, if you put in a piece of iron, it sinks because it's more dense than water. But I can 'float' a piece of steel, a plate of steel, or a steel rod on the surface of water—when I say 'float,' I say it with quotes because it's not floating, it's surface tension.

"You see, down below here we have molecules that are all pulling in and out of the surrounding area by what are called Van der Waals forces. They're attracted to each other, something like the center of a bicycle, the spokes all pulling in. However, the little guys up here on the surface can only reach out across the surface and down, there's nobody up above. So there is this attraction, this pulling together almost like a skin, and the physicist, not being too creative thinking in terminology, said let's call the tension on the surface 'surface tension.' "

Where was this perfectly executed lecture heading? He drew a series of liquid drops showing how they build in size and begin falling away from the faucet, or beaker lip or whatever it was they are attached to. Just before breaking away, the drop is held by a thin thread, and then it falls free. "It is perfectly round. There has never, ever been or ever will be a teardrop. There is no such configuration . . . You will never see a teardrop, they do not exist. I'm sorry, it just doesn't happen. Because the interelectory forces are pulling in all directions . . . So, that's the way you form drops, that's the appearance of drops, and there are textbooks that are misleading because they say blood falls in a teardrop shape."

And then MacDonell walked away from the jury and resumed his place in the witness chair. The real point, of course, wasn't the physics lesson, *per se*. It was to demonstrate MacDonell's mastery of the subject, his ease of expression, his self-confidence, his ability to correct textbooks that contradict him. It left observers, and the jury, with the impression—no, the knowledge—that guy knows his stuff.

Legghio then brought the lecture to its corollary point, one to do with the evidence. Which was, how does the physics of surface tension and all that science come to bear on analyzing blood evidence at the scene of a crime?

MacDonell explained: Blood will form uniform drops if

left to the forces of gravity and surface tension. Smaller than uniform drops mean an application of outside force, and the smaller the drop, the more the force. Drops of one size might mean the victim was hit with a baseball bat traveling at 25 feet per second. Much tinier drops, smaller than a millimeter, come from the huge forces generated by bullets.

And then they got to the crux. MacDonell, with the court's permission—witnesses normally are not allowed to hear or see other witnesses unless they have already testified, but in his capacity as an expert witness an exception was made—had sat in on Woodford's testimony of the day before about castoff blood and the size of its droplet components.

Legghio: "Do you recall at all his answers as to what size castoff droplets of blood could be?"

MacDonell: "I'm sure it was three to six millimeters in diameter."

Legghio: "Do you agree with that testimony of Mr. Woodford?"

MacDonell: "No. That's much too large. You can get some that large, but in all the castoff experiments we do . . . You get spots very much smaller, much smaller than that. The only way you would get that would be to have something like a baseball bat and just swing it very slowly."

And, of course, everyone knew they were dealing with a gun here, not a baseball bat, so what was Woodford talking about?

Legghio had MacDonell look at some of the crime-scene photos of blood stains that had been introduced as evidence by Townsend. About all that MacDonell and Woodford would agree on is that the spattered blood had come from Leann's ear. Then MacDonell began a series of questions once again designed to reinforce the already solid impression that Woodford was a rookie—almost a rank amateur—compared to the good professor when it came to who knew what about blood. In fact, whatever evidentiary point Legghio was leading to would be lost when the court would recess for lunch, but the evidentiary point was irrelevant—another lecture was the purpose.

It included this bit of narrative from MacDonell about how to determine the trajectory of a drop of blood while discussing People's Exhibit 96:

Legghio: "The drop under the word 'pattern'—you say that is about one millimeter?"

MacDonell: "Yes."

Legghio: "How do you know that?"

MacDonell: "I have a calibrated eyeball. It is, well, maybe 1.1 wide and approximately two in length. That would be about—I'm estimating—about an 18-degree angle of impact. No, it's about a 22-degree angle of impact. You can do that very quickly. There's nothing magic about it. You take 1.1, divide it by two equals .55, and that's the sine of the angle of impact, so we hit arc sine and we get—oh, I meant 33, just over 30, not 23. This is now 33 degrees, 33.4, and I did that to demonstrate how easy it is, whether you understand trigonometry or not. And most of my students have at one point in time—they haven't used it much—but it's a very nice application of mathematics.

"And when you've got the angle impact like that, you can then say 'All right, it struck at this angle' by putting a protractor. And then as you project these back, you can come to a point in space which is at or above the origin of spatter."

Judge Cooper interceded: "Apparently this particular presentation will take some time this afternoon, yes?"

Legghio: "It will, Your Honor."

Cooper: "All right. We'll recess for lunch. Members of the jury, we'll give you until 1:30. My favorite thing to do is to tell you get in the car, go far. Do not, do not go to the cafeteria, do not wander in this building. Do not discuss this case amongst yourselves or with anyone else. Don't allow anybody to discuss it with you. Don't listen to the news on the radio. Don't watch the news on television. Do not pick up any newspapers regarding this particular case. See you back in the jury room at 1:30."

The jury departed, the spectators walked out. It was 12:10 p.m. and MacDonell had been on the stand less than an hour. It had been a very fruitful 50 minutes. The foundation was well laid for the important conclusions and inferences yet to come.

Pat Carter, a friend of the Miseners, an electrician who would see every minute of the trial, came up to a reporter. He was forlorn. "Is that the heavyweight witness you were talking about? He's got quite a way with a courtroom, don't he?"

Yes, indeed. And Carter hadn't seen anything, yet.

1:50 p.m. The jury walked into its box and Legghio continued with a subtle dig at Woodford.

Legghio: "You were present in the court yesterday, again, with the judge's permission, and you had an opportunity to listen to Mr. Woodford's testimony, correct?"

MacDonell: "Yes, I did."

"You heard the phrase 'gravity drops'?"

"Yes . . . The proper term is "passive drop," which means just a free-falling drop that is created by gravity breaking away from a source of blood."

Legghio handed MacDonell the shirt Fletcher was wearing when police arrived at his house following the 911 call. MacDonell said it looked like the same shirt he'd seen when it had been sent to his laboratory in New York on November 30, 1999, at Legghio's behest. Coincidentally, the shirt had been personally delivered by Woodford, with MacDonell examining it by stereo binocular microscope.

Legghio: "Did he assist you or direct you where is it you should conduct your visual examination?"

MacDonell: "Yes, he—well, I spread this out and I was having a problem finding any spatters, any stains that looked like blood, so he found one which I concurred looked like it could be a stain caused by blood. It was the right color. The fiber optics are very high intensity, so you can virtually make a shirt of this color appear very, very light, and that allows more contrast between—if there is a stain of any kind that's darker than the material, it enhances the contrast.

"So, I looked at that and ultimately took a photo micrograph through the stereo binocular microscope—it was a Polaroid shot—and then I looked further. He informed me, as I recall, there were two spots on here, but could not find the second one. That was the only one I photographed. He believed them to be the result of projected blood, which would be, in that size range, consistent with the energy of a gunshot or high-velocity impact spatter. I disagreed with that at that time. It is on the surface of the fibers, and that's why I took the photograph, the photo micrograph, to show it."

Legghio had him remind the jury how many times he has examined similar articles of clothing in criminal investigations or trials. "A great many. I would say hundreds of times. I won't say thousands of times, but I've looked at garments hundreds of times."

Legghio: "So, that's the picture of one stain that you said looked visually consistent with a blood stain on the shirt?"

MacDonell: "Yes. It could be a blood stain. It's a stain."

"Did you see any other stains that appear to you to be blood stains on that shirt?"

"No, I didn't."

"You were in the courtroom yesterday and today, correct?"

"Yes."

"You heard Mr. Woodford's testimony?"

"Yes."

"Did you hear his testimony that he found just all kinds of little specks of blood on the shirt?"

"There are pins there [on the shirt] and I looked with a 20-power microscope and high-intensity elimination, and I was unable to see anything except where the pins go through the cloth. I'm not saying there's not something there, but with this kind of equipment, I ought to be able to see it."

"So, do I understand your testimony, then, when you were in Corning, New York, and you had what you consider to be acceptable or near-perfect laboratory conditions, the only spot or stain that you saw on the shirt is the stain that you captured in that photograph marked 'Defendant's LL'?"

"That's correct."

Having attacked Woodford's conclusion that there were numerous small blood stains on the shirt, Legghio then attacked a more important conclusion made by the prosecution's blood expert that the one stain they agreed on got there as a result of high-velocity bloodspatter, the kind of fine-misting generated by a bullet expelling microscopic droplets of blood at high speed.

MacDonell said that while he still wasn't convinced the spots were blood, he was certain they had not resulted directly from high-velocity bloodspatter.

"It has to be a surface transfer," said MacDonell. In other words, the blood hadn't spattered on Fletcher's shirt directly.

It had spattered onto something else, first, and then Fletcher's shirt had come into contact with it.

"How can you make that distinction?"

"Well, the dark areas are shadows. That's where the light does not penetrate down into the garment so you can see the weave pattern more clearly. On the surface, right in the center on two top fibers that are jumping across, as you can see, there is blood on each side of a depression which has no blood in the fiber, here. If it were projected as a round ball, which it would be in the air, these areas down in here would be stained as well as just the surface. And then there are other little lighter spots on the top of the weave that, again, are consistent with contact but not with projection."

"Is it your opinion, then—let me ask this. Do you then disagree with the opinion by David Woodford that whatever you saw on that shirt was high-velocity impact spatter?"

"It's not that. It's transferred blood. I disagree with that, yes."

Woodford's testimony—and Townsend's case—appeared to be unraveling.

Thirteen days after Woodford's appearance in Corning with Fletcher's shirt in hand, MacDonell flew to Michigan to visit the murder scene. He walked through the entire house, but naturally enough spent most of his time in the bedroom where Leann had been shot.

He examined the ceiling and other places that police might have missed spots of blood. He examined the floor, the walls, around and under the windows, camera and tape measure in hand.

He found what he was looking for, he told the jury. "I found several small stains of blood. I found one stain on the north wall, which would be on the wall where the bedroom door is. It was near the light switch, which is just inside the room . . . And there was one stain there which had all the physical appearance of a blood stain. I went over to the window, which was on the opposite wall, the south wall, and in the easterly part of the south wall I looked at these windows and found three other small stains.

"I of course measured all of these, I photographed them, and then I sampled the very smallest of all these four stains

I had found, and I took that back to my laboratory and performed a presumptive test for blood on it."

Legghio offered to make a sketch of the room on the large white board, then asked MacDonell if he preferred to make the sketch, himself. "I don't know how good an artist you are," said the professor. "I'm not bad."

"I can't spell, so . . ." responded Legghio, drawing laughter from the audience in reference to his verbal scuffles of two days earlier with Dr. Dragovic.

MacDonell got up and went to the board and outlined the room, putting in doorways, the bed, light switches, windows and the like, all the while recounting dimensions for the jury—of room size, door width, etc.

And then he drew, in red, the four stains of blood he found—three on the window screen on the south side and immediately below the light switch on the north side.

Legghio then moved to have three photos taken by MacDonell of the stains admitted as Defense Exhibits MM, NN and OO. Exhibit OO was a close-up of the blood stain by the light switch.

"Clearly it is heavier on the bottom," said MacDonell. "By gravity, there is more blood on the bottom. It is coming down, that is clear from the point, as well, so having the geometry of the drop I can tell it's descending. It's eight degrees to the left of vertical."

And the significance of the picture of the drop and the angle from which it landed?

"They do show directionality, which goes back toward the bed, in that general area . . . it comes up at an eight-degree angle going up toward the bed . . . It's clearly coming down from the right to the left."

That the blood came from the direction of the bed was crucial. The prosecution's theory was that Leann had been shot while kneeling on the floor. If MacDonell could establish a different point of origin, the prosecution's theory would be proven wrong at the start of the defense case. What's more, police photos showed a large blood stain on the bedspread, which had been in place on the bed when they arrived. It was the prosecution's contention that the blood had gotten on the bedspread after Leann was shot on the floor, that the force of the bullet had jerked her body over to the bed, where her profusely bleeding ear had come into contact with the spread before she fell to the floor.

MacDonell said the prosecution was wrong. It was simple physics, he said; the force of the bullet, while carrying plenty of killing power, was incapable of propelling Leann's body from where the prosecution said it was—kneeling on the floor—to the bed against the wall.

Legghio asked, "Now, Professor, do you recall the testimony yesterday that the prosecution's expert opined that Mrs. Fletcher was on her hands and knees, approximately nine and a half inches away from the bed?"

"Yes, sir, I heard that."

"And do you also recall that Mr. Woodford had testified that Mrs. Fletcher . . . was anywhere between 14 inches to 18 inches off the ground?"

"Yes, I remember that."

"And do you further recall the testimony that the height of the bed here is approximately 22 and a half inches?"

"One-half."

"Do you agree that a single .45-caliber shot to the head, no exit wound, would cause the head to thrust nine and a half inches—without even discussing the height differential— thereby creating the contact blood stain?"

"Only in Hollywood. No. That doesn't happen."

"How do you know that?"

"Physics."

"Okay. But you weren't in the room and you weren't there when the bullet went in the head."

"Right."

"So how is it that you can arrogantly state you know that the head or the body didn't move nine and a half inches?"

After several objections by Townsend, MacDonell testifies that he has fired many bullets into recovery tanks for testing purposes and into a variety of substances. Bullets, he says, "do not impart a destruction that moves the object being shot."

Legghio: "You talked about Hollywood. Is there such a mental concept that you shoot somebody, they jump back with the force of the bullet?"

MacDonell: "Yes, especially in *Dirty Harry*. Never happened in real life."

"*Dirty Harry*, Arnold Schwarzenegger–type movies?"

"Yes."

"Is there a scientific principle upon which you base your opinion that Mrs. Fletcher's head could not have moved nine and a half inches from point of impact toward the bed?"

"Yes. Again, from physics, and also having seen people commit suicide and see that they do not get blown one side to the other. With a .357 Magnum, for years the most powerful handgun made, Mr. Bud Dwyer committed suicide on camera. He shot in the mouth, the energy transfer was such that there was no noticeable movement other than he dropped immediately, which is what people do. . . . From the physics, the deformation of the projectile, the disruption of the tissue, intracranially specifically, will transfer the energy levels so low that you probably won't see the head move, even if the bullet does not exit. That is physics."

"My question is this: Can a bullet, even a large bullet, ever push the body or portions of the body? I mean, is there enough energy when that bullet goes in that it actually pushes the body or pushes the head?"

"No. It cannot. You have what is called the kinetic energy from the bullet. We know the weight of the bullet in grains— in this case 230. Seven thousand grains to a pound. We know its velocity is 855 feet per second and we take kinetic energy equals velocity squared times the mass or the weight. When you calculate the amount of energy . . . and apply it to a head absorbing it—the head weighs nine or ten pounds—you cannot move the head hardly any noticeable amount."

MacDonell buttressed his theory that Leann had been shot while sitting on the bed, and produced photos he had taken of a human model he hired at his laboratory. The model, while leaning over to pick up the single bullet not yet in the clip—while holding the gun and the clip in the same hand— could have shot herself in such a way that accounted for all the various types of blood smears and their angles as shown in police photos.

The photos were admittedly awkward, but who was to say that a novice gun user wouldn't end up in an awkward position while trying to pick up a bullet while attempting to load it in a clip? In any event, from Legghio's perspective, it was better to have an awkward theory than one that defied the laws of physics.

MacDonell's direct examination ended—or seemed to—moments later, after one final, crucial point, one that refuted prosecution testimony that the crime scene had been tampered with.

Townsend claimed that blood found under the gun was evidence that Fletcher had placed it there.

Legghio: "Can you indicate to the members of the jury whether that causes you any concern that underneath the gun were found blood stains?"

MacDonell: "No. When the shooting occurs, blood is projected and therefore it will travel faster than gravitation for a moment, until air resistance slows it down. But it merely has to be projected on the carpet before whatever is on top of it fell or was dropped, and that's not at all unusual."

Legghio announced the conclusion of his direct examination of Professor MacDonell at 3:15. Judge Cooper ordered a ten-minute recess before the cross-examination would begin.

The Miseners walked out in shock. Said Pat Carter: "Doesn't look very good, does it?"

MacDonell, who wrote the FBI's book on blood evidence, had refuted nearly every conclusion Woodford had made crucial to the prosecution. There weren't a lot of flecks of blood on Fletcher's shirt; the blood that was there wasn't from high-velocity blood mist; it was a violation of the law of physics to claim both that Leann had been shot while kneeling on the floor and that her bleeding ear had come in contact with the bedspread; and the fact that the Smith & Wesson was found atop some blood was not evidence of a contaminated crime scene.

It was a case that would be won or lost on the forensics, Legghio had said before trial, and his expert had seemingly destroyed Townsend's.

Several months after the trial was over and a verdict rendered, MacDonell would say when asked about Woodford for this book:

"He's not a bad guy. He just doesn't know what he's talking about. He doesn't know the subject. What he testified to, he was honest as far as he knows, but he just doesn't know what he's talking about. When he came to my lab, I had fiber-optic illumination on the shirt and he couldn't show me what he claimed was there. It's funny, I couldn't see it under ideal laboratory conditions. Make sure you write that it's not the science at fault. The science is clear. This isn't like forensic psychiatry, where they can't even agree on what day it is. This is very clear science. It's the people doing it that make mistakes.

"Woodford's not adequately prepared to give expert testimony on bloodstain interpretation. It's clear from his reports and his testimony that he does not understand the subject. He shouldn't give testimony unless he improves significantly."

A SHORT BIRD STORY

After the jury left, Townsend, Lisa Ortlieb, Sgt. Hendricks and Woodford huddled. The trial's outcome might very well hinge on the upcoming cross-examination and whatever damage control Townsend could put together in a few minutes.

Though there was a sense of urgency, Townsend and Ortlieb didn't look panicked. Anything but. A close look at Townsend, in fact, revealed what the patrons of Hazel Park's working-class bars might have called a shit-eating grin.

The 10-minute break stretched to 30. The smokers on the jury needed to race outside for cigarettes and by the time they were done, had caught an elevator back to the third floor and gotten the clerk's summons to Cooper's courtroom, it was 3:45.

They thought they would be hearing from Townsend, and they would, but first there was a surprise final couple of questions for Dr. MacDonell by Legghio, stunning questions that started Townsend off very nicely on his mission of damage control.

"Your Honor, I informed Mr. Townsend that I forgot to ask the professor two questions before I concluded my direct examination. Doctor, after you did your examination of the photographs, did you later receive some information from the state police about the supposed—or what you thought was bloodspatter in the room?"

"Yes."

"What was that information, if you recall?"

"I was informed that the blood on the window and by the light switch was not human blood."

"And did that—let me ask you this question: If in fact—well, let me ask you this question—" for the first time in the trial Legghio appeared flustered "—if the blood under the light switch and the blood on the screen were not human blood, would it change your opinion at all or your conclusions or deductions that you arrived at regarding the bloodspatter and how Mrs. Fletcher had been shot?"

"No. It would support it, but it doesn't negate it."

"Thank you, Professor. I have nothing further."

Huh? There was a stunned look to many observers in the court, and a noticeable rustling in the jury box, a snapping to of attention. It was as if people were trying to digest what they'd heard.

Legghio had gone on at length about the drops of blood MacDonell had found that had been overlooked by police, that hadn't shown up in any of their photos. And that the directionality of the blood pointed right to the bed.

And now he was asking his witness—*after* he had said he was done and had turned him over to Townsend—if it would be important if he found out that the blood was *not* human blood? And the witness had said it didn't matter? What was going on? Reporters turned to their peers, wondering if they had missed something. They hadn't.

The explanation would have to wait for a few minutes.

Townsend rose, and began what would be a spirited cross-examination. By the time MacDonell got off the stand at 5:05, he no longer seemed so wise. He was still professorial, all right, and still on top of his material, but he came off also as a gun for hire, too eager to come up with theories to please, even ill-prepared. What had begun triumphantly for Legghio and his client would end in something far less.

What Yogi Berra had said about baseball games would prove true of a witness's testimony, too: "It ain't over till it's over."

"Good afternoon, Professor. How are you?" began Townsend, and then he got out the knives and began carving.

He established that MacDonell's laboratory was something less than listeners might have envisioned earlier—that it was, in fact, in MacDonell's house, that it had no employees, that it had never been certified by any agency.

"I thought I read some transcripts from the past—and correct me if I'm wrong—didn't you at one time tell a reporter that you probably were entitled to be included in *The Guinness World Book of Records* [sic] because you testified in more courts on more subjects than any other human being? Did you say that?" asked Townsend.

"I think it came up and I agree with it."

Townsend had him run through the litany of areas he had testified to—fingerprint identification, bloodspatter, firearms identification, gunshot residues, Breathalyzer and blood-alcohol cases, general physics, chemical analysis, gunpowder granules, shoe-print identification and blood clotting. Townsend even got him to confess that he'd testified once in an area in which he admitted no particular expertise. "I even testified once in forensic psychiatry, that's the subject. I'm not a forensic psychiatrist, but the topic came up of auto-erotic masochism and I seemed to be the only one, other than the state policeman, that knew what it was, and that's what the case was about, so that was the topic once, but I'm not a forensic psychiatrist."

The image was clear: Here was a guy who saw himself as an expert in all things, even when he wasn't.

"It looks like you've testified in quite a few homicide trials as well, is that correct?"

"Yes."

"You testified in the O. J. Simpson case, criminal case?"

"Yes."

"Testified for the defense?"

"Yes."

"And also testified—I believe you testified in the O. J. Simpson civil case, too, is that correct?"

"Yes, I did."

"Testified for the defense in that."

"Yes."

Townsend wasn't playing the race card, he was playing the guilt-by-association card. Cooper runs a tight courtroom, tolerating little spectator reaction. The O. J. acknowledgment was one of the few times all trial when an audible buzz went through the courtroom. The Simpson trial may have polarized the country, but it didn't polarize Oakland County, Michigan, where a huge preponderance of the population is convinced that he killed his wife and Ronald Goldman and got away with murder through courtroom shenanigans. Admitting a role in that was practically an admission of guilt of some kind.

(MacDonell testified that the blood in Simpson's socks seemed to have been pressed into the material in an artificial manner, the implication by the defense being that it was put there by police planting evidence.)

Townsend asked him how many reports he'd filed on the Fletcher case.

"I didn't write an actual report."

"You received all kinds of police reports from us to Mr. Legghio to you, is that correct?"

"Yes."

"All kinds of photographs?"

"Yes."

"And you were able to review and examine all of those, is that correct?"

"Yes, I was."

"Didn't you feel it was necessary that you should write a report to put down your findings that would give the State the opportunity to review your findings and maybe consult with somebody or check with somebody regarding those findings?"

"If I was asked to, I would have written a report. I'm frequently asked not to write a report, either by the defense or the prosecution."

"Let me ask you specifically in this case, were you asked by Mr. Legghio to write a report?"

"No."

"You were not?"

"No."

(Legghio looked as if he were trying to hold down a live fish in his throat. At the very beginning of the trial, with the jury out of the room, Townsend had protested to Judge Cooper that the prosecution had not received any copies of reports from MacDonell despite promises from Legghio that they would; Legghio had responded by saying he was sorry and frustrated, too, but despite having repeatedly asked MacDonell to issue a formal report on his findings, nothing had ever come in.)

Townsend asked MacDonell what kinds of reports had been sent to him.

Amazingly enough, MacDonell seemed to have no idea.

"There were a lot of reports relative to work notes, and mainly photographs is what I look at. I don't really read many reports unless they're technical reports. I looked at the crime-scene sketch. I compared it to my own measurements."

"I'm asking you what you received."

"I received, I think, just about everything that I could have." Titters in the court. "I didn't notice anything missing. I had an autopsy report. I think I got everything. I just don't know."

"You read all the police reports in this case about all the various statements that were made, the interviews that were conducted by all the individuals, is that correct?"

"No. I don't usually read interviews. I may have received them, but I don't read them."

"How can you reconstruct something unless you have all the information for it?"

"The information that I use is physical evidence, not hearsay."

Townsend then referred him to Defendant's Exhibit UU, one of the photos of MacDonell's model trying to re-create a possible death scenario.

"That photograph—can you describe that photograph for the jury? What is your model doing?"

"She is bending in an attempt to reach toward a cartridge on the floor and holding a pistol in her right hand and a clip also in the right hand."

"Now, obviously you did that for a reason, is that correct?"

"Yes, to document a possibility."

"And why do you have the model holding the gun in that manner?" (She was holding the gun opposite the way one might expect someone to hold a gun, with the thumb near the trigger and not the fingers. If the thumb had pulled the trigger, Leann could have shot herself from a farther range than if the forefinger pulled the trigger, and Legghio needed the gun at a distance to account for the stippling on her skin.)

"No particular reason . . ."

"Were you advised that the theory of the defense was that that's the way she was holding the gun?"

"No. It was a possibility that we discussed. He didn't— Mr. Legghio didn't advise me to consider it as anything more than a possibility, which I evaluated."

"And that she was reaching for a bullet. You recall seeing these photographs that there's a bullet lying over there, right?"

"Right."

"And, so, what were you attempting to show in that photo?"

"That if she were reaching for the bullet with the left arm extended and the right hand containing the pistol in some configuration, it places the ear in a position to spatter blood under the arm in the crotch area and back into the room."

"Did you know that the gun at the scene was fully loaded and had a clip in it?"

"I didn't know about the clip. I think there was, yes."

"Do you know why a person would reach down, pick up a bullet to put in a fully loaded weapon? In other words, why would somebody do that?"

"Well, if they had a clip that wasn't full or didn't know it was full they might think they could load it."

"Wouldn't you normally unload the—take the clip out of the gun before holding it to your head like that?"

"I wouldn't."

They returned to the subject a few minutes later.

Townsend: "Under one of your theories—again, I show you the photograph of the girl with the gun to the head, picking up the bullet—if this is an accurate theory, that would mean that she's got a fully loaded gun with a clip in it, holding it to her head?"

MacDonell: "Correct."

There was a second clip, the one not in the gun, that Fletcher claimed he had asked her to finish loading. In MacDonell's photo, not only is the model holding the gun in one hand, but she's holding the second clip in the same hand while reaching with the other hand for the bullet on the floor.

"You've got her holding both the gun and the clip?"

"That's correct."

"Why would a person do that?"

"I don't know why people do a lot of things . . . The reason she's holding it in my reconstruction, or possible reconstruction, is that it ultimately fell on the floor and it's on top of blood. If it's on top of blood, it couldn't have been there before the shooting."

Townsend had gotten MacDonell to make his point for him. The clip *was* found on top of the blood on the floor. The prosecution contends Fletcher put it there while phonying up a crime scene. The defense must account for how the clip came to rest on the blood if Mick didn't put it there. Ergo, Leann must have been holding the clip and the gun and the gun went off and the clip fell on top of the blood expelled from her ear. If convolution were required, so be it.

And then it was time in the cross-examination that many had been waiting for—to get back to the mystery of the blood MacDonell had found, the blood that Legghio had harped on so strongly earlier, the same blood that was so important in pointing toward the bed as the death spot, but which seemed wasn't even human.

The police had taken numerous pictures of the crime scene moments after arriving. The blinds on the windows are clearly closed in them, the same windows where MacDonell found three drops of blood.

"Are the blinds down?" Townsend asked.

MacDonell replied, "They appear to be, yes."

"Would you agree with me that blood droplets cannot go— would not be going through the blind unless you saw evidence of it on the blind?"

"Correct."

"I mean, it can't go around the blind and attach itself to the window."

Snickers in the court.

"If they were in that configuration, they wouldn't go through the blinds."

"Then there came a point in time that you authored a report, or a letter, obviously something different?"

"Correct."

Townsend asked MacDonell if he knew that the Michigan State Police had gone back to the house after being notified that MacDonell had found some other blood stains. He was. Townsend asked him if he was aware that when the police went to the house they found a dead bird in the house. Again, he said he was aware.

"And that there had been quite a bit of other blood stains in the house as a result of that?"

"I wasn't aware of that. I just recall there was a dead bird."

"You were aware that the stains came back as non-human blood, is that correct?"

"I was told that."

"Now, it being non-human blood, then obviously it cannot be used for computations with regard to any type of point of origin, or impact, is that correct?"

"Correct . . . It's an extreme coincidence that the location of them projects back to the area where I believe the shooting occurred, but it's still possible."

Townsend was nearing an end, with several more points to make. He asked MacDonell if he was aware that blood had been found in the hairs and other detritus in the trap of the bathroom sink.

"Human blood?" asked MacDonell, showing that perhaps he had at least been paying attention during Woodford's testimony. It had not been tested as to type, a clear oversight.

"Just traces of blood. Were you aware of that?"

"Beef blood? Steak? I was aware that something had been found, but I wondered if it was human blood."

"I'll ask that again: Were you aware there were traces of blood found in the trap of the sink?"

"I was told that, yes."

"As a criminalist, would that not be significant to you? Assuming they weren't cooking or butchering steak in the bathroom sink, would that cause you any concern as a criminalist?"

"I would be suspicious that someone had cut themselves or got blood on them and washed it off in the bathroom sink."

And then Townsend returned to something he'd been dancing around earlier—that MacDonell is a professional witness who will testify to and about all manner of topics. But this time he wanted to point out that the price had to be right, and it was a very high price.

Townsend: "Professor, can I ask you how much your retainer was on this case?"

MacDonell: "$3,500."

"And how much do you charge an hour?"

"Four hundred, today. At the time I was retained, it was $350, so I have to honor the lower figure."

"Three-fifty an hour. And can you indicate for me how many hours you've put into this case?"

"I honestly can't. I will have to go back and look at the folder, the outside jacket where I keep a rough log of time. I'm very generous with the time I give, so I honestly don't know. I charge for trips, but for working the lab, I don't remember how many hours I put in. Maybe ten."

Townsend had one last brief line of questions regarding why blood spatter wasn't found in the barrel of the Smith & Wesson, but the exchange didn't amount to much, and he turned the professor back over to Legghio for redirect.

MacDonell said he did not see the dead bird that police photographed when they came back to the house on January 7, 2000. And he said that he did not see the amount of blood when he was in the house that showed up on police photos.

"This wasn't there at the time I was there," he said, looking at a photo.

Legghio got into the record that MacDonell held a patent for a device he invented for processing fingerprints and that he has often testified for the prosecution, and he got MacDonell to say that the photos of his model were only meant to suggest that there ways to explain the blood evidence other than that Leann was shot on the floor.

At 5:05 p.m., the witness was excused and the trial adjourned for the day.

After the trial, Ortlieb and Townsend would still chuckle at the thought of MacDonell's poor performance upon cross-examination. And the bird blood had been a continuing source of mirth.

Townsend said after the trial that when they first heard that MacDonell had found blood stains apparently overlooked by police, the first thought was: Did he dare tamper with the scene? And then immediately dismissed that option as too far-fetched. "We thought, 'Surely they can't be stupid enough to doctor the evidence.'"

Police were told, went back to the scene and found the blood MacDonell had mentioned, and other spots of blood, some large—as well as the dead bird. "It turned out a bird had gotten in and flew into some walls," he said. In fact, it had happened several times while the Fletchers had lived

there; one of those times was the notorious incident where
Mick beat the bird to death in front of his wife and daughter.

Lisa Ortlieb wasn't nearly as circumspect as her boss.
Speaking of MacDonell after the trial, she said: "To call him
pathetic would probably be rude, so I shouldn't say that," her
feelings fueled by what she alleged had been a lie told her
by MacDonell when she briefed him before his testimony.
She claimed he misled her. "He told me one thing in the hall
when I was talking to him and testified in court to the direct
opposite."

In fact, during the cross-examination, Townsend had asked
MacDonell briefly about being less than forthright with the
assistant prosecutor. MacDonell first denied talking to her,
then when she was pointed out to him referred to her as "that
gal"—hardly a term to endear him to a young female prosecutor who has specialized in the rights of women victims.
MacDonell denied any falsehood in court, saying his recol-
lection had been faulty at first but was accurate during testimony.

As for the testimony about the blood during Legghio's
direct examination, Townsend smiled broadly and said, "Fine.
We both thought, 'Let him talk all morning about bird
blood.'"

Chimed in Ortlieb: "He made $600 talking about bird
blood. He spent two hours talking on it. What was he making?
Three hundred an hour? Oh, $350? Okay, he made $700 talking about bird blood. I still to this day don't know where they
were going with that."

Jury foreman Rob Jensen admitted after the trial to being
flabbergasted when Legghio came back after seeming to have
finished with MacDonell to ask him whether it would change
his conclusions if it turned out the blood in question wasn't
human.

"I was really shocked," he said. "I thought Legghio made
a big mistake. They spent all this time talking about this blood
by the light switch. *All this time!* Blah, blah, blah—and then,
it wasn't human blood, was it? The blood on the wall, the
blood on the window. If he'd just not done that, it would
have made his case better . . . Sitting on the bed made sense.
So why did he have to be deceptive like that? And that's not

MacDonell, that's Legghio. He's asking the questions. Why the hell would he let him talk about that?"

Why, indeed. It was a question that would stick in people's minds till the verdict came in, and even after. Was it something Marla McCowan had to bring to Legghio's attention during the recess, forcing him to reopen his examination of his star witness? Or was it somehow a tactic gone bad, a willful stratagem to leave the image of the blood in the jurors' minds for as long as possible, then come back after what he knew would be a recess when he first seemed to be done with MacDonell and then do his oh-by-the-way?

If Legghio knew it was bird's blood but wanted to get across that something in one of the drops got MacDonell thinking about looking toward the bed, why not just have him tell it to the jury straightaway, without leaving the impression MacDonell based some grand conclusion by confusing bird blood with human blood?

"Professor, what did you find upon your examination that seemed missing from the police photos?"

"Four spots of blood, three on the window and one by the light switch."

"Did you think they were significant at the time?"

"Yes, they were angled so that they seemed to come from the bed. And once I had begun to think of the bed as the source—where Leann had been shot—all the other evidence, such as the blood on the bedspread and blood on Leann's body, began to make a lot more sense. In fact, by the time I was done looking at the evidence I was convinced that she had to have been sitting on the bed when she was shot. It's the only way it all made sense."

"Now the police subsequently found that the blood got there in the days or weeks after the shooting. Do you recall what they said it was?"

"Yes. Bird's blood."

"So we know it wasn't Leann's blood. Did that change anything about how you thought the shooting might have occurred?"

"Well, obviously it was just a coincidence in that the blood first directed me toward the bed, but all the other evidence still points to that being where Leann was shot.

The floor makes no sense and that theory still defies the laws of physics."

But that was not how the questioning went.

After the trial, Legghio would seem confused that people thought it was an issue. He was, he said, just recounting what happened when MacDonell entered the bedroom, how quickly he could spot evidence, what a master he was of the scene. "I went to the house with him and it was like watching a master at work. He was brilliant," said Legghio, who added that whether it was bird blood or not was irrelevant, anyway. The point was that Leann could not have been shot on the floor the way the prosecution said, and leave blood on the bed. That was physics, MacDonell had said, and the jury believed him.

The cross-examination, most courtroom observers agreed, had been brutal. The prosecution witnesses and team gathered around Townsend to congratulate him as spectators trooped out for the day. The Miseners, no longer dismayed, laughed and joked in the hall, and would still be telling MacDonell jokes the next day before court began.

Still, though, not all of MacDonell's testimony had been undone. The blood on the bedspread was hard to explain in the prosecution's version of events. And the physics of a tiny bullet and a big body seemed unrefuted.

What the Miseners and the press thought about MacDonell was beside the point. Townsend, Ortlieb and Woodford wouldn't have been nearly so satisfied—or had such a pleasant night away from the court—had they been able to look into the jury's minds.

What the prosecution wouldn't find out for weeks was this: MacDonell's testimony, despite Townsend's rebuttals, bird blood or not, had been far more effective than many would have supposed. Once the jury began deliberations, about the only thing they agreed on at first was that they didn't believe the prosecution's theory of events. They didn't just doubt that Leann had been shot while kneeling on the floor. They were *sure* she *hadn't* been.

They believed the physics lesson, particularly the three engineers. And all 12 of them believed MacDonell's theory—

that Leann had been shot on the bed. She had been sitting on the bed, they agreed, and not kneeling on the floor, when the bullet was fired that ended her life and left her lying in a pool of blood.

Woodford came up to MacDonell after the day was done to introduce himself in person and shake his hand. Though Townsend had tried mightily to discredit MacDonell, to make him look like a charlatan, the fact remained that he was a acknowledged by his peers as the master of bloodstain evidence, something of a living legend in the world of criminal forensics, and Woodford wanted a private moment with him.

Woodford was in for a comedown. As MacDonell recounted after the trial: "I told him, 'You really shouldn't have given any evidence in this case.' Before he testifies at any more trials, he really needs to learn more. He's got a science background—he's a serologist—but he's no physical scientist."

DEFENSE DAY 7

The family was still abuzz before court about what they perceived as Townsend's dismantling of Professor MacDonell. But the newspaper headlines barely touched on the cross-examination, except to mention the line about *The Guinness Book of World Records*. They played up his discrediting of the bloodstain evidence against Fletcher.

Thursday wouldn't be as dramatic as Tuesday's back-and-forth with the good professor. The next three witnesses Legghio put on would less colorfully but coolly and dispassionately continue to build a solid defense.

Frederick Wentling took the witness stand at 9:37. He was an independent firearms examiner and, as a 26-year member of the Pennsylvania State Police, an extremely credible defense witness. No mere hired gun, he was a former state trooper who had been been a firearms instructor for fourteen years and had overseen seven other examiners for nine years.

Wentling had testified in numerous state and federal trials, had been trained by the FBI and had done lab work on firearms for the Pennsylvania State Police, the FBI and the US Treasury Department.

He told the court that he had been hired by Legghio in late April to review all the police reports in the case, including autopsy and crime-scene photos and ballistics tests, and had also examined Fletcher's Smith & Wesson. Unlike the prosecution witnesses, he had conducted single-action tests on the gun. After a bullet had been racked and chambered, it required just 5.75 pounds of pull to fire it, compared to 12.5 pounds when it was in double-action mode.

And, he said, that weight need only be applied briefly as the trigger did not need to move much to fire the gun. "On a high-quality firearm—and this is a high-quality firearm—the movement of the trigger is almost imperceptible."

He said that the incomplete stippling pattern in the autopsy photos of Leann's face—her hair prevented a complete pattern—made it more difficult to determine precisely how far the gun was from her ear when it was fired.

Then he buttressed MacDonell's point that Woodford's theory of events—and the prosecution's—that Leann had been shot while kneeling on the floor, with the force of the bullet lifting her up and over to make the blood stain on the bed, was impossible. It was, he said, a simple matter of a basic law of force, one known to all high school science students. "If the bullet from the gun was capable of knocking me over, then it would knock me over when I shot it, because every action has an equal and opposite reaction. The bullet can't hit with any more force than the recoil of the gun."

The body wouldn't be flung up and over? asked Legghio.

Wentling said you can test this counterintuitive point by shooting a bullet into a mannequin. "Nothing occurs. It just sits there. You can punch someone harder than a bullet hits."

Townsend on cross-exam tried to recover, without success. But what happens, he asked, when a powerful .45-caliber bullet enters the head but doesn't exit? Doesn't it have to expend all that kinetic energy somehow?

"Kinetic energy is potential energy, and most of it is converted into heat," said Wentling.

Townsend then pulled one of the old tricks out of the prosecutorial bag: If you can't impugn the testimony, impugn the witness. As he did with MacDonell, he asked how much Wentling was getting paid. It was $100 an hour for examination time, $150 for courtroom time and $30 an hour plus expenses for travel time.

What Townsend didn't tell the jury was that he had his own professional witness on the witness list, Rod Englert, a former cop who makes a living testifying on forensics for prosecutors around the country. Legghio had fired a warning across Townsend's bow before trial, writing him that if he dared bring Englert to court, he did so at his own peril. Englert was never called to testify.

Townsend didn't put Englert on the stand.

On redirect, Legghio did more damage. Leann's hair had

never been tested for gunpowder residue. The closer the gun when fired, the more residue there would be. He asked Wentling for comment, and he replied: "It is common practice to remove it, to properly bag it and submit it to the laboratory for analysis."

After the trial, in an interview for this book, Wentling said he'd been approached by Ortlieb in the hall and challenged on the physics of whether or not Leann's body could have been moved over to the bed. "I told her, 'There's not prosecution physics, or defense physics. There's just physics. Go ask a high school physics teacher. The idea that a bullet that weighs less than half an ounce can lift and move a grown woman is ridiculous."

And he was very critical of the firearms testing by Lt. Thomas of the state police, who had neglected to test the pull required to fire the gun if it were in single-action mode. "This was critical to the case. The examiner doing the work was very remiss in not doing that. It was very unusual to miss that."

Legghio didn't ask Wentling—but he should have—if he'd ever come across cases in his long career where it seemed as if a death might be homicide but it was determined upon investigation that the victim had shot him- or herself accidentally, with the thumb on the trigger? Was it so far-fetched to think Leann might have died this way, too? A reporter asked Wentling those questions months after the trial. His answer? "It's not something that happens every day, but in the real world it is not an unusual thing." He and his investigators, he said, had come across several such thumb-trigger deaths in his years with the Pennsylvania State Police. Murder had always been the first suspicion, and had been ruled out by other evidence.

But Legghio didn't ask those questions. It would be one of his rare oversights in a brilliantly argued case.

John Gifford, a private investigator took the stand at 10:55. He'd been an Indiana cop for eight years and a special agent for the FBI.

He'd driven from the gun range to the house on Hazelwood three times, once at 11:30 a.m., once at 11:50 and once at 12:08. Driving the speed limit, it had taken him 18 minutes the first two times and 14 the last.

When he left the stand, there was a murmur of "What was that about?"

It seemed inconsequential. There certainly wasn't much to cross-exam.

But in his closing arguments, Legghio would use the testimony to assail the prosecution's theory of events. Given the time the Fletchers left the range, considering how long it took even under optimal conditions, there wouldn't be enough time, Legghio would argue, to have sex, commit a murder had been and clean up all by 12:48, when about the only incontrovertible thing about this case happened—the 911 call.

After a recess, Patrick Besant–Matthews took the stand. Tall, wearing wire-rim glasses, he is a Michael Caine look-alike. A native of London, where he got his M.D., he studied forensic pathology at the Walter Reed Army Medical Center, had been with the Institute for Forensic Science in Dallas, was a medical examiner in Anchorage, New Orleans and Dallas, had been a teaching physician at George Washington University, the University of Washington in Seattle, the University of Texas in Austin and the University of Colorado.

He had been certified by a number of pathology boards, was a member of the American Academy of Forensic Science and had taken two blood-pattern courses taught by—who else?—Herbert MacDonell.

His area of specialty was mechanical trauma, including that caused by firearms. He considered himself, he said, an expert on how bullets react with human bodies, had written parts of five books and numerous scientific articles on the subject, including a chapter on firearms in a recent book published in Scotland called *The Pathology of Trauma*.

He had been brought on the case in April and, like Wentling, had studied all the reports and evidence. He had also made two trips to the Fletchers' house, along with Alexander Jason, a crime-scene specialist from San Francisco.

Legghio asked him if Leann's hair should have been bagged and tested for gunpowder. "We did it all the time." And his opinion on how far the gun was from her ear when it went off: "At least seven or eight inches but probably around fifteen."

The attorney showed him photos of the inside of Leann's right thigh, marks Dragovic had called abrasions. They weren't abrasions, said Besant–Matthews. They were streaks of blood, not scratches. Legghio was buttressing a point made earlier that if she'd been shot on her knees, there was blood on both thighs that couldn't be accounted for.

Then Legghio brought him to the main point he wanted him to make, about the possibility the bullet had picked up Leann's body and moved it up and over. Earlier, while recounting his years of expertise, Besant–Matthews had said, regarding perceptions of how bodies react to bullets: "There's a great deal of myth out there. I think we get it from Hollywood."

Now, it was time for specifics. Could a .45-caliber bullet move a 133-pound woman six inches up and nine inches over? "No. It can't do that. It doesn't happen. A bullet weighs half an ounce. The head weighs twelve and a half pounds and is attached to a body. We've all seen pictures of D-Day. Bodies hit with bullets fall forward, not backward. And they were getting hit with far higher impact than the bullets here."

And what about the hands? Did he bag hands in his practice? "Countless times. When you have a case that is of significance, if you feel there is a potential of trace evidence on the hands, you put bags on the hands. That keeps the hands from coming into contact with the sheet or anything else."

Finally, Legghio asked about the police theorizing that the crime scene had been staged because the gun was lying on top of some blood, that it had been placed there by Fletcher after the fact. Besant–Matthews said the mere presence of blood under the gun was meaningless. Why? Because the blood is expelled from the wound and falls faster than the gun, which falls on the pull of gravity alone. "Blood often gets to the floor first."

Besant–Matthews was excused at 3 p.m. His testimony and Wentling's convinced the jury, its members would later acknowledge, that Woodford and the prosecution were wrong in their theory of events. Leann could not possibly have been shot on the floor. After the trial, McCowan said that they also had been instrumental in her belief in Fletcher's innocence—

not for the testimony in court, but in the preparation leading up to the trial. She'd had some doubts, but they had convinced her of the plausibility that Leann had suffered an accidental self-inflicted wound.

Believing the prosecution was wrong about where Leann was shot was one thing. But convincing them that Mick hadn't simply shot her elsewhere would be something else entirely. Besant–Matthews had also made a point for the prosecution that the jury would find crucial—while Leann could have been shot from as close as seven inches, his best guess was closer to fifteen. How crucial remained to be seen.

The day ended with a bit of drama, a prelude to the four minutes of high drama that would play out in court the next day, when the courtroom and jury would hear the infamous 911 tape that had called police to the scene way back on August 16.

Legghio wanted the tape introduced into evidence. Townsend argued against it, saying it was a way for Fletcher to, in effect, testify in the trial without having to be cross-examined. Cooper decided to play the tape in her chambers, then rule.

An hour later, she came back to say she was provisionally allowing it in, but would take the night to reconsider. She would later review case law and decide that the tape fell into the category of an excited utterance and it was played Friday morning before an enthralled courtroom.

At 4 p.m., the trial was adjourned for the day.

Inside the courtroom, Legghio told reporters they would hear for themselves how dramatic the tape was, and it would be clear no one could play-act such a scene.

They ran outside into the hallway to get a response from Townsend. "I'd like to see his psychiatric degree," he said sarcastically. As for his opinion on the playing of the tape, he said: "I don't think the defendant should benefit from his own doing. But I'm not concerned. I don't think it will hurt us. I think they'll see it for what it is. A fabrication."

The reporters scurried off to meet their deadlines. Townsend re-entered the courtroom, his demeanor changed now that the reporters were gone, hurried over to Legghio, slapped him on the arm, flashed him a big grin and said to him good-naturedly, "You know what I just told them? I told them I'd like to see your psychiatric degree."

Legghio leaned over and said something to Ortlieb. They both laughed. Then Hendricks said something to Legghio and there were laughs all round.

Inside, Hendricks wasn't so jovial. He was worried. Badly worried. The case seemed to be getting away from them. From open-and-shut to in-doubt. Maybe Townsend had taken Legghio too lightly. Legghio seemed to have an answer for everything. Things were going bad, and with the 911 tape coming up in the morning, it seemed as if they were about to get a lot worse.

JUDGE COOPER

By luck of the blind-draw system that assigns criminal cases to circuit court judges, Judge Jessica Cooper has presided over more than her share of high-profile, media-glare cases.

She oversaw two of Jack (Dr. Death) Kevorkian's trials on homicide charges involving patients he helped commit suicide. The second, as a result of Kevorkian's notorious appearance on "60 Minutes", where he was shown twisting the dials on his poison-gas machines, which effected the death of Thomas Youk, 53—a sufferer of Lou Gehrig's disease—ended in a guilty verdict and a long prison sentence. Unfortunately for Kevorkian, by that time he had split with Fieger and insisted on representing himself, proving the adage about attorneys who do that having fools for clients.

At his sentencing, Cooper said: "You dared the authorities to stop you. Consider yourself stopped." And then sent him off for 10 to 25.

Thanks to those and other prominent and controversial cases, the room in the Oakland County Courthouse that is reserved for camera crews, technicians and overflows of reporters and media attending trials had long carried a permanent, tongue-in-cheek sign saying: "Cooper's Media Room."

Cooper became a judge by accident, and her path to one of the most prominent judgeships in one of the most affluent counties in North America is at times mystifying even to her.

"I'm a product of the Sixties," she says. "And I'm a city person. How I got to the suburbs is anybody's guess."

Cooper is a tiny woman, soft-spoken both off and on the bench. Attorneys long ago learned not to mistake either her size or her demeanor for weakness of any kind. Upon entering the small suite of offices that housed her, her clerk, secretary and court reporter, visitors were greeted by a sign on the wall: "No Whining." She is a scholar of the law—she is also a professor at the Detroit College of Law on the campus of Michigan State University, specializing in the nuances of evidentiary law—sure of herself, confident in her rulings, the unquestioned monarch of her domain. She is almost hidden up high behind the bench in her courtroom, but she can be ferocious when need be, and intimidating upon command.

Rob Jensen, the jury foreman for the Fletcher trial, would describe her afterwards as: "very neutral to everybody. Very fair. She seemed like the coolest person, but everybody in the jury was terrorized by her. She commanded authority. Here was a person who looked at you and you knew she was an authority figure."

Needless to say, when Cooper told the jury at each of their recesses and adjournments not to discuss the case amongst themselves or with anyone, they obeyed.

She was born in Los Angeles but moved to Michigan as a baby and grew up in Detroit, graduating from the city's premier high school, Cass Tech, in 1964. Detroit was a far different place in those days, still the center of the automotive universe, a forested city whose canopy of towering American elm trees had yet to be ravaged by Dutch elm disease. The buses ran on time and, while it was a city with many problems, most of them involving the gaping racial divides, no one yet called it Murder City.

Cooper went to undergraduate school and law school at Detroit's Wayne State University. While in school, she clerked for three years at a law firm specializing in labor law, and after graduating from law school in 1973, worked in appellate law for two years before starting her own firm in 1975, sharing space with another attorney as she struggled to build a practice.

"In those days, there weren't a lot of women practicing law," she says. And not a lot of work.

As a child of the Sixties, Cooper began specializing in civil rights cases. "Those were the days when they'd tell you, 'I'm sorry. We don't hire women.' Nobody understood it was a violation of Title VII." And she did a lot of probate work, one of those few niches into which women attorneys had been funneled and were allowed to prosper. As the civil rights cases would wend their laborious way through the federal court system, probate law paid the bills.

In 1978, on a lark, never suspecting she could win, in fact expecting to get trounced, she ran for judge of the 46th District Court in southern Oakland County. The incumbent was a character—some would say that is far too polite a description—who had been around Southfield politics forever. A Neanderthal, he had been mayor before becoming a district judge.

He wore red robes on the bench, of all things, and used to keep his own chart of what time of the month women committed crimes. Not time of month as in early, middle or late, but time of the month relative to their menstrual cycle. He was sure he would eventually be able to correlate crime with menstruation, especially the crime of shoplifting.

"I thought his practices were an invasion of privacy and I was very much feminist oriented," she recalled in an interview in her office following Mick Fletcher's trial.

Inside her offices was a poster that read: "Justice, justice thou shall pursue."

And justice she pursued in what she and everyone else thought would be a Quixotic run at the incumbent judge's office.

"I was at some political party and they said, 'Look, nobody can possibly beat him. But, you know, just to let him know he can't get away with this kind of thing, we need a woman to run against him,' " she recalled. "It was not a thing I was going to win. It was for the principle of it."

The police didn't like the judge, either, and so, to her surprise, the conservative police union and the ultraliberal feminist lawyer found themselves working together. The union campaigned for her door to door, her theater group went door to door, her female clients, no matter what time of month, went door to door.

And she won the election by 770 votes. She was 33. Her legal firm had just begun showing signs of being a *real* practice, a way to pay bills and take a vacation now and then and maybe even put something in the bank—"money had just started coming in"—and suddenly *that* career was over and this new one had begun.

It was clear from the start that, although there were too

few women judges and far too much old-boy-networking among the lawyers that came before her, Cooper was not an accidental judge. She was a natural talent on the bench, the kind losers walk away from thinking they had a fair trial.

She won re-election in 1984 with 75 percent of the vote, then ran for the more prestigious circuit bench in 1986. She was the district judge in Southfield, at the southern—and less affluent—end of Oakland County. Southfield abuts Detroit and its once lily-white make-up was fast being diluted by an influx of blacks, who for the first time in southeastern Michigan's history were able to find realtors who'd sell them houses in the suburbs, and Chaldeans, a fast-growing subculture of immigrants and their kids who had bought many of the gas stations and party stores in the inner city and were proving to be the latest success stories in the American melting pot.

Conventional wisdom, then, was that you couldn't get elected to Oakland County's circuit court from one of the south-end cities or towns.

Cooper won a six-year term, this time with 60 percent of the vote. "You should never tell me I can't do something."

In 1992, she easily won re-election, then lost a truly quixotic vote for the state Supreme Court in 1994—candidates run officially as independents, but are nominated at state-wide party conventions and the court is notoriously politicized. She ran as a true independent, without party backing or financial support just to protest the system—"I hate it; it's so ugly"—and shocked everyone by getting half a million votes.

In 1998 she was once more re-elected to the Circuit Court and at the time of the Fletcher trial was running for second district of the State Appeals Court, where she would be able to stop trying felons and move on to her real love—legal scholarship. "There's a time in your life when you say, 'Enough.' I shouldn't be in the public eye," she said, admitting a weariness for TV reporters racing after her, deluges of e-mails, hate mail and, particularly in the Kevorkian cases, death threats and armed guards.

"I want to fade into the background. At 54, I want to get more into academics. The Appeals Court is getting more and more politicized and I want to get in there and say, 'Hey, let's do the analysis. Let's call things right down the middle.

Politics has no business here.' That's been my flag for a while, so I guess I'll have to go up there."

And then there was the sheer psychic weight that dealing with murderers, rapists and other assorted felons on a daily basis for 20 years presses down on you. "I think I've seen more things than I've ever needed to see," she said. "And I've learned more things than I've ever needed to learn. I've seen people who had no souls behind their eyes."

But the limelight wouldn't be fading, and the reporters wouldn't be going away, yet, in the spring and summer of 2000, which had been phenomenally busy seasons even for the energetic Cooper. There would be at least one more set of eyes to look into.

Cooper taught a seminar on trial practice at Emory Law School in Atlanta in early May, then got married on May 27 to engineer Clarke Cunningham, taking a week's honeymoon in Vermont before coming home to begin the Fletcher trial—Legghio had requested a delay which would have extended the honeymoon, but she would have none of it.

And during the long trial, she continued to commute the 75–90 minutes each way, back and forth to East Lansing each Tuesday night, to teach evidentiary law at DCL.

Sometime that summer, she found time, too, to house-hunt, make some bids, buy a dream house and move.

"I'm insane," she'd crack to those who questioned her schedule.

Though she was a product of liberal times and causes, Cooper was a tough sentencer when it came to felonies of violence, and while defense attorneys respected her for her fairness and her knowledge of the law, they didn't necessarily look forward to judgment day.

Jack Kevorkian got 10 to 25 after his second-degree murder conviction in 1999, despite pleas by the defense that a long sentence would amount to a death sentence for the ailing, elderly eccentric. Henry Hearns, the younger brother of world-champion boxer Thomas Hearns, got 27–52 years for his conviction of second-degree murder in the shooting death of his fiancée following an argument at a party.

Those were sentences for second-degree murder, and Mick Fletcher was up on murder one.

THE 911 CALL

On Friday, June 23, the jury—and the packed courtroom—heard the tape of the dramatic 911 call Mick Fletcher made in the moments after his Leann had been shot. The prosecution had fought against its being played in front of the jury and entered into the court record. It was Townsend's contention that not only was the tape dramatic for its content, it was drama of the theatrical variety—Fletcher was playing a role, a role that Townsend could not challenge directly because the accused had not, and was not going to, take the stand.

The tape, Townsend argued in a motion before Judge Cooper, was a way for Fletcher to, in effect, testify without the burden of cross-examination. Cooper took the motion under advisement, but on Thursday had announced that she would allow it and that it would be played in open court on Friday.

Months after the trial was over, she consented to explain her ruling involving what was arguably the most important piece of evidence presented at the trial. Cooper has a well-deserved reputation as a judge who seldom makes an appealable error of law, and she explained that her decision to allow the tape was one in a series of precautions she took along the way to reduce the chances of a guilty verdict, should one come down, being overturned.

"My ruling was by the book," she explained.

With Mick being unavailable for cross-examination about the tape, it fell under the category of hearsay, which is normally prohibited in trial proceedings, but for whose allowance there are a number of exceptions. One of the more prominent of these is if the hearsay is a so-called "excited utterance," most notably in the case of a dying man or woman, the presumption in law being that a dying person is more likely than not to be telling the truth. Whether he or she is or isn't is still a matter for the jury to decide, but the exception to the hearsay rule at least gets it into the record.

While Townsend had argued against the admission of the tape, he would later acknowledge is was a *pro-forma* objection, that he had little expectation of winning the point. Cooper listened to the tape in her chambers with her court reporter, Karen Hollen, who produced a transcript. And then she allowed its admission, later explaining that Michigan case law and precedent were clear on the issue, and that to keep the 911 call out of the proceedings would have opened the door in case of a guilty verdict.

"Jeez, I wish I could tell you my impression of it," she said of the tape. "But it came under the definition of an excited utterance and if you don't let it in, it's an appealable issue. It doesn't matter if I think it's an excitable utterance, but: Does it come under the definition?"

So, Townsend lost his motion, and Legghio gained the right to enter the tape, as dramatic a four minutes as anyone could remember in this or any courtroom. Later, during their deliberations, the jurors would listen to it several more times, as well as read along with the printed transcript.

Spectators sat transfixed, most of them staring at Fletcher as, for the first and only time in the trial, they would hear the voice of the man accused of killing his wife and unborn child—and not just killing them, but shooting her in the back of the head with a Smith & Wesson seconds after depositing a load of sperm in her vagina.

The court seemed to hold its collective breath as the tape began. The Miseners and their relatives fought to hold back sobs, their gasps and sniffling audible against the keening, wailing voice of the distraught man on the tape. Either truly distraught, on the verge of hyperventilating throughout, or—as Shelly Smith of Channel 7 might have described it—an actor giving the performance of a lifetime, with his life in the balance.

911

Fletcher: "Eh, eh, eh. Oh." (The "ehs" that appear on paper to the ear were more like a series of high-pitched, quickly grunted "EEs"; most of what Fletcher said should probably have been re-created on paper in capital letters, to better capture the seeming urgency and the panic sound in his voice, but it was not. In a novel, nearly all of what Fletcher would say would take an exclamation point, as well.)

911 dispatcher: "Hazel Park 911 Emergency."

Fletcher: "Heh, heh, heh." (Louder, more desperate-sounding than the previous "ehs," sounding like someone not on the verge, but in the midst, of all-out hysteria.) "My wife. Heh, heh. She just shot herself in the head. Oh."

Dispatcher: "I'm sorry. I can't understand you. Can you calm down, please?"

Fletcher: "My wife shot herself. Oh."

Dispatcher: "Okay. Your boy shot himself?"

Fletcher: "My wife."

Dispatcher: "Okay. I can . . . Okay, and where is this at?"

Fletcher: "23757 . . ."

Dispatcher: "Okay."

Fletcher: "Hazelwood."

Dispatcher: "Okay. We'll get the ambulance en route."

Fletcher: "Oh, my God."

Dispatcher: "Are you sure you're the only one there alone with her?"

Fletcher: "Yes. Yes. We'd, we'd just, oh."

Dispatcher, apparently to ambulance crew: "Woman shot herself at 23757 Hazelwood."

Fletcher: "Oh. Oh. Oh."

Dispatcher: "Okay. Where is she? Is she . . ."

Fletcher: "She's on the floor. We were . . . We were . . . She was sitting on the bed. I went to the, into the bathroom. I come back out . . . Oh."

Dispatcher: "Okay. She's in the bedroom?"

Fletcher: "She's on the floor. There's blood all over. Oh, my God."

Dispatcher: "Is she breathing? Can you tell if she's breathing?"

Fletcher: (Loud, quick panting.)

Dispatcher: "Can you tell at all?"

Fletcher: "There's nothing. She's on her face. Should I roll her over?"

Dispatcher: "Okay."

Fletcher: "I'm going to roll her over. Oh, sweetheart. Oh, oh, oh my God."

Dispatcher: "We have cars coming. We have cars on the way. Is there anybody else in the house with you?"

Fletcher: "No, I'm alone. My daughter's at her parents' house."

Dispatcher: "Okay. Where, where's the weapon at this time?"

Fletcher: "It's lying on the floor. It's in the . . ."

Dispatcher: "Lying on the floor?"

Fletcher: "It's on the floor."

Dispatcher: "Okay."

Fletcher: "It's on the floor."

Dispatcher: "Okay."

Fletcher: "Oh. Honey. Honey. Oh, oh, oh. Jesus, it's right through her head."

Dispatcher: "Okay. We're on the way. Okay?"

Fletcher: "Oh. Okay."

Dispatcher: "We should be there shortly."

Fletcher: "Honey. Honey."

Dispatcher: "If you panic, you can just stay on the line with me."

Fletcher: "I'm here."

Dispatcher: "Okay. Until the police get there."

Fletcher: "The gun is . . . Should I put the safety on the gun?"

Dispatcher: "No. Just leave it alone. Okay? Do not touch the weapon."

Fletcher: (Panting)

Dispatcher: "Okay. The officers will secure the weapon. Please don't touch anything in the room."

Fletcher: "Oh, sweetheart."

Dispatcher: "Okay?"

Fletcher: "Oh, my God."

Dispatcher: "Is the front . . ."

Fletcher: "Oh, my God."

Dispatcher: "Sir, is the front door unlocked so we can get in?"

Fletcher: "Yes. Yeah, it's open."

Dispatcher: "Okay."

Fletcher: "It's open. Oh, my God. It's all over. Oh, oh, sweetheart."

Dispatcher: "Okay, sir. I know this is hard for you, but you need to help me. You have to calm down a little bit."

Fletcher: "What can I do? What can I do?"

Dispatcher: "Just relax and wait till the officers get there. Okay? Again, if you can't see her breathing or anything, just step out of the room. Okay? And let the officers come in and help you. Okay?"

Fletcher: "She's half naked. We, we were gonna be . . ."

Dispatcher: "I'm sorry. What's that, sir?"

Fletcher: "She's half naked. Should I cover her?"

Dispatcher: "That, just don't touch anything in the room. She's fine. It's fine. Okay? Just leave her the way she is so we can get there and the medical team can assist, okay?"

Fletcher: "Okay."

Dispatcher: "Okay. Is she on any medications or anything?"

Fletcher: "Not that I know of."

Dispatcher: "Not that you know of?"

Fletcher: "Not that I know of. Oh, jeez, there's blood on me."

Dispatcher: "Okay. There should be a car rolling up. Let me know when they show up, okay?"

Fletcher: "Okay. Oh, oh, oh, God. Oh, please help me."

Dispatcher: "Just take, just take some deep breaths. Come on. Relax. You've got to relax. I know it's hard. It's okay. Slow down. Slow down. Come on."

Fletcher: (Panting.) "Why? Why?"

[Note: The questions, and one to follow, seem to be rhetorical, of the Fates or God, not of the dispatcher.]

Dispatcher: "Should be there in just a moment. Just try and relax a little bit."

Fletcher: "Why?"

Dispatcher: "Okay? So you can help us out 'cause we're going to need to talk to you. Okay?"

Fletcher: "Yeah."

Dispatcher: "Okay."

Fletcher: "My God. Oh, my God."

Dispatcher: "We've got the ambulance en route."

Fletcher: "Eh, eh, eh, eh . . . How could she do this? How could she do this?"

Dispatcher: "I don't know."

Fletcher: "Oh, oh."

(Interruption as dispatcher says something to police at the front desk.)

Fletcher: "Oh, my God. I can't believe this."

Dispatcher: "And you say you have kids, also, but they're gone?"

Fletcher: "I've got a little three-year-old girl."

Dispatcher: "Okay, and she's gone? Okay? There's no one else in the house?"

Fletcher: "No."

Dispatcher: "Okay."

Fletcher: "I have a three-year-old girl."

Dispatcher, talking to police: "Talking to her husband."

Fletcher: "Jesus."

Dispatcher: "Did you hear a gunshot go off, sir?"

Fletcher: "Well, yeah. I came outta the john . . ."

Dispatcher: "Okay. Were you arguing at the time, or any problems?"

Fletcher: "No. Not at all. She was . . . We just got back from the firing range. That's why we had the gun out."

Dispatcher: "Okay."

Fletcher: "And . . ."

Dispatcher: "You just got back from the gun range today?"

Fletcher: "Yeah. We were just there. Just. We had the gun out, and . . . Oh, my God."

Dispatcher: "Okay. Okay. Like I said, don't touch anything in the room, okay?"

The next voice on the tape is officer John Heisler of the Hazel Park police, who has arrived at the scene and is talking to the dispatcher: "Who's the caller?"

Fletcher, responding to the dispatcher's last request: "I'm not, I can't even be in there."

Hazel Park officer, Sgt. Craig Fowler, is heard on the tape, talking to Heisler: "The husband is inside the house."

Fletcher: "There's a cop here, now."

Dispatcher: "He's in there, now? Can you see him? Okay?"

(Fletcher steps outside.)

Heisler: "We're out with him."

Dispatcher: "They're there with you, okay, sir? Okay, hang up and talk to them. They're there with you, okay, sir? Okay? Hang up and talk to them."

Fowler: "Step out front, sir."

Fletcher: "Thank God."

Dispatcher: "Step outside."

LAST PROSECUTION WITNESS

Townsend had one last witness, Sgt. William Harvey of the Oakland County Sheriff's Department, who took the stand at 11:30 Friday morning. The purpose of his testimony was to rebut MacDonell's suggestion that the shooting could have occurred on the bed, and to say that if it had, the crime scene had subsequently been tampered with.

Harvey, who had 21 years of service with the county, was in charge of its Special Investigations Unit, which handled most of the department's major crimes, including armed robberies, serial rapes and, of course, homicides. He had been an investigator since 1987 and testified that he'd been involved with upwards of one thousand investigations, had been the lead investigator in about a dozen cases and was secondary investigator 40 or 50 times. He also said he'd been qualified as a bloodspatter expert in one District Court trial and six or seven times in Circuit Court.

His training in bloodspatter evidence consisted of a seminar conducted by one of the leaders in the field, Dr. Stuart James, whom he'd met on a case; two training sessions in Florida that included several hours on bloodspatter; and other seminars that included "portions of bloodspatter, which are gone over and evaluated." He also used James's textbook on bloodspatter in investigations.

Harvey began his testimony by saying that if Leann had fired the gun while sitting on the bed, the gun should have kicked back to the other side of the room, away from where police found it, next to her extended arm, on the floor, though he acknowledged "there are obviously variables; it could have bounced on carpeting or whatever, but I would have expected it to be in this general vicinity."

Before Townsend could proceed, Legghio interrupted. "Your Honor, excuse me. I believe he's asking the witness opinions and yet he's not been qualified."

Townsend then moved to have Harvey qualified as an expert witness in bloodspatter analysis. Legghio asked to *voir dire*, that is, to more fully explore Harvey's background before agreeing to his status as an expert.

Whether it was the stress of a long trial, or the residual emotions from the drama of the 911 tape, Legghio was hardly the placid gentleman he'd been for most of the proceedings. He was brutal and dismissive, disdain dripping from his voice as he conducted his *voir dire*.

"Do you think that physics at all plays a role in bloodspatter evidence?" Legghio asked.

"All the rules you follow—basically, these investigations, these experimentations, have already been conducted by scientists. By no means am I a scientist, I'm a criminal investigator. The ground rules, the math, that is already done. You have your procedures to know that the blood droplet comes out as a sphere, not as a teardrop, this has all been established by the scientists. So basically, to do bloodspatter, you'd don't have to have nuclear or astrophysics, you don't have to have advanced degrees . . . There are rules you follow through the textbooks, such as all droplets are circular when they hit, spines indicate direction, things like that. It's not rocket science, it is just recognition/interpretation."

"I'm not asking you whether or not you read astrophysicists' books and mechanical engineering and engineering mechanics, what I'm asking you is, Do you believe that the law of physics applies to blood stains and the flight of blood?"

Legghio was anticipating a defense by Harvey against claims that Leann couldn't have been shot on the floor, that laws of physics in that scenario could not account for the blood on the bedspread. He was using the *voir dire* to get in some early cross-examination.

"Yes. I do."

"Can you tell the members of the jury how many college-level physics courses you have had?"

"Absolutely none."

"How many college-level chemistry classes have you had?"

"One."

Legghio hit him with a curve.

"Can you tell me, what is sine? I don't mean a stop sign."

"Mathematically—you mean s-y-n?—it's a mathematical formula."

"For . . . ?"

"I use it off of . . ."

"How do you spell it, by the way?"

"I don't know. I'd have to look in my adding machine or whatever."

An adding machine or whatever? Legghio couldn't have written the script any better. The reference to sine and upcoming references to cosine and tangents referred to Mac-Donell's explanation earlier that bloodspatter experts use the rules of trigonometry to help fit the bloody pieces of the murder-scene puzzle together.

"Why would you go to an adding machine?" said Legghio, straightfaced. "What do you use that for?"

"It's got the sine on it already?"

The engineers on the jury were chuckling inwardly. It would be difficult, indeed, for this expert to redeem himself in their eyes.

"What about cosine?"

"Don't know."

"What is cosine?"

"Don't know."

"Well, what about tangent? What's the tangent? What is a tangent?"

"I'd have to go back to the textbooks. I don't recall."

"So, let me see if I understand this. Are you able to give the members of the jury a brief, yet articulate definition of the word 'sine'?"

"No."

"And not for cosine?"

"No."

"How about tangent?"

"No."

"Now, have you taken any elevated mathematics courses at the college level?"

"No. My college is in criminal justice."

"How about serology? Do you have any kind of background in blood? The viscosity of blood? The surface tension of blood?"

"No training other than my dealings with serologists."

Legghio held up the textbook written by James, and Harvey acknowledged it was his guide book.

"Did you know that Professor MacDonell trained Dr. James?"

"I know they worked together."

"Did you know that book you studied from has a statement that says, 'Special recognition is given to Professor Herbert Leon MacDonell, a renowned criminologist of Corning, New York'?"

Townsend objected, way too late. "I understand maybe this is for cross-examination but I thought this was *voir dire*."

"All right, I'll reserve," said Legghio.

"Other than the courses you took, have you had any other type of formalized bloodspatter interpretation or analysis?"

"No."

"I would object to this witness's qualifications, Your Honor."

Townsend asked Harvey how many hands-on cases he had been involved with in bloodspatter. Harvey said it was "fifty, sixty, maybe a hundred."

And how did Harvey assist other agencies or police departments? "What I do is slightly different than what Lt. Woodford does. Being a crime-lab technician, he goes in and measures the scene, he does the measurement of angles, the re-creations, the elastic strings. I go in and interpret the stains that exist and attempt to re-create what occurred in there, both through the photographs and the blood on the floor."

Townsend asked Cooper to grant Harvey expert status. Legghio said he didn't have the proper background.

"The sergeant has specialized knowledge that may aid and assist the jury in the determination of fact," said Cooper. "To the extent that he does not have a background in mathematics or physics goes to the weight and not to his qualifications to aid and assist the jury. He has hands-on experience and that may aid and assist the jury with regard to his determinations."

And so they continued. Harvey was in.

Townsend asked him about the photos MacDonell had taken of a model in a seated position on a bed. Harvey said that if Leann had been shot in this fashion, with the gun in her right hand when it went off, high-velocity blood mist should have sprayed out to the right. And that blood should instantly have started pouring out her nasal passages or wound. "There should be a blood trail from here over to the final resting spot."

"Do you see any?" said Townsend, referring to actual photos of the scene.

"No. This is one of the problem areas." Cooper asked him to move over in front of the jury so they could see the photos better. "The blood trail starts in this diamond of this pattern right here and continues across. There's your final resting spot within that general vicinity and that's where you have this mass amount of blood. This is called pooling blood, where the blood just leaches out from the body. But you can see the blood trail starting here and it continues right along to where Leann is lying down. This is what bothered me when I first saw the crime-scene photographs. If she was over here, this bleeding should not occur. Bleeding is going to be immediate, it should start immediately and continue to the final resting area. There should be no breaks. No void areas. In this case, there is an obvious void area."

Harvey also said that photos of the scene showed blood under where the gun had been when police arrived, and that the area beneath the gun should be void of blood. And that he disagreed with MacDonell that the blood could get there normally as a result of being projected from the body faster than the gun would fall by force of gravity. "It has been my training and my understanding that when the brain stem is severed, there is no pumping of blood, the blood is not going to come out with any velocity. So, I don't see how the blood droplets could get there before the gun."

Townsend asked Harvey if it's proper for police to try to fit evidence to a theory and Harvey said that, no, the proper thing to do is go into a crime scene with an open mind and let the evidence shape the theory. And that one should never throw out evidence just because it doesn't fit a theory.

Townsend had no further questions.

Legghio attacked Harvey with the same vigor he'd displayed earlier. He asked about a crime tape both he and MacDonell had alluded to, one of a man shooting himself in

the mouth with a .357 Magnum before live cameras, a tape
that has become a standard teaching tool at police seminars.

"You said the blood gushes out immediately?"

"Yes."

"Because that's how you said that there would be this trail,
right?"

"Should be, yes."

"But then just a minute ago you said that blood doesn't
pump out quickly after a shot in the head, did I understand?"

"From the pressure of the nasal passages, when they let
go inside the pressure within a controlled closed area like the
cranium, that's going to come out quickly."

"You indicated to Mr. Townsend that you were asked by
him last summer, 1999, to look at these photos and autopsies?"

"That's correct."

"Did you write any reports back then of the things you
did?"

"No, I didn't."

"But you did author a report on June 6th, 2000?"

"That's correct."

"Is this report based on something you did recently?"

"This is based on my examination prior to [Fletcher's pre-
trial exam in September of 1999] and my consultation, my
examination with the evidence and with the other investigators right up until the 6th."

"Have you been to the crime scene?"

"No, I have not."

"Am I to understand correctly, you looked at the crime-
scene photographs and you used a magnifying glass?"

"No, actually what I used is a fingerprint loupe."

He pulled it out and showed the jury.

Legghio asked him if he knew that medical technicians
had touched the body upon their arrival? He did. That blood
smudges and fingerprints showed she'd been touched on both
arms? He did. And that Fletcher claimed to have at least
touched the body? Maybe moved it a bit?

Legghio then asked if he agreed with testimony by Dr.
Besant–Matthews that when the brain stem was severed,
"there would be a complete loss of muscle control and the
body would drop like a sack of potatoes, so to speak?"

"Should be, yes."

Legghio showed him Defendant's Exhibit GG, the one showing a big blood stain on the bed.

"Now, if Mrs. Fletcher were kneeling on all fours, 14 inches off the ground there, and if she went down when she was shot and dropped straight down . . . if she is shot next to the bed and her head is way over past the computer stand with feet [partially] under the bed, how does her body, if it dropped like a sack of potatoes, make contact with the bed?"

"I don't know what energy or how much force she hit that side of the bed. I don't know whether she bounced, I have no idea. All I know is the blood trail starts here and she ends there. How she gets there, I don't know if I can testify to that."

"You indicated, I believe, that you find it suspicious that the gun and the magazine have blood below them?"

"If you take it in its totality, they have blood below them and they have blood on top of them. Combining the two, yes, I do."

"Now, did you realize the report Mr. Woodford prepared said that the blood on top of the gun—in addition to high-velocity blowback spatter, there was also a portion of the gun that had a contact stain?"

"Correct. I believe it's near the ejection port."

"And did you, when looking at the form of Mrs. Fletcher, note that there appeared to be a contact blood stain nearly parallel or perfectly aligned with the firearm were she to be lying on top of it before being rolled off?"

"Show me the photograph."

"I will. Showing you what has been marked Exhibit E and have you take a look at that, do you see a blood stain on her forearm, a more pronounced blood stain further down from the wrist?"

"Yes, I do. I see the stain, yes."

"Now that stain aligns with the contact stain, I would suggest to you, on the firearm immediately adjacent to that stain, would you agree?"

"If you rolled her over, it would be in the same vicinity, yes. Whether it's a mirror image, I can't tell."

"Thank you, sir. I have no further questions."

"I have no redirect," said Townsend.

"Thank you. You may step down," said Cooper.

"I'm sorry, Your Honor. I do. I forgot," said Townsend.

He asked Harvey if he could see a void area in Leann's hands. It was a question they'd clearly rehearsed, for Harvey was ready with an answer and an explanation of a void's importance. There should be a large area on a victim's hand void of any sign of blowback high-velocity blood because the gun would block the mist from hitting the hand. But he could not see any such void area in the crime-scene photos.

At 12:30, Harvey stepped down. He certainly hadn't been the decisive rebuttal witness Townsend had hoped for. His training seemed thin, and his testimony about sines, cosines and having to check his adding machine had given observers one of the few lighter moments in the trial. There was also the irony, duly noted by jurors, of his eagerness to testify solely based on looking at photos, while Woodford had made such a show of just the opposite.

"That was priceless," John Fletcher would later say to his wife of Harvey's performance.

Legghio had put more doubt in the jury's minds—not that they needed any, they would say later—about the credibility of the prosecution witnesses. He hadn't been to the crime scene, he hadn't written up his report for some six months, until just before the trial, and he'd made what might turn out to be an important acknowledgment—that there seemed to be matching stains on the gun and Leann's arms. If her body had rolled over the gun after it fell beneath her, the prosecution couldn't be right about the need for Mick to grab it from the other side of the room and plant it next to her before police arrived.

It had been a good morning for Legghio, he was certain of that.

CLOSING ARGUMENTS

At 9:16 a.m. on Monday, June 26, two weeks after they began hearing testimony, the jury entered Judge Cooper's courtroom to hear closing arguments in the case. Since the state has the burden of proving its case beyond a reasonable doubt, it gets to go first and then it gets to finish up with a rebuttal of defense arguments.

"Good morning, ladies and gentlemen," Townsend began his 32-minute summation. "Before I begin, I'd like to personally thank you. We've noticed that—it's been quite a long trial and quite a few witnesses—we've noticed you've paid very close attention to the witnesses and the evidence and taken a lot of notes. On behalf of myself and my office, on behalf of the victim, I would like to thank you for your close attention in this matter."

Townsend told them of a young woman they'd gotten to know a bit during this trial, a young mother who loved her daughter, who had a special relationship with her, who could never have committed suicide. And then, interestingly, since he was the county's expert prosecutor on forensics and this case had been billed as one of clear-cut forensics by his office since Fletcher's arrest, Townsend said:

"Ladies and gentlemen, I'm going to ask you, and actually I'm going to urge you, that when you consider the evidence in this case, you use your common sense when you look at the evidence. I urge you to use your everyday life experiences when you analyze this evidence in this case. For if you do, because this is a common-sense case, the evidence will become clear to you, the evidence that's there, as well as the evidence that's not there. High-velocity mist. Gunpowder residue. Evidence that would have been there had she shot herself in the head. Blood and mist that would have been on the comforter but does not exist."

What had begun as a case of forensics, with the prosecution trumpeting many months earlier the supposedly damning bloodspatter on Fletcher's green Oxford shirt, had become a case not of science but of common sense. Not of measurements and scientific testing so much as: Come on, you think it was a coincidence she got shot the one and only day she went to a shooting range in her life? It was a change in focus that would have made even more sense to Townsend if he could have seen into the collective mind of the jury and seen how little it thought of the forensics.

Townsend then went to motive. "Right from the beginning we know Michael Fletcher did not love Leann. He had a different interest. That interest was Judge Susan Chrzanowski, whom he was having a very detailed love affair with, a very intimate affair with, for well over a year, year and a half." And then he read two of Fletcher's e-mails to the judge, including one that concluded with: " 'I miss you already. I am so anxious for the day when I never have to say that again. That's my hope for the future, anyway. I love you, Susan. Mick.' "

From motive, he got to the strength of his case—the seemingly non-common-sensical series of events that happened in the bedroom of the house on Hazelwood, as recounted by Fletcher.

"The defendant tells police, well, I had gone to work and then I returned and then we dropped off Hannah, then we went to the gun range. She was afraid—she didn't like shooting, so we came back and we were going to have sex. That's what he told the officers.

"The facts and the evidence, I suggest to you, show something different. The facts show that Leann had fresh semen in her vaginal cavity. She was found naked from the waist down, so tests were conducted and there was fresh semen. And if you also recall, the defendant's undershorts were taken and also examined by the Michigan State Police and that there was semen in his undershorts. I suggest to you what the evidence actually shows is that in fact he had sex that day, prior to the death of Leann.

"He further tells the police that while she's sitting there, sitting on the bed, while she's naked from the waist down, while she's waiting to have sex with him, that at this point in time he's decided to load his gun and that he loads a full clip, that he puts one bullet, one round, into the chamber. He then tells the police that [he] started loading the second clip again, Leann is waiting to have sex with him. But he's having a hard time loading the clip and therefore, since he's having a hard time, he gives the second clip to Leann to load.

"Again, I ask you when applying that, does that make sense, is that reasonable? You have a complete novice at guns, somebody that doesn't like guns, somebody that is afraid of guns, and I suggest to you has no idea on how to load a clip, and he's asking her to load the weapon."

Townsend then got to the forensics. He said that if MacDonell's theory was correct and that Leann had somehow pulled the trigger with her thumb, there should have been high-velocity mist on her hand. But tests showed none of it. Other tests showed that the Smith & Wesson was a heavy depositor of gunpowder residue but none was found on Leann's hand. And that police firing tests concluded the gun had to have been between 12 and 18 inches from Leann's head when it was fired.

Townsend reminded them of the photo of MacDonell's model, the one with her holding both the gun and the clip in her right hand, with her thumb on the trigger. "It comes down, again, to common sense and everyday life experiences. First of all, would Leann, who hates guns, who is afraid of guns, would she have ever touched it? Would she ever put her thumb into the trigger of the gun? If she's got the clip, would she ever do anything like that? I suppose if we just completely devoid ourselves of our life experiences and common sense, I suppose anything—anything—is possible. But is it reasonable? I suggest to you, absolutely not. There was no reason for Leann to touch that gun and she wouldn't have touched that gun."

Finally: "I think the evidence has shown that at the scene the defendant washed his hands. I forgot to mention one thing. Also recall as far as the phone, the cordless phone that was taken, there was no blood on that. There was blood found in the sink of the trap [sic] and I think that's important. If you find blood in the trap of the sink, according to Mr. Wood-

ford, that would have taken a great quantity or a large amount
of blood in order to even get that testing. He's been testing
it for 19 years. It's the first time he was able to even come
up with a showing that is indeed blood.

"When I asked his one expert, Dr. Besant–Matthews,
'Well, Doctor, do you find it significant that there's blood in
the trap of the sink?' He goes, 'No.' I go, 'Why don't you
think it's significant?' 'Well, I don't think it's significant because he had moved the body. He had touched the body.'
And I asked him 'So he had blood on his hands so he washed
them?' And his response was 'Well, wouldn't you? Would
you want that sticky stuff on your hands?'

"Ladies and gentlemen, I suggest to you that if I had gone
out and seen my wife—or a person goes and sees a wife or
a husband lying on the ground, that they're bleeding, don't
know if they're alive or dead, don't know the extent of their
injuries, the first thing they're going to do is attempt to find
out, is to embrace, to cradle, to comfort. I don't think I'd go
wash my hands and then decide to call 911.

"Ladies and gentlemen, the defendant may have washed
his hands at the scene attempting to get the blood of Leann
Fletcher off his hands. But, ladies and gentlemen, the blood
of Leann Fletcher will always be on his hands. It will be on
his hands for the rest of his life.

"Ladies and gentlemen, I ask you to hold the defendant
accountable for what he did on August 16th, 1999. I ask you
to hold him accountable for his actions. I ask you to return a
verdict consistent with the evidence in this case and consistent
with justice in this case. I ask you to return a verdict of guilty
of murder in the first degree."

It was a powerful summation, made all the more powerful
by its brevity. Wisely, Legghio asked for 10 minutes to mar-
shal his resources. The jury was excused at 9:50 a.m. and
came back at 10:02.

It was a hard act to follow. Legghio followed it brilliantly.
For an hour and 45 minutes he tore into the prosecution's
theory of events and motive, and he ripped into its witnesses.
He savaged Woodford, in particular. He was alternately calm
and passionate, quiet and thundering. It was a performance
worthy of a client whose future was at stake. Michael Fletcher

would soon be either going home to his parents and the best meal his mother could make him, or he would be going back to jail, possibly for the rest of his life, with no possibility of parole.

"During the course of trial, and even probably during the course of my closing argument, I sometimes have a tendency to be irreverent," Legghio said, after, like Townsend, thanking the jurors for their attentiveness. "I have a tendency to be somewhat disrespectful, maybe, perhaps to witnesses or even authority."

He was actually warning them of the disrespect and irreverence toward witnesses and authority that lay moments ahead.

"And if you found that was inappropriate, if you thought I was inappropriately aggressive with a witness or if I conducted myself inappropriately, I apologize. But I will tell you, I take my job very, very seriously. I try not to take myself too seriously, but I take this job very seriously. And so if I have at all offended you, do not hold that against my client."

He made a few more introductory comments and then got to the heart of things: lack of motive.

"I think that the very, very threshold issue that you have to deal with when you go to the jury room is why—why—would Mick Fletcher kill his wife? Now you'll hear law by the judge that says motive is something that you may consider but the prosecution doesn't have to prove it. They don't have to prove it, which, I don't know, is a bit of an oxymoron to me. Their whole case from the day that you walked in this courtroom is that my client murdered his wife in cold blood.

"And that's the motive. Because, you know, if you're going to go in that room and deliberate about bloodspatter and stippling and gunshot residue, I think at least the threshold issue that you better be crossing is, Why is this guy killing his wife? He's 29 years old. He just passed the bar a couple of years ago. He's a fledgling young lawyer. He has a three-year-old daughter. Why would you murder your wife?

"You have heard not one—one!—not one drop of evidence that my client has an assaultive behavior, whatsoever, that he's an angry man or a pent-up person or an assaultive person. And in fact, if you use your common sense as Mr. Townsend wants you to do, what you'll deduce, I think, using a little bit of psychology here, is that my client has all the classic behavioral patterns of avoidance and denial. He's a classic guy who doesn't want to deal with issues.

"He moved out of the house three times. Is he dealing with the issue? No. He's filed a divorce. Is he dealing with the issue? Well, he's taking steps, he made a pronouncement to the world, you know, I'm going to divorce my wife. And what does he do? He moves back in.

"What does Susan Chrzanowski say? 'He left me three times.' In fact, one time she even said, 'On the day my divorce was final, he moved back in with Leann.' Now, if that's not a message . . . He's engaged in a behavior pattern where there's flight rather than fight. He's left his wife three times, and his baby, and filed for divorce. Why would you go and kill your wife?"

Then, in a line of reasoning that jury members would later say was crucial in shredding Townsend's theory of motive, Legghio said: "Quite frankly, I think if you examine that relationship with Susan Chrzanowski, examine her testimony, do you really believe that stuff? 'Oh, if I knew he was having sex with his wife, I'd just—well that would be it!' Yeah, right . . . They say he wants to be with the judge. Whenever he wanted to be with the judge, he was with the judge. He was with her three times, he left her three times. So it's not that.

"Why did he kill her? Because he didn't want the judge to find out his wife was pregnant? Really? . . . Do you really think that if Leann had kept on living and had this baby and Mick said, 'You know what? I'm sorry we had another child but I'm done, I just can't do this,' do you really think Susan Chrzanowski wouldn't take him back? In a heartbeat. In a heartbeat.

"And so the prosecution says, 'The reason he's willing to kill his wife is because he doesn't want her to find out she's pregnant. Well, lordy, lordy. When she dies, the whole world knows she's pregnant. He was going to keep her pregnancy from the judge if he killed her? *Duh!* Do you honestly believe that? And so now the judge says, 'Gee, Mick, now we're together. Let's see, your wife died under suspicious circumstances, a gunshot to the head.' Well, that's going to make for a very rosy, long-term investment in the relationship, isn't it?"

*   *   *

Having apologized in advance for sometimes being "somewhat disrespectful" toward witnesses, Legghio went on to become very disrespectful. He mocked Cleyman, tried to take Dragovic down a peg or two and downright savaged Woodford.

(Legghio needn't have apologized in advance to the jury. When the twelve of them began their deliberations later that day, they would find themselves agreeing that they thought Dragovic was arrogant but trustworthy; that Cleyman had made a precipitous rush to judgment based on far too little; and that they downright hated Woodford, whose stubborn refusal to comment on defense photos showing blood on Leann's thigh—blood that was hard to explain if she'd been shot in a kneeling position, as he contended—nearly single-handedly destroyed the credibility of much of the police witnesses in their eyes. He had no way of knowing, but when Legghio criticized those three, he was preaching to the converted.)

"Sgt. Cleyman was absolutely sure, he knew the minute [Fletcher] walked down the stairs of the police department, he was guilty as sin. Well, Sergeant, how did you know that? 'Well, one, he was a defense attorney. And two, he took his wife to the shooting range. I've been married 13 years, I haven't taken my wife there. And he didn't have any blood on him. I knew right then. I knew right then. Stone-cold killer.' Really? How interesting."

Of Dragovic? "I like Dr. Dragovic and he presents himself well as a good expert witness. But I suggest to you that there is a fair amount of professional, systemic, institutional arrogance attendant and attached with his testimony."

Legghio criticized Dragovic for being so quick to determine from the stippling pattern that Leann had been shot from 12 to 18 inches away, while admitting under cross-examination that different forms of gunpowder have different stippling patterns and that he didn't know what kind of powder was in Fletcher's gun, or even what caliber it was.

He criticized Dragovic for saying a lack of blood mist on Leann's right hand was critical, while not knowing her hands had been swabbed for gunpowder residue the night before.

Most telling, Legghio presented a blow-up to the jury of

some of Dragovic's testimony from June 12. "This is what I call institutional or the systemic arrogance," said Legghio. On the 12th, he had asked Dragovic if Leann's hands were bagged when the body got to the Medical Examiner's Office. Dragovic had said, as the enlarged words pointed out to the jury, that they had been.

"The bagging of hands in this particular case where we're talking about blood mist is important," said Legghio, "because you can use your common sense about rubbing on the cloth and rubbing on the body bags. Why didn't he just simply say, 'You know what, I do a lot of autopsies. I think they were, I'm pretty sure they were, and as a matter of procedure we usually do it?

"I mean, he doesn't just say it once. Were her hands bagged? They were? 'Yes.' They were? 'Yes.' Can you show a photograph? 'I don't take photographs of bagged hands.' So the bags were removed prior to photographing? 'The bags were removed prior to photographing.' Amazing. Once, twice, three times he tells you, 'I certainly know it. They were bagged.'

"I think this is problematic. Why so committed? So committed to provide you testimony, sworn testimony under oath, that he knows. And not just once, not like, 'You know, oh gee, I misunderstood your questions now that I look at it.' No. Three times. He knows. He's certain of it. That's someone who is unwilling to say, 'You know, I think there could be some margin of error.' No, none of that at all. It is Drag's way."

The jury didn't like Woodford and neither did Legghio. He had infuriated the defense attorney when he refused to comment on photos of large blood stains on Leann's thigh during cross-examination, and now it was payback time. He attacked Woodford's claim to be an expert in bloodstain patterns, having taken two courses in 12 years but never having been published, nor belonging to any related organizations.

And then, sarcasm dripping from his voice, he paraphrased some of his earlier back-and-forth with Woodford involving a display Woodford had made to show the jury different forms of bloodspatter:

" 'Well, Mr. Woodford, you're the expert. Will you tell

the ladies and gentlemen of the jury what size are these cast-off [blood] patterns? Do you know? 'No, I don't. It's in the book.' All right. Well, go take a look. 'Castoff patterns, according to the book, are three millimeters to six millimeters.' 'Really? And this is your exhibit?' 'Yes, I created this.'

"And what did Professor MacDonell say? In front of you, using a measuring device, he measured this [exhibit] and said there are numerous, numerous castoff stains of a millimeter or less. Now why is this important, besides the fact that it may be a bit embarrassing for Mr. Woodford? Besides the fact that he doesn't really know blood stains that well [that he should] come in here, in my opinion, and testify as an expert in a first-degree premeditated homicide case."

Legghio attacked not just Woodford but the logic behind thinking the blood in the sink was critical. " 'That's proof, there it is,' say the People. Really? So then why does he say on the phone [the 911 call]—if he's going to wash his hands and come back to this staged crime scene—why does he say, 'I've got blood on me'? It defeats the entire purpose."

Legghio disputed Townsend's contention that it was evidence of guilt that Fletcher had not hugged Leann and got more blood on himself. "Oh, my God, why would you grab somebody like that? Would you not think, 'I might be hurting them more'? 'I don't even know what I'm doing'? You would pick somebody up? You would dare move that body?"

Legghio attacked police procedures at the scene—nobody bagged Leann's hands, a crucial oversight, leaving subsequent tests for gunpowder residue in doubt. Crime-scene photos show her hands covered in blood; the one photo of her hand during the autopsy the next day shows nearly all the blood is gone.

Legghio also questioned Townsend's assertions that Fletcher had sex with Leann before killing her. It made for a nasty mental picture—of a homicidal villain able to get an erection and ejaculate even though he knows he is about to murder the woman he's having sex with, and murder in the most gruesome, bloody fashion. But in fact, pushing the claim did nothing for the case, except to help demonize Fletcher.

In fact, the evidence was nowhere near conclusive and even hurt the case, by making the time-line so much more jammed up. There was very little time as it was between leaving the gun range and calling 911. Trying to prove sex occurred, too, seemed superfluous to observers. Why the emphasis on it? Because it painted such a horrible image that it was worth it?

Legghio brought up during cross-examination and again in closing that sperm is considered fresh within 72 hours of ejaculation, so the sperm in Leann's vagina could have been deposited before the weekend even began. And the test of Fletcher's underpants wasn't done for many months, until just before the start of the trial, and then revealed seminal stains, which may have been proof of nothing more than bad laundry habits.

"So, there is no proof that these people had sex immediately before this," said Legghio. "There's no proof of that whatsoever, but that is what I think you are encouraged to believe."

Legghio criticized Woodford for his insistence that there were many blood-mist stains on Fletcher's shirt, yet even pooled together were too little for a DNA match, even though other blood-mist stains in the room were big enough to be seen with the naked eye.

Finally, Legghio got to what had been bugging him since the early days of the trial—and had been bugging the jury, too—Woodford's refusal to comment on Defendant's Exhibit W, which showed blood running off Leann's thigh. " 'How did it get there?' " said Legghio to the jury, re-creating an event still vivid in their minds. " 'I don't know. I'm not going to give you any opinions. I gave my opinion. I'm not going to look at pictures and give you opinions.' 'Wait a minute, you're an expert, this is what you're supposed to do. Did you look at this? Tell the jury what you make of that?' 'I'm not doing it. I won't do it.'

"If I was aggressive with him or seemingly disrespectful, I'll tell you where it came from. It came from frustration when you come in front of a jury, you testify about bloodstain analysis, you testify you're an expert. You're providing testimony on this man who's facing a first-degree premeditated murder and you say, 'I'm not going to answer your question'? 'You're not going to answer my question? He's facing murder. And you're not going to answer how that blood got there, Mr. Woodford?' 'Don't ask. I gave you my theory.' "

(Legghio's disregard for Woodford wasn't just for the jury's benefit. He would say later: "Woodford looked like a buffoon.")

Legghio finished rebutting Woodford's forensics by saying he had failed to explain blood mist on the bedroom mirror; that the physics were irrefutable that Leann could not have been shot on the floor and then propelled up and over to the bed; and said that Woodford's own diagram of the gun included bloodspatter on the right side of the gun, which would have been impossible had Fletcher pulled the trigger.

Legghio thought the last point, alone, would be telling in the jurors' minds. He hadn't spent much time during the trial on the diagram. "I laid the snare," he would say after the trial, explaining why he saved closing arguments to stress the point. "It was a Perry Mason moment, and you *never* get that. A defense attorney *never* gets that. It's uncontroverted. It's Woodford's own diagram. If there's bloodspatter there, how does he grab the gun and pull the trigger? He can't. It's impossible. But it is consistent with Leann picking the gun up."

(After closing arguments, Townsend would respond to reporters: "I don't know how he held the gun. But I know who held the gun.")

Legghio wrapped things up by returning to the time-line. The Fletchers arrived at the gun range at noon. They fired at least 40 rounds, based on the target later found on the couch in the front room, and left about 12:25. They drove home, which, according to test drives done by Legghio's private attorney, took between 14 and 18 minutes. "If you sit down and add these times up, you'll see that my client had about seven minutes to get out of the truck, leave the targets across the couch, go into the bedroom, have sex, ejaculate, shoot her, go in the bathroom, wash up and call 911."

Legghio reminded the jury that his client had a presumption of innocence, no matter how unsavory his personal life or how much they might dislike him. He told them that in the English system there is a verdict called "not proved" and they might want to think how that seemed to apply here, that this was a situation where the People's case was "not proved." He thanked them for their time, asked them to return a verdict of not guilty and sat down. It was 11:45 a.m. Time for a recess.

*   *   *

Townsend began his rebuttal at noon. He told the jury that Cooper would explain to them that closing arguments are not evidence and that Legghio's closing went well beyond the evidence and shouldn't be considered as such.

"I noticed in his closing argument that he pretty much attacked everybody. I guess this has got to be the world's largest conspiracy in the history of Oakland County. And by God, we've got Judge Chrzanowski, we've got Officer Lehman, also the ET or EMT, the medical technician that arrived is in on this conspiracy, we've got Sgt. Cleyman, we've got, I guess, the entire victim's family involved with this, we now also have Dr. Dragovic involved with this conspiracy as well as Mr. Woodford."

For the first time in the trial, Townsend seemed personally perturbed at his opposition. He then addressed the 911 tape.

"I want you to listen to that tape several times, too, because I think if you listen to it, you're going to be able to see through it. And as I stated in my initial summation, one's actions speak far louder than one's words. If that weren't the case, then all a person would have to do is if they murder somebody, 'Gee, let me just call in, I'll act upset, I'll act excited, I'll act frantic,' and they're all done."

And then he tried to repair the damage to the state's claimed motive. "Mr. Legghio says, well, everybody would have known that Leann was pregnant. Again, that's wrong because if the police bought the story, if the police believed it to be an accident, nobody would find out about it . . . The only reason it came out is because there were charges and it went to trial."

Townsend took another shot at Legghio. "He talks about blood in the sink. I tell you what: Mr. Legghio has got an explanation for everything in this case. But you know what? He has to. And I don't blame Mr. Legghio. If I was Mr. Legghio, I suppose I'd do the very same thing, because all this evidence has a tendency to hurt his client. In fact, each of this evidence, by itself, is sufficient to convict the defendant as to the crime that was committed.

"Well, let's talk about that blood because that's one of the last things he talked about, with regard to the blood in the sink. He goes, 'Oh, that blood in the sink. Well, that could have been, we don't know if it's human blood, we don't know if it's animal blood, it was never submitted for DNA.' You heard Mr. Woodford testify when they do that test, it's the first time in nineteen years that he found blood in a sink, and that in order for him to find the blood . . . I suggest to you that it's not animal blood. I don't believe that they were cutting up food or cutting up steaks that morning while they were there at the house.

"I suggest to you the reasonable inference was that it's human blood. I think you can fairly infer that from the evidence. Was it submitted for DNA? No. There just wasn't sufficient enough evidence or blood to submit it for DNA."

Townsend briefly defended each of his witnesses in turn, and their conclusions and then returned to the weakest part of his case: motive.

"Motive does not have to be proven. But I tell you what, ladies and gentlemen: I think everybody wants to come up with an idea why somebody would do something. I've been doing this for quite a while and I can tell you now, I can't get into the mind of a murderer as to why certain people do certain things. We do know that he had an extensive love relationship with Judge Susan Chrzanowski. We do know that he had lied to both Leann and to Judge Chrzanowski. . . . We do know that Judge Chrzanowski had indicated to him basically if she knew that there was any type of intimate relationship or any type of sexual activity or closeness, that would end the relationship.

"What went through his mind on that day? I don't know. I certainly know that there were reasons for it and reasons that I can't possibly explain to you."

Townsend then reinforced a point that would be at the heart of the long jury deliberations that lay ahead: "As far as the gun itself, the gun should have been to the right. [If] she was sitting on the bed, it should have been to the right, rather than to the left, where it was found. . . .

"Ladies and gentlemen, you've heard the entire case. You've heard all the evidence. . . . This is not a grand conspiracy in Oakland County. There's not a conspiracy between Judge Chrzanowski, Officer Lehman, Dr. Dragovic, Mr. Woodford and all the witnesses that came before you. It just doesn't happen that way.

"Ladies and gentlemen, Leann Fletcher did not shoot herself. And I guess that's why I say, use common sense. And I agree with Mr. Legghio: Please do use common sense in analysis of all the evidence in this case . . . I'm going to ask you again, when you go into deliberations, to return a verdict consistent with the evidence and consistent with justice.

"Don't give the defendant what he wants. Give him what he worked for. Give him what he earned. Give him what he deserved. Return a verdict of guilty of first-degree murder. He's earned it."

Judge Cooper instructed the jury that they could only base their decision on the evidence presented and her instructions about the law. She defined for them reasonable doubt—"doubt that is a fair, honest doubt growing out of the evidence or the lack of evidence. Now it's not merely an imaginary or possible doubt, but it is a doubt based on reason and common sense. A reasonable doubt is just that: a doubt that is reasonable after a careful and considered examination of the facts and circumstances in this case."

She told them they must not consider the fact that Fletcher didn't testify as evidence of guilt, that they were free to believe or disbelieve any witness as they felt fit, that they were free to assess a witness's bias or prejudice, and that an expert opinion was just that: opinion, and not fact.

She told them that first-degree murder required four elements—that the defendant caused the death, that the defendant intended to kill, that the act was premeditated, even if just for seconds ahead of time, and that it was deliberate, a result of considering pros and cons.

Cooper also told the jury that under Michigan law—[unlike in some other states]—that even though Fletcher was charged with first-degree murder, they were free to judge him guilty of the lesser charge of second-degree murder, which didn't involve premeditation.

She then pulled two numbers out of the 14 that were placed in a box before the trial, blindly pulled out numbers five and twelve, and those two members of the jury were excused from further duty.

At 12:49 p.m., the jury walked out of the courtroom and into the jury room. Within seconds, they would begin debating Fletcher's fate.

DELIBERATIONS

As the jury began its deliberations Monday afternoon, the Miseners were sure of a quick guilty verdict, the Fletchers were equally confident of a not guilty, and both Legghio and Townsend knew juries well enough to be aware that predictions were useless, especially in a case relying so much on forensics and with so much conflicting testimony.

No one could have foreseen the dramatic circumstances that would unfold in the jury room over the next four days—four days of building tension and agony for the two families as they paced the hallway outside Cooper's courtroom—or the unprecedented and highly controversial way the jurors would attack their deliberations.

What no one knew as the ten men and two women began their deliberations—two women out of the original pool of 14 jurors were eliminated by blind draw at the end of the trial—was the remarkable unanimity they had toward crucial aspects of the case. Had Legghio known what was in their minds, he would have been ordering up cold champagne on his cell phone. Townsend would have been dismayed. And the Miseners would have been in absolute disbelief.

There wasn't much time left in the day. The first order of business was to take a quick vote, not that anyone expected it to be decisive. But it would give them a starting point for their discussions.

Rob Jensen, a senior engineer at General Motors' sprawling Technical Center in Warren, had earlier been selected jury foreman. "Somebody said, 'Who wants it?' Nobody said anything. It was like dead quiet. It seemed like a year. I've got a pretty outgoing personality, so after nobody wanted it, I said, 'Well, if nobody wants it, I'll volunteer.' I couldn't even

get the words out of my mouth and they were like, 'Yeah!' "
he recounted.

Jensen asked if they wanted to vote and then they did so,
orally. It was seven for conviction, four for acquittal, one
unsure. Then, in their first 15 minutes in the jury room, they
agreed that, given Leann's love for Hannah and her family
and her excitement over the new baby, suicide was impossible. Not that it had been brought up as a practicable defense,
but the jurors decided to rule it out anyway, and they did.

That still left a range of options to discuss—not guilty,
guilty of first-degree murder, guilty of second-degree murder
or guilty of manslaughter. They went back and forth for a
while, haphazardly discussing the case, making no progress,
very much disorganized and without a blueprint for how to
proceed before they broke for the day.

That night, Jensen decided to try to get things organized,
and the next morning, at his suggestion, they began to get far
more systematic, as befitting a jury with three engineers. It
also included a small-town postmaster, the woman who
owned the dog-bakery in affluent Birmingham and the older
woman who had said at jury selection that she'd be able to
overlook the issue of adultery because her father and husband
had committed it.

Jensen asked Cooper for a flip chart and markers, where
they could start writing things down on big sheets of white
paper. He wrote down reasons that people thought Fletcher
was guilty and reasons that they didn't. They put together a
chronology of events. They compiled a list of things they all
agreed on, and a list of all those they didn't.

These were people who had spent nearly three weeks sitting in judgment of the kind of high-drama, life-and-death
issues most people only read about in bad novels or see on
made-for-TV movies. They'd seen gruesome color photos of
Leann in a thick, red-black sea of her own blood that had left
some of them crying. They'd watched at close range as a
young judge had told of her affair. They'd watched her cry.
They'd listened to the heart-rending testimony of the Miseners and their loss. And they'd had to keep it all inside. Not
one of them had been able to talk about the trial with a spouse
or friend, they hadn't even been able to discuss it with each
other during their many recesses and lunch hours and all those

boring times sitting around waiting to be summoned back to the court. Now, finally, they were able to talk about all the amazing events they'd seen or heard.

They quickly discovered that doubts they thought might be theirs and theirs, alone, were doubts they all shared. Despite their differences regarding guilt and innocence, as Jensen began totting up things on the giant sheets of white paper—some 25 of them would eventually fill the walls of the small jury room—they quickly realized they were in nearly unanimous agreement about many of the major elements of the case.

And what they agreed on was, they didn't buy almost any of the elements of Townsend's case against Mick Fletcher. What they agreed on was:

- They didn't believe much of the forensic evidence against Fletcher.
- They thought Townsend did a lousy job of placing Mick in the bedroom at the time of the shooting.
- They distrusted or outright disliked many of the prosecution witnesses. They thought some of them were incompetent and suspected others of lying.
- They disagreed with Townsend's version of a motive—that Mick had killed Leann to keep the judge from finding out he had been having sex with his wife all along. They agreed with Legghio's closing arguments that the judge would have gone right on forgiving Mick and would have taken him back in a heartbeat. And they thought that it made no sense whatsoever to stage a crime scene that involved getting ready for sex if you were trying to hide the fact that you were having sex with your wife.
- Most telling of all: They agreed with Legghio's witnesses that Leann could not have been shot on the floor if there was any accounting for the blood on the bedspread. MacDonell and others had said that was a violation of the laws of physics, and the jury, particularly the three engineers, agreed with them.

Jensen, in a two-hour interview at his home after the trial, had this to say about Townsend's witnesses:

"Nobody on the jury disagreed with this: Everyone was thoroughly—I want to say disgusted—with the way the police handled the investigation. Not Mr. Townsend, who was a class act all the way, but some of his witnesses really infuriated the jury. Part of the people who [were] originally thinking not guilty, a lot of it was everybody just had this rage against the police in this case. People were even using the word 'conspiracy.'

"You gotta get to the truth, and I didn't get that impression from a lot of witnesses for the prosecution. It sounded to me like 'This guy was guilty,' and they were going to say whatever it took to get him convicted. . . . It seemed to me the witnesses were tailoring their testimony [and] that infuriated me."

As for Sgt. Cleyman, who admitted under cross-examination that he had used the words "stone-cold guilty" in assessing Fletcher after his interview with him at the Hazel Park police station just after the shooting, Jensen said: "To us on the jury, it scared the hell out of us.

The jury thought Dr. Dragovic was believable but they thought he "came off as an arrogant ass."

As for Woodford, he came off worst of all. "Here was a guy who was actually getting upset on the stand," said Jensen, "and he was refusing to testify off photographs for the defense but he would for the prosecution. There were people on the jury who literally very aggressively hated this guy. They didn't like this guy at all."

Late in November, ABC's news show "20/20 Downtown" finally aired its coverage of the Fletcher trial, calling it "The Final Verdict." It was supposed to air earlier in the month but was bumped in favor of coverage of the much-delayed results of the Gore–Bush presidential election.

The daily media covering the trial weren't granted access to the jurors. They were allowed to leave by a back exit following the trial, and court officials refused to give out their names and phone numbers. But, in a move that angered the local media types—press, radio and TV—"20/20" was allowed to play by a different set of rules.

The show's producers were allowed to contact jury members, and a week after the trial, Cooper turned over her courtroom and the jury room for five and a half hours of filming, with the jury members being interviewed in two rows of chairs in the courtroom, and then re-creating their long deliberations in the jury room.

On camera, the 10 jurors who agreed to take part in the show concurred that they thought the prosecution case was weak and its witnesses biased and unreliable. One of the engineers said supposed blood evidence on the sleeve of Fletcher's shirt "was one of many elements the jury didn't believe."

Who had problems with the credibility of the prosecution witnesses? "I think we all did," was the answer.

Did the lack of credibility hurt the prosecution case? "Yes, it did," answered Gloria, the older woman, who said the lack of motive was particularly troubling for her. "If he wanted to prove to the judge that he wasn't having sex with Leann, he certainly wouldn't have set up a murder scene with her getting ready to have sex."

So, in their minds, they had no motive, unreliable and untrustworthy prosecution witnesses, weak physical evidence and an impossible explanation of events by Townsend.

That second day of deliberations, had Legghio and Townsend been able to listen in to the proceedings in the jury room or able to see what was being totted up by Jensen on those white sheets, it would have seemed like a slam dunk: Certainly all of those things had to at least add up to reasonable doubt, and reasonable doubt meant not guilty. Legghio couldn't have added another item to a wish-list of things he wanted the jury to believe at the beginning of its deliberations.

But this wasn't the usual case, and it wasn't the usual jury. Unusual events and unusual deliberations still lay ahead for the twelve jurors.

On the prosecution side of the ledger, the jurors still had to account for a dead woman. How could this shooting have happened? Holding the gun with her thumb on the trigger, as MacDonell suggested, seemed ludicrous. And they had a defendant who had committed numerous acts of adultery, looked way too smug and cocksure to their eyes as he sat in court each day, and who just irritated the hell out of them.

Surprising—shocking, even—was how the 911 tape was

perceived. Legghio had argued for its admission, and Town-send against its being heard by the jury. As it turned out, they were arguing the wrong positions.

The jury didn't believe the tape. Instead of convincing them of Fletcher's innocence, it helped convince at least some that he had pulled the trigger.

Some jury members, including Jensen, thought it included too much information, that it seemed more like his way of laying out his whole alibi than merely calling in a state of panic to report a shooting. Why talk about where they'd been that morning? Why say they had gone back to the house to have sex?

"The whole damn defense was on the tape," Jensen would say later.

The owner of the dog bakery agreed Fletcher was genu-inely emotional, but for reasons Legghio hadn't predicted. "We all agreed he was emotional on this tape, as you would be if you just shot someone."

One of the engineers had another unforeseen reason for saying the tape was the deciding factor in switching him from "not guilty" to "guilty": Fletcher had called his wife by pet names and not by her given name. "If something happened like that to one of my family members, I imagine I would be screaming their name. He didn't do that. He called her 'honey' and 'sweetheart.' "

Jensen agreed. He had a young son who had nearly choked on food once, and Jensen remembered calling him by name in panic. "In a moment of extreme panic, you'd go back to their regular name."

The *honey* and *sweetheart* stuff sounded too much like alibi-setting to some of them, too phony, too much for the benefit of the 911 operator and the official record. Add one surprise for the prosecution.

When they voted again on Tuesday after compiling their lists—it was eight guilty, four not guilty. Two of the not guilties were adamant.

Led by the engineers, the jury decided on a new tack: They would become crime-scene investigators, too. They sent out a note asking for masking tape and a tape measure.

"Masking tape? What do they want with masking tape?" Sgt. Hendricks wondered.

They used it to to help turn the jury room into the Fletcher bedroom. They marked off where the body was, they marked off blood, they marked off the bed and dresser.

They also asked for a copy of a transcript of the 911 tape to read as they listened to it, for an inventory of all items admitted into evidence and for something to magnify the photos they had spread out on the table.

One of the engineers did that one better. He carried around a miniature pocket microscope as part of his work, and they used it to look at the green Oxford shirt Mick had worn the day of the shooting. Woodford had left numerous pins in the cuff of the shirt where he said there were drops of blood. The jury, though, agreed with MacDonell that there was nothing there.

And then the jurors began their crucial play-acting, with the one named Bob playing the role of Leann as he pretended to be shot in the head, and pretended to be mortally wounded as he fell to the ground of the jury room.

And the more Bob fell, the more unlikely it seemed that Leann could have held the gun in any way that explained the trigger getting pulled, the wound being behind the right ear and the gun falling where it fell.

There was just one thing wrong with their role playing. They weren't acting out events as the prosecution said they must have occurred. They were acting out a different scenario, one Legghio had never had a chance to address or rebut. Sure, his own witness had suggested the shooting could have occurred on the bed, but he didn't say conclusively that it had. He *had* said conclusively that the shooting could not have taken place on the floor and had suggested the bed as an alternative scenario by way of establishing reasonable doubt.

Had Townsend based his case on the theory that Leann was shot on the bed, Legghio would surely have tried to rebut that, too.

The jury took MacDonell one step further. They decided the shooting *had* taken place on the bed. And using the table as the make-believe bed, Bob would hold out the gun, pretend to pull the trigger and then he and the gun would fall. Over and over he did it, and the gun never ended up where it did in the police photos.

Wednesday was a day off for the jurors. The entire courthouse was closed in the morning so employees could attend the funeral of an assistant prosecutor, and in the afternoon Cooper had to listen to motions on other cases.

Thursday, they resumed deliberations, resumed their crime-scene reenactments and resumed their votes. It was now coming out 9–3 for conviction. They hadn't voted on whether it would be first degree, second degree or manslaughter. There was no sense arguing that unless they could agree on guilt or innocence.

As Jensen later explained, the crime-scene reenactments were a way of taking the back-door approach. They had unreliable or little forensic evidence, in their mind, linking Fletcher to the crime. But if they could come at it with inductive reasoning—more proof they were engineers—and eliminate Leann as the source of the gun being shot, then by logical elimination, it would have to be Mick who did it. The play-acting might cause the rest of the hold-outs to see how unlikely that was; then they'd be left with no other explanation except that the husband did it.

A couple of the jurors weren't sure this was legal, though. They weren't sure if proving Leann didn't do it was the same as proving he did. They sent out a hand-written note to Cooper.

"We have a legal question. If we decide that it was impossible based upon the evidence that Leanne [sic] shot herself, are we allowed to decide that the defendant shot her?"

Judge Cooper wrote back at the bottom of the same lined white sheet: "Please sit down and very carefully re-read all my jury instructions."

She hadn't told them they couldn't, which must mean they could.

By the end of the day, the vote was 11–1, with Gloria still holding out for acquittal.

"Just out of pure carelessness, she may have reached over and picked that gun up to get it off the bed and it could have gone off," she said later. "We know Leann's fate. Leann is dead. She is not coming back. We have the fate of a young man sitting in that courtroom—who I really don't like—but it's still a life in the balance."

Townsend was heartened by the jury's note to Cooper. It showed they were close. At least they weren't sending notes out saying they were hopelessly deadlocked, as you might expect on the third day of deliberations.

Said Townsend's boss, David Gorcyca: "It seems to me they're hung up on the central issue of the case. If Leann didn't shoot herself, the only one who could have done it was Michael Fletcher. There is no other logical explanation. . . . I think it was favorable for the prosecution."

Legghio tried to frame it in a better light. "I don't find the note to have any significance or insight," he said.

The Miseners didn't know what to make of it. Having expected a guilty verdict on Monday, by now they were fearing the worst.

"Trust me, it's okay," Townsend consoled them. "Trust me."

It was a horrible time for both families. The Miseners and friends would gather at one end of the hall outside Cooper's courtroom, the Fletchers and their friends at the other end. "We prayed a lot," said John Fletcher. "And we stared out the window a lot. It was probably the worst four days of our lives."

The Miseners kept thinking: How will we get through another trial if it's a mistrial? Then, worse: What if he gets off? "If there were even a chance they would let him go, I don't know how we would survive," said Lindy. "We need justice for our sister."

At one point, according to Darla, the woman who had been in charge of Hannah's case for the Family Independence Agency, came up to the Fletchers and said: "I just want you to know, Mrs. Fletcher, that regardless of what happens in there, we plan on telling Hannah the truth." Her truth, not the jury's truth, in case it was not guilty.

Friday morning, it was still 11–1 for guilty. Gloria asked Bob for one final reenactment. The gun went off, Bob fell from the bed (table), the gun landed in the wrong spot, again. Gloria had seen enough. "You couldn't get the gun in the

right spot. That was the determining factor for me," she'd say
later.

Another vote. Twelve–zip. Relief swept through them.
What had been anguished, and at times extremely vocal, deliberations, had gotten over the hump.

Now that they had decided Mick did it, what crime, exactly, was he guilty of?

Jensen saw it one way only: First degree. Given the trip
to the gun range it was hard to believe any subsequent death
wasn't part of a planned effort. "If it looks like a duck and
quacks like a duck, it's a duck."

But the first vote on degree surprised him. Seven said
second-degree murder, three said first degree and two were
undecided.

Once again, things would get heated up. What seemed
over, wasn't.

Some said they didn't want to vote for first degree, because
that was an automatic life sentence, and what if they were
wrong? Jensen reminded them that the judge had instructed
them to disregard punishment, that their job was only to decide on guilt or innocence and on what charge. "They pissed
me off," he'd say later. "They didn't have the balls to go with
the sentence."

Others argued that the prosecution case was so weak they
couldn't justify first degree. Others thought maybe it was truly
second degree, that the trip to the gun range had been innocent, but once they were back at the house and the gun was
sitting there, he acted on impulse and killed her.

They broke for lunch, the two main factions adamant.
When they returned, Jensen surprised them by giving in. He
knew in his mind that Fletcher was guilty of first-degree murder and he wasn't going to let a hung jury result. No way
would this go to another trial and another jury, which might
set Fletcher free.

"I gave a little speech, and I said I would compromise to
second degree if we could agree on a verdict. The woman
who owned the dog bakery agreed to switch to second degree,
too, and so did the third one who had been holding out for
first degree." The undecideds came aboard. It was finally settled, and a note to that effect was sent out to Cooper, whose
clerk passed the word on to the attorneys.

An adrenaline rush went through those waiting out in the halls. The long wait was over. Legghio came out and told the Fletchers the verdict was coming in, to hurry in and get a seat in the front row.

The courtroom was ringed with bailiffs, which the Fletchers took to be a good sign. They must be worried about an outbreak of violence from the Miseners in case it was not guilty. One of the bailiffs reinforced that feeling when he leaned over and whispered to them: "I want you folks to know this is not because of you."

The "20/20" folks had even asked the Fletchers if they could buy them a victory dinner the night the jury came back, at the posh Townsend Hotel in the nearby upscale suburb of Birmingham, filming the happy reunion with Mick, of course.

Darla hoped against hope that the food she'd bought and stored in the freezer and fridge at home hadn't been a waste of money. She was going to cook Mick a week of his favorite foods—rib steaks from her favorite meat market in Port Huron, burritos, country ribs, cheesy potatoes ("It's a casserole, but you can't say the word *casserole* around Mick, so we call it cheesy potatoes"), lasagna, a roast, and enough potatoes to have mashed potatoes night after night.

The extended Misener family trooped in, pulses racing, terror in their throats.

The courtroom was soon packed. A dozen sheriffs lined the room, half of them separating the spectator pews from the defense and prosecution tables.

Lindy began to cry. Jeni Hughes was crying. John Fletcher gulped. Jack Misener looked ill. Gloria looked, as she had throughout, resolute. When everyone was seated and the prosecution and defense were at their places, Cooper said: "We have the deputies in the courtroom for a reason," she said quietly, but forcefully. "This *will* remain orderly. Bring in the jury."

There was a minute's delay. The tension could get no higher. The door opened, the jurors came in in single-file and took their seats.

"I have received a note from you that you have reached a verdict. Is that correct?" said Cooper.

"Yes, your honor," said Rob Jensen.

"What is your verdict?"

Rob Jensen said quietly: "Guilty of second-degree murder."

It all seemed somehow anticlimactic. The courtroom gave a collective sigh. And then broke into cheers.

Fletcher, in a blue-gray suit, slumped forward, his first sign of emotion since arguing about a tie three weeks ago.

The Fletchers slumped, too. Darla began crying. The jurors were thanked and dismissed as the media descended on both families, the Miseners joyous, hugging, crying and laughing at once, the Fletchers in stunned disbelief. Cameras, microphones and notebooks were stuck in their faces, but soon their dozen or so friends and family members had formed a ring around them, giving them some space. Mick was led out without a chance to talk to them. The media were told to gather in the courtroom lobby two floors below for interviews. The Fletchers, unable to face the horde, were allowed to leave by a side exit and depart unimpeded.

"I want everyone to know: Nobody won here," said Jack Misener moments later, down in the lobby, his voice breaking. "I can't have my little girl back."

"We're just glad there's justice for Leann," said Gloria. "We would have preferred first-degree murder, but we're satisfied."

Legghio gave the obligatory comments to the press and said an appeal would be filed. "This is a case that had reasonable doubt written all over it," he said. "I thought we were going to be celebrating."

Privately, he would admit: "I was physically ill. Physically ill. I honestly thought we had won the case. I honestly believed we had scientifically and forensically undermined the prosecution case. It was painful. It was painful. Not just because I was the attorney, but because I had a client going downstairs in shackles."

The nature of the verdict—second degree—was even more of a shock than the word "guilty." "Nobody can rationalize or understand how they got second degree," he said. "It's so antithetical to the case. The prosecution and the defense both tried a first-degree murder case. They took four days to pin the tail on the dog. They knew what they wanted to come out with; they just needed a way to rationalize it in their own mind to get there."

"There was never a doubt in my mind that he was innocent," John Fletcher would say later. "We know he's not capable of it. We sat through the trial. I thought he was going to be acquitted. All I know is my son isn't capable of doing it. I'm proud of Michael. He was a good kid. He was every father's dream. He respected his parents. Every promise he made he fulfilled."

"Isn't that sad?" Jack Misener would counter. "How much do you have to prove? I don't think I could still be in denial, even if it was my child."

The Fletchers went home. Their physician had prescribed some mild tranquilizers in case of bad news. "I just went to bed," said Darla. "I couldn't get out of bed for days."

Every time she opened the refrigerator, Mick's food was still sitting there staring at her.

THE SENTENCING

Friday morning, July 28, was a day of portent, and the weather outside seemed scripted to match. Powerful things were about to happen. The morning was hot and Michigan-muggy, the kind of stifling combination of heat and humidity visitors this far north never expect. You can find its match in the Everglades, and in the bayou country around New Orleans, but not many other places on earth.

The state is surrounded by the Great Lakes, and filled with thousands of inland lakes, streams and rivers. When the humidity builds, it builds thick, giving the air a gelatinous feel as you walk through it. But a cold front was approaching that day, fast and furious; it was the kind of incoming weather guaranteed to set off massive thunderstorms as the inrushing cold air could no longer hold the water hanging suspended over the state.

Tornadoes were likely, thunder and lightning a certainty, and as early arrivers walked toward the Oakland County Courthouse, the day had already turned to near-night. Streetlights had come on, cars pulled into the parking lot with headlights on.

Seven sheriffs are on duty in Judge Cooper's courtroom. One of them sweeps people with a portable metal detector before they can enter. The TV and radio stations are back en masse. Each row is jammed with bodies packed in tight. A growing crowd waits in the hall, as the light outside the hallway windows is sucked away like air from a vacuum. A black, roiling, thick angry cloud is rolling over the woods and pastures visible from the third floor of the hall windows. CRAASH! A bolt of lightning is followed immediately by thunder, and opaque sheets of rain materialize instantly.

The thunder and lightning seem fitting, God's wrath and judgment coming to join with Cooper's.

Word has gone out through the crowd that there will be a one-hour delay before court begins. Legghio can't get here on time. Fletcher's parents, sick at heart, sit at the left of the front pew, silent, looking lost in thought. The extended Misener family is much more animated, greeting each other, leaning toward each other to share a story or two. This is the day they've been waiting for.

News accounts in recent days have quoted Townsend as saying he will ask for much more than the sentencing guidelines for second-degree murder call for—between thirteen and a half and twenty-two and a half years, plus two years for using a gun in the commission of a felony. He will, he says, ask for life in prison. Legghio has scoffed in print at that suggestion and says he will appeal the verdict, in any regard.

Finally, the clerk announces Cooper's arrival. She has the always-weighty task of sentencing someone to prison, and she seems in a rare dark mood. A cell phone jangles and she snaps that whoever has their phones need to turn them off. Moments later, Legghio enters the courtroom.

"Good morning, Your Honor. May I approach?"

"Would you like to explain where you've been?" she asks frostily, clearly not pleased at the delay.

"I did call your office yesterday morning," he offers in explanation. It hardly lightens Cooper's mood. Scheduling conflicts aren't an excuse to her this day. He's got a client on his way to jail, and that should have been his first concern.

Fletcher is brought in. There won't be any more arguments about whether ties match or not. With the jury gone, he is marched in in his Day-Glo orange prison jumpsuit that reads "PRISONER" on the back.

Thunder booms, even through the closed doors of the courtroom. And booms again.

Fletcher is seated in the jury box and the sparring over the pre-sentence report begins.

In Michigan, sentencing guidelines control the minimum amount of sentence. Those convicted get X amount of time for the crime itself, plus extra months for any of a wide number of militating factors, for which points are assessed and jail time accrued. Was a gun used? Was there violence? Were other felonies committed at the same time? Was there an effort to interfere with a police investigation? And so forth.

Legghio has been given a copy beforehand of the pre-sentence report done by court officials, which totals up the extra jail time. In fact, the recommendation is for life in prison, which Legghio can reduce by successfully arguing objections to the various findings.

Legghio objects to points for predatory behavior. If it were second-degree murder, there was no time for predatory behavior. The judge disagrees. "I will allow that," she says.

He argues against points for three or more contemporaneous felonies, arguing the jury found him guilty of two counts and the judge dismissed a third count. She disagrees, saying that while other charges had not been filed, his guilt means his statements to police at the scene and subsequently were felonious lies.

Legghio then requests a separate hearing, to be scheduled on another day, on each of these and other disputed findings.

Cooper answers, her normally quite quiet voice forceful and emphatic. "Mr. Legghio, I sat through the trial. I don't feel a hearing is necessary. If there are findings to be made, I am in a position to do that."

He starts to protest and she cuts him off. "I will not argue with you. I am not in an adversarial position with you. I've made my ruling. Let's move on."

They move on the points for another charge, a threat to the administration of justice, arising from Fletcher's 911 call. If he had murdered Leann, then the call was a phony, and a phony call to 911 is an attempt to interfere with the administration process, argues Townsend.

Legghio is apoplectic. "The only time I've ever seen this administered is when someone in jail has threatened a jailer," he says. "They've already assessed points for contemporaneous crimes. If contemporaneous crimes cover four events, you can't cut it off at three and then apply the other here. I challenge Mr. Townsend to show me one other case where that has ever been scored."

The judge rules against him. All told, Fletcher scores an additional 115 points, which pushes him into the life range, should the judge choose. And by now no one has any doubts at all about Cooper's intentions.

(At one point during the scoring process, Cooper refers to Woodford's testimony. "I believe what Mr. Woodford testified that there was copious amounts of blood in the trap of the sink . . . his word was—I wrote it down—'copious.' " She was wrong. Woodford never used that word in his testimony. The first time he referred to it, he said it was "a fair amount" and later amended the description to "significant." Significant as "significant" is, it's hardly the same thing as copious.)

Michigan law calls for victim-impact statements prior to sentencing. They generally have no bearing on the sentence, but serve to let victims stare a perpetrator in the eye and let him or her know what they think.

At murder trials, it is a painful, heart-rending part of the proceedings but one that often serves as the beginning of the healing process. Gloria Misener is first.

"Hannah was playing a game of marbles on the floor with her grandfather and she picked up a marble with blue and gray streaks. 'Isn't this a beautiful marble?' Then she put the marble down and said, 'Please, God, send my mommy back to me for ever and ever.' Then she laid her head down on my shoulder and hugged me. Mick, you've said how much your daughter meant to you. Well, she's never asked about you even once.

"Our daughter was the sunshine of our life, and she looked forward to each day. She loved spending each day with her daughter, and they had such a special bond. Hannah cries for her mother each and every day. I told her . . ."

Loud sobs and sniffles sound from some of the family behind her. She pauses and continues, like always at this trial and related proceedings, a bedrock. "I told her if I could go to heaven and send her mother back, I would. She asks us, 'How did my mommy die?' What should we tell her, Mick? That her father put a gun to her trusting mother's head and pulled the trigger? Some day she'll find out. What a horrible thing that will be! We lost our second grandchild, too. Maybe it would have been the boy you said you always wanted, Mick.

"I hope they find you in the same humiliating position they found Leann—half naked on the prison floor, dead."

Absolute silence in the court. Mick sits as he has throughout, impassive. He hasn't looked Gloria's way, nor will he look at those to follow.

BOOM! The storm breaks the spell and Lindy gets up and walks toward the lectern.

"Leann was an incredible mother, daughter and sister," she says, addressing Judge Cooper. "He has brought such incredible pain to so many people. The pain will last all the rest of our lives, but so will our memories. He's on the way down from the position he had for himself. Maybe he'll realize what a meager human being he is, and maybe then he'll realize what a treasure he had in Leann.

"We won't spend our lives hating Michael Fletcher, for then he'd destroy us, as well. We're strong. We'll persevere. Michael Fletcher thought he had it all, and now he has nothing."

Fletcher's face is frozen, but he is rocking very slowly back and forth, now.

More sobs, sniffles, blowing of noses from the crowd.

Lori Mays, another sister, goes to the lectern. "This past August has changed our lives forever. We are truly heartbroken. I've got four children of my own, and they loved Leann. My son was 14. I'll never forget the look on his face when I told him Leann was pregnant, and then the next day had to tell him she was dead. He's been in counseling ever since."

Lori told of a combined birthday party a month before the shooting for her eight-year-old and five-year-old. Leann came early with 200 balloons and filled them with water. Later, the kids would bombard her, drenching her. Lori snapped pictures of Leann, wet and joyful. "She never got to see them."

More sobs and sniffles.

Another anecdote: She came home recently and one of the boys was tearing up a page of the newspaper. "Don't rip the paper," she told him.

"But it's got a picture of Uncle Mick in it."

"Michael Fletcher's parents can visit him in jail, but we can only visit Leann in the cemetery," she concluded.

*   *   *

Then came Jeni Hughes, Leann's best friend. "Leann was more than a friend to me. We used to joke that we were sisters in a previous life, and we always wanted to raise our children together," she said. "The pain and grief is more than anything I've ever imagined. I only knew her for eight years, so I can't imagine what her family feels like.

"I wake up every morning and pray it was just a nightmare. But then I look over and see her cat laying next to me and I know it wasn't. Your Honor, please remember what Michael Fletcher has done to all of us. He sentenced us to incredible pain for the rest of our lives.

"I used to say to Leann, and it would always make her laugh: 'If I was any better, there'd be two of me.' I'll never say that, again."

Family friend Pat Carter goes last: "I just met the Miseners five years ago. Leann was a rare and unique flower in this bouquet of people on this planet. She was not only physically beautiful, but there was an inner light that came from her that made you glad to receive its warmth. . . . What kind of father leaves a legacy this cold, this heartless to his precious daughter?"

Finally, Cooper tells Townsend it is his turn to make a closing statement. He rises. "The family has made such an elocution, I don't think anything by me is necessary."

Legghio stands and walks over to the jury box to stand at his client's side. Mick stands, too.

"Your Honor, this is a contested case, and my client, through his attorney, has steadfastly maintained his innocence. This is not a guilty-plea situation. What makes this task so difficult is everyone comes to you with a singular vision—to cause the greatest damage, to render the toughest sentence you can. We ask you to bring some sensibility and calmness to a very charged situation. Without you, Your Honor, we ought to go back to a time of lynching.

"I'm imploring you, Your Honor, despite the media frenzy . . . I'm asking the court to take a reasoned and balanced approach when it comes to imposing a sentence. Before he came to this court, he was not unlike others. There are thousands of pictures of him in family albums. He has a warm and loving family that stood by him every day. And they're here today. He was a productive member of society before he came to court, and he can be, again. He will be."

All eyes shift to Cooper, who asks: "Michael Fletcher, is there anything you wish to say?"

Fletcher stands and says quietly, without emotion: "On the advice of counsel, no."

"I've spent 22 years on this bench, and I've presided over innumerable trials involving all manner of heinous crimes," says Cooper. "In all those years, I've never seen a crime so incredibly cold-blooded or heartless. You killed your wife, who was pregnant with your child. Your daughter, Hannah, will live her whole life without her mother.

"The jury didn't believe you and the story you told the police, and I don't, either. I don't understand what kind of monstrous arrogance caused you to think you could get away with murder. I don't have any doubts how to sentence you.

"It is the sentence of the court that you be sentenced to life in prison."

Loud cheers erupt. Misener family members jump up and hug each other, tears pouring down. John and Darla Fletcher slump in the pew. Fletcher is quickly led from the court as reporters and camera crews surround Gloria and Jack Misener and their kids. Lindy hollers out, sarcastically: "Goodbye, Mick."

"I feel the family can finally start to heal," says Lindy moments later. "We have justice for Leann. That's a start."

Someone asks her about what she thought of Mick's demeanor. "He was smug. Nothing changed. He was actually laughing. If he was so innocent, why didn't he stand up and say what happened?"

Did she have doubts about the sentence? "I was worried about getting through my speech, but not about what I was going to say. I had no doubts in my mind."

Gloria: "He got his sentence, but we still don't have our little girl."

John Fletcher, still professing belief in his son's innocence, responded: "If I thought for a second that Mick had done it, I'd have a certain amount of anger myself," claiming the media frenzy over the fact that his son was a lawyer and his lover a judge was to blame for much of this. "If he'd been a pizza man, and she'd been a waitress, none of this would have taken place."

Later that same day, in one of those remarkable coincidences, punishment, albeit much milder, was meted out to Chrzanowski, too. The Michigan Supreme Court suspended her with pay, pending a hearing the next month, for having assigned cases to her lover and then ruling on them.

EPILOGUE

Brian Legghio did the seeming impossible after the Fletcher trial—he took on an even more high-profile case, at least to those in the younger demographics. The popular white rapper Eminem, AKA Marshall Mathers III, a Warren native, was arrested in June, just as the Fletcher trial was about to start, and charged with assault after he pulled a gun in the parking lot of a Warren bar and threatened to kill a man he saw smooching his wife.

The gun? A Smith & Wesson.

At a hearing on August 31 in Warren District Court, to determine if the case should move on, Legghio was photographed standing behind his client, with the photo running in color on the front page of the Metro Section in the next day's *Detroit News*. Legghio got the judge to allow his client to remain free so he could continue a national tour.

Coincidentally, the very first hearing on the Eminem case was on June 8, as jurors were being selected for the Fletcher trial. And it was held in front of none other than Susan Chrzanowski.

It got even more coincidental and curious at the August 31 hearing. That hearing was scheduled for Judge Dawnn Gruenburg, Mick Fletcher's other lover. But Gruenburg recused herself because her father, Roy, had once been Eminem's lawyer. What's more, she and Mathers had grown up in the same neighborhood and knew each other.

Dawnn showed up at the hearing, though, and as Eminem left the court, she had a smile and a wiggle of her fingers for him.

Later, at the subsequent hearing in Circuit Court in October, Macomb County Prosecutor Carl Marlinga told the judge he was seeking 17 months of jail time for the rapper. Legghio entered a not-guilty plea, got the hearing adjourned until December and got the judge to allow his client to remain free on a bond of $10,000. (More of the small-world nature of southeastern Michigan: Marlinga was in the midst of running for re-election against Susan Chrzanowski's father, Robert.)

In addition to threatening to kill the man, it was alleged Eminem smacked him with the butt of the gun three or four times. The alleged victim, John Guerra, also filed a civil suit, seeking a jury trial and damages in excess of $25,000.

Eminem also faced charges in Oakland County for a separate incident involving a threat with the same gun against the manager of a rival white rap group, the Insane Clown Posse. It was alleged that Eminem pulled the gun after the manager called him a homosexual in front of Eminem's wife.

Later, the wife, Kim Mathers, attempted suicide, then moved out and filed for divorce.

Legghio stood to get more business, too, if members of the Fletcher jury ever ran into legal trouble. Following the verdict, jury members took turns doing a trial post-mortem with both the prosecution and the defense, to see what the jury found compelling, what it didn't, what it liked, what it disliked, etc. When it was Legghio's turn, several of them asked him for his business card, a pretty high compliment for the losing attorney.

"Just in case, you know?" said jury foreman Rob Jensen. "Because we were so impressed with him."

Legghio remains convinced of Fletcher's innocence. Those who watched talk shows on the O. J. Simpson case may remember some of his lawyers steadfastly sidestepping questions about whether they thought their client was innocent by using the old dodge of "Under our system, everyone is entitled to a defense," or "The prosecution didn't prove the case beyond a reasonable doubt." Legghio is more forthright.

"I do not believe that he is guilty of killing her. I honestly believe that. This guy would walk away. He is the most non-confrontational guy. He is the classic example of what a lot of guys have as a character trait, particularly when it comes to women and issues and confrontation. Men are avoidance–denial people. We're poor communicators. We do anything but deal with the issue. He tried leaving Chrzanowski three times. This guy is just incapable of doing some act or deed that is so irrreversible."

Legghio said that he and Marla McCowan, because of the admittedly odd timing of Leann getting shot immediately after she'd been to the firing range the first time, initially thought that Fletcher had shot her by accident, then, fearing no one would believe him, had lied about the circumstances. "But MacDonell convinced us. He said, 'If he'd shot her, he'd have been covered in blood.' "

Legghio said the trial continues to haunt him, particularly the comment by some jurors that the 911 tape—which he fought to get admitted—is what pushed them to conviction. "This has been and is the most unsettling verdict of my career, both in terms of the evidence and in terms of my feelings for my client," he said. He said the case wakes him up in the middle of the night and continues to pop into his head unbidden. "I always think about the case. On a regular basis."

Susan Chrzanowksi remained embroiled in her own legal troubles long after the trial was over. She was removed from the 37th District Court with pay, $118,285 a year, by the Michigan Judicial Tenure Commission, an arm of the state Supreme Court, in July, the same day Mick was being sentenced to life in prison.

At issue were the 64 cases she assigned to Fletcher between April of 1998 and August of 1999, while they were having an affair—and which netted him some $17,000 in legal fees, the vast majority of his earnings for that period. Not only did she assign the cases, but she heard them, too. During that same period, the other three Warren judges combined gave him 22 cases worth $6,000 in work. What was worse, she was accused of lying to police. In her first interview with Sgt. Larry Hendricks the day after the shooting, she said the affair with Fletcher had ended in March, even though she had had sex with him just two days earlier. And she denied having spoken to Mick after the shooting, though in fact she had returned a page from him and talked to him briefly on the phone.

Also in July her attorneys met with retired Supreme Court Justice Charles Levin, who had been appointed a special "master" to conduct a hearing on her case. At the July meeting, groundwork was laid for a trial in August.

The process was cumbersome and confusing. The Tenure Commission had recommended her removal pending formal hearings and the justices of the Supreme Court had concurred. Levin would issue his own opinion, which the eight-member Commission could either agree with or overrule at its own hearing later. Both Levin's and the Commission's decisions would then be weighed by the full Supreme Court.

She faced a wide range of outcomes, from an immediate return to the bench, to suspension with pay, suspension without pay or even disbarment.

At her hearing in September in downtown Detroit, family members testified that if Chrzanowski gave untruthful answers to Hazel Park investigators in the days after the shooting—and the cops testified that she did—it was because she was in a state of shock and not responsible for her actions.

Gregory Townsend was a star witness—for Chrzanowski. Continuing the kid-gloves treatment she got at the Fletcher trial, he testified on her behalf, saying: "She volunteered information. She answered questions fully and completely." And he said that she had seemed truly ashamed of the whole affair when she came face to face with him for the first time following revelations of her affair. "Judge Chrzanowski, when she first saw me, broke down in tears. I believe she was very embarrassed."

When she got on the stand, the judge also said that any misinformation was a result of her shock and confusion and wasn't willful. "I don't know what they asked and I don't know what I answered," she said under oath. "I was not thinking about my professional life. I was thinking, 'Oh, my God, someone is dead and they're saying that he killed her, and I've been going out with him.' And then they told me she was pregnant."

As to giving Mick Fletcher legal work, she admitted passing assignments his way but said that no court rules prohibited such conduct and that male judges routinely give work to "their buddies."

Another witness was a lawyer friend named Stephen Rabault, who had gone to help her out when she found out Leann had been killed. "She was clearly distressed, crying, very upset," he testified. "It took some time to generate a dialogue. She was not in a position to communicate with them [police] or anyone else." (Rabault happened to be Legghio's first partner upon entering private practice.)

On December 9, 2000, Levin issued his finding in a 50-page report, which shocked most legal observers. He absolved Chrzanowski of misconduct, a finding the Tenure Commission was expected to appeal to the Supreme Court early in 2001.

Levin agreed that her emotional state in her interview with Hendricks made it impossible to conclude willful deceit. And he said that however distasteful it might have been that she funneled cases to her lover, there was no rule against such judicial behavior and that, in fact, judges routinely assign a disproportionate number of cases to close, if platonic, friends.

He did mention an e-mail in which Chrzanowski talked of an upcoming sexual rendezvous and then promised Fletcher she would throw him "an extra appointment or two" beforehand. "The messages do not, indeed, look good," wrote Levin, adding that the Judicial Tenure Commission had not established "a policy respecting disproportionate assignments to close personal friends."

Macomb County Prosecutor Carl Marlinga, who had filed charges against her because of her dismissal of drunk-driving charges against one of Fletcher's clients, said after Levin's ruling that "I feel bad I ever got this whole thing rolling. It did cross the line, but this was not a person who was trying to hide and duck and weave. She took full responsibility and she understands what she did was wrong."

Her attorney said he would ask the Supreme Court to reinstate her immediately pending a possible appeal.

The Chrzanowski name no longer held its polling-booth magic. Chrzanowski's dad, Robert, who preceded her on the Warren bench and later moved up to Circuit Court before retiring, had surprised everyone by announcing his candidacy for Macomb County prosecutor. A long-time Democrat, he ran as a Republican, and rumors began floating around that the fix was in.

As was mentioned earlier, Michigan's Supreme Court is notoriously politicized. Candidates are nominated at party conventions, but run without party affiliation as part of a charade that the court is above party politics. Just the opposite. Under Republican Governor John Engler, the court grew even more political, and that wasn't easy. The court even began, on its own, without being asked in the form of appeals or lawsuits, going back and overturning previous court decisions and eradicating liberal precedents.

The rumors that were floating—and at least one columnist for *The Macomb Daily* in Mt. Clemens gave voice to them in print—was that if Chrzanowski would be a sacrificial lamb against Democratic incumbent Marlinga, his daughter would ultimately keep her seat on the Warren bench. (Levin is highly respected and no one would dare accuse him of being part of any such fix, but the rumors persisted.)

Marlinga trounced the elder Chrzanowskí by a two-to-one margin to win a fifth term.

It continued a string of losses for the family. In the August primaries, another relative, E. J. Chrzanowski, had finished a distant third in the Republican primary for Macomb County Sheriff (an election that was necessary because the long-time incumbent, William Hackel, had just begun serving a long jail term for raping a woman at a convention while his wife was in their room on another floor), and an uncle, Richard Chrzanowski, was second by fewer than 2,000 votes out of 32,000 cast in the Republican primary for county treasurer.

The Miseners and Fletchers got embroiled in a bitter and costly struggle over Hannah. Following Mick's arrest, the Miseners refused the Fletchers visitation. Mick's parents saw their granddaughter a total of two hours between her mother's death on August 16 and Christmas of 1999. Eventually a court order was granted and the Fletchers began seeing her, first in a supervised setting at county child-care facilities, then on alternate weekend visits in March of 2000.

Those visits didn't last long. Two weeks before the trial in June, news was leaked to the press—the Fletchers and Legghio think it was a concerted effort by public officials—that the county's Family Independence Agency was investigating unspecified allegations of child abuse against the Fletchers and in the meantime their visitation rights were being terminated.

Their attorney, James Williams, called the allegations frivolous but said state law prohibited him from discussing details. "My clients are fine, Christian people, and no one ever accused them of anything like this. If you'd meet them, you'd conclude they are closer to walking on water than any of us. This is a travesty. This is just one more attempt to harm the Fletchers at the expense of poor, little Hannah."

At the trial, the rumor spread that the allegations involved sexual abuse. Lisa Rodela called them "evil people" as she walked by the Fletchers with friends out in the hall during a break in the trial one day. Months after the verdict, people were still asking, "So, whatever happened to those sex-abuse charges?"

According to the Fletchers, they were contacted by FIA officials based in Oakland County, demanding a visit to their house. Subsequently a visit to their Marysville home was made by St. Clair County child-welfare officials, who told them there had been an allegation that they had been locking Hannah in her room.

John showed them to Hannah's nursery, which has no lock on the door. The only explanation he could come up with was a lightweight screen, about two feet high and with a thin metal frame, that they placed across Hannah's open doorway when she spent the night. The Fletchers said they used it with their other grandkids, too, and if one of them wandered out of their room during the night, the screen would fall, hit the floor and awaken one or the other of the grandparents. Maybe Hannah had said something about it and it had been misconstrued.

St. Clair officials filed a report saying the allegations seemed groundless, but by then, the trial was over, the Miseners were seeking to adopt Hannah and the general perception remained that the Fletchers were child abusers. Their visitation rights were not reinstated pending the adoption proceedings and ongoing court custody battle. None of the daily newspapers ran a story that the original allegations had proven baseless.

Despite their son's verdict, the Fletchers continued to fight, through their attorney, for custody of Hannah. The result was a foregone conclusion—the court was clearly not going to turn over custody of the four-year-old to the parents of the convicted murderer when the parents of the murdered wife wanted her.

At a hearing in Oakland County Family Court on August 7, a week after he was sentenced to life in prison, Mick's parental rights were terminated by Judge Edward Sosnick, but his parents fought on.

Fletcher appeared at the hearing in his bright orange jail uniform, and pleaded no contest to charges that he was an unfit father.

That same day, heartbroken at the impending loss of their granddaughter on top of the loss of their son, whose innocence they continued to maintain, Fletcher's parents filed a petition seeking custody of Hannah. They fought the Miseners for custody until late October, even undergoing physical examinations and psychological testing at their own expense to prove their worthiness.

Finally, with the handwriting evident, the Fletchers said they would drop proceedings if the Miseners would make a "gentlemen's promise" to allow them to visit their granddaughter.

The Miseners agreed, with Gloria telling a reporter that while she didn't want to deprive Hannah of her other grandparents, she needed some assurance first that they wouldn't proclaim Mick's innocence to her. Then, on November 20, ABC aired a "20/20 Downtown" show on the case. The Miseners were enraged at a comment made on air by Darla, who said that while she loved Leann and thought she was sweet, "she had another side, too."

The Miseners' adoption of Hannah became official on November 28, and shortly after, they told a reporter they'd never let the Fletchers see their granddaughter, again. They were still angry about the TV show and accused the Fletchers of refusing to return things they'd taken from the Hazelwood Avenue house in the days after the shooting. The Fletchers say they took some items back at Mick's direction and others because they assumed they'd be having Hannah some of the time and would need them.

After the formal decree was made final by Judge Sosnick that allowed the Miseners to officially adopt Hannah, the judge invited Jack and Gloria into his chambers. When they walked in, they were greeted by a surprise party. In attendance were many of the principals, including Townsend and Ortlieb, Hazel Park police chief David Niedermeier and some of his officers, and Dr. Dragovic. Champagne was popped and cake cut. Their compassion for what seemed a fitting end to this whole sad affair was understandable, especially given the belief by most in attendance at the party that they'd played crucial roles in putting a cruel murderer behind bars. Still, it struck some as unseemly that the party would be held in the chambers of the very judge overseeing the case, on county and taxpayer time. The Fletchers weren't notified about the final proceedings.

No one who knew the Fletchers could doubt their love for their granddaughter—Darla was the one who moved in with Mick and Leann for a week when Hannah was born, sleeping on the couch next to the baby's bassinet; they'd redone one of their bedrooms in their Marysville house into a nursery, filled with toys and stuffed playthings; and they'd babysat frequently for Hannah, as they did for their other grandchildren. (When the trial was over, they resumed babysitting five afternoons a week for Ben's infant daughter.)

The day the adoption was final, the Miseners began making plans to have Lindy adopt her, in turn. Hannah's last name was changed to Misener.

Mick Fletcher was taken first to the foreboding Jackson Prison—the largest walled prison in the U.S.—for processing, and then transferred to the western part of the state in Muskegon, a more modern facility.

Having spent $250,000 on his trial—forcing them to remortgage their home and sell off a prized show Corvette—John and Darla Fletcher could not afford an appeal. Instead, one was filed on Mick's behalf by Peter Van Hoek of the State Appellate Defender's Office, a branch of the state's Supreme Court. In his application for a state-appointed appellate lawyer, Fletcher listed $150,000 in unpaid legal bills owed by his parents and $75,000 in student loans.

Said Marla McCowan in a candid admission: "That's for people who spend all their money on the trial and have nothing left for an appeal. But Van Hoek is as good as they come. You couldn't buy a better appeals attorney."

Among possible appealable issues—any ruling could be years off—were improper jury conduct involving their coming up with their own theory of events and then play-acting their way to a verdict; and Cooper's refusal to toss out the charges involving the death of an unborn infant before the trial. She tossed them out midway though, after the jury had heard them, and some jurors later said the baby's death played a part in what they thought Fletcher's sentence should be.

McCowan, who had attended law school with Fletcher but didn't get to know him until she asked Legghio if she could help with the case, remains convinced of Fletcher's innocence, and angry, even bitter, at his conviction. "My take on his guilt or innocence is that he is not guilty, period. Looking back, it seems like I dedicated nearly ten months of my life and my career to proving his innocence. I would do it again in a minute if I thought it could help. The number one lesson is that there is no justice when cases are tried in and by the media. My hope is that Fletcher will someday get another trial. Speaking of appeals, a reversal of his conviction is the only way Michael Fletcher will ever get out of prison.

"If it makes Judge Cooper feel better morally or ethically to keep him behind bars forever, then that is what she will do. Her 'judgment' in that regard has nothing to do with principles of law. That was proven when she invited her husband to attend Michael Fletcher's sentencing. Somehow, it was personal to her, and she will continue to act accordingly. All of these factors make the appeal so important."

McCowan said her sense of Mick's innocence arises not from having grown close to him, but from having spent so much time with the defense witnesses, who convinced her during preparation for trial that Fletcher couldn't have done it, and that Leann, quite plausibly, could have. "Somewhere along the line, the jurors shifted the burden onto us to prove that he didn't do it, and when we didn't, they came up with a conviction by default. The injustices of this case are almost unbearable for me to think about."

McCowan went on maternity leave in December and her first child was due in January.

Jessica Cooper won election to the four-county second district of the Court of Appeals and finished up her tenure as a trial judge. She got the recommendations of both the liberal *Detroit Free Press* and the conservative *Detroit News* and trounced her opponent by 102,000 votes, even beating him in his home county of Macomb. In her county, Oakland, she got 61 percent of the vote.

Having promised some juicy reflections on the trial and on Fletcher if elected to the Court of Appeals, following her win, she was more judicious. "I really said all I had to say about Fletcher at the sentencing," she said.

Her files, she stressed, would make it clear to her successors that Fletcher, to her mind, should never get out of jail. Her campaign literature referred to her role in both the Kevorkian and Fletcher cases.

In an interview for this book she said that the one thing that convinced her of Fletcher's guilt more than anything was Woodford's testimony that there had been copious amounts of blood in the sink and yet none on the phone that Fletcher used to call 911. If he had washed that much blood off his hands before making his call, he was obviously guilty.

On Dec. 1, 2000, Officers Cleyman, Hendricks, Welch, Arthur, Weimer and Heisler received unit citations by Chief David Niedermeier and were honored at a banquet for their roles in the case.

John and Darla Fletcher continued to maintain their son's innocence.

"I knew before this whole thing even started—beyond a shadow of a doubt—but the trial proved to me that there was no evidence," said John more than three months after his son was sentenced, sitting in the front room of his home during one of the weeks he pulled the evening shift at work. "Every day we went to court, and I'd come home at night feeling more reassured that my feelings were right.

"I understand how it looks. I understand the implications. But, first of all, Mick's not that stupid. Remember those shows—'The World's Dumbest Criminals'? If Mick had done it, he'd have qualified. Let's face it."

"For him to have done it," said Darla, "he absolutely would have had to have lost his mind. And he would not have recaptured his mind so quickly if he'd done something like that. This is just totally not him."

The family was trying to rebuild as much as it could—

Halloween decorations still remained on the front porch, and he and Darla were in the midst of house-breaking a new Shi-tzu, Gerty. They hadn't been able to see Hannah for months. As Christmas of 2000 approached, Amy and Darla had just visited Mick upon his transfer to Muskegon, where his mother, for the first time since the family car was pulled over on the freeway and Mick had been arrested some 15 months earlier, was able to give him a hug.

What made John the angriest was watching the "20/20" news show that ran in November and seeing jurors describe how they discarded the prosecution's theory about the chain of events and re-created their own.

"I'm just thankful every day—it didn't turn out the way we wanted—but I don't go to bed at night wondering if there was anything more we could have done," said John. "Because we did everything we could. If we had spent a million dollars, we couldn't have had a better attorney than Brian. We're not in the poorhouse, but I don't know if I'll be retiring at 55, like I'd planned."

"I've never been prouder of my parents in my life than I am now, seeing how they've handled this," said Amy by phone from El Cajon, after a trip to Michigan to visit her brother in prison. "They've been battered and pounded. But even during the custody hearings they told me if they got custody they'd let the Miseners have visitation because that was the right thing to do. I was like, 'What!' but my dad, 'No, no, it'd be the right thing to do.' "

John can no longer stand to watch his favorite TV show, "Law and Order." He doesn't believe so clearly in bad guys and good guys anymore. And he no longer believes in capital punishment. "Imagine how many innocent people are in jail. People who couldn't afford a quarter of a million dollars for a defense."

Their outside Christmas tree lights were up, too, on a re-porter's last visit. There was a wreath and an angel on the door.

Darla was finishing up a pink tutu for Hannah for a would-be Christmas present. "It's the last thing she asked me for. But I don't know if I'll ever have a chance to give it to her."

* * *

Sheryl Tortigian, Woodford's assistant with the Michigan State Police, gave a presentation in October at the annual meeting in Tucson, Arizona, of the International Association of Bloodstain Pattern Analysts—an organization of some 650 founded by Professor Herbert MacDonell. The topic was the Fletcher case and how the bloodstain evidence was processed and then used to gain a conviction.

MacDonell was furious—partly because he thought it improper for a case on appeal to be discussed, but more so because he remained convinced that Woodford and Tortigian badly misinterpreted the blood evidence and helped send an innocent man to jail. MacDonell said he remained silent during Tortigian's presentation, but will be making one of his own at next year's gathering in Tucson.

MacDonell said Woodford saw evidence that wasn't there (the myriad of supposed blood-mist dots on the shirt that didn't exist) and put Leann in a position where it was physically impossible for her to be given the other stains (kneeling on the floor). Moreover, says MacDonell, Woodford missed the evidence that was there—Leann's blood was sprayed around the small bedroom, in 360 degrees. Fletcher was a fairly big man. If he had shot Leann from close range, his body would have served as a shield. "It would have had to have blocked some of the blood," said MacDonell. "But there was blood in all four directions. It wasn't intercepted. It was all over the room. There was no place for Fletcher to be in that room. I don't see how he could have been in that room and fired the shot. I don't think he was involved. It's at the least reasonable doubt.

"At our next meeting, I'm going to say, Okay, you heard one side of this case last year, and now you're going to hear the other side," said MacDonell after the convention. "I'm going to blow Woodford out of the water."

Frederick Wentling, the 26-year Pennsylvania state cop and firearms expert, remained convinced that Fletcher is innocent. And he said so in the strongest of terms in an interview after the "20/20" show for this book. Stressing that what he was about to say came from a retired cop and not some shill for defense attorneys, he used the words "I was stunned" to characterize what he said was the poor quality of the police investigation and of their subsequent testimony at trial, which he read in transcript form. He said, for example, that it was inexplicable that in a case where the suspect claims he loaded a gun and chambered a round, which meant it was cocked, that the firearms examiner wouldn't test the pull required to fire the gun in single-action mode.

"Initially I told Brian when he called to see if I'd help in the case—like I tell everyone—'I'll be happy to look at the evidence and the reports, but generally the police get it right.' Boy, did I have to eat those words! The police didn't get it right. They tried to make the facts fit into their theory and when you do that, bad things happen. The facts just weren't there."

While acknowledging the obvious, that he can't know for sure that Fletcher is innocent, "there's nothing in my experience as a firearms expert that leads me to believe he did it." He said the time-line was too short and there was much too much blood scattered around the room, in every direction, for Fletcher to have done it without getting covered in blood. "Once I was in the room and saw it, I was convinced. That room is just so small and there was blood everywhere. He should have had a lot of blood on him, and he didn't. You just can't shoot someone from a foot away and not get blood all over you. It's just not possible."

His reaction to the jury reeanctments on "20/20" and the play-acting that led to the guilty verdict? "Jesus Christ! It's stunning. That's just poor engineering," he said, taking a shot, so to speak, at the three engineers on the jury. "The photos of where the pistol is relative to her body didn't strike me as out of line or odd from the hundreds or thousands of cases I've done. I wouldn't have expected the gun to have gone flying. I wouldn't have expected it to be far from her body. I would have thought it would be close to her hand or even still in it. Just look at suicides. You normally don't see firearms fall away. Usually they're near the body."

As for the seemingly far-fetched possibility that she accidentally pulled the trigger with her thumb, he said the examiners he supervised had been involved in several cases over the years of similarly inflicted deaths, where murder was suspected at first because of the odd circumstances but later it was proved that the death was caused by the thumb and was accidentally self-inflicted.

"You have a woman who is an absolute novice and her husband is not well skilled—he leaves the gun cocked, we could convict him of stupidity, very easily. But this is how tragedies occur. She doesn't know the gun is cocked, she wants to remove it from the bed, she reaches over and grabs it and is unfortunate enough not to have her thumb hit the trigger guard and BANG! You don't have to be aiming.

"I told someone the strange thing about this case is the prosecution acted like the defense normally acts, and the defense acted like the prosecution. Normally the prosecution argues its case on the facts and the defense throws up road blocks. Here, the roles were reversed. The defense was the one arguing facts.

"The whole case is one of the strangest cases I've ever been involved in. The way the prosecution and police acted like this was some game they had to win. As if it was personal. The way the police did things. You talk about a railroad job. He should never have been convicted."

Jeni Hughes continued to wake up hoping it had all been a nightmare and seeing a cat, instead. Lori's oldest boy was able to stop counseling. The Miseners and all their children made plans for Christmas, 2000, dreading that holiday as much as they'd dreaded Christmas, 1999. But Jack Misener, the holiday decorator, sad heart or not, looked forward to getting out the boxes of stuff and spending the week or so it would take to get everything up, just so.

By early December he wasn't done, yet, but already the yard and outside of the house included giant replica lollipops stuck into the lawn, huge candy canes, a towering angel, two Santas and a snowman.

Hannah was enrolled in preschool at the same elementary school in Troy that her mother used to attend. She was in counseling. And she continued to tell people about the things she used to do with her mom, and think up possible ways to out-trick God and get her mother back.

Ben Fletcher, who went into the Hazelwood Avenue house to get his brother's things out of the bedroom the night of the shooting, will always remember what he saw and smelled in that room, but the nightmares seem to have passed.

"I'll never be able to get it out of my mind. It was absolutely one of the most horrific things I've ever seen or had to go through in my life. At the time I just tried to block it out as much as I could because I knew my brother needed my support, he needed someone with a rational mind to support him.

"For a long time I blocked it out, but a couple of months after it happened I would have sleepless nights just thinking about it. Walking into that room and that smell. I'd fall asleep and wake up and have that smell in my nose."

Danielle Blais, one of the friends much of the world seemed to think Mick never had, wrote Fletcher after his transfer to Muskegon: "We love you and always will," she said.

Jennifer Davis mailed him a joke a day when he was in the Oakland County jail. "I didn't think it would last so long," she said. Weeks turned into months, and now very likely into a lifetime. Now, she drives across state for four or five hours on occasion to see him, the last time with his aunt. "We let him know we're all thinking about him."

At least some of the jurors continued to have doubts. One of them, a young man, told "20/20 Downtown:" "I think maybe there is some doubt that he didn't do this. What if we're wrong? That's what I keep thinking. Everyone feels that possibly he wasn't guilty, right?"

The reporter, Elizabeth Vargas, asked the other nine jurors whom her producers had gathered for her, if they all felt that way. Was there one percent doubt, two, ten? she asked. No one put a number to it, but one of the engineers, not Jensen, said: "With the evidence, I think we have to have that much doubt."

Dr. Dragovic, who watched the "20/20" show with the three of his children who are in law school, said the doubts the jurors had weren't because Fletcher might be innocent— Dragovic is convinced of his guilt—but because of the preparation put in by Legghio and McCowan. And, by comparison, a lack of preparation by the prosecution.

"Brian Legghio—I give him a 10. He opened up every

avenue. He chipped away bit by bit, planting doubt," he said. "With no evidence in their favor, they were able to raise doubts left and right. Legghio clearly demonstrated himself as a master. A master. That's what separates a great defense attorney from the attorneys you usually see in court every day, who just shoot from the hip. I didn't know him before; I turned into his fan."

As for Townsend, Dragovic, a hip-shooter himself when the mood suits, said: "You learn from trials. We learned from this one. This will sound like criticism. It's constructive criticism. The defense spent far more time on preparation than the prosecution. They spent far more time with me than the prosecution did. I think the prosecution thought the evidence would be so overwhelming that they got complacent. We could have spent more time demonstrating the evidence and provided the jury with more information.

"I think there was a lull that set in. They thought the evidence was so straightforward, all they had to do was present it. But that's not enough when you're going against an attorney like Legghio."

From the time Fletcher's shirt was confiscated the day of the shooting, until the lab tests came back a week before the trial, the prosecution and police were convinced that Leann's DNA would show up in the so-called blood mist on the sleeve, proving conclusively, in open-and-shut fashion, that Fletcher shot her at close range. When the tests came back with the shocking result that there was no DNA profile for Leann on the shirt, it was too late to come up with a Plan B. Townsend would be stuck relying on witnesses the jury would hate; in the meantime, Legghio and McCowan had found the best experts they could.

As an example of Townsend's relaxed, overconfident approach to the trial, Dragovic offered two examples. One, he had been on vacation in Europe before the trial and didn't find out he was going to be the first witness until he arrived home the night before the trial began and had a message on his phone telling him he was first up—a shocking lack of preparation given the stakes. Two, before his reappearance as a rebuttal witness on the last day of the trial, Marla McCowan asked him what he was going to testify to; Dragovic had to tell her he didn't know, because Townsend hadn't discussed the line of questioning with him ahead of time.

The Miseners got a phone call one day from someone conducting a survey for Philip Morris.

"No one here smokes," said Jack Misener.

"Doesn't Michael Fletcher live there?"

"No. He lives in Jackson State Prison."

A pause on the other end, then: "I'll put down he's on an extended vacation."

"A life-long vacation," said Jack.

Townsend has a new memorial to the bad guys in his small office. It sits atop the small table just to the left as a visitor enters, right next to the framed newspaper photo of Jack Kevorkian, the one with the caption, "Do I look like a criminal?" This newest addition to his collection is a framed color photo of Mick Fletcher, also bears a caption.

Lisa Ortlieb has the same framed photo in her office, with the same caption. The photo was taken indoors and the color of Mick's face is a bit off. It has a green tint. He's in his bright, almost Day-Glo, orange Oakland County prisoner uniform.

The caption at the bottom reads: "He never thought he would be a convicted criminal."

AFTERWORD

"The No. 1 rule for everybody is one spelled out by Sir Arthur Conan Doyle through the mouth of Sherlock Holmes. 'You cannot advance theories before knowing facts.' If you create a theory, you fall into the trap of trying to fit the facts to your theory."
— Dr. Ljubisa Dragovic, discussing the philosophy behind his approach to his work during an interview with a reporter more than a month after Michael Fletcher was sentenced to life in prison.

Did Michael Fletcher kill Leann Fletcher? A jury said he did. A judge agreed and sentenced him to life in prison. She will do all she can to make sure he leaves jail only when he's dead and ready for burial.

There certainly is room for doubt, though, beginning with jury members, themselves. They deliberated for four days, then brought in a verdict of second-degree murder, a verdict that stunned everyone, since the prosecution's whole case and theory of events was that this was a carefully orchestrated, planned and executed murder, a murder that may have taken months to carry out.

Fletcher had been too nice and too sweet in those months between the time that he moved back into the house at Easter of 1999 and when Leann died on August 16. His seeming change in attitude wasn't a change at all, but part of the plan.

When Mick bought a card the morning of the shooting and inscribed words of love and affection to his newly pregnant wife, they were just more of the alibi being put into her hands and into place.

When he took her to the shooting range, the intent was

clear, said Greg Townsend. It wasn't to have Leann Fletcher practice her shooting, it was to get gunpowder on her hands, corroboration for a claim he'd make later in the day that she'd shot herself.

This was, all sides agreed going into the trial, during the trial and after the trial, either first-degree murder or it wasn't murder at all.

Until that Thursday afternoon when the jury walked back into Judge Cooper's courtroom and jury foreman Rob Jensen pronounced Mick Fletcher guilty of second-degree murder.

To this day, the police, the prosecution, Judge Cooper and the extended Misener family are sure that an evil, calculating cold-blooded murderer got trapped by his own arrogance and is now where he belongs, in jail, serving a life term. Gloria Misener told him at his sentencing that she hoped they'd find him dead on his jail cell floor one day, naked from the waist down.

Mick Fletcher, in their eyes, is so evil that he can engage in the act of sex, get an erection and reach ejaculation knowing all the while that the instant he is done, that when his sperm is fresh in her vagina, inches away from the nearly microscopic little baby that is attached to Leann's uterus, he is going to pick up his Smith & Wesson and shoot her in the head, killing, in the most bloody and violent way possible, this woman he is joined to now.

That is a nasty, nasty image, and one that Townsend wanted to plant clearly in the jury's mind, even though it made the actual time-line that much more congested and gave that much more credibility to the defense claim that there wasn't enough time to have committed the murder.

But that's the creature Townsend is convinced he put away, and that's the creature he wanted the jury to see, not the handsome guy with the sexy spit curl dangling over his forehead sitting there in front of them.

Though they brought in a murder verdict, the jury itself seemed hardly sure of its work. The week after the trial, court officials turned over their court- and jury room to the producers of "20/20 Downtown",—getting the kind of cooperation their print brethren could never receive—and the ten jurors who chose to participate in a filmed post-mortem.

What they told "20/20" was so startling that the show's producers decided to forgo the hours of gavel-to-gavel footage they'd shot of the trial, decided to forgo the forensic evidence, decided to forgo Judge Cooper's dramatic condemnation of Fletcher at his sentencing, and show, instead, for virtually the entire hour of the show which ran on November 20, 2000, reenactments of the jury process.

It shocked the Fletchers, who feared the show would portray their son as a murdering devil.

It shocked the Miseners, who expected the same.

It caused Brian Legghio to feel like vomiting and left him depressed. It left Greg Townsend muttering that all the producers wanted was entertainment value and not truth.

What "20/20" presented was extremely sympathetic to Mick Fletcher. If your only knowledge of the case was gleaned from watching that show, you couldn't have reached any other conclusion than this: Mick Fletcher got railroaded.

The jury, en masse, sitting together in front of reporter Elizabeth Vargas, said that they found the evidence weak; they thought the prosecution's witnesses were incompetent, unreliable, or, worse, lying. They also dismissed the prosecution's theory of motive as preposterous; and they agreed with Legghio that Leann Fletcher couldn't possibly have been shot where the prosecution said she was, on her knees, while her head was bent down over the floor, after having sex with her husband.

"Reasonable doubt." Everyone who has ever watched TV, seen movies or read books has heard that term. Almost no laymen really know for sure what it means. But to most people, if you said a jury didn't believe the prosecution witnesses, didn't believe the forensic evidence against the accused, didn't believe the motive and didn't think the deceased was shot where the prosecution said she was shot—well, if that doesn't seem to be at least reasonable doubt, what is?

Do I think Mick Fletcher is innocent? When the trial began, I only knew what I'd read in the papers. I figured he'd done it. As the trial unfolded and the prosecution's evidence seemed so assailable, I began to have doubts. Lots of them, at least a reasonable amount. I don't know if Mick murdered Leann. He's the only one in the world who does know. He may very well have killed his wife. But I do think that with all those doubts the jury admitted to, and which are covered more in depth in the chapter in this book on the deliberations, they were obligated to return a not guilty verdict.

After discussing the case at length at Rob Jensen's home after the trial, I thought their actions were egregious, and I was convinced of it after watching "20/20".

The jury decided Leann had been shot on the bed, a scenario Legghio never had a chance to argue against. They thought they could prove a negative, deciding that it was impossible for Leann to have killed herself, even though their final proof for that theory was an embarrassment of illogic and bad science.

The jurors put tape on the floor of the jury room to reconstruct the Fletcher's bedroom. Then, pretending to be on a bed that wasn't there, holding the actual murder weapon while only pretending to fire it, they couldn't get the gun to land where it should. Even a prosecution witness, Sgt. William Harvey of the Oakland County Sheriff's Department, had answered a question from Townsend about where the gun likely would go if fired by someone on the bed by saying he agreed it was unlikely the gun could have ended up where it did, but added: "Now there are obvious variables. It could have bounced on carpeting or whatever, but I would expect it to be in this general vicinity."

The Fletcher bedroom was extremely cramped, a small room made all the smaller by the bed, a chest, a computer stand, a computer tower and the like. Pretending to fire a gun, pretending to give it a recoil, pretending to be shot, pretending to fall from a bed that isn't there, pretending to be in a differently configured room that was cluttered with real objects— doing all of that and then sending someone to jail for life because of the way the gun bounced? Preposterous.

The last holdout wanted one more play death. When the gun landed in the wrong spot again, she voted to convict. And what if, on that trial, the gun had taken a fluke bounce and rolled the opposite way? That fluke roll would have made Fletcher innocent?

The play-acting struck both MacDonell and Wentling as absurd. Both have been around firearms their whole careers; one wrote the book on blood evidence for the FBI and the other is a former Pennsylvania state cop who was a firearms examiner for 24 years. Both say there is no scientific validity in the game of pretend the jury played.

What the jury tried to do was fulfill another of Sherlock Holmes's maxims. Eliminate the impossible and what you have left, no matter how unlikely, is what happened. They decided it was impossible Leann could have accidentally shot herself, therefore Mick had done it. Professor MacDonell, in an interview for this book, said he had been involved in a case of a rifle shooting under similar circumstances—the weapon slipped in someone's hand and the thumb discharged it with disastrous results—and that in any event, just because something was highly unlikely was proof of nothing. There is a one-in-two-billion chance, he said, of a sperm achieving its goal, and yet we are all testament to the reality that unlikely events can and do occur.

There are two extremely unlikely chains of events that might have happened in the Fletcher house on August 16, 1999. Neither is remotely likely. One of them happened.

Scenario A: A woman who is afraid of guns, who just got back from her first-ever visit to the gun range, decides to pick up the gun when her husband is out of the room. For some stupid reason her thumb—her thumb? Of all things?—ends up on the trigger, somehow exerting the pressure needed to pull it, and she accidentally shoots herself in the head, just at the instant her husband—an unfaithful husband, by the way, whose lover is going to be enraged when she finds out his wife is pregnant—happens to be out of the room.

Come on. What are the chances? The very first time she ever goes to the gun range she just happens to get shot later? Why would she pick up the gun? Why would her thumb end up on the trigger? How could blood, any blood, end up in the drain trap? That all this could happen and the husband be innocent is preposterous.

Scenario B: A man with absolutely no history of violence, who has been known all his life for walking away from fights—heck, he even drives his wife nuts when he won't argue with her—who has never so much as slapped his wife during all their troubles and separations, is suddenly going to turn into a murderer? A cold-blooded, premeditated murderer?

So, let's see, he hatches a plan to take his wife to the gun range so she'll get gunpowder residue on her hands. Then, to get her back to the house where he can kill her, instead of going where they're supposed to go, which is to her parents', he asks her if she wants to have a quickie. And so they race home. But having set up this elaborate plan, having got the baby over to the in-laws', having got gunpowder on her hands, having lured her back to the house where he's going to shoot her within minutes, instead of killing her right then and there, he waits until she's done going to the bathroom.

Never mind that there isn't a woman in North America who goes to the bathroom without washing her hands and never mind she's in a tiny bathroom just across the hall and he surely hears the faucet running, he decides to go ahead with it anyway? I mean, if the reason behind all the plans made that day was to get gunpowder on her hands, once she washes them, wouldn't you go to plan B: killing her another day?

What else? Oh, yeah, he's got this incriminating book on crime-scene evidence, which sets off alarms to the cops, but if he's so busy studying crime-scene evidence, why shoot her from 12 inches or whatever when he can just put the gun to her head and kill her without leaving any tell-tale stippling?

And, oh, yes, from the time they get home from the gun range till the time the 911 call is made, there's only going to be eight or ten minutes, but he decides to pack as much as possible into her last day by having sex before murder. Even though the whole point of killing his wife is to keep the judge from finding out he's having sex with his wife, his plan for getting away with it is to set up a fake death scene that involves getting ready for sex with his half-naked wife? He's going to cover up his sexual relationship with his wife by calling 911 and saying they were about to have sex when the gun went off?

There's more. Everyone agrees that a killing machine like a Smith & Wesson .45 creates a cloud of high-velocity blood mist, a fast blowback aerosol of minute blood particles flying through the air. And even though he shoots her at close range, presumably getting blowback blood mist all over his hands, his shirt, just about everywhere, by the time the 911 ambulance arrives four minutes later—so quickly, in fact, that Leann, mortally wounded, still has electric heart palpitations, proof she has just been shot—Fletcher doesn't have any blood on him, nothing visible in his hair, on his face, anywhere that is seen by any of a series of cops who interrogate him over the next few hours.

He's on the phone for four minutes to the 911 operator, so if he cleaned up, he had to do it before calling, but after pulling the trigger. He shoots her, he phonies up the death scene—including, inexplicably, dragging or pushing her so that all of one foot and part of another are under the bed—he washes all trace of this cloud of blood mist off his arms, face, hands, even hair, then he calls 911 and talks to them for four minutes. And when the ambulance arrives Leann's heart is still beating.

Preposterous? Absolutely.

Two preposterous scenarios. Yet, one of them was probably real.

Is it likely Leann shot herself? Of course not.

But is the alternative any more likely? No.

The trouble with this case is, you can't believe anything. There are two very strange chains of events. Maybe Mick is an unbelievably cold-blooded psychotic; maybe this otherwise brilliant man really did plan this murder for months, pretending to be the loving husband to throw everybody off the scent, but was so stupid that the best plot he could come up with was to kill her in such suspicious circumstances (going to the gun range first, being alone with her in the house later) that he would be the first, obvious and only suspect.

Maybe Leann, in a hurry to have sex and then go get her daughter, starts grabbing a bunch of the gun stuff off the bed, grabs the gun and clip in one hand, goes to stand, slips, tries to brace herself, her thumb hits the trigger, BLAM!

The Miseners all say it is impossible Leann could ever have touched the gun under any circumstance, for any reason. Therefore, Mick had to have touched it, and fired it. But she'd fired it numerous times just minutes earlier. Maybe, despite its awesome power, having held it and fired it and hit a target, it no longer seemed so fearful. Maybe it was something she would, and did, pick up. And doing so killed her.

The jury agreed with the Miseners, even though they disagreed with nearly every element of the prosecution. And so they convicted him.

On the "20/20" show, at least one of them was already wracked with doubt that they had done the right thing. Another said he imagined that everyone on the jury had doubts, that you'd have to, given the weakness of the evidence.

As for me, I keep coming back to motive. It isn't necessary, legally, to prove motive, but I can't believe that if this was a murder, it happened without one. To believe the prosecution's final motive, the one it used in the trial, you have to believe that Fletcher's love for Judge Chrzanowski was so strong, that when he found out his wife was pregnant, in order to keep the judge from finding out, he hatched a remarkably stupid plot to kill her. The judge's love was that important to him. And yet, this is the same judge, who divorced her husband and the same Mick Fletcher who moved back home to his wife the very day the divorce was final. The same judge and the same Fletcher who hadn't exchanged a single e-mail, or card, or poem—of all the e-mails, cards and poems detectives unearthed—in the last four months of their relationship.

Like everything else in this case, the motive doesn't add up. One is left—if Mick did it—with a huge, seemingly unanswerable *why?*

One thing I have no doubt of is that nearly everyone seems to have violated the No. 1 rule as promulgated by Sherlock Holmes, Sir Arthur Conan Doyle and Ljubisa Dragovic.

Brian Legghio said after the verdict was announced that this case had reasonable doubt written all over it. The jurors disagreed.

For sure, they and I agree, it had rush-to-judgment written on it, and "fitting facts to theory." The judgment may have been correct—that Fletcher killed his wife in cold blood—but I'd feel a lot better about it if the final judgment hadn't had so many snap judgments along the way. Reading the police reports and my subsequent interviews with everyone involved, it's striking how many people say they know "instantly," "right away," "as soon as," or some such variation, exactly what happened.

Gloria Misener made a rush to judgment when she said said, "Oh my God, Jack, he shot her," the moment the Troy police said there'd been a shooting. Maybe that was a cruel alignment of fate, too. When her daughter had told her she was going shooting, Gloria joked that she hoped Mick hadn't taken out another life-insurance policy on her. (As it turned out, they didn't have any policy on Leann.) But perhaps the thought had been planted, and when Troy police told her there'd been a shooting, out it popped.

Gloria said in an interview for this book: "We knew from the minute the police came exactly what happened." But of course she didn't know. Until she got to the police station, she thought the shooting had happened at the firing range. She doesn't come from a gun family. She didn't know if they can fire easily or not. She didn't know if her daughter had been holding it and stumbled and fell in front of a dozen witnesses. She didn't know if it had happened at the range. She hadn't been told any of the particulars by Cleyman or Hendricks. The state police investigators hadn't even gotten to the scene and begun piecing the bloody puzzle together. How much did her assertion sway police?

The night before, they had gone out to dinner to celebrate the new baby her daughter was going to have with Mick. That morning they took Hannah to babysit. If you thought your daughter's husband was capable of planning her murder, would you have been celebrating that they were having another child just the night before? If you thought him capable of pulling that trigger, would you casually agree to babysit while they went to the gun range? But when you're told there's been a shooting, the first thought is that it's murder, and a planned murder at that?

But Gloria Misener is entitled to make all the rushes to judgment she wants.

What of the police? Welch said Gloria's statement that the son-of-a-bitch did it told him he was on the right track. Cleyman appalled the jury when he told them on the witness stand that he was "stone-cold certain" Mick was a murderer, when he hadn't been to the murder scene and based it on little more than seeing Mick walk into jail, and having seen a History Channel show on the Kennedys a couple of nights earlier.

His boss, Chief Niedermeier, says events proved Cleyman right and that his certainty on August 16 was nothing more than the good instincts a good cop cultivates over the years. But did his seemingly premature leap to "stone-cold" certainty, combined with Gloria Misener's anger and self-assurance of her own at the police station aim him and other cops toward fitting fact to theory?

Officer Barner wasn't a homicide investigator. Relatively new to police work, he was by all accounts a crackerjack undercover cop, whose forte was casing and arresting B&E punks. He heard the Hazelwood call on his police radio and zipped to the scene in case he was needed. He wasn't. He was at the site a minute or two, then left. He told himself and others that it looked like a phonied-up crime scene and the husband did it. "I remember thinking at the time, and I told the other crew member, 'This guy just killed his wife.' That was my initial impression," Barner, who eventually arrested Fletcher, would say a year later. Was he right? Maybe. Did he have any experience or knowledge base to arrive at his quick conclusion? No. Was it a rushed judgment? Of course.

Dennis Welch got to the scene and thought something was fishy because Fletcher didn't have much blood on him, and if it had been his own wife, "I'd have been covered with blood."

Larry Hendricks, in an interview after the trial, said: "The scene seemed staged to us." This quick judgment from a cop heading up his first homicide investigation, who never even saw the body at the scene. He thought the gun should have kicked farther away from the body, that everything looked "too neat." Fair enough. Good police instincts? Possibly. Still, the state police were hours away from the real nuts-and-bolts stuff of measuring bloodspatter and trying to figure out what had happened and where.

Welch, Hendricks and Cleyman may have been right all along. But the fact remains they come from a small force where murders are rare and the kind of crime-scene tampering they were sure had happened is a once- or twice-a-career event you don't get any practice for. A classic example? Hendricks is going to head up the investigation, and he's at the Hazel Park police station just four blocks from the murder scene. So why in the world would they cart the body off before he got there? He was pulling up when the body was coming down the sidewalk. Couldn't they have let Leann lie there a few minutes more, till the lead investigator could at least survey the scene?

And that begs the question, of course, of why none of

them, if they were so sure they were dealing with foul play, would do the basic next step of ordering that Leann's hands be bagged so as to leave any evidence such as gunpowder or blood mist inviolate.

Officer Lehman, the first cop at the scene, was another to jump to conclusions. Was he right? Perhaps. But he jumped, nonetheless. When he arrived, he saw Mick Fletcher standing outside the house, smoking a cigarette, holding a cell phone. His written report later that day emphasized Fletcher's relative calmness, and he was used as a prosecution witness to paint an entirely different picture of Mick than came across on the 911 tapes.

And, yet, a reading of the transcript of that tape gives another perfectly plausible reason for Mick to be out on the lawn. Lehman saw him as an actor who was calmly smoking a cigarette and seemed not very agitated. But from the defense point of view, he has been warned repeatedly by the 911 operator not to touch anything at the scene. And he'd been asked several times to please try and calm down:

"Like I said, don't touch anything in the room, okay?"
"I'm not. I can't even be in there." Then, "there's a cop here, now."

The cop is Lehman. Is Fletcher calm? Or is he so freaked out by what's in the house that he can't even be there? Is he doing what a cigarette smoker does in times of stress—smoking? Has he been able to follow the dispatcher's advice and calm down?

Two ways to look at it. The cops' way was to see it as evidence of duplicity.

Fitting fact to theory? After Fletcher had been interviewed off and on for more than two hours, he was on the way out of the station with his attorney. As Cleyman escorted him to the door, he told Fletcher he had a beautiful daughter. Fletcher responded by saying that Hannah was his angel, his life. Cleyman brought up Hannah, and Mick answered. Later, Cleyman would say his brief response was further proof of his guilt because he hadn't mentioned his wife, either. But he'd just spent two hours talking about his wife, their activities together that day.

"They thought they'd figured it out in hours," said Legghio. "It goes back to the old argument of investigation by inclusion. That which builds a case gets included in the case. That which doesn't seem to fit or doesn't fly or doesn't bolster the case gets excluded."

I think the Hazel Park cops' reaction to the day's events were heart-felt, honest and industrious. Wentling, a retired cop who has spent the preponderance of his time in the witness box over the years testifying on the behalf of prosecutors, is far harsher. He says that not only did the Hazel Park police and state police fit their facts to their theory, they were incompetent to boot. However you look at it, clearly Sherlock's maxim was violated repeatedly on August 16, 1999.

Legghio used the word "systemic" several times in his closing arguments. The system may very well have been right, but there's no question that the system made a concerted, organized effort, steamrolling along in one straight direction from the first minutes at the scene right through the adoption proceedings for Hannah.

It involved police—"I think it was all just part of the natural antipathy that exists between police and attorneys; nothing makes a cop happier than getting a lawyer," Legghio said after the trial—the medical examiner, the prosecutor, judges and child-welfare officials. Cooper's harsh sentence and faith in Mick's guilt stemmed from David Woodford's testimony about blood in the drain trap and a word she said he used to describe it. She said in an interview for this book that the convincing evidence for her that Fletcher was guilty was Woodford's testimony that there had been "copious" amounts of blood in the sink and that there was none on the phone Mick used to call 911. Only a guilty man washes his hands before calling 911.

During sentencing, Cooper said: "I believe what Mr. Woodford testified to was that there was copious amounts of blood in the trap of the sink . . . his word was—I wrote it down—'copious.' "

Except Woodford never said it. Neither my notes of the trial, the official transcript nor the original computer discs of Cooper's former court reporter, Karen Hollen, show Woodford using the word. No actual blood was found. The gunk in the drain trap tested positive for the presence of blood but whatever was there was too tiny even to be tested for a DNA profile, and that's tiny, indeed. Woodford implied, in his words on the stand, that the presence of any blood in the trap must have meant "a fair amount" was there before the last person to use the sink turned on the water. Later he amended it to "a significant amount."

The jury didn't believe a word Woodford said. Professor MacDonell said during the trial that the tests for blood are so sophisticated that one drop in a tub full of water would cause a positive result, and to him its presence in the trap wasn't significant. Trace amounts of blood could linger there depending on how much water was run through. (For this book, he went further, saying that drawing meaningful conclusions from a presumptive test for blood "is ridiculous." Moreover, he said, Woodford was so clearly incompetent on the subject of bloodstain evidence that he shouldn't even be allowed to testify at trials.)

But Cooper discounted MacDonell and gave more power to Woodford's testimony than even Woodford meant. She sentenced Fletcher with the picture of copious amounts of blood in the sink. Systemic? (And then there's Woodford's infamous, flustered, red-faced refusal to testify off defense photos moments after willingly drawing conclusions from his own photographic blow-ups for the prosecution.)

Or how about the system seeming to change its view about whether there was blood on Fletcher, and what it meant? At his arraignment in August and his pre-trial hearing in September, the prosecution said the obvious blood mist on his shirt was conclusive proof of his guilt, that the blood could only have gotten there if he was inches away from Leann's head when she was shot. But the shirt ended up having so little blood, if any, that it couldn't even be tested for DNA. So, at the trial, the prosecution's theory was that a *lack* of blood on Fletcher was proof of his guilt—one, he must have washed it off, and, two, in any event, if he wasn't guilty he would have cradled his dead wife and got blood all over himself.

Or the selective use of witnesses at trial? Officer Lehman testified that when he arrived at the scene, Fletcher was fairly calm. It was, said Townsend, a sharp contrast to the Fletcher on the phone. But the reports Officers Welch and Hamel filled out that day show a hysterical Mick Fletcher, even hours after the shooting. Welch wrote that he had to help Fletcher walk, that he kept collapsing to the ground and breaking out in sobs. Maybe it was all the work of a gifted actor, but there was nothing calm about it.

Fletcher had a presumption of innocence up until the moment the jury voted 12–0 for his guilt. But the presumption was theoretical, not practical.

For example, when it came time at his arraignment to set bail, the prosecution argued against it, claiming he was a flight risk, and presented evidence that by then the cops and prosecutors knew was false. Or should have known.

Upon Barner's arrival as part of a surveillance team to Fletcher's parents' house in Marysville—to keep an eye on Fletcher while an arrest warrant was being readied—he saw a fifth-wheel trailer being unloaded . . . or loaded. He couldn't tell in the dark. Of course his first thought was that this guy might be getting ready to make a run for it. But within seconds he had run the plate through Lansing and got back the answer that the vehicle was registered to another Fletcher, one who lived in Holland, who was in his 60s.

In any event, how stupid would you have to be to flee police in a huge, oversized fifth wheel that goes about 60 m.p.h. top end and has your name, "FLETCHER," printed in big letters across the back of the trailer? Especially when there's a Corvette sitting in the garage.

No, the police and the prosecutors knew by then the vehicle was not evidence of anything whatsoever, yet they told Hazel Park Judge Keith Hunt that the fifth-wheel showed Mick to be a flight risk, the judge agreed and put Mick in jail without bail. "What was he going to do with a trailer? Load up his furniture and flee?" said Legghio after the trial. "It was disingenuous. Clearly, clearly disingenuous," said Legghio.

If he committed the crime, you might argue, who cares if the system cheated to keep him off the streets? Still, we pretend to take the presumption of innocence very seriously in this country. At his arraignment, legally, Fletcher was still an innocent man. Yet, on that silly evidence, he was deemed a flight risk and worthy only of jail.

*   *   *

As for the good Dr. Dragovic, no one ever questioned his moral authority or integrity. He is brilliant and dedicated, but even he acknowledges that his zeal in the past to see homicide where co-workers saw accident or ambiguity—second-guessing them, looking over their shoulders and even asking to redo their work—once made him extremely unpopular when he was an assistant medical examiner in Wayne County.

Yes, he was right in some of those cases. He was wrong in others, too. Repeatedly, Oakland County jurors said he was wrong in judging the assisted-suicide cases of Dr. Kevorkian as murder, and even his supporters wondered if Dragovic had crossed the line into advocacy in his battles with "Dr. Death."

Legghio says a nearly instantaneous judgment of homicide in the Leann Fletcher case—before Dragovic knew the caliber of the weapon and the type of gunpowder, both of which affect stippling patterns, or whether Leann was right-handed or in need of glasses, factors that might be relevant—shows the doctor violated his favorite saying, too. And it was Dragovic, himself, in an interview for this book, who said it was clear to him what had happened as soon as Leann's body was wheeled in to him for the autopsy. "Right then and there it was clear," he said. Right then and there, before she'd been cleaned up, before he'd done *any* of the work that goes into an autopsy. Another violation of Holmes's maxim?

Dragovic is convinced Fletcher is a murderer, though even he would probably admit he's never erred on the side of caution when it comes to seeing evil in the corpses that lie on his table. No one has ever accused him of seeing accidental death when there's been murder. He has, over the years, been accused of seeing murder where there wasn't.

If Mick Fletcher killed his wife, he's where he deserves to be. And he is as evil a character as ever came through the Oakland County courts.

If Leann died as a result of some horrible, implausible, but real accident, then he's the unluckiest man on the face of the earth. Because if that's the way it happened, then he lost his wife—yes, he was cheating on her, but he also left a beautiful, powerful judge who made far more money than he did to take one last stab at making his marriage work—he lost his beloved child, he lost his unborn second child and he lost his freedom, likely forever, for something that was the fault of the Fates.

There are very intelligent people, well meaning, who are sure Mick Fletcher got what he deserved. There are others, equally intelligent, equally well meaning, who are sure an innocent man sits in jail, likely forever.

One other thing that happened that day: Two families were tragically and horribly changed forever. The Miseners lost their most beloved member, a combination of sunshine and angel who touched everyone she came into contact with. The Fletchers lost a daughter-in-law they loved, they lost their son, handsome and brilliant, and they lost their granddaughter.

Hannah, of course, is the biggest loser of all. She lost her mother, her father and two of her grandparents, and one wonders how she'll ever recover.

AN INTERVIEW WITH MICHAEL FLETCHER

AUTHOR'S NOTE: Against the advice of his appellate attorney, Michael Fletcher agreed to respond to written questions nine months after his guilty verdict, as this book was going to press. The comments have been trimmed but the language that remains is his. There was no opportunity for follow-up questions. Except for a brief interview on the ABC news show "20/20" these are his only on-the-record comments about that fateful day in August and subsequent events.

Q. How do you spend your time? Can you describe for me a typical day and week?

A. Although I've recently changed facilities, and have as of yet no set routine, I'll describe what I did with my time at the last facility.

Almost immediately, I was hired as the housing unit librarian. This appealed to me, because I didn't even have to leave the building. Monday through Friday, I sat and read books for two hours, and little more. Those inmates who enjoy reading almost always prefer to read suspense novels, and those are kept in the main library in another building. The books in the library I worked in were primarily educational materials. For some reason, those types of books are like kryptonite to prison inmates. As such, I didn't have much work to do, and oddly enough, those ten hours a week (sometimes even less) constituted a full-time position. Go figure.

Every other day, I worked out in the weight pit. As for the rest of my time, I spent it at my typewriter, reading books, and watched "Jeopardy!" twice a day. I also spent a good amount of time listening to the radio.

Since everything is pretty much done for you, even your laundry, you're pretty much free to spend your time as you like. It's pretty strange for me, not having a hundred or so different responsibilities tugging at me all the time, but then again, I suppose I'd have to be foolish to complain, given the circumstances.

As far as weeks are concerned, every day is pretty much the same for me. The only thing that changes is the television schedule, and church on Sunday.

Q. **What do you do for recreation or amusement?**
A. See above.

Q. **You were an avid reader. Are you allowed to read what you want? Do they censor or restrict the books or magazines you are allowed?**
A. Given the life of leisure that I've recently been provided with, I have the opportunity to do more reading than I ever have in the past. There are silver linings. . . .

Materials relating to weapons, explosives, etc. are prohibited as I understand. Since my tastes in literature tend to center around philosophy, theology, technology, and any decent fiction that I can get my hands on, these restrictions haven't proven to be a bother in the least. Although there is this Aryan Nation/Neo-Nazi fellow up the hall that's trying to sell a photocopied edition of the *Anarchists' Cookbook*. I told him that I wasn't interested.

Q. **According to police and prosecutors, death threats were made to you upon your admittance to the prison system. Rumors were flying among the men in blue. I know this firsthand because I was told them. Has there been any truth in that, as far as you know? How do you get along with your fellow inmates?**
A. That's pretty funny, actually. I will assume that you already have a pretty good idea as to why police and prosecutors would want to spread rumors of that nature, and perhaps want to believe them true themselves. I suspect you've figured that out for yourself during the course of your research and interviews with them, by the way you've worded this question as well as the next.

Before even getting to prison, I received letters of support from inmates. Many of them just wrote to tell me that they were praying for myself and my family, their belief in my innocence, and wishing me luck for a speedy and successful appeal. Not once have I ever received correspondence that was negative in any way, let alone threatening. That is, of course, excluding creditors.

Consider this: an attorney goes to prison. Where else on earth could a lawyer be of more practical value? Forgive me taking a risk at sounding distasteful, but one could easily, if not accurately, analogize ringing the dinner bell in a Third World country.

Given that I've been trying to keep myself busy, I spend the majority of my time working alone. However, when I'm out and about, I'll sit around and converse just like everyone else. Much of this time I spend answering questions of a legal nature, as you might guess, and overall my fellow inmates have seemed appreciative.

Q. **Will you be doing, or have you done, any jailhouse lawyering on behalf of your fellow inmates?**

A. As I mentioned earlier, I frequently answer questions and discuss legal issues. From time to time, I'll review briefs and other paperwork. But for the most part, I've been too busy doing other things to involve myself in research or document preparation. Should I change my mind in the future at some point, there will certainly be no shortage of clients, however.

Q. **Can you recount for me those few moments from the time you went into the bathroom, heard the shot and came back out? Your thoughts, reactions, etc.**

A. Our house was very small and very old, with painted plaster walls. So when the gun went off, I felt the sound as much as heard it. I suppose that anyone who has been shocked by an unexpected and extremely loud noise can relate to the heart-stopping effect it had on me.

Admittedly, and regrettably in retrospect, my first concerns were not for Leann's safety or welfare. In that brief moment it took for me to exit the bathroom and go down the hall to the bedroom, I was thinking about the hole she had just blown through one of the dressers, the floor, wall, or possibly her computer or printer. I expected to find her standing there holding the gun, shaking like a leaf, with her mouth slightly open and her lower lip quivering as it always did before she started to cry. The first words out of my mouth would have been "What the *hell* are you doing?" or "Are you insane, woman?"

We had expressions that we used when one of us would screw up in a big way. Mine for hers was "pulling a Leann" (her phrase for my mishaps was identical, except for the name of course). In short, my first thought was that she had just pulled a Leann, and it was destined to be one of her many classics. It would've been one of those things that I was mad about at first, but laughed about later. I can't explain why this thought was my first mental response. Perhaps a psychologist would say that subconsciously I didn't want it to be anything more than that. All I know is that it would've been preferable to come home and find that she had burned the house to the ground with everything we owned in it, than to see what actually did happen, or even have the memory of it.

Q. **The prosecution seemed fixated on the thought you had sex with Leann and then killed her, even though it made a tight time-line even tighter. When did you last have sex with her, if not just before the shooting?**

A. Prior to responding to your question directly, I would first like to address what I believe is the larger issue here. Namely, I would like to discuss the justification, or lack thereof, for their assertion, and why it was important to them.

There are several physical indicators that a pathologist will look for in order to determine whether or not a female had engaged in sexual activity immediately prior to death. These observations are routine procedure, and questions in this regard are also routine when the issue is raised.

Oddly enough, the prosecution failed to ask any questions with regard to these physical indicators during their direct examination of the forensic pathologist that had performed the exam. They were asserting that I had sex with my wife just prior to the shooting, yet they failed to even attempt to extract evidence of this from the only witness that could have provided it. The defense, on the other hand, performed this routine line of questioning upon cross-examination of the same witness. Normally, this would be a risky thing for defense counsel to do, because the prosecution had failed to produce the evidence, the defense had nothing to refute. In addition to the fact that the witness was called by the prosecution. In this case, however, the responses of the witness were anticipated. That is, there were no physical indicators present which suggested that my wife had been involved in sexual activity just prior to her death. The prosecution's own witness admitted this.

The prosecution also failed to establish any kind of time-line with regard to the events. Time-lines are important in any case, particularly to prosecutors in this type of trial. Since the prosecution bears the burden of proof (they're *supposed* to bear the burden, at any rate), it is important that they establish that their theory as to what occurred actually fits within a given time frame. In other words, they have to demonstrate that an individual could have carried out the activities they are alleging, or at least had the opportunity.

The prosecution also called a witness that was able to approximate the time of our departure from the gun range. Furthermore, they had almost an entire year to investigate how long it takes to drive from that point to our home during typical Monday lunch-hour traffic. This, again, is routine procedure that was strangely overlooked by a prosecutor with a wealth of experience; far more than my own, at any rate. As the evidence demonstrated, elicited from the prosecution's witnesses at that, Leann and I were only in the house for a few minutes prior to the 911 call. For the prosecutor to claim that I did all of the things they assert, and then allege that I was able to have sex prior to, is ludicrous. In fact, if the prosecutor claims that it was possible for a man to *only* have sex, and nothing more, within that time frame, he must certainly be speaking from his own personal experience. And my sincerest sympathies are extended to his wife.

The question remains as to why the prosecution would

make such an assertion, the lack of evidence to support it notwithstanding. After all, having sex with your wife is perfectly legal, so far as I know, and it is certainly not an element of the crime of murder. Furthermore, I was never charged with criminal sexual conduct or any other offense for which having had sex would even be legally relevant. So why was this claim made in the first place? Why was it so important to them? The answer is really quite simple, and it involves human nature.

I would venture to guess that most people can relate to the scenario where an accused man is being led into a court-house, he's usually wearing handcuffs and surrounded by police. We see this on the news all the time, with a reporter giving his rendition of the allegations being leveled against the individual. If the alleged crime is particularly heinous in nature, there is a tendency for people to point a finger, and hope against all hope that the accused individual gets nailed to the wall. This is done without regard as to the evidence, if any, that officials may or may not have to support the accusation.

Although I won't venture to guess as to why it is that people are so willing to assume guilt without basis, whether it is an innate desire to have faith in their government's institutions, a rush to judgment in order to satisfy one's sense of justice, or the ease of assuming the worst about a complete stranger. Whatever reason(s) lie behind this reaction, the fact is that it exists. No one is more aware of this than people who understand the nature of our criminal justice system, particularly those who work within it. It is also understood that the more heinous the accusation is, that natural reaction is proportionately stronger.

To accuse a man of executing his pregnant wife has a powerful effect in the community. Whether or not there is any evidentiary support for the claim, they have effectively made a monster of him. But when they assert that he had sex with her before committing the crime, they create something even more appalling. Namely, a perverted monster. They wanted to have the world hate me, especially the jurors, before the trial even began. It was the only way they could convict me.

The answer to your original question is Saturday, August fourteenth, late in the evening. We had gone out to a restaurant with our daughter and Leann's sister Lindy and her husband Marc. After that, we dropped Hannah off at Leann's parents' place, and the four of us went out to catch a movie. When we returned to collect our daughter, we decided to announce Leann's pregnancy to her parents. I had taken Hannah aside and told her to tell Grandma and Grandpa that she was going to have a little brother (Hey, a guy can dream, can't he?). Anyway, Hannah spilled the beans, and it was quite cute. Of course there were hugs and congratulatory expressions that normally follow such announcements. We stayed and talked for a while. During the ride home, Hannah fell asleep, so I carried her into her room and tucked her in bed when we arrived. When I went into our bedroom, Leann let me know that she was "in the mood." It was the last time I made love to my wife.

Q. When did you first realize you were a suspect?

A. When foul play is suspected, the spouse is always a suspect. Always. However, I never had any indication that they were considering foul play until just prior to my leaving the police station.

For the three-and-a-half hours or so that I was there, a detective (I believe his name was Welch) sat with me in a small room. He was compassionate in his mannerisms toward me, and continually offered his sympathy. It was this man who took my written statement. Oddly, the prosecution never used this statement, nor did they call Detective Welch to the stand. He was the same officer that brought me to the station from the house.

During the last few minutes I was there, Detectives Hendricks and Cleyman came into the room. Hendricks asked me why Leann picked the gun up. I told him that I didn't know. I thought this was an odd question, given what I had already written. Unless I was a psychic, any answer I could have possibly given him would have been pure speculation.

Cleyman was seated across from me when he addressed me. His tone was harsh, as though he were trying to emulate the "tough cop" persona. He said, "Well, I have a problem with people loading guns and having sex."

I was quite taken by surprise, shocked even, that an officer would say something like that to a man in my position and after what I'd been through. I began to repeat what I'd already told Detective Welch, and what I'd written down for them.

As I was recounting the events for the umpteenth time, he sat there rolling his eyes and bobbing his head, doing his best to demonstrate the fact that he had already formulated his opinion before coming into the room.

It was at that time that Roy, the attorney who came in to be with me, got up and took me out of there.

I had worked closely with police as an attorney, from both sides of the court, prosecution and defense. I was well aware that some cops use the tough-guy approach in order to shake out any inconsistent statements. This is not necessarily because he is a suspect.

It wasn't until later that we discovered that both Hendricks and Cleyman had already made up their minds at that point. The real investigation was over. What was in fact happening was an effort to find anything possible to support their opinion, as opposed to finding out what actually happened.

Q. You are a lawyer. Why didn't you simply ask to speak to a lawyer the moment the police took you to the station?

A. At the time I was taken to the police station, I was not a lawyer. I was a man who had just moments before been kneeling over the body of his wife. It was the most horrific and gruesome sight I had ever witnessed, and the fact that it was my wife, who only moments before had been smiling at me, created a sense of dread within me that is beyond description. I was in shock for days afterward, and legal concerns had no place in my mind. It took hours for me to even write out the brief statement for Detective Welch; I could barely hold the pen in my hand.

Marcia, the secretary at Roy Gruenberg's office (where I shared office space), paged me after a reporter called to ask questions. I called her from the station, and she told me that Roy was on his way. This was after I had been there for a couple of hours or so, perhaps three.

Q. **You went to the movies with Leann's sister that weekend. You went out to dinner with her parents. Obviously you socialized with the Misener family. What is your reaction to Gloria's immediate conclusion that you had killed Leann on purpose, and the rest of the family agreeing with her so readily?**

A. Yes, I frequently socialized with my in-laws. Furthermore, there isn't anything that I wouldn't have done for any of them if asked. At the same time, I am all too aware of Gloria's personality traits, as well as her position in the family.

If you review the report Detective Cleyman prepared with regard to Jack and Gloria's reaction to being told that their daughter was dead, you will notice that Gloria never even shed a tear. Her only reaction was a "grim" facial expression, and her statement "That son-of-a-bitch shot her" (I don't know why she had to insult my mother). She then proceeded to draft a statement, using bold, smooth penmanship. Cleyman indicated that Jack, on the other hand, completely lost it, which under the circumstances would be expected, I should think. I mean, imagine being told that your daughter, your baby at that, had just been killed. Yet Gloria's first reaction was to lash out, without even being apprised of the facts.

Simply put, this is the way that Gloria typically reacts or deals with anything that affects her adversely. She casts blame upon anyone whom she perceives as being worthy of it, and she never backs down, regardless of circumstances. She once, according to Leann, held a grudge against her own brother for purchasing a tombstone for their stepfather, whom she apparently disliked. Leann told me that she had refused to even speak with him for a decade. Although I'm not a psychologist, I think that perhaps this is some form of coping mechanism that Gloria developed a long time ago. I always felt sorry for her, actually. Harboring so much bitterness and animosity is much harder on the person who holds it, as opposed to the subject of it, and you can see it on her face.

Once this personality trait is taken into account, it's easy to understand why the family consistently backs her up in virtually any situation. To not do so would merely invite family discord of epic proportion. They are a very tight group, with all but one of the siblings living within Oakland County, and that one exception lives less than forty minutes away. In fact, the only brother, who is in his forties, still lives at home with Jack and Gloria. Without a doubt, the family is matriarchal, and Gloria is the head.

Another consideration, with regard to the family taking the position that they did, was the press. Although none of them were in a position to say anything authoritative with regard to the alleged incident, the Miseners were suddenly placed in a position where anything they did say was considered newsworthy, but only because of the sensationalism that the case generated.

Had the situation been reversed, that is, if I were the one who had been killed, my family would have hoped against all hope that it was an accident, consoling Leann instead of accusing her. They would have supported her, or at the very least held a neutral position in the unlikely event that she would have been charged with a crime (absent the accusation of Gloria, it is unlikely that I would have been charged). Knowing this, it was difficult for me to hear them claim that I had killed Leann, as simply and matter-of-factly as if comparing such an act to taking out the garbage. That they would consider me even capable of doing such a thing was a lot to handle.

What upset me most, however, was their behavior. At my wife's funeral, they removed the cards from the flower arrangements that my family had sent, cut my face out of the family pictures that were displayed . . .

Q. Did you want to take the stand at your trial, and, if so, why didn't you?

A. Since the prosecution failed to produce evidence that established my guilt, counsel advised me against it. There are several reasons for this. Prior to the trial, I had been locked in a little cement box for nearly eleven months. I hadn't seen the sun in any of that time, and I was pasty pale. I was unable to get a haircut for the three months or so prior to going to court. In short, I looked like hell. There was also the bitterness factor. That is, I held so much anger against the police, prosecutor's office, and the way the Miseners had behaved with regard to my wife and daughter, my attorneys were concerned with how the jury would interpret my demeanor.

In a case where you are clearly holding the upper hand, it is risky for the defendant to take the stand unless it's necessary. You do not want to risk having certain jurors take a disliking to the defendant because of the way they look or react to questions. The jury has no idea what a person has been put through, either physically or emotionally.

There is a natural tendency to want to stand up and declare your innocence, and I felt every bit of that within me. However, I had to defer to counsel on the matter. Post-trial statements from several of the jurors indicated that they had made up their mind prior to the trial even beginning. As such, it is unlikely that my testimony would've had any effect on the verdict.

Q. Why didn't you at least make a statement at sentencing, stand up and say that this was a godawful accident and that you were innocent? What could possibly have been the downside?

A. The best way to answer your question is with a question. That is, what did I have to gain? The judge had already made up her mind as to what she was going to do; this was made readily apparent by the way she scored the guidelines. She was involved in her campaign for the Court of Appeals, and had virtually every press representative you could ask for in the court room. After the trial was over, she even cited my case as an example of her qualifications for the job she was vying for . . . She even had the gall to call *me* arrogant, when I had done nothing but remain silent throughout the whole ordeal.

All of this was expected. As such, counsel had advised me to refrain from "casting my pearls before swine." I had absolutely nothing to gain by doing so, and everyone who really knows me believes that I'm innocent at any rate, and those who watched the actual trial itself with any degree of objectivity, knew at the very least that the prosecution had failed to prove otherwise.

Q. **What do you think happened in that bedroom while you were in the bathroom? Did you and Brian Legghio ever entertain the thought of suggesting suicide? Do you think that is a possibility? Perhaps Leann followed you to your meeting with Judge Chrzanowski the night before and wanted a dramatic payback.**

A. What I *think* happened is this: Leann couldn't, or didn't want to, get the bullet loaded into the magazine I had handed her. She had never done this before, and it does require a bit of dexterity and strength in the fingers (there's also the possibility that she didn't want to break a nail—she was a manicurist, and was usually careful about doing things like that). So instead of loading the clip, she would place it with the gun in the safe on the dresser, saving me the loading task for later. I had never told her that I already loaded the gun, and in fact she might have believed that the magazine she was holding was intended to be inserted into it. Nevertheless, I believe she reached over and took hold of the gun, believing it not to be loaded, placing her thumb on the trigger, and her fingers on the back side of the grip. The reason I have for envisioning this is because of the forensics. The blood spatters on the right grip would not have been there had the gun been fired in a conventional manner. That is, if either her right or left hand had held the gun as it was intended to be held, that portion of the grip would have been covered by her hand. At any rate, even the prosecution seemed to concede, during their rebuttal summation, that the gun must have been fired in this fashion.

We don't know whether Leann squeezed the gun while picking it up, or if she applied the pressure as she was attempting to stand. The spattering on the mirror indicated that she was still on the bed (the mirrored dresser was located at the foot of the bed, where the gun was lying on its case; Leann was sitting closer to the pillows at the other end). The spatter on the bedspread indicates the same. Furthermore, we don't know how far Leann was leaning toward the gun case at the time the firearm discharged, or whether she had righted herself prior to. Given these variables, I cannot say what I believe happened with any degree of certainty in this regard.

Of course, when investigating and preparing for a trial, all possibilities are considered. But when the forensics are taken into account, it seems unlikely that Leann would have held the gun in that fashion if she had intended to kill herself. But for purposes of the trial, the issue was left open to conjecture. That is, the question was not ours to answer.

No one could ever convince me that Leann committed suicide, however. I knew her well, well enough to know that she could never do such a thing. Not only would she never do something like that to herself, but she could never do something that would hurt our daughter, or our child she was carrying. We were as happy as we had ever been in a long time, especially with a new baby on the way. She had no reason to want her life to end. Even if she had the desire and will to do such a thing, it would not have been with a gun. In my heart, I will always believe that her actions were nothing more than leaning over and taking hold of an object that she meant to put away, without a reason to think twice about what she was doing, or how she was doing it.

Needless to say, it is difficult for me to reflect upon the possible scenarios, although I've replayed them in my head a million times or more since that day. Not only because it involves the death of my wife and child, but also because of the role I played. Had I put the gun in the safe myself when I got up to leave for the bathroom, or even told her that it was loaded, my wife would still be with me, and I would've been able to experience becoming a father for the second time, the indescribable feeling of holding your child for the first time. This reality haunts me to this day, I think about it often, lamenting my irresponsibility and the cost of it. In some ways, I believe that although I was convicted of a crime I did not commit, it is easier for me to cope with it when I consider the things I should have done differently. Perhaps a small part of me believes that I deserve it. I know that this is something that I will carry with me for the rest of my days.

With regard to your "payback" scenario, I believe that you should save that idea for your next book, it sounds intriguing. Again, there is no way that anyone could ever convince me that Leann's death was a suicide. Furthermore, Leann would have never even thought up something like that. I'm not saying she wasn't smart, because she certainly was, but it's not something she would have ever considered. Leann once told me that if she ever saw Susan, she would kick her butt. I didn't know if she was actually serious or not, but she was confident that Susan wouldn't go to the cops afterward. She was smart enough to figure *that* out. At any rate, I would expect Leann's reaction to be more along those lines, certainly as opposed to inflicting harm, or worse, upon herself.

Q. Do you in any way feel betrayed by Judge Chrzanowski? Is there anything she could have or should have said or done to help you out?

A. Susan's testimony benefited the defense far more than it assisted the prosecution. This is evidenced not only by post-trial statements made by the jurors, but as bad as that jury was toward the defense, they couldn't bring themselves to believe that my relationship with Susan was any kind of motive. Hence the second-degree verdict, without premeditation. Susan cooperated fully with the proceedings, and she told the truth. We were confident that this would benefit us, and we were proven correct.

Although I was unable to speak with her, I am confident that Susan knows I am innocent. She knows me better than anyone. She knew that I still loved Leann, despite our prior problems, and despite my feelings for her. She also knew that my little girl is the most important thing in the world to me, and that I could never do anything that would hurt her in any way. However, if she had said anything along these lines, it would've discredited her. The headlines would read: "Judicial Mistress Tries to Save Boyfriend!" The press would have been all over it, and the prosecution would have used her statements to try and support their silly theory.

In the court room, proof and truth are mutually exclusive things. And unfortunately, all too often, one comes at the expense of the other. In this case, the truth served us best.

Q. Where does an appeal stand now? And what is the timing from what you hear regarding the soonest it could be heard or acted upon?

A. Appeals take at least a year or so to get through the first level. God willing, this will not be necessary for us. We currently have a very powerful motion to remand for a new trial in front of the new trial court judge, Rae Lee Chabot. The motion is based upon the improper conduct of the jury during the deliberation process, as seen on the "20/20" program that aired last November. The experimentation, we argue, was improper, because they were considering evidence not produced at trial. This conduct violated the court's instructions, as well as denied my right to a fair trial. That is, jurors cannot be witnesses, particularly outside of the court room.

The initial hearing date is scheduled for April 25. Presumably, an evidentiary hearing will be scheduled soon after, with the jurors testifying as to their conduct in the deliberation room. It should be quite interesting. Given the strength of our argument, which is buttressed by the "20/20" video, which is fairly dispositive with regard to the issue, we are quite optimistic, but cautiously so. We are hopeful that the new judge will offer a fresh, if not a little more fair, perspective. At any rate, she is not currently campaigning, which I think is a definite bonus.

Q. How optimistic are you that an appeal can be successful?

A. If an appeal is necessary, it is difficult to gauge. Reversals are rare, particularly in the state system. State judges are elected, and reversals, even though they might be perfectly just and appropriate, are often held against a judge during elections by their opponents. This is especially true of high-profile cases. The federal system, on the other hand, is run by judges who sit by appointment. As such, they are free to rule without the political/job security concerns. As such, particularly because my case is high profile in nature, I have a bit more faith in the federal system. We have strong appellate issues, however, and my appellate counsel has certainly earned his good reputation. He has managed to garner just decisions from the state appellate courts with regard to cases having far less compelling issues than my own. As such, I am guardedly hopeful that if an appeal is necessary, we will be successful without having to take the case to the federal level.

What matters most to me is my daughter. The only hope she has lies with our success. The longer the process takes, the longer she will be forced to live in a household that would raise her to believe that she is one-half monster. This is more than I can bear; it has become my driving force in seeking a remedy.